Suffering and Sentiment

Suffering and Sentiment

Exploring the Vicissitudes of Experience and Pain in Yap

C. JASON THROOP

UNIVERSITY OF CALIFORNIA PRESS

Berkeley / Los Angeles / London

University of California Press, one of the most distinguished university presses in the United States, enriches lives around the world by advancing scholarship in the humanities, social sciences, and natural sciences. Its activities are supported by the UC Press Foundation and by philanthropic contributions from individuals and institutions. For more information, visit www.ucpress.edu.

University of California Press
Berkeley and Los Angeles, California

University of California Press, Ltd.
London, England

Library of Congress Cataloging-in-Publication Data

Throop, C. Jason.
 Suffering and sentiment : exploring the vicissitudes of experience and pain in Yap / C. Jason Throop.
    p.   cm.
 Includes bibliographical references and index.
  ISBN 978-0-520-26057-3 (cloth : alk. paper)—ISBN 978-0-520-26058-0 (pbk. : alk. paper)
    1. Medical anthropology—Micronesia (Federated States)—Yap.   2. Pain—Treatment—Micronesia (Federated States)—Yap.   I. Title.
 GN296.5.M626T57   2010
 306.4′610966—dc22   2009029171

Manufactured in the United States of America

19 18 17 16 15 14 13 12 11 10
10 9 8 7 6 5 4 3 2 1

This book is printed on Cascades Enviro 100, a 100% post consumer waste, recycled, de-inked fiber. FSC recycled certified and processed chlorine free. It is acid free, Ecologo certified, and manufactured by BioGas energy.

This book is dedicated to the memory of my friend Kirk Ellard, who demonstrated to us all the virtues of graceful endurance in the face of suffering.

Contents

Illustrations

Acknowledgments

First and foremost, I would like to thank the people of Yap who so generously accepted me into their lives and who shared their cares, concerns, and understandings of what it means to lead a life the Yapese way. *Siroew ngoomeed ma karimagaergad!* For reasons of confidentiality I cannot directly name all of the individuals whose insights have informed this work. I hope, however, that my deep appreciation for the time, trust, and confidence that my numerous Yapese teachers, friends, and family gave to me is evident in the pages that follow.

Of those I can mention by name, I would like to thank the following individuals for being such patient teachers: Bomtom, Charles Chieng, Carmen Chigiy, Martin Dugchur, Charles Falmeyog, Al Fanechigiy, Henry Fangalbuw, Peter Fatamag, Ansilem Filmed, Francis Filmed, Stan Filmed, Gisog, Guper, Gurwan, Laguar, Basil Limed, James Lukan, Claudius Maffel, John Mangfel, Cyprian J. Manmaw, Agnus Marlee, Martina Gisog, Thomas Mo'on, Dr. Victor Ngodan, Leo Pugram, Lourdes Roboman, Ruw, John Tamag, Padre Thal, John Thinum, Elvira Tinag, Peter Tun, John Wayan, Cyril Yinfal, and Julie Yuru. I was also very fortunate to have had two extremely knowledgeable and gifted language teachers in Francisca Mochen and Taman Kamnaanged. And I am indebted beyond words to my research assistants, Sheri Manna and Stella Tiningin.

Given that this project has taken nearly a decade to complete, there are many individuals, institutions, and agencies that have played key roles in helping out along the way. Of these, I would first like to respectfully mention the Council of Pilung and the Yap State Historic

Preservation Office. I am very thankful for the generous support granted by various staff members at the Yap State Memorial Hospital; the Yap State Department of Education; the College of Micronesia, Yap State Campus; the Yap State Archives; and MARC at the University of Guam.

I would like to acknowledge my appreciation of funding granted through the Department of Anthropology at UCLA and the Social Science Research Council and Andrew W. Mellon Foundation's International Dissertation Field Research Fellowship Program. I am also very grateful for receiving a UC Faculty Development Grant that allowed me a quarter off from teaching in the fall of 2008 to work on the final draft of this book.

There are many scholars who have generously contributed directly to the ideas that are developed in the following pages. That the boundaries between friendship, mentorship, and scholarship are thankfully fluid ones, I owe a deep heartfelt thanks to: Keira Ballantyne, Niko Besnier, David Brent, Carole Browner, Bob Desjarlais, Nalini Devdas, Jay Dobbin, Jennifer Dornan, Alessandro Duranti, Jim Egan, Nicole Falgoust, Angela Garcia, Linda Garro, Kevin Groark, Douglas Hollan, Uffe Juul Jensen, Charles Laughlin, Mary Lawlor, Sherwood Lingenfelter, Ted Lowe, Cheryl Mattingly, Jill Mitchell, Amira Mittermaier, Keith Murphy, Angela Nonaka, Masaru Noritake, Justin Richland, Joel Robbins, Don Rubenstein, Elinor Ochs, Warren Throop, and Sarah Willen. In addition, I would like to thank two of my graduate students, Mara Buchbinder and Hanna Garth, for reading over and commenting on an earlier draft of the book. I would also like to acknowledge the very helpful comments of three anonymous reviewers. Finally, I owe a great amount of gratitude to my editor Reed Malcolm for his support and many insightful suggestions throughout this process.

Parts of the book benefited greatly from questions and comments arising from presentations given to the Department of Anthropology, the Meta-Epistemology Seminar, and the Mind, Medicine, and Culture Seminar at UCLA; the Department of Anthropology and the Psychodynamic Seminar at UCSD; the Department of Anthropology and the Department of Occupational Therapy and Occupational Science at USC; the Culture, Life Course, and Mental Health Workshop at the Department of Human Development at the University of Chicago; and UCLA's Center for the Interdisciplinary Study and Treatment of Pain. I thank all of the organizers and participants for giving me such insightful feedback and critique.

There are many friends I would like to thank who were there for me through thick and thin during the research and writing of this book. The most sincere gratitude and love to: Tej Bhatia-Herring, Alex Burke, Melanie Cua, Alex Dakoglou, Keith Ellard, Kirk Ellard, Tim Gideon, Matt Goforth, Matt Harrell, Michael Herring, Phillip Lipscomb, Matthew Minter, Susanne Rattigan, Joshua Thompson, and all of the members of the Bar Ethnography and Sushi Tuesday collectives!

Finally, I owe perhaps the greatest debt of all to my families, both my adopted Yapese family and my Canadian family. To all of my parents, grandparents, siblings, and cousins, the suffering that went into bringing this book into being was for you.

Jason Throop
Los Angeles, California

Selected parts of the introduction and conclusion are drawn from an extensive reworking of the previously published article "Articulating Experience," *Anthropological Theory* 3, no. 2 (2003): 219–41.

Parts of chapter 3 and chapter 7 are drawn with some modification from the previously published article "From Pain to Virtue: Dysphoric Sensation and Moral Sensibilities in Yap (Waqab), Federated States of Micronesia," *Journal of Transcultural Psychiatry* 45, no. 1 (2008): 253–86. Reproduced by permission of SAGE Publications Ltd., London, Los Angeles, New Delhi, Singapore, and Washington, D.C.

Parts of chapter 3 and chapter 6 are drawn with modification from the previously published article "On the Problem of Empathy: The Case of Yap (Waqab), Federated States of Micronesia," *Ethos* 36, no. 4 (2008): 402–26. Reproduced by permission of the American Anthropological Association.

A Brief Note on Transcription, Yapese Orthography, and Data Collection

There have been a number of different orthographies used for Yapese. I have chosen to rely upon the orthography that has been adopted by the Yap State Department of Education. One drawback in using this orthography is that it does not always match up with Jensen's (1977a) dictionary or with the various ethnographies that I cite throughout the book. A very important advantage, however, is that it is the orthography that is being currently taught in Yapese schools.

As Elinor Ochs (1979) has argued, transcription practices are theory laden. The choices we make regarding what aspects of talk and interaction are represented through textual means are inescapably a reflection of our own analytical and interpretive interests. Such choices, in turn, do much to shape the form in which our observations take. In this book I have chosen to follow two very different approaches to transcribing my data that align with two different analytic aims.

Throughout most of the book I present individual narratives in terms of a free translation of the original Yapese. That is, I have chosen not to provide the original Yapese in interlineal translation. This is due to the fact that my analytical interests are focused more centrally on exploring the overarching content of individual narratives and the way in which painful experiences are both personally and culturally configured within them. This strategy for representing talk is, of course, much more familiar to cultural and psychological anthropologists.

In a few different sections of the book (in particular chapter 8) I provide in contrast a microanalytic examination of much more delimited stretches of talk and interaction. This data is drawn primarily from videotaped interactions between a local healer and one of her patients. Given my microanalytic focus, these transcripts more closely approximate forms that linguistic anthropologists are familiar with. The transcription conventions used in these cases were slightly modified from those proposed by Sacks, Schegloff, and Jefferson (1974) in one of their seminal papers on conversation analysis. They are as follows:

((sits down))	Material between double parentheses provides extralinguistic information, such as gestures, bodily movements, positioning, etc., as well as paralinguistic information such as volume.
(pain)	Words between parentheses in the English translation indicate information that is understood by native speakers but not explicitly stated in the Yapese morphemes.
(???)	Question marks inside of parentheses mark inaudible talk.
[	Square bracket between turns indicates a point where one speaker overlaps with another.
. . .	Three dots indicate an untimed pause in speech.
F;	Initials for speakers are separated from their utterances by semicolons.

All told, the data collected for this book includes sixty-five interviews with thirty chronic pain sufferers (each interview was conducted in Yapese and ranged anywhere from thirty minutes to four hours in length), videotaped healing sessions (over thirty hours' worth), and observed healing sessions between local healers and fifteen chronic and acute pain sufferers, as well as twenty-five successive pile sorts that focused on the categorization of a number of Yapese terms for internal states. In addition, I was able to conduct four months of research at the Yap State Archives going through all of the attorney general's correspondences as well as all of the local periodicals printed in Yap since the 1950s. In these records and periodicals I found much important information pertaining to a more general understanding of some key Yapese cultural values. It was also through my archival research that I was able to gain a better sense of the history of a number of social, legal, and health-related concerns from the perspective of the state government.

Furthermore, I had the opportunity to conduct two weeks of research at the Micronesian Area Research Center (MARC) at the University of Guam in January 2003. There I had access to one of the world's largest libraries and archival collections devoted specifically to

Micronesian cultures and history. Through my research at MARC I obtained copies of a number of important collections of Yapese mythology as well as documents from a number of early ethnologists and merchants who either lived on or visited the island in the nineteenth and twentieth centuries. Finally, at the request of the village I lived in, my colleague Jennifer Dornan and I conducted a four-week GPS mapping and oral-history project. While not directly related to the goals of my study, the information I gathered about the history of various house foundations and past political alliances in the village contributed significantly to developing my current understanding of how the experience of pain fits into broader cultural frames associated with the significance of work, endurance, effort, and suffering as core virtues in Yapese society. Other interviews conducted for the study included conversations with the attorney general of Yap State, the head linguist for Yap State's Department of Education, the director of Yap State Public Health, three members of the mental health program at the state hospital, one of the hospital's doctors, and the doctor who runs the only private health clinic on the island.

With my archival research, the oral history and mapping project, the successive pile sorting tasks, and my everyday conversations and observations living in a Yapese household and community for what amounted to fifteen months spread out between the years of 2000 and 2005, I believe that I was taught much about a number of core cultural virtues that importantly inform the ways in which individual sufferers sought to give meaning to their experiences of pain. In addition, by conducting interviews in conjunction with videotaping interactions between local healers and their patients, I was able to collect data that reflects both retrospective accounts of past experiences of pain in the context of particular life histories and naturally occurring discourse and interaction surrounding the real-time experiencing of dysphoric moments. With the exception of individuals listed in the acknowledgments, all other names used in this book are pseudonyms.

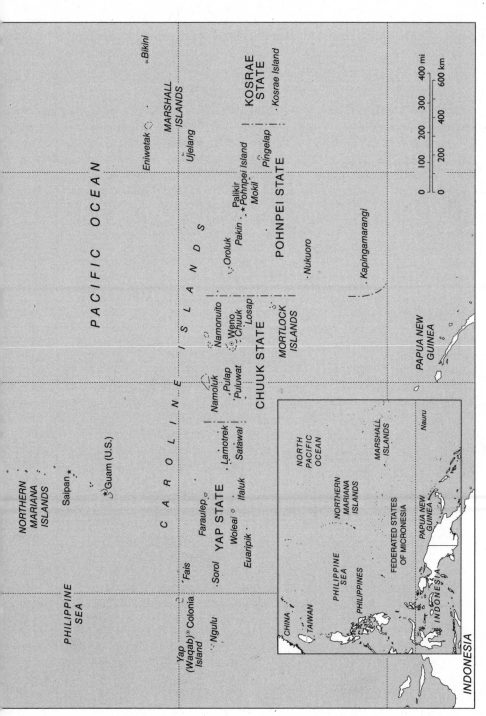

MAP 1. Micronesia.

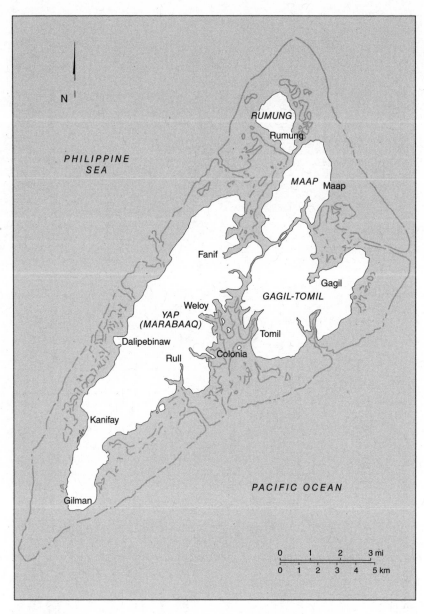

N

PHILIPPINE
SEA

RUMUNG
Rumung

MAAP Maap

Fanif

Gagil

GAGIL-TOMIL

Weloy

*YAP
(MARABAAQ)*

Dalipebinaw

Tomil

Rull

Colonia

Kanifay

PACIFIC OCEAN

Gilman

| 0 | | 1 | | 2 | | 3 mi |
| 0 | 1 | 2 | 3 | 4 | 5 km |

MAP 2. Yap.

Introduction

There we sat, cross-legged, quietly facing each other with my digital recorder between us. Humidity still clung to the air despite the slight breeze that had arrived with the beginning of sunset. Twilight had brought the anticipated annoyance of mosquitoes; it had also brought a play of light and shadow that made it almost impossible for me to make out Fal'eag's facial expression in the already darkened space of the community house. Reaching for my basket, I somewhat apprehensively began feeling around for some betel nut to chew. I had come to find such moments of silence between us comforting. And yet at this moment, I was anything but comfortable. Should I say something? I wondered. Or was it better to prepare my betel nut, begin chewing, and wait. As I had come to learn, it was always better to wait.

After a few minutes Fal'eag began speaking again. This time his voice was distant, like he was still lost in the shadowy world of reverie that seemed to have consumed him when our conversation had last stopped. The pain, he said, had been unbearable. It was like nothing he had ever felt before; he could not find the words to describe it. It was a pain so intense, so insufferable, that it was all that he knew. He could not feel his body, only pain. It was, he said, a pain for which "it would have been good had I died." At that moment I was thankful for the encroaching darkness. It was better for both of us that I was unable to make out whether or not there were tears in his eyes.

Pain is a basic existential fact of our distinctly human way of being-in-the-world. To be human is to be vulnerable to both the possibility and inevitability of suffering pain. Woven into the fabric of our existence, pain is an experience that calls forth questions of meaning, morality, despair, and hope. As such, pain is imbricated throughout a wide spectrum of possible human experiences. It is implicated in our most empathetic connections to others. It arises in the most inhumane acts of violence. Throughout its various manifestations, a foundational property of pain's existential structure is its capacity to enact a transformation in the subject who experiences it, whether for good or for ill. And yet, pain itself may be transformed through the particular meanings, values, ideals, and expectations that we bring to bear in dealing with the existential possibilities and limitations that it evokes. As much as pain is a foundational aspect of our existence as humans, it is variegated in its forms of manifestation and significance.

Rooted in a critical dialogue with attempts to theorize subjective experience, morality, and social action in anthropology and philosophy, I set out in this book to address both the vicissitudes and existential structure of pain in a particular cultural context. Specifically, I examine the cultural and personal patterning of experiences of both chronic and acute pain sufferers on the island of Yap (Waqab), which is located in the Western Caroline Islands of Micronesia. Situating subjective experiences of pain in light of local systems of knowledge, morality, and practice, I investigate the ways pain can be transformed into locally valued forms of moral experience within the context of particular individuals' culturally constituted lifeworlds. I focus in particular on the limits, challenges, and possibilities that individuals face when attempting to transform their pain from an experience of unwanted "mere-suffering"—what Emmanuel Levinas terms "useless suffering"—to more positively valenced forms of moral experience (Levinas 1998).

Generally speaking, this work has two goals. The first is to provide an ethnographic description of pain's significance in the context of local understandings of subjectivity, social action, and morality. To this end, a significant portion of the book is devoted to discussing the social, historical, and moral contexts that provide the background against which Yapese individuals' understandings of pain are articulated. These local understandings may at times uniquely inform individual sufferers' personal ascriptions of meaning to their experiences of pain. Such understandings importantly serve to pragmatically structure the everyday interactions of individuals suffering with a painful condition.

The second goal of the book is to address a number of long-standing debates in both philosophy and anthropology over the concept of "experience." Here, following Thomas Csordas's phenomenologically grounded observation that perception does not begin, but rather, "ends in objects" (1990, 9), I seek to investigate those processes of meaning-making by which pain may be variously configured into a coherent or disjunctive experience for individual sufferers through time. Both of these goals are pursued in the context of an examination of the ways that narratives of chronic and acute pain sufferers articulate with local ethical modalities of being. In Yap, such virtuous modes of being are rooted in the idea that certain forms of suffering are deemed to be of moral worth.

While these two goals may at times appear to follow rather distinct pathways, they both inform the overarching aim of this book, which is to advance a cultural phenomenology of morality and experience that speaks to the always complex and dynamic texturing of human subjectivity. Taking my inspiration from the phenomenological tradition and the work of Edmund Husserl, Martin Heidegger, Emmanuel Levinas, and others, I suggest an approach to subjectivity, suffering, and morality that expands what I have come to see as rather unsatisfying characterizations of lived experience in the discipline of anthropology. Often failing to grapple with the full richness of experience in our observations, research, writings, and theorizing, we as anthropologists have largely relied upon fully articulated forms of experience in our attempts to capture the lifeworlds of those with whom we are ethnographically engaged. Looking for certainties, coherences, and structures we have often overlooked the ambiguities, the confusions, the gaps, and the ambivalences that arise in the midst of our own, and our informants', experiences as lived. In this work, I thus want to propose a means by which to begin expanding our view of experience to include a spectrum of articulations that range from the most formulated and explicit to the most inaccessible and vague. It is precisely for this reason that I have sought to investigate some of the most dramatic, unassumable, and compelling forms of human experience: experiences of pain and suffering.

The anthropology of suffering has indeed become a vibrant field of study that has already significantly challenged a number of core assumptions in contemporary culture theory (Kleinman, Das, and Lock 1997). Many of these studies have pushed the boundaries of anthropological theorizing and practice precisely because they have attempted to understand some of the most incomprehensible and inhuman acts of torture, humiliation, violence, and genocide (see Asad 1993, 2000;

Das, Kleinman, Ramphele, and Reynolds 2000; Das, Kleinman, Lock, Ramphele, and Reynolds 2001; Hinton 2002, 2005; Scheper-Hughes and Bourgois 2004; Tambiah 1996; Trnka 2008). For instance, scholars like Veena Das (2007) and Valentine Daniel (1996) have struggled to find ways to understand and represent unbearable forms of suffering, pain, and violence in such a way as to never lose sight of the palpable human realities that exist at the limits of the sayable, the knowable, and the reportable. In advocating a turn toward examining what is at stake for individuals in the context of their everyday cares and concerns, Arthur Kleinman (2006), Douglas Hollan (2000, 2001), and Unni Wikan (1990, 1992, 2008) have each in their own way further pushed us to rethink the complexities inherent in the relationship between personal experiences of suffering, concrete social realities, and cultural forms of understanding. Thinkers like Nancy Scheper-Hughes (1992, 2002), João Biehl (2005, 2007), and Paul Farmer (1998, 2003) have for their part proposed critical ethnographies that reveal the complex global, economic, and material realities that have given rise to a myriad of forms of inequity, oppression, and dispossession underpinning social suffering on both local and personal scales.

Deeply inspired by this body of work, this book draws primarily, though not exclusively, from phenomenological and existentialist approaches to the problem of suffering. It shares with much of the work cited thus far a concern for examining the lived realities of individuals suffering with various forms of pain, hurt, and loss. It also shares a call to recognize the various ways that human suffering may compel us to rethink some of the most basic assumptions in social scientific and anthropological theory. Finally, it is equally committed to detailing how the brute facticity of suffering may become enfolded in the practice of everyday life. It contributes most significantly to this literature, however, by foregrounding the problematics of experience and temporality as key sites for understanding the articulation of suffering in meaningful and moral terms.

Foundations and Pathways: The Vicissitudes of Experience and Pain

There are certain ideas in anthropological theorizing that are foundational. Because these concepts provide the ground upon which anthropologists are able to construct their theoretical edifices, these constructs are often taken for granted and tend to remain unquestioned. As such, they become part and parcel of what Edmund Husserl (1962) might have termed an anthropologist's "natural attitude." A core concept that has risen to prominence in anthropological theorizing and which has, up until relatively recently, been left largely unexamined in critical literature, is the concept of "experience."

While experience has remained a key, if largely understated, construct throughout much of the history of the discipline, its proliferation throughout recent anthropological writings is truly remarkable. To wit, experience has become foundational for a number of divergent perspectives in anthropology, including feminist theory, phenomenological anthropology, psychological anthropology, medical anthropology, and critical ethnography (see Good 1994; Kleinman 2006; Mattingly 1998; Turner and Bruner 1986). In all of these approaches, while a prominent reliance upon experience is evident, its definition and operational properties remain largely elusive. This lack of conceptual clarity may in fact be tied to the very taken-for-grantedness of experience in social theory (see Desjarlais 1994, 1997; Jay 2006; J. Scott 1991; D. Scott 1992). Indeed, social scientists often look to experience not only as a central area of investigation, but also as the ground upon which all later speculation, description, and explanation are erected.

Increasingly, however, there have been a number of scholars who have come to critically question anthropology's unexamined reliance upon the concept of experience (see Desjarlais 1994, 1997; Geertz 1985; Kleinman and Kleinman 1991, 1996; Mattingly 1998; Jay 2006; J. Scott 1991; D. Scott 1992; Throop 2003a, 2003b; cf. Needham 1973). Perhaps most radically, Robert Desjarlais (1994, 1997) has proposed that the cultural, historical, and political underpinnings of the concept of experience necessitates that it no longer be considered a universal category underlying all human existence. Anthropologists should instead, he suggests, challenge and replace the concept with ways of being-in-the-world that do not rely upon and perpetuate its pervasive "intellectualist" and "subjectivist" connotations. This is a call that has to some extent been taken up by those anthropologists advocating a turn to embodiment in anthropological research and theorizing (see Bourdieu 1977; Csordas 1993, 1994a, 1994b, 1999, 2004; Jackson 1983, 1989, 1996; Wacquant 2003; cf. Throop and Murphy 2002).

In many ways, the inspiration for this book grew directly from an ongoing interest in this relatively recent concern with the concept of experience. This is a concern that is deeply rooted in a number of long-standing debates in philosophy and the social sciences over the structures and dynamics of subjective life and social action (cf. Agamben 2007; Good 1994; Mattingly 1998; Jay 2006). Generally stated, these debates have revolved around two competing theories of experience, which the philosopher Calvin Schrag (1969) has labeled "coherence" and "granular" theories. Granular theories tend to take experience to be disjunctive, fragmentary, discordant, discontinuous, formless, and punctuating at its core. Coherence theories, in contrast, characterize experience as conjunctive, integrated, concordant, continuous, meaningfully formed, and temporally structured. Victor Turner (1986) has perhaps expressed this tension most clearly from an anthropological frame in his much-cited distinction between "mere experience" and "an experience." According to Turner,

> Mere experience is simply the passive endurance and acceptance of events. . . . *An* experience, like a rock in a Zen sand garden, stands out from the evenness of passing hours and years and forms what Dilthey called a "structure of experience." In other words, it does not have an *arbitrary* beginning and ending, cut out of the stream of chronological temporality, but has what Dewey called "an initiation and a consummation." (1986, 35)

Experiences of pain and suffering have somewhat unique existential attributes that make them especially interesting for speaking to debates over the structures and dynamics of experience. There is now a growing body of work in the social sciences that characterize pain as evidencing polar tendencies that seem to parallel granular and coherence theories of experience (Daniel 1996; Das 2007; DelVecchio-Good et al. 1992; Das et al. 2000; Kleinman, Das, and Lock 1997; Kleinman 2006; Trnka 2007, 2008). Broadly speaking, there is a prevalent assumption in this body of literature that pain is a complex phenomenon that seems to display an inherent ambiguity. Pain at times obdurately resists meaningful conceptualization, while also often succumbing to culturally shaped systems of categorization, classification, and narrativization. As Elaine Scarry (1985) argues, the experience of pain is potentially "world-destroying." In the intensity of its lived immediacy it is a phenomenon that "occurs on that fundamental level of bodily experience which language encounters, attempts to express, and then fails to encompass" (Kleinman et al. 1992, 7). As such, pain can be characterized as a disjunctive or granular experience par excellence. And yet, there are also a number of important studies (e.g., Good 1992, 1994; Garro 1990, 1992, 1994; J. Jackson 1999; Kleinman 2006; Kirmayer 2007; Throop

2008a, 2008b; Trnka 2007, 2008) that have sought to demonstrate how individual sufferers are able to give meaning to their experiences of pain, at least retrospectively. From this perspective then, pain appears at times to be a conjunctive or coherent experience as well. As we will see, such differing articulations hinge importantly upon different *temporal orientations* to pain and suffering.

Pain's ambiguity and its relevance for theorizing experience is further amplified in its vacillation between at times strictly physical, and at times strictly psychical, varieties of experience. In light of many of our commonsense assumptions about the relationship between mind and body, it seems self-evident to say that pain is a somatic experience.[1] Understood as an affliction of the body, pain in the context of biomedically informed North American folk models is often colloquially labeled a "sensation." In the philosophy and anthropology of pain, however, the connection between "pain" and "sensation" is seldom so clear-cut (see Throop 2008a).[2] So-called physical pain and psychical (emotional) pain, much as Kirmayer (1984a, 1984b) has noted for processes of psychologization and somatization, are in fact poles along a continuum of possibilities, both personally and culturally influenced, to interpret and communicate dysphoric experiences in terms of mental or bodily idioms of distress (see also Kleinman 1980; Kleinman and Kleinman 1991). That it is at times hard to discern whether individuals are speaking of their pain and suffering in terms of purely physical or psychical varieties, or in terms of some difficult to parse combination of the two, is again testament to the often-elusive qualities of the phenomenon we gloss in English with the term "pain." Again, it makes pain all the more interesting for a study that hopes to speak to problems regarding the articulation of experience.

Articulation, Attention, and Experience

Following Vincent Crapanzano, my interest in experience and its possibilities for articulation into different modalities, including moral ones, is rooted in a general concern with both "openness and closure, [and] with the way in which we construct, wittingly or unwittingly, horizons that determine what we experience and how we interpret what we experience" (2004, 2). Central to these determinations of actual and possible horizons of experience are processes of articulation. By articulation, I am referring here not (at least primarily) to the capacity to communicate to others the contents of one's subjective life through various expressive forms including language. Rather, I am referring to the ability to give what may otherwise be indefinite or ambiguous varieties of experience a definite form through symbolic and embodied means.[3] Indeed, as Susanne Langer observes, "Visual forms—lines, colors, proportions, etc.—are just as capable of *articulation,* i.e., of complex combination, as words" [emphasis in original] (1942 [1996], 93). To quote Cassirer, articulation thus includes those symbolically mediated (though not necessarily exclusively linguistic) processes through which "the chaos of sensory impressions begins to clear and take on fixed form for us" (Cassirer 1955, 107; cf. Hallowell 1955). Not all varieties of experience are equally amenable to articulation, however. In fact, as Crapanzano makes clear in investigating what he terms "imaginative horizons," there is experience that "insofar as it resists articulation, indeed disappears with articulation, has in fact been ignored" by culture theorists (2004, 18). Building from William James's (1890) call to reinstate "the vague and inarticulate to its proper place in our mental life," Crapanzano's work thus evokes questions as to whether such unformulated varieties of experience are necessarily deferred in our attempts to provide them an articulate shape and meaning. His writings also point to the problems of how, and the extent to which, such inchoative varieties of experience may undergo formulation and expression. In many ways, we are reminded here of Edward Bruner's caution that while there "may be a correspondence between a life as lived, a life as experienced, and a life as told, . . . anthropologists should never assume the correspondence nor fail to make the distinction" (1984, 7).

These differing modalities of experience present us with the possibility that inarticulate or unformulated varieties of experience are not themselves reducible to a singular category.[4] Instead, such varieties of experience entail various forms that may themselves be each amenable to differing degrees of articulation, an insight that I will return to discuss in the conclusion of this book. If anthropologists are truly interested in exploring the fullest range of experience cross-culturally, as well as those processes of articulation that may serve to render those experiences coherent in both meaningful and moral terms, greater attention needs to be paid to those experiences that reside on the fringes of our abilities to articulate, verbalize, and interpret. Accordingly, it is time for us to establish what I have termed elsewhere an "anthropology of ambiguity" (Throop 2002, 2005). It is precisely for this reason that pain's at times intransigent opacity and active resistance to formulation makes it especially compelling as a site to examine how processes of meaning-making are implicated in the articulation of experience and its ensuing objectification (see also Crapanzano 2004, 81). As such, inquiries into the articulation of experiences of pain and suffering may provide potential insight into how pregiven personal and cultural tropes, narratives, and images may alternatively conflict or conjoin in the structuring of subjective life.

When speaking of the articulation of experience it is crucial, I argue, to take into account the role of attention. The focus of attention as a discriminating faculty in the organization of experience was recognized as early as William James's writings on the stream of consciousness (1890). In his words, "in a world of objects thus individualized by our mind's selective industry, what is called our 'experience' is almost entirely determined by our habits of attention" ([1892] 1985, 39). According to James, attention is "taking possession by the mind, in clear and vivid form, of one of what seem several simultaneously possible objects or trains of thought. Focalization, concentration, of consciousness are of its essence. It implies withdrawal from some things in order to deal effectively with others, and it is a condition which has a real opposite in the confused, dazed, scatterbrained state which in French is called *distraction,* and *Zerstreutheit* in German" (1890, 403–4).[5]

Insights similar to James's were taken up and elaborated by Edmund Husserl (1962) in his discussion of the role of attention in the subjective constitution of objects of experience. Attention's role in configuring experience is also a theme that is directly implicated in Husserl's (1962) analysis of those forms of phenomenological modification involved in shifting from a natural to a phenomenological attitude—a process that I will return to discuss more thoroughly in the conclusion (see Duranti forthcoming).[6] While such pragmatic and phenomenological insights have been key to developing an understanding of the place of attention in the structuring of subjective life, it is clear from the perspective of anthropology that one must speak of the organization of attention in the articulation of experience *in relationship to cultural processes.*

There have been diverse attempts within anthropology to examine the role that culture plays in differentially articulating patterns of attention, conceptualization, and sensation in the structuring of experience cross-culturally (see Berger 1999; Berger and Del Negro 2002; Csordas 1993; Kirmayer 1984; Leder 1990; Ochs and Shieffelin 1984; Throop 2003, 2005).[7] One particularly generative contribution, however, is found in Thomas Csordas's notion of "somatic modes of attention." Drawing on Schutz's (1970) and Merleau-Ponty's (1999) phenomenological insights, Csordas defines somatic modes of attention as those "culturally elaborated ways of attending to and with one's body in surroundings that include the embodied presence of others" (1993, 138). By grounding attention directly in the existential structure of our bodily ways of being-in-the-world, Csordas wishes to highlight the various ways that culture can serve to pattern one's attention to bodily sensations in relation to perception, sociality, and motility. As he explains, to "attend to a bodily sensation is not to attend to the body as an isolated object, but to attend to the body's situation in the world. . . . Attention *to* a bodily sensation can thus become a mode of attending to the intersubjective milieu that gives rise to that sensation. Thus, one is paying attention *with* one's body" (1993, 138). It is, he holds, in the organization of attention in relation to the body that experience becomes patterned according to both "preobjective" and "objective" modalities (see Throop 2005).

Csordas's insights, along with the work of others (Berger 1997, 1999; Berger and Del Negro 2002; Leder 1990; Levy 1973, 1984), lend support to what I have termed elsewhere an attentional-synthetic approach to the cultural patterning of sensation and feeling (Throop 2008a). Such an approach pivots on differences found in specific cultures tied to the functioning of attention and memory. To borrow James's apt terminology, it is *collectively structured forms of selective attention* to the various sensory, affective, conative, and cognitive dimensions of subjective life that account for observed differences in the articulation of experience in differing cultures or communities. Accordingly, it is also such collectively structured forms of selective attention that account for observed variations in individuals' culturally and personally patterned experiences of pain. It is, in short, the patterning of attention that is implicated in the transformation of painful sensations into meaningful, morally valenced, lived experiences.

From Pain to Virtue

> The stimuli that cause physical pain to which the emotions react are constant in history. But the capacity for enduring and tolerating pain, which is different from its stimuli, has varied in the history of civilization . . . we can "give ourselves up" to suffering or pit ourselves against it; we can "endure"

suffering, "tolerate" it, or simply "suffer"; we can even
"enjoy" suffering (algophilia). These phrases signify styles of
feeling and of willing based on feeling, which are clearly not
determined by the mere state of feeling.

Max Scheler, 1963

I did not go into the field with an explicit interest in exploring the role
of morality and virtue in the context of the personal and cultural articulation of lived experiences of pain in Yapese communities.[8] Yet while
living on the island it did not take long for me to recognize how local
understandings of pain were embedded in moral sensibilities that
viewed certain forms of suffering as virtuous. Moreover, as I worked
through my field notes, interviews, and videotape data in the months
after my return to Los Angeles, I found that my data spoke strongly
to the extent to which pain may be meaningfully configured as a coherent experience precisely when it is recognized as indexical of an individual sufferer's previous history of virtuous comportment. As will be
evident in the pages that follow, a focus on virtue and morality thus
became central not only to understanding the emplacement of pain in
everyday life in Yap, but also to my own theorizing of the articulation
of experience in the face of unassumable suffering. Such moments were
often revealed in the very intense pain undergone by the individuals
who were generous enough to share their time, insights, and suffering
with me.

Much like the anthropology of suffering, the anthropology of morality has become an increasingly significant contributor to contemporary
culture theory (see Howell 1997; Zigon 2008). That issues of morality
are deeply intertwined with problems of suffering is most certainly
implicated in the fact that many anthropologists interested in morality
and ethics have also been actively engaged in researching suffering in
its cultural, social, economic, and personal contexts. Whether focusing
upon the complex dynamics of local moral worlds (Kleinman 1999,
2006; Garcia forthcoming), the critical assessment of regimes of power,
truth, and oppression (Asad 1993; Mahmood 2005), the practical ethical
implications of ethnographic engagements (Castañeda 2006; Meskill
and Pel 2005), the embodiment of moral ideals (Lester 2005; Rydstrøm
2003), or the relationship between practice, value, and virtue (Lambek
2008; Parish 1994; Mattingly n.d.), this literature has offered much in
the way of situating morality within an anthropological frame (cf.
D'Andrade 1995; Scheper-Hughes 1995).

Of particular significance for my purposes here, however, is a recent work by Kathryn Linn Geurts (2002) that examines the cultivation of moral sensibilities among Anlo-speaking peoples in southeastern Ghana. Her work brings us back full circle to how it is that questions concerning the articulation of experience and the patterning of attention may be directly related to the formation of ethical modalities of being. Drawing specifically from Csordas's (1990, 9) contention that "the goal of a phenomenological anthropology of perception is to capture that moment of transcendence in which perception begins, and, in the midst of arbitrariness and indeterminacy, constitutes and is constituted by culture," Geurts argues that the process of learning to appropriately focus and isolate elements of fluctuating sensations in culturally appropriate ways is a mode of organizing experience that may be implicated in "ways of understanding and expressing morality" (2002, 74).

Geurts suggests that moral sensibilities are significantly tied to our routine ways of attending to bodily sensations and through those sensations to the social and physical worlds within which we are enmeshed. That is, moral values can be understood as residues of *collectively structured modes of selective attention*. Borrowing from the language of Michel Foucault (1985, 2005), we can thus say that the organization of attention as mediated through our sensorium can be directly affected by differing hermeneutics and technologies of self. That is, the cultural organization of attention is often implicated in the ethical work "that one performs on oneself, not only in order to bring one's conduct into compliance with a given rule, but to attempt to transform oneself into the ethical subject of one's behavior" (Foucault 1985, 27).

Well in-line with these insights, this book investigates the ways in which local understandings of subjectivity, social action, and morality can work to recurrently orient individuals to first selecting and then recasting certain elements of their experience of pain in light of core cultural virtues. In the process, dysphoric experiences are configured such that they are no longer merely held to be unwanted painful sensations. Instead, the experience of pain may come to be viewed as basic to the cultivation of moral sensibilities as individuals work to endure through them. Tracing the paths that individual sufferers struggled to navigate in working to fashion their dysphoric experiences into virtuous ones is thus a means to highlight the ways in which granular experiences are, and are not, translated into more coherent varieties. Most simply put, transitioning from pain to virtue is largely reflective of varieties of experience that shift from granularity to coherence.

Additionally, transformations of pain into virtue can be seen as importantly implicated in the formation of particular ethical modalities of being.

Part of this ethical work, as we will see, is importantly enacted through existential, practical, and discursive acts. Indeed, the cultural phenomenology that I ascribe to is one that attempts to take language seriously (see Desjarlais 2003, 6), while also not ever reducing experience exclusively to the linguistic categories, local grammars of suffering (Ochs and Capps 2001), and discursive acts that most certainly inform it. To this end, in the concluding chapters of this book I examine the ways in which individual sufferers and their interlocutors subjectively, interactionally, and discursively work to select, delimit, disambiguate, and in the process objectify, elements of their lived experience of pain in the context of retrospective, present, and future-focused orientations. Such temporalized efforts after meaningful objectification speak to important questions concerning what Trnka (2008, 19) has characterized to be possible differences between pain's "communicability"—the ability to meaningfully express or describe pain—and its "shareability"—the ability to intersubjectively share pain in experiential or embodied terms (cf. Das 2007). They also help to shed light on dynamic processes of meaning-making that might otherwise be elided in the context of everyday interaction.

It is very important to note the emphasis that I am placing here on differing orientations to time. As I hope to show throughout this book, it is only in situating collectively structured modes of selective attention *in time*—be that in the form of past, present, or future orientations—that we will be able to capture more accurately the richness, complexities, and dynamics of subjective life (cf. Biehl, Good, and Kleinman 2007). In fact, one of the basic assumptions that first guided this research was that the way in which attention is arrayed in time impacts the extent to which experience may be configured into coherent or granular varieties. Whether attention is directed back over an already elapsed span of experience, is oriented to the flux of the present moment, or is projected forward to impending but yet-to-be-realized possible futures, may make a difference in how an individual's subjective life is configured in both personal and cultural terms (see Throop 2003a). The ongoing dynamic flux of subjective life and the various shifts in attention that accompany it greatly complicates any simplistic dichotomy between granularity and coherence. In advancing a temporally grounded approach to experience, this book thus seeks to destabilize this dichotomy while still addressing questions concerning the relationship between forms of subjectivity and culture by exploring the dynamic ways that Yapese cultural logics may at times embed experiences of pain in a meaningful landscape of moral sensibilities.

The Path from Here

Having outlined the motivating problematics that led to the research upon which this book is based, I would like to now provide a general overview of the paths we will explore in the pages to come. In the first chapter, I briefly introduce Yap before situating my fieldwork in the context of the island's precolonial, colonial, and postcolonial history. In the process, I review the practical and methodological aims of my research, as well as the extent to which those aims were able to be effectively realized given the social, historical, and cultural constraints that I confronted working on the island as a nonlocal researcher.

In chapter 2 I begin providing a substantive ethnographic account of the significance of pain and suffering in Yapese social life. Specifically, the chapter outlines the importance of a number of core cultural virtues and corresponding moral sentiments that serve as a psychocultural and ethical basis for the patterning of everyday life. Of central concern in this chapter is an examination of how a culturally elaborated dialectical relationship between people and land is centrally implicated in local models of ethical subjectivity and virtuous comportment. These models are dynamically inscribed somatically and sensorially in the experiences of suffering *(gaafgow)*, work-induced exhaustion, fatigue, or tiredness *(magaer)*, endurance, perseverance, or striving *(athamagil)*, and compassion *(runguy)*. Extending this initial foray into subjectivity, morality, and virtue, chapter 3 investigates Yapese moral sensibilities in relationship to a number of Yap's core cultural idioms. This includes an examination of the idioms of purity and order, hierarchy, relationships, exchange, and food production and consumption.

Chapter 4 transitions to sketch the contours of Yapese articulations of subjectivity, embodiment, and social action. The chapter explores how local conceptions of mind, feeling, emotion, sensation, and other bodily processes intimately linked to pain are broadly figured in Yapese understandings of subjective experience. This provides a foundation for the following chapter, which examines the relation between these local understandings of subjectivity and issues of expressivity. Here, I discuss the valuation of privacy, secrecy, and concealment in relation to questions of social agency. More specifically, I seek to demonstrate how secrecy, privacy, and concealment are collectively linked to ethnopsychological assumptions regarding the moral significance of self-monitoring, self-mastery, and nonexpressivity. Such forms of self-vigilance are qualities or capacities essential to approximating core models of what it means to be a good person, to lead a good life, and to flourish.

In chapter 6, I discuss more specifically local medical theory and the place of pain within it. I examine the ways in which experiences of pain are culturally configured through detailing how varieties of pain are linguistically encoded, at both levels of lexical and grammatical representation. I then shift to examine how pain is situated within the context of those local understandings of subjectivity, social action, and morality discussed in the previous chapters. In so doing, I argue that pain is understood in Yap as a form of suffering that may be categorized either as an unwanted (and largely granular) dysphoric experience in terms of mere-suffering, or as a virtue experienced (in a more coherent manner) in the context of suffering-for others.

The next two chapters turn specifically to an analysis of individual narratives of suffering with pain. Chapter 7 draws from narratives derived from interviews to explore how individual sufferers give meaning and value to their suffering. Many individuals did so by variously aligning their painful somatic experiences with local understandings of ethical modes of being. Here the emphasis is placed upon examining how available cultural idioms of suffering help to configure sufferers' understandings of their pain, the unique ways in which individuals are able to personalize such idioms, as well as those instances in which, even in the face of such retrospectively cast narratives, experiences of pain may yet actively outstrip efforts at articulation.

By comparison, chapter 8 relies upon observational and videotape data of interactions between a local healer and one of her patients as a means to microanalytically explore "dysphoric moments." In particular, I examine how the brute force of pain experienced purely as mere-suffering from the perspective of the sufferer, can present an opportunity for other actors to attempt to shift the sufferer's frame of reference to understanding suffering in light of a -for structure, a structure imbued with temporality, meaning, and virtue. In the process, I propose the notion of "indexical markers of cultural virtue," which are semiotic vehicles that mediate between conjunctive and disjunctive varieties of experience. Such a mediation is accomplished, I suggest, through organizing disparate events, intentions, and actions that may otherwise seem to be confined to discrete, point-like moments in time, into an incipient, and yet meaningfully configured, temporal frame. This frame links moments of otherwise unassumable pain to past or future orientations that stretch beyond the confines of the present.

Finally, the book concludes by examining how the varieties and vicissitudes of dysphoric experience examined in the previous two chapters may speak to the development of a cultural phenomenology of moral experience. Building upon the work of Edmund Husserl and Emmanuel Levinas, among others, I suggest an understanding of moral experience that goes beyond any of the often simplistic and partial renderings of human existence traditionally offered in the context of granular and coherence theories of experience. In so doing, I suggest a prolegomena to an experienced-based ethics that actively addresses a continuum of possible engagements with other social actors spanning from distanced objectification to intersubjective alignment to unassumable alterity. Moreover, I speak to what experiences of suffering and pain may have to say specifically to such an ethics and to possibilities for shifting between differing orientations toward others and oneself in either a mode of typicality or uniqueness. Such an approach to understanding morality and experience seeks to attend equally to the existential realities of our uniquely human ways of being-in-the-world and to the personal and cultural idioms, tropes, and narratives that arise from and give shape to such modes of being. Finally, I reflect upon the extent to which ethnographic practice may be implicated in such an ethics by examining what I term, following Husserl, the anthropological attitude and the ethnographic epoché.

CHAPTER I

Girdiiq nu Waqab ("People of Yap")

Avoiding my gaze, Paer looked out over her garden. She had planted this garden close to the house, she said, to reduce the distance she had to walk to get food when her grandson was visiting. Her leg was hurting a lot these days and it was just not possible for her to get to her favorite taro patches and gardens without some help. Her present pain seemed to be evocative of past suffering, however; at that moment our conversation shifted rather abruptly, I thought, to her memories of gardening for Japanese soldiers during the war. "During that war there was great suffering, suffering that was put upon us," she said. "Very great suffering that the Japanese gave to us. We all stayed and we all worked. And there was work and that is how it went."

The story of pain in Yap cannot be told without first understanding the place of suffering in the island's rich and at times difficult history. Perhaps most famously recognized in anthropological circles as the inspiration for David Schneider's (1984) critique of the concept of kinship, the island of Yap is located in the Western Caroline Islands of Micronesia. Unlike the coral atolls that constitute some of its closest neighbors, Yap is a volcanic high island that is the exposed area of a large submarine ridge. Yap proper actually consists of four main islands—Yap (Marabaaq), Gagil-Tomil, Maap, and Rumung—that are each separated by narrow water passages that have been, with the exception of Rumung, linked together by manmade land bridges, roads, and paths. While it is much larger than the neighboring coral atolls, Yap proper is still a relatively small area with a land mass of approximately 38.6 square miles and an estimated population of 7,391 inhabitants (Yap State Statistical Bulletin 2000). Having endured four waves of colonial governance (Spanish, German, Japanese, and American), today Yap proper is the administrative capital of Yap State, one of the four states (Yap, Pohnpei, Kosrae, and Chuuk) that comprise the Federated States of Micronesia (FSM), an independent nation that holds a compact of free association with the United States.

Economically, most Yapese individuals participate in some combination of wage labor and subsistence farming based primarily upon the cultivation of taro, yams, bananas, breadfruit, and chestnut (Lingenfelter 1991, 392; Egan 1998). In many villages fishing still contributes importantly to daily subsistence. Most salaried workers are employed by the government, the small private sector, and the service industries that have arisen in response to the growing influx of American, European, and Japanese tourists. For many individuals, cultivating and selling betel nut at local stores and to individuals who export to Guam and other islands in Micronesia is an important source of household income.

Languages spoken include Yapese, English, and a number of Outer Island idioms, including Ulithian, Woleaian, and Chuukese (Yap State Census 1994). Yapese, a reported first language for over 95 percent of the island's inhabitants, is a nominative-accusative Austronesian language in which the canonical word order is verb-subject-object (see Ballantyne 2004). Yapese is distinct from the languages of Palau and the other Caroline Islands (Lingenfelter 1991, 391) and has long defied historical linguistic attempts to classify it either as Western Malayo-Polynesian or Oceanic (Kirch 2000, 191; Ross 1996). During the time that I was conducting my fieldwork, many individuals under the age of fifty-five spoke English as a second language, while many individuals under the age of thirty spoke English fluently.

Precolonial History

While there are numerous competing archeological and historical linguistic accounts of the various waves of migration that contributed to the settlement of Micronesia (see Kirch 2000), there is a growing consensus that Yap was inhabited well before Gifford and Gifford's (1959; see also Takayama 1982) original estimation of 1800 B.P. (cf. Dodson and Intoh 1999). As is true of all cultures, precontact Yap was not only the product of local refinements on the cultural forms that arrived with its first inhabitants. It was also importantly shaped by a long history of interaction and trade with other peoples and traditions spread throughout the Western Pacific and beyond (Egan 1998, 35; Kirch 2000, 191). In fact, Yap proper long held a position at the center of an expansive trade network whose size and complexity led a number of scholars to term it an "empire" (Hage and Harary 1991, 1996; Kirch 2000; Lessa 1950).

Beginning sometime between 300 and 800 A.D., Yap participated in an elaborately interlinked system of mutual-exchange relationships stretching from Palau, located 280 miles to the southwest (the site of aragonite limestone quarries that were essential for the production of Yap's stone money called *raay*), through a total of fourteen islands and atolls extending from Yap's closest eastern neighbors (Ulithi and Fais) to Puluwat and Namonuito, two atolls located over eight hundred miles to the east. While there are a few researchers who have explored the trade relations between Palau and Yap (see Gillilland 1975), it is the link between Yap and the eastern atolls that has garnered the most attention by scholars working in the region (see Alkire 1965, 1980; Descantes 1998; Hage and Harary 1991, 1996; Hunter-Anderson and Zan 1996; Kirch 2000; Lessa 1950; Labby 1975; Lingenfelter 1975).

The system of formal relationships *(sawëy)* between Yap proper and the Outer Islands was arranged as a chain of hierarchically cast linkages between islands.[1] In this system, the links progressed from the lower-ranking atolls in the east to the higher-ranking atolls and islands to the west. The highest-ranking positions were attributed to a number of estates in the villages of Gatchpar and Wanyaan in what is presently the municipality of Gagil on Yap proper (Alkire 1965; Lessa 1950; Egan 1998). A basic form essential for understanding a great many different varieties of social relations in Yap, the transactions between each individual island participating in the *sawëy* were understood in terms of a series of dyadic relations between a higher-status island and a lower-status trading partner. In each case, the relationship between islands was predicated upon an exchange of gifts and tribute. Gifts, such as bamboo, turmeric, and foodstuffs flowed east from a higher-status island to a lower-status island. Tribute, in the form of shell belts, *beagiy* (woven textiles made from banana fiber), and coconut fiber rope, flowed in the opposite direction (see Egan 1998).

As a number of my friends and teachers explained to me, this exchange was understood in terms of an interchange of care *(ayuw)* on the part of the higher-status island and respect *(liyoer)* and the part of its lower-status trading partner. These two forms of activity represent the outward manifestation of a dynamic of feeling that I will explore in later chapters as founded upon an exchange of suffering *(gaafgow)* and compassion *(runguy)*. As Egan notes, the system was set up "with the westerly island being accorded higher status" and having necessary "obligation to support its eastern subordinate (especially after it had been hit by a devastating storm or typhoon)" (1998, 36).

Colonial History

While interaction with surrounding peoples in the Western Pacific was a reoccurring aspect of everyday life in precolonial times, Yap did not enter into sustained contact with Europeans until the mid- to late 1800s, though there were a number of earlier instances of contact beginning as early as the mid-1500s (Hezel 1983; Labby 1976, 2). While Yap managed to avoid frequent contact with Europeans for much of this period, Yapese communities were not fortunate enough to avoid the devastating epidemics born from exposure to a number of European diseases. Estimates of the precolonial population of the island range anywhere from twenty-eight thousand to fifty thousand inhabitants (Labby 1976; Hunt et al. 1954; Schneider 1955). By the time of the first census conducted by the Catholic mission in 1899, however, the population had shrunk to just under eight thousand. Yap's population reached an all-time low during the American Navy's first census in 1946, with merely 2,478 inhabitants (Egan 1998, 43; Hunt et al. 1949; Useem 1946, 4). As Labby argues, the "process of depopulation had, of course, definite effects on Yapese culture . . . [for even as early as the period when] the German Wilhelm Müller was doing his ethnography in 1908, he found that depopulation had irreparably upset the process of the hereditary transmission of ritual information and priestly position and that the Yapese religious system was in a state of near collapse" (1976, 3). As Egan (1998, 43) argues, this devastating loss of life also dramatically altered local social and political dynamics, since only a very few "people were available to hold the many landed positions, resulting in the concentration of many positions in single hands" (see also Lingenfelter 1975).

It is hard to say how much exposure to such epidemics may have affected local attitudes toward Europeans. As Hezel attests, "Although not entirely hostile to foreigners the Yapese had always been unpredictable in their treatment of visitors. . . . They had taken two Spanish vessels that had come to fish for bêche-de-mer in the 1830s, brutally murdering the crews, and had driven out [the British trading captain Andrew] Cheyne on his first trading visit to the island a few years later" (1983, 263). Even after his first failed attempt to establish trading relations with the Yapese in 1843, however, it was Cheyne and his new-found German business associate Alfred Tetens who first managed to establish semiregular trading relations with Yap in the 1860s.

While Spain had maintained its claim to Yap and the Caroline Islands since their "discovery" in the mid-1500s, with the closest Spanish garrisons and missions located in Guam and the Philippines respectively, this claim was nominal at best. Instead of a garrison or a mission, the first significant colonial presence in Yap came in the form of the establishment of a trading post for sea cucumber and copra by the German trading company J. C. Godeffroy and Son in 1869. It was not long after this that the most successful trader to establish residency in Yap, the Irish-born American David O'Keefe, was washed ashore in December 1871 after losing his ship *The Belvedere* in a typhoon (Hezel 1983, 263).

While other traders had difficulty motivating Yapese communities to produce copra and collect bêche-de-mer, O'Keefe discovered that motivation for such work could be quickly garnered within the context of the local system of exchange. O'Keefe's success was tied in particular to his access to steel tools and his newly acquired Chinese junk that he put to use in helping Yapese communities procure much valued large aragonite limestone disks called *raay*. For centuries, Yapese sailors had made the hazardous 280-mile ocean trip to Palau in order to spend years quarrying and crafting this "stone money" with shell tools. As Hezel notes, the "labor and risk involved were enormous, since the disks, often weighing a ton or two and measuring six feet in diameter," had to make the return trip to Yap by raft and canoe. In the process of acquiring stone money, many "lives were lost and men were maimed" (1983, 266). As I learned from talking with many of my Yapese friends and family, the worth of each piece of stone money is tied directly to the hardship and suffering that went into its acquisition. The most valuable pieces of stone money are those that are associated with a loss of life, while the least valuable tend to be those that were acquired through O'Keefe. Again resonating with ideas that will be explored in subsequent chapters, value, like virtue, is thus quite literally calibrated in Yapese cultural logic according to a *metric of suffering*.

At the height of O'Keefe's trading career, Yap was not only a major player in the copra trade in the Caroline Islands, with twenty to thirty ships visiting its shores every year to pick up the average of fifteen hundred tons of copra that were produced annually (Hezel 1975, 9; 1983, 281), but also at the center of a major political conflict between Spain and Germany. Increasingly worried about Germany's expansionism in the Pacific, Spain decided in 1885 that it was time to secure their longstanding claim to the island by establishing an administrative settlement on Yap. Spain, having spent the better part of a week preparing for the official flag-raising ceremony to celebrate their occupation of the island, was beat to the punch by a German ship that "raced in and, amid a din of beating drums and loud cries, immediately hoisted the German flag on Yap, claiming the Carolines for the Kaiser" (Labby 1976, 3). When word of Germany's attempt to annex Yap reached Spain, "thousands of angry demonstrators in Madrid stormed the German embassy and tore down the coat of arms, which they dragged through the streets and burned in the Puerto del Sol" (Hezel 1983, 311). In order to avert the possibility of war, both sides agreed to arbitration through the Vatican. Pope Leo XIII recognized Spain's sovereign right to the Carolines, while giving Germany permission to continue their business and trade operations in the region (Hezel 1983, 312–13).

In 1886 Spain finally established its first garrison and administrative center on Yap. Along with the newly appointed governor of the Western Caroline Islands came six Capuchin missionaries who established the first Catholic mission, located just above a number of small buildings that served as the first government hospital on the island (Hezel 1995, 11). As Hezel notes, this newly founded Spanish administrative and missionary presence on Yap did not, however, have much of an impact on daily life (1991, 1995). According to Hezel, in spite of the goals of the Spanish officials and missionaries, "the Yapese ate, worked, danced, and reveled in their men's houses as before, venturing into the colony only to sell copra, replenish their supply of liquor, and witness one of the occasional religious fiestas. Very few showed any real interest in becoming Catholics, much to the disappointment of the Capuchin missionaries" (1995, 82). As Egan observes, the Spanish government was also quite ineffectual in settling disputes between Yapese communities and intervillage warfare continued as it had for centuries (1998, 39). The Spanish colonial rule of Yap was not long lived, however. The financial destitution at the end of its defeat in the Spanish-American War led Spain to sell its Micronesian possessions to Germany in 1899.

German rule brought a number of significant changes to Yap, including the establishment of a system of municipalities that were imperfectly based on the local system of intervillage alliances and counter-alliances. This restructuring, which included the banning of intervillage warfare, was an attempt to ensure that information concerning German colonial regulations, policies, and work programs could be dispersed through a newly established council of eight chiefs *(piiluung)* from the highest-ranking villages (Egan 1998, 39; Hezel 1995, 105). The German colonial regime conferred with the council to help mobilize a Yapese work force that was used "for exhausting work on all . . . public projects" (Hezel 1995, 105).

With the outbreak of World War I the Yapese witnessed the arrival of yet another colonial power to their shores. Having declared war on Germany in accord with their ongoing alliance with Britain, Japan wasted little time in taking control of Germany's Pacific Island possessions (Egan 1998, 40; Hezel 1995, 146; Labby 1976, 4). Japanese colonial rule began in 1914, although Japan was not granted international recognition of its possession of the island until a League of Nations mandate was negotiated in 1920. It continued its rule until the American Navy took control in 1945.

The Japanese had a more extensive colonial presence than either Spain or Germany. Japan also exerted a much stricter rule over the island's inhabitants, a rule that was, in part, tied to an explicit belief in the "inferiority" of Yapese cultural traditions and Japan's mandate "to 'civilize' the Micronesian people" (Hezel 1995, 169; Labby 1976, 5). Japan's "civilizing" process included mandatory participation for all Yapese children in five years of Japanese schooling, the banning of men from sleeping in the men's houses *(faeluw)*, the prohibition of many traditional exchange practices (such as Yapese intervillage *mitmiit*), and the outlawing of all traditional religious practices (Egan 1998, 40; Labby 1976, 5; Peattie 1988; Poyer 1995, 224). With the coming of the war all able-bodied adults were further required to participate in Japanese work projects that included building a garrison and other fortifications, constructing the island's first airstrip, and providing food for Japanese soldiers (Labby 1976; Poyer 1995).

In response to their concerted efforts to change local lifeways, the Japanese met much resistance. For instance, even though the new colonial regime worked to enact its changes through a council of Yapese "chiefs," the individuals filling these positions were often younger Yapese men who were "appointed and were rarely legitimate leaders recognized by Yapese" (Egan 1998, 41; Lingenfelter 1975, 189). Filling a role that was very much a part of the Yapese traditional political system, these young men served as the eyes and ears of the legitimate traditional chiefs who were older, did not speak Japanese, and yet still wielded power in the villages where they continued to meet regularly in secret. According to Hezel (1995), the great rise in conversions to Catholicism at this time formed a further means of passive resistance in as much as it helped to put a barrier between the converts and the colonial government.

The number of Japanese living in Yap was comparatively small for much of the duration of their colonial rule, with only 275 individuals in 1931, six hundred in 1935, and approximately fourteen hundred at the beginning of the war (Poyer 1995, 224; Peattie 1988, 180–81). Not long after the first U.S. air attack on Yap on March 31, 1944, however, the number of Japanese in Yap skyrocketed with the arrival of seven thousand military personnel who were to form a new secondary line of defense in the Western Pacific (Poyer 1995, 227). The increased presence of Japanese troops on the island, combined with Japan's use of Yap as a point for "funneling air power to forward bases," resulted in American air strikes becoming a relatively routine occurrence on the island (Poyer 1995, 229). Indeed, many elders I spoke to recalled the last year of the war as a time of great suffering *(gaafgow)* and fear *(rus)*. It was a time when one could never be certain how many days would pass before there would once again be the dreaded sound of approaching planes, inevitably followed by calls to run to caves or the woods for shelter.

During my time in Yap, memories of the war and reflections on the Japanese colonial regime were a common topic of conversation with the elders whom I befriended. However, it was not until my colleague Jennifer Dornan and I set out to conduct an oral history and GPS mapping project at the request of my host village that I got a real sense of the extent that the war and the Japanese occupation had impacted day-to-day life on the island. Every day as we walked through the village with a number of elders who were helping with the project, we saw evidence of destruction to house foundations, paths, and sacred sites. We also heard from the elders of how the Japanese had torn down the women's house *(dopael)* in order to build a kitchen to feed the soldiers. In yet another part of the village we found two empty Japanese gasoline drums buried in the middle of one of the village's highest-ranking and most auspicious foundations. These two gas drums, the elders recalled, served as restrooms for the soldiers. The destruction of such sacred sites, paths, and community meeting houses *(p'eebaay)*, when combined with the scarcity of food and the forced work regimes, left many people who lived through that period with ambivalent feelings toward the Japanese, to say the least.

That said, much like Labby (1976) and Poyer (1995) before me, I discovered that even despite these hurtful memories, most individuals also expressed considerable compassion *(runguy)* for the Japanese soldiers. By the end of the war, they were starving, hiding in the woods, living without shelter, and "reduced to a plight worse than that of the Yapese" during the war (Labby 1976, 5). This, as we will see, fits well with local understandings of morality in which a dynamic of suffering and compassion is central. Moreover, almost everyone I spoke to was careful to distinguish between how comparatively well they were treated by Japanese civilians prior to the beginning of the war and the harshness with which they were treated by the Japanese military.

Like many important events in Yap's history, the indelible marks of the suffering endured in the face of the war have been inscribed in one of the most significant aesthetic forms in Yap, dance. A good example of how these experiences of the war are preserved in collective memory is found in the following dance chant. This chant was composed by one of contemporary Yap's most esteemed dance experts, an elder named Tinag who lives in the district of Rull, and was purchased by the village I lived in. At the time of my fieldwork it was performed regularly in the form of a bamboo dance *(gamaal)* for tourists visiting the village.

I have decided to share this rough translation of the dance, which, despite its obvious shortcomings, still conveys in rather vivid terms the suffering that was endured by many Yapese during the war.

> Humbly, let me tell you a story of suffering that we endured during the war.
> This story that we are singing we have heard passed down from one generation to the next.
> This story is a story of suffering that makes us feel great compassion for those who came before us.
>
> For one full year they were lost running from one valley to another.
> The only reason the soldiers came to Yap to live among us was to take control of us.
> And yet whenever they spoke of Yap, they said that they were going to help our island.
> We left our homes and they lived in our villages while we fled to the valleys.

And now we are finally ready to talk about what happened to us.
When it was morning we started looking for streams.
Coming from the east was a distinctive rumbling sound in the sky.
A group of birds spread all over our island.

We were groping, running, and we could not find our way.
We thought that we would not even reach the door of the hole we had
     dug in the ground like a home of a land crab where we would run
     to hide.

And beyond anything that we could expect or imagine, we were living in
     a hole like crabs. Where it was dark and the kids were crying.
It was killing them, the hunger, and the children were starving.

The sky is closed to us, as is our hope.
They come down in torrents to the ground.
They shoot in the area where we had been forced to work.
The fear is killing us, we hit the ground because the whole island
     is shaking.

Everything was falling in one direction.
When the sun set, we came out from inside the hole up to the
     surface, groping.
We were hungry, but the soldiers controlled our taro patches so you
     could not go look for food there without being seen and punished.
This is the suffering of one year's duration.

Like in the children's game where you are always running, we went from
     one valley to another.
Everything was getting worse, new kinds of sickness came to us, sores
     came to the children, and we had no self-worth, no hope.
We could not even dream that one of us would survive.
All of our minds fell in one direction, frustrated, depressed,
     without hope.

The end of the war heralded the arrival of the fourth and last wave
of colonial governance. The American Navy took control of the island
in 1945 and assumed rule over Yap for the next six years as part of the
new Trust Territory that consisted of the Caroline, Marshall, and
Mariana islands (with the exception of Guam). Unlike Japan's concerted attempt to "civilize" the inhabitants of Yap, the early American
policy of "minimal interference" (Labby 1976, 6) produced a climate
wherein a number of traditional practices were reestablished. While it
is hard to say exactly how pervasive the restoration of these traditions
was, scholars like Hezel have likened it to "a cultural renaissance" (1995,
276–77). As Labby (1976, 6) and Lingenfelter (1971, 273–82) observe,

this cultural renaissance included restoring some of the traditional religious and ritual practices, rebuilding a number of the traditional men's houses *(faeluw)*, and constructing traditional canoes. *Mitmiit* exchanges, funeral ceremonies, and traditional dances were also taken up once again (Hezel 1995, 277).

The rekindling of such traditions was no doubt further aided by the strict control the navy exerted over visitors to the island. Indeed, aside from navy administrators, visitors to Yap were primarily restricted to a number of American researchers and anthropologists—including most famously David Schneider, a participant in George Murdock and Douglas Oliver's Navy and National Research Council–funded Coordinated Investigation of Micronesian Anthropology team (Bashkow 1991).

During the years of navy rule the professed primary focus of the American colonial administration was to help rebuild damaged facilities, improve health care and sanitation, establish an educational system, and aid with economic development (Hezel 1995, 257–61). To this end, the navy managed to recruit a small labor force by offering wages to Yapese workers who set out to fix many of the island's roads, build a new hospital, and construct a number of elementary schools and dispensaries in Yap's various municipalities. Much like the Germans and Japanese before them, the Americans also attempted to institute a council of elected chiefs to represent each of the districts to help relay information and requests from the Navy administration to the villages. Although, as Labby (1976, 6) maintains, these newly elected "chiefs" were largely ineffectual due to the atrophying of their powers during the war years.

In 1951 the U.S. Department of the Interior took over administration of the island. As a result, a number of salaried positions tied to public services and the local administrative bureaucracy were now available to be filled by Yapese workers (Labby 1976, 6). The continued economic isolation of the island was still readily evident, however, in the fact that the living standards in Yap and the rest of Micronesia had greatly declined since prewar levels (Egan 1998, 44; Useem 1946). So much so that in the early 1960s the United Nations took an active interest in the United States' management of the Trust Territory, ultimately pressing the American government to invest more money in the region and to begin developing plans to establish self-governing communities in Micronesia (Egan 1998, 45). The United States, with an ongoing strategic military interest in the area, responded by funneling money into the Trust Territory. This money helped to institute a number of government-run service programs, aided with various projects being set up in conjunction with President Kennedy's newly constituted American Peace Corps, and greatly extended the administrative bureaucracies in the various districts.[2]

After well over a decade of negotiations that were punctuated by the fractioning of the various districts comprising the U.S. Trust Territory of the Pacific Islands into four distinct polities, Yap was established as the administrative capital of Yap State, one of the four states comprising the FSM. Along with the Republic of the Marshall Islands, the FSM signed its Compact of Free Association with the United States in 1986, and as such became recognized as an independent nation that has chosen to "freely associate" with the United States. In return for this free association, the United States agreed to provide the FSM with access to a number of U.S. federal programs, free entry of its citizens into the United States for work or education, the use of American currency, the continuing interlinking of U.S. and FSM postal services, as well as large annual payments for use in further developing the nation's political, educational, economic, and health-based initiatives. The first compact came to an end in 2001, with negotiations for an amended compact beginning well before that time. The amended compact, which offers much less in the way of funding and entails a much greater emphasis on accountability on the part of the FSM national and state governments, was implemented on May 26, 2004.

Postcoloniality, Tradition, and Modernity

It is impossible to examine postcolonial contemporary Yapese society without recognizing the interplay, and at times evident tension, between the rhetorics of tradition and modernity. I became aware of this tension on my very first trip to the island in September 2000. Stepping off the plane from Guam, I vividly recall walking past the immigration checkpoint and being greeted by a young man and woman wearing traditional dress. The young man was wearing a *kafar*, a carefully wrapped combination of cotton, banana fiber, and hibiscus around his waist. The young woman was wearing an *oeng*, a skillfully woven grass skirt. As I approached them, the young woman, all the while avoiding eye contact, smiled and placed a *nuunuw* (flowered lei) on my head. She then handed me a pamphlet that contained tourist information and a map of Yap, before quietly welcoming me to the island.

After getting my bags and walking through customs I entered the airport's open-air waiting area. Lined with backless benches filled with Yapese families awaiting the departure or return of friends and family, the area also contained a handful of American, Japanese, and European tourists preparing to leave the island en route to Guam. I recall a lot of activity. Yapese men and women working for each of the five major hotels—all but one of which were located in the main port town of Colonia—held up signs, greeted their guests, and helped visitors get their bags aboard the vans that would take them to their respective destinations. All the while, local families said their good-byes to loved ones departing the island or greeted those who had just returned home.

I noticed that unlike my official greeters, everybody in the airport, with the exception of a few individuals who I would later learn were Outer Islanders, was wearing Western clothes. Wardrobes mostly consisted of some combination of shorts, T-shirts, and flip-flops *(zories)*. As I made my way to the van that would take me to my hotel, I recall thinking that the airport parking lot also evidenced a tension between tradition and modernity. In addition to containing various models of cars and trucks, the parking lot had a few local structures built with pandanus-leaf roofs and bamboo benches. Here people sat while talking, laughing, and chewing betel nut. The airport itself was designed to echo the structure of traditional meeting houses *(p'eebaay)* with its open-air waiting area framed by a highly peaked roof.

My destination that day, Colonia, locally called *Donguch* (the Yapese term for "small island"), is the island's main port town. Colonia's layout is itself indexical of the impact of transnational economic, social, and political forces on local ways of being-in-the-world. For instance, Colonia is the location for the island's major businesses, the small tourist industry, the high school, the Yap State Campus of the College of Micronesia, and the government of Yap State. As directly reflected in the makeup of the town, there is absolutely no doubt that postcolonial Yap has been greatly impacted by its history of contact, conflict, exchange, and interaction with the various colonial regimes that claimed control over its shores. This fact has indeed been recognized in all the major published ethnographies of Yap, which have detailed the many ways in which contemporary Yapese society has been importantly transformed through missionization, colonization, and increasing integration into world economic systems.

FIGURE 1. A view of Colonia. Photo by the author.

Life in the villages, while certainly more "traditionally" organized than life in Colonia, has also clearly been greatly transformed by such forces. At the time of my fieldwork, many, but not all, houses had access to electricity, running water, and telephones (and midway through my third field season in 2002, cell phones). Many homes also had refrigerators, radios, television sets, VCRs, and various other household appliances. Depending on the socioeconomic status of the particular village or family, houses ranged from modest traditional homes to structures built out of wood and corrugated steel to Western-style concrete constructions. Many families had access to a car or a truck. Renting Hollywood movies, drinking Budweiser or Coca-Cola, eating rice, ramen noodles, and canned tuna, while talking about Compact negotiations, September 11, Iraq, and American politics, were all often a part of everyday village life. Most schools had computer facilities and access to the Internet. Hip-hop, reggae, and rap music was played on the local radio station and on stereos and CD players across the island. The extent of intergenerational difference in terms of style of dress, fashions of speaking, and general comportment were readily apparent to me even very early in my fieldwork.

That said, it would be a mistake to overlook the fact that there is still a prevalent recognition by many Yapese individuals and students of Yapese culture that there are important continuities to be found between contemporary and "traditional" cultural forms. Yapese cultural logic has certainly been shaped by particular historical trajectories. However, it has also played, and continues to play, an important role in patterning the always selective local incorporation of nonlocal forms of understanding, acting, consuming, and valuing (cf. Robbins 2004, 6–15; Sahlins 1981, 1985, 1995). Outsiders have long commented upon the "conservative" nature of Yapese society. The Spanish, German, Japanese, and American colonial regimes all remarked upon what they perceived to be Yapese "resistance" to change and modernization. These colonial regimes also observed that Yapese individuals and communities seldom adopted foreign goods, practice, or beliefs without careful deliberation.[3]

I believe that one reason for the pervasive perception of the apparent "resistance" and "conservatism" so often attributed to Yapese communities is, at least in part, a result of the fact that local understandings of subjectivity, social action, and morality are enmeshed in a system of cultural virtues predicated on the valuation of deliberate, thoughtful action, a theme that I will explore in much greater detail in later chapters. As I have come to understand it, Yapese "resistance to change" was never simply resistance or conservatism as such. It was more accurately a reflection of the valuation of carefully assessing ideas, goals, values, and technologies, whether introduced from within or outside of Yapese communities. Indeed, while there is an overt cultural ideology that places a great value on maintaining longstanding traditions, Yapese people have always been quick to adopt new ideas, materials, and technologies when such innovations are understood to be of some benefit or can be understood to align with previously established norms and values.[4] The result of this stress on deliberate action is that novel ideas, values, and practices were seldom adopted unthinkingly or simply because they happen to align with a particular individual's personal needs, desires, and wants.

To be clear, some individuals do act without thinking, just as some people are highly skilled at using community goals as a means to achieve their own personal ambitions and advancement. There is as much of a range of variation in the individual internalization of these ideals as in any other community of practice. Those individuals who were skillfully able to manipulate the system by aligning putative community goals with their own ambitions and desires were, however, at times highly regarded. Those who were not skilled in this delicate negotiation between personal desires and collective goods or who transparently acted in accordance with their personal ambitions were looked down upon and often socially criticized.

Yap at the time of my fieldwork was thus as much about money, computers, TVs, VCRs, video games, movies, and top-forty music as it was about taro patches, gardens, fishing, canoes, rafts, betel-nut chewing, magic, ancestral spirits, and local medicine (cf. Lingenfelter 1993). There were often significant differences in the extent to which specific individuals internalized nonlocal values, and perhaps not surprisingly there was a great difference between the younger generations and their elders in this regard. Like all aspects of Yapese social life, however, there are always multiple levels at which these tensions between tradition and modernity are played out.

As Egan suggests, in thinking about these complex relations between tradition and modernity in contemporary Yapese society, we must always appreciate the fact that "social reproduction . . . has involved negotiation and uncertainty. Outcomes were never predetermined, and, in many cases, 'continuities' resulted from older relations being reproduced for different reasons and through entirely new means. . . . [And accordingly, the] Yapese have tried to make elements of an older cultural order—as they have received it—relevant in post-colonial contexts" (1998, 84).

Yapese culture, like all cultures, is thus "situated and linked within wider cross-cultural histories" (Descantes 2002, 227). And yet, Yapese ways of being-in-the-world have a defined integrity such that local norms, practices, values, and modes of comportment are never simply a pliable refraction of "the pervasive colonial culture" (Descantes 2002, 227; cf. Sahlins 1981, 1985, 1995).

Emplacing Ethnography

> The self-conscious, reserved manner of the Yap people, which Krämer rightly ascribes to them, is indeed a true impediment for the investigator.
>
> Wilhelm Müller, 1917

It is a truism that every ethnographer faces significant challenges in conducting research and that knowledge accrued through such endeavors is always, necessarily, selective and partial. Despite researchers' attempts to ensure some degree of methodological rigor in the hope of asymptotically approaching a nonbiased (i.e., "objective") account of what it is they have experienced, observed, and learned through fieldwork, anthropological knowledge, however carefully enacted, is always mediated through the subjectivities of the researcher and his or her acquaintances, informants, friends, and teachers. The knowledge that is accrued through ethnographic research is thus best understood as an *intersubjective achievement*. It is a reflection of a complex set of interactions between those historical conditions and social trajectories within which a researcher is emplaced and the sedimentation of cultural, educational, and idiosyncratic influences upon the subjectivities of the ethnographer and the specific individuals he or she interacts with in the field.

An excellent case in point is found in Ira Bashkow's (1991) account of the various ways in which the trajectories of colonial history played a crucial role in shaping the course and outcome of David Schneider's research on the island between the years 1947 and 1948. As Bashkow (1991, 170) notes, Schneider came to the field with an early interest in psychoanalytic theory and in exploring the functional dynamics of Yapese culture and personality.[5] Inspired by psychoanalytic theory, Schneider attempted to engage in careful self-examination while in the field, which, as Bashkow observes, can now be considered almost prescient in its anticipation of the reflexive turn in ethnographic writing that occurred some thirty years later.

What is most interesting about Schneider's psychoanalytically inspired reflections, however, is the fact that he provides us with an important glimpse into the dynamics of his negotiations with his Yapese informants—what Schneider called in the context of his notes, "rapport." It is true that Schneider never fully understood the extent to which his research was directly impacted by local interpretations, expectations, and political maneuverings, which where all significantly shaped by Yap's colonial history. And yet, as Bashkow demonstrates, his notes give us considerable insight into the various ways in which Schneider's "own identity was construed by . . . [the Yapese], in relation to their experience of colonial domination, and in the context of his own identification with victims of oppression" (1991, 171). Almost forty years after the completion of Schneider's fieldwork, James Egan asserted that "the overall field context continued to be shaped by historical forces that flowed from the colonial past into contemporary economic and political relations" (1998, 70). Egan also discovered, as had Catherine Lutz (1988) in Ifaluk, that he was situated within a locally defined nexus of kin and sociopolitical relationships.

Like most fieldworkers, the unique path I took to being socially positioned in Yap was based partially on serendipity, and partially on my own personality and my ability (or inability in many cases) to become a competent member of a Yapese community. It was also partially based on many of the historical conditions and political maneu-verings that have been so insightfully examined by Bashkow (1991), Egan (1998), and Lutz (1988). While issues tied to confidentiality prevent me from detailing the exact path I took to find my social place-ment in Yap, I too was situated within local social, political, and moral landscapes in my being associated with a particular house foundation *(tabinaew)*, in a particular village *(binaew)*, as a child *(faak)* of particu-lar Yapese parents *(chiitamangin/chiitimangin)*.

Like Egan (1998), I too found that this social positioning conferred a number of advantages and challenges for my research. In being posi-tioned as a child—that is, as a landless, needy, suffering, and lower-status person who is reliant upon the compassion of a landholding higher-status caregiver—my adopted Yapese parents were put in the position of having to assume the obligation of ensuring that I was properly socialized, cared for, and safe. By being granted a position within the community as an "insider"—a placement that both Egan (1998) and Lutz (1988) recognize as being an important strategy for gaining control over outsiders living in the community—I was thus granted access to forms of knowledge that are only accessible to active members of Yapese families and communities.

Another implication stemming from this social positioning, however, was that in being associated with a particular family, in a particular landed-estate, village, and municipality I also faced, along with others in my community, the serious restrictions that are placed on social mobility within Yap. This in turn necessarily limited access to forms of knowledge that resided outside of the circle of relations that defined the particular social networks within which I was emplaced (see also Egan 1998). Given the complex hierarchical structure of Yapese society, there are distinctive restrictions placed on where an individual can go, what paths he or she can walk on, what villages he or she can visit, and who it is that he or she can talk to or interact with.

It is important to note in this regard that during my time sitting in on a Peace Corps language training program, I was fortunate to become close friends with my language teacher, Taman, who hailed from the municipality of Maap. This friendship led, upon my third trip to the island in the fall of 2002, to my being able to place my colleague, Keith Murphy, with my teacher's family for a six-week stay. I made regular trips to Maap to visit my teacher and my colleague and I spent more than a few nights at their house. My friendship with Taman combined with the fact that one of my two research assistants hailed from Maap resulted in my being afforded the possibility of feeling quite comfortable conducting research in two differing municipalities. While it is true that I, like Egan, felt most comfortable in my home municipality of Dalipebinaw (the municipality where my Yapese family lived), I also found myself increasingly at ease when traveling or working in Maap.

In Yap, as is true of many cultures in the Pacific region, there is also great emphasis placed on ensuring that men's and women's activities and obligations, as well as the forms of knowledge associated with them, are carefully separated. There are numerous ways in which activities are distinguished according to gender, including the very basic, and important, fact that it is traditionally the role of men to supply the family with *thum'aeg* ("meat" or "fish") and the role of women to provide the family with *ggaan* ("food," which refers primarily to taro and the various other starch-based vegetables grown in Yapese gardens).

Given such restrictions on interaction between the genders I decided early on that it would be necessary to locate at least one female research assistant who could accompany me whenever I was conducting interviews with women. I was fortunate early in my third field season to have the opportunity to meet Keira Ballantyne, a PhD student from the University of Hawai'i, who was conducting a few months of research on the island in order to gather data for her dissertation in linguistics. While in Yap, Ballantyne had been working closely with two research assistants whom she had trained in transcription. Ballantyne was kind enough to introduce me to the woman who would become the first of my two research assistants, Sheri Manna.

Manna, a woman in her early sixties, also lived in my municipality, Dalipebinaw. With a sharp intellect combined with a great sensitivity to, and interest in, Yapese language and culture, Manna proved to be an invaluable asset to the project, helping not only with interviewing women, but also with the many hours that were devoted to transcribing and translating interviews.[6] She, along with my Yapese mother, also spent countless hours answering what must have seemed to them to be an endless stream of questions about Yapese language, history, tradition, ethnomedicine, and ethnopsychology.

Given the social limitations placed on traveling to municipalities in which Manna did not have close friends and relatives, I soon found it necessary, however, to seek out a second research assistant who hailed from another part of the island. I was led to look for an assistant from Maap given my familiarity with the municipality combined with the fact that traditionally individuals from Maap often have close social and political ties with individuals in the northeastern (relative to Dalipebinaw) municipalities of Rumung, Gagil, and Tomil. Again, I was lucky to be introduced through another of my language teachers, Francisca Mochen, to Stella Tiningin, a woman in her late thirties who had attended university in both Hawai'i and Guam, and who had previously done interviewing for the Historic Preservation Office. While Manna and I worked together for all of the interviews conducted with women in the western, central, and southern municipalities of the island (Fanif, Rull, Kanifay, Dalipebinaw, and Gilman), Tiningin and I worked together in the northeastern municipalities.

The challenge that had the most profound effect on my research, however, was my having to face the prevalent Yapese valuation of the ideals of privacy, secrecy, and concealment (cf. Petersen 1993; chapter 5). As I will explore in greater detail in later chapters, privacy, secrecy, and concealment were importantly integrated into multiple levels of the social fabric in Yap. This social fabric is one that is kept intact through a diffuse social distribution of power and knowledge. Indeed, at all levels of Yapese social life there are a number of cultural checks and balances in place to ensure that power and knowledge never accumulates solely within the purview of one person, one family, one village, or one set of village alliances.

Traditionally, for instance, this diffuse distribution of knowledge and power was evident at the level of village leadership. In each village, there is not one, but three "chiefs" *(piiluung)*: a chief that represents the voice of the women *(piiluung ko binaew, lunguun paweelwōl)*, a chief that represents the voice of the young men *(piiluung ko pagäl, lunguun pagäl)*, and a chief that represents the voice of the ancestors *(pilabthir ko binaew)*. Each chief speaks for a differing sphere of knowledge, competence, and power in the village. The very word that is used for chief, *piiluung*, is literally translated as "many voices." This highlights the fact that the individual holding one of these three positions is not understood to speak for himself. Instead he is understood to

speak for those individuals in the village whose interests and competencies he represents. Ideally then, it is not personal opinions or prejudices
that are to guide a chief's decision-making and expression at the level
of village affairs, but those of the individuals his voice is held to represent in the village. It should not be personal but collective goals and
desires that are expressed through the chief's voice in the context of
village affairs.[7]

One of the reasons given to explain the traditional threefold structure of chiefly authority in Yap—a structure that is replicated on a
number of different social levels—is that it ensures that one individual
is never able to take control of too much power. With three chiefs
sharing the differential spheres of power in the village, there are always
two individuals to keep the third chief's influence in line with the
concerns of the other members of the village.

At the level of the island, this threefold structure was traditionally
replicated in the competencies and responsibilities of the three highest
ranking villages and in the two systems of village alliances representing
the side of the chiefs *(ban piiluung)* and the side of the young men
(ban pagäl) whose disputes were resolved through seven foundations
that were understood to embody the power of women as mediators
(ulung somol). At the level of the family, the same structure held with
regard to the spheres of knowledge, competence, and power that were
distributed between the mother, the children, and the father. In the
context of this system, as Egan (1998, 76) explains, "No one possessed
more than a few disconnected pieces of the grand political puzzle of
Yapese knowledge, though each piece could only have meaning when
joined with other parts. Keeping knowledge secret and segmented
prevented the possibility of anyone learning too much and using their
accumulated information to press new claims to authority." This broad
distribution of knowledge and power by means of secrecy and concealment is further rooted in a local epistemology in which the transferring
of knowledge from one individual to another is held to necessarily
occur within a dynamic exchange of sentiments—suffering and sacrifice
on the part of the individual receiving the knowledge and compassion
and care on the part of the one giving it.

While I will elaborate upon this dialectic of suffering and compassion
in subsequent chapters, it is important to point out that my own abilities to make connections with people, to learn from them, and to
gather knowledge about their cares and concerns was often very much
mediated through my own experiences of suffering, as well as through

my abilities to demonstrate compassion when witnessing the suffering of others. On this accord, a number of key turning points in my field-work that led to my greater incorporation into my family and community came only after I had engaged in particularly difficult community work projects, and in a couple of cases, not long after I had unintentionally injured myself and had become sick. In one instance, I had to undergo treatment from a local healer who put my shoulder back into place after I had slipped and fallen off a makeshift coconut-tree bridge. In a second instance, I had to be flown for emergency medical treatment in Guam. In both cases, my own pain and my ability to endure in the face of it led to a palpable shift in my relations with my family and other members of my community who expressed compassion for my suffering. In both cases individuals interpreted my decision to stay in Yap to continue my research despite these hardships as evidence of my willingness to endure suffering for the benefit of others, others who were sometimes understood to be my Canadian parents, sometimes to be my teachers in Los Angeles.

Perhaps the most vivid demonstration of this embedding of knowledge within the exchange of sentiment, however, came after I had first witnessed a young girl, whom I call Tinag, have two broken bones in her forearm put back into place by a local healer without anesthesia (see chapter 8). As I sat witnessing the intensity of her pain, as Tinag screamed, cried, struggled, and pleaded with her father and the healer to stop the procedure, I could not help but embody her suffering in the form of quiet tears. At that moment, watching her father bravely try to comfort his suffering daughter, sitting still, with tear-filled eyes, I had a crisis of faith. What was I doing here? Why should I attempt to document such private suffering and pain? Was my presence not just making things worse for everyone involved? What right did I have to witness such hurt and such fear?

Just as these questions were rushing through my mind I noticed the healer, Lani, who also had tears in her eyes, look over at me. Our eyes met for what could not have been longer than a split second, but apparently it was long enough for her to register my response to the situation. At first I was embarrassed, worried that somehow I had overstepped my bounds. From what I knew already of Yapese expectations concerning the expression of emotion I knew that I was failing miserably in living up to the ideals of mental opacity and emotional quietude. At the end of the session, however, Lani came over to talk to me. She said softly, "I saw you crying over there," and smiled, tears still fresh in her own eyes. I nodded and may have apologized. She put her hand on my shoulder and told me that I could stop by anytime. She wanted to help me with my research. From that moment on I became a regular at Lani's house, meeting many people with her gracious help and introduction, some of whom ended up sharing their experiences of pain and suffering with me.

CHAPTER 2

From Land to Virtue

As we sat on the veranda to protect ourselves from the intense afternoon heat, Tina began telling me about her first years living in her husband's household. When she first came to her husband's estate she was suffering. She had five cooking pots to take care of: hers and her children's, her husband's, his mother's, his grandfather's, and his father's. During this period many families still adhered to the strict food preparation rules in which a husband's food was prepared and consumed separately from that of his wife and children.[1] She recalled that she was not allowed to set foot in her father-in-law's taro patch nor was she allowed to eat chestnut from either her father-in-law's or mother-in-law's chestnut trees. She was forbidden to drink or eat coconut and was only given one betel nut tree to get her betel nut from. Able to cut only one small part of a branch of betel nut a day, she had to try her best to make it last. Perhaps most difficult of all, however, was the fact that her mother-in-law never allowed her to eat when they went to work in the gardens and taro patches. Each morning, the two of them would prepare food for the children and the men, and then they would leave immediately for the gardens. Her mother-in-law repeatedly told her: "Don't you eat because if you eat you will destroy the garden, be sure to help the taro patches and gardens, don't you eat." She had no choice but to keep working, suffering, and enduring.

This chapter details an indigenous model of social structure (Robbins 2004) that is rooted in Yapese understandings of a rhetoric and dynamic of sentiment. Significantly, the psychological and moral underpinnings of this model include the negotiation of relationships as mediated through a dynamic interplay of viscerally palpable experiences of suffering *(gaafgow)*, endurance *(athamagil)*, work-induced exhaustion *(magaer)*, and compassion *(runguy)*. In examining such local configurations of social life, I will lay the groundwork for detailing the ways in which experiences of suffering generally, and experiences of pain more specifically, are intimately linked to Yapese moral sensibilities and ideals of ethical modes of being.

Before I turn to outline this constellation of morally valenced sentiments, however, it is first necessary to examine previous ethnographic accounts of the interconnections between land, gender, power, and social relations. Centrally implicated in Yapese understandings of social life is the concept of *magaer*—the sensation or feeling of work-induced exhaustion, tiredness, or fatigue. *Magaer*, I argue, is an example of a morally configured sensory attunement, what Thomas Csordas (1993) would call a somatic mode of attention. Of central concern here is how *magaer* relates to a pivotal cluster of moral sentiments that include suffering; endurance, perseverance, or striving; compassion; and shared pain *(amiithuun)*. Together, these moral sentiments pattern everyday practices that generatively contribute to the perpetuation and contestation of norms, values, and ideals informing everyday social life. As such, these moral sentiments importantly configure individual experiences of suffering with pain.

Tabinaew: A Dialectic of People and Land

David Schneider's early descriptions of Yap suggest that Yapese society evidenced a dual descent system. On the one hand, patriliny could be understood as an "artifact" of those social configurations surrounding the hierarchical organization and control of land. On the other hand, matriliny was "psychologically real" inasmuch as it was a basis for engendering solidarity between individual clan members who were otherwise dispersed through differing landed estates (Egan 1998; Schneider 1949, 1953, 1962). For the most part, this interpretation of Yapese kinship was supported in the subsequent ethnographic work of Mahony (1958) and Lingenfelter (1971, 1975). It was not until Schneider's student David Labby began attending to local models emphasizing the relationship between landed estates *(tabinaew)*, matrilineal clans *(ganong)*, and labor *(magaer)*, however, that a clearer picture of Yapese sociopolitical life was inscribed in the ethnographic record.

Previous ethnographies of Yap had recognized the centrality of the *tabinaew* (landed estate) in configuring social and economic relationships, political hierarchy, and kinship. It was Labby's insight into the centrality of work and labor in mediating intergenerational land transactions, however, that provided a basis for a new understanding of the structures of Yapese social life. Namely, it revealed that what had been previously characterized as a dual decent system was in fact a social system arising from ongoing histories of transaction between successive exogamous matrilineal clans negotiating rights to landed estates through an exchange of service, labor, respect, and care.

Traditionally (and in many ways still today), Yapese social structure was radically hierarchical, articulated according to historical relations in the form of matrilineal links constituting clan membership *(ganong)* and affiliation with a particular *tabinaew* (Egan 1998; Labby 1976; Lingenfelter 1975; Schneider 1984). In the case of the former, the emphasis is placed upon shared affiliation between all of those who are connected through "one-belly" to a specific matrilineal clan.[2] Each clan traces its origins to a founding female ancestral spirit *(nik)*. In the case of the latter, emphasis is placed upon an individual's life history working on a particular estate and moving progressively through different age- and merit-based statuses (Labby 1976; Lingenfelter 1979). In this system, political status and rank are understood as rooted directly *in* those landholdings that constitute a particular estate or *tabinaew* (Lingenfelter 1975, 1977). It is the *tabinaew* that serves as a central basis for understanding Yap's complex sociopolitical structure.

The term *tabinaew* encodes a wide semantic range that encompasses anything from references to a particular household or dwelling to the "person or persons who are related to the speaker through ties to the land" (Schneider 1984, 21). According to local conceptions of personhood, power, and place, each *tabinaew* and all of the various house foundations, taro patches, and gardens associated with it, is invested with particularized histories and ranks that reflect the labor of differing successive clans upon that land (Labby 1976). As such, the status and rank of a particular landholder is tied directly to the land of his or her *tabinaew*. In fact, status, rank, and authority are never understood to be qualities inhering in specific individuals *qua* individuals, but are instead viewed to be historically sedimented in the very land itself. Individuals are understood as merely representing the "voice" *(lunguun)* of the land that is held to be the true seat *(gil ii lunguun)* of power, authority, and status (Egan 1998; Labby 1976).

It cannot be stressed enough that in Yap it is the land, and never the individual(s) associated with the land, that is imbued with rank, position, and authority. It is the land, as a material accretion of particular histories of labor-based exchange between successive generations who each once held title to that land, which is recognized as the source of power and authority. For instance, in speaking for the land, an individual is never considered a "chief" *(piiluung)*. It is instead the foundation and its associated land that is considered to hold such a status—*Buut ea piiluung!* ("Land is the chief!). Authority, rank, and status are thus inscribed in the land. The person is merely considered to be its vehicle or conduit, its "voice." Moreover, speaking for the land is not a right that is granted to every member of a given estate or *tabinaew*. One's right to speak in public, in the context of the community meeting house *(p'eebaay)*, is determined according to one's gender, maturity, and position within the *tabinaew*.

It is important to recognize that an individual's connection to land is never simply given. In the end, each individual is responsible for earning his or her right to first establish and then to maintain such ties to the estate's land. In this light, as Schneider phrases it, "people say that a child 'is formed on the *tabinau*,' stressing residence and activity and the relationship of child to *citamengen* [father] over any simple rule of recruitment by birth" (1984, 22). One should note the emphasis that is placed here on activity—activity that is framed within the context of respectful service to a higher-ranking individual (the father) whose clan currently holds title to the estate. For it is precisely this activity or service that is held to be the means by which a child is understood to form a relationship with, and thus become formed by, the *tabinaew*. According to Schneider, the *chiitamangin-faak* (father-child) relationship is centrally configured according to an ethic of *doing*, not an ethic of *being*.

Generally speaking, Schneider is correct to note that social relationships in Yap are not primarily understood as predicated upon pregiven qualities inherent in persons. That said, people do readily recognize that such qualities exist and that they do vary from one individual to the next. Moreover, while these relationships are largely viewed as resulting from the participants' actions, it is also the case that relationships are seen as importantly rooted in the flux of sentiments, motives, and feelings that are understood to generate those actions. Forms of doing, modes of comportment, codes for conduct, and performance, as well as those moral sensibilities and feelings that are understood to be generative of social action, are thus each foregrounded as central to the configuration of relationships in Yapese communities.

Personhood and Place

The beginning of an individual's relationship to land as well as his or her social recognition as a person is initially established through the act of naming (Kirkpatrick 1977). A Yapese individual is connected to the land through his or her name in a very distinct and immediate way. Names, as Schneider (1984, 22) observes, are inextricably linked to a specific *tabinaew* through a particular house foundation or *daaf.* In some cases, names of persons correspond directly to a particular house foundation and to specific plots of land affiliated with the *tabinaew*. An "individual given such a name counted these lands as actual parts of himself and had exclusive use of their resources" (Egan 1998, 104).

For most estates, the highest-ranking house foundation usually serves as the house foundation for the head of the *tabinaew*. In precolonial and early colonial times it was also thought to be the home of the estate's ancestral spirits *(thagiith)*. The landholdings of a particular *tabinaew* include a number of different foundations, each invested with differing ranks and forms of authority or *lunguun* ("voice"). Much like many other aspects of Yapese social life, an estate's collection of house foundations and their associated landholdings are never located in one central configuration. They are instead diffusely interspersed amidst the lands of those differing *tabinaew* that together constitute the Yapese village or *binaew*.

The particular ranks associated with differing house foundations represent the historical accretion of labor, effort, and exchange that were enacted by successive generations on behalf of that particular foundation. The rank of a particular foundation not only reflects its specific position within the hierarchy of *tabinaew* constituting the village *(binaew)*, but is further situated within an island-wide system of ranking that is based upon the delineation of different "castes," both landed *(piiluung)* and nonlanded *(pimilngaay)* (Egan 1998; Lingenfelter 1975).

As Egan notes with regard to the differential ranking of taro patches *(maqut)*, in this system "the efforts of generations made a taro patch culturally productive and 'high' not only by maintaining and enhancing its fertility, but also by associating the taro patch with the honors earned by estate people who made some special contribution to the overall order of sociopolitical relations. The place established by estate ancestors within this order became bound to the land upon which they lived, imbuing its soil with essences that were passed on to the very taro grown within it" (1998, 135).

Because each individual is thought to be a composite of ahistorical sex and clan identities and historical age, eating, and landholding identities tied to a particular *tabinaew,* "all persons are isolated in distinct social positions" (Kirkpatrick 1977, 313). In other words, within the relationally defined hierarchical organization of Yapese social structure that is articulated according to a "topographic idiom" of differentially ranked landed estates, no two individuals can inhabit equivalent social positions (Egan 1998).[3]

Naming and Being-Anchored-to-the-Land

Bestowing a name on a child was, and for the most part still is, the responsibility of the elders representing the *mafen,* the collection of individuals who constitute the clan (*ganong*) that currently holds the title for the estate. Each *mafen* traditionally consisted of the children's father and uncles, as well as the father's mother, sisters, and sister's children. All of these individuals share the same affiliation to the *ganong* that has most recently earned the right to the title of the land. Accordingly, it is the responsibility of the *mafen* to oversee the actions of the members of the most recent clan to arrive at the estate. In contrast, the newly arrived clan, consisting of the children and the children's mother, are expected to work the land in service of the children's father, who is the individual currently carrying the voice or *lunguun* of the estate's authority as vested in the land.

It is through working the land and serving the *tabinaew* that the children's mother and the children themselves eventually earn their right to take over partial responsibility for the land in subsequent generations. I say partial because the term *mafen* technically refers to all of the clans that still hold residual rights to the estate, which can consist of clans representing as few as three, or as many as seven, previous generations (see Egan 2004, 30; Lingenfelter 1975; Schneider 1984, 25). The children and their mother are expected to work the land, expending their effort, energy, and labor in order to earn a right to claim that land in the name of their clan when the children's father, who is ideally of a differing clan than his wife and children, passes away. In this way, at "its most fundamental level, Yapese land tenure, marriage, and the social relations within the *tabinaw* were all predicated upon the exchange of a woman's agricultural labor for rights given to her progeny in the estate of her husband" (Egan 1998, 106).

An estate or *tabinaew* is never simply the domain of a single clan. It is instead effectively a material anchor for ongoing histories of transaction between clans over successive generations. As both Labby (1976) and Egan (1998, 2004) explain, the logic of an ongoing dynamic of land-giving and land-receiving clans is clearly reflected in the often-cited Yapese saying, *tafeandad, tafean be; tafean be, tafeandad*—"our land belongs to someone else, someone else's land belongs to us." Indeed, while personal identity, including one's status, rank, caste, and position, is connected to the house foundation that is the source of one's personal name, an individual's identity and responsibilities are always stretched over multiple estates through one's clan affiliation. This represents the historical trajectory of the *ganong* through various estates over numerous generations.

Every Yapese individual then, as Egan summarizes, "at once honored the claims of people of other *ganong* whose ancestors had held the estate in past generations, just as he or she was respected by people of other lands as a descendent of former owners of those lands" (1998, 111). As one friend explained to me, the ongoing dynamics of land-giving and land-receiving operated such that the concepts of "ownership" and "boundary" were never directly applicable to local ways of construing the dialectical relationship between people and the land. In his words, "In the past we did not have boundaries, we had relations." Accordingly, if there was a particular relationship recognized between two villages or estates then the land between them was conceptualized as "us all the way to them and them all the way to us."

Egan (1998, 108), in part building upon Labby (1975) and Schneider (1984), insightfully recognizes that this system is founded on a complementary unit of inheritance consisting of the cross-sibling dyad. Here it is the paternal aunt who has the responsibility to monitor the behavior of the children and their mother in order to ensure that they respect and care for her brother and the land that her clan currently holds title and authority over. As mentioned earlier, it is also largely the responsibility of the paternal aunt to name the children, a name that gives the child a direct connection to a particular foundation *(daaf)*. This name thereby establishes the child as a person who has the right to work to earn title to the land associated with that foundation.

The act of taking a name from the foundation for a particular child is a process that can be likened to awakening the estate's ancestors: *ma puug ea yaam roodaed* ("we wake our dead"). This association makes very good sense given the fact that names associated with a particular foundation referred to "ancestors who had lived and worked on the land and who were seen to remain there after death as spirits, the *thigith*" (Labby 1976, 18). If for any reason a woman believes that her sister-in-law or her brother's children have not taken adequate care of her brother or the clan's landholdings, that they have not viscerally embodied their responsibilities to the estate through actively enduring through suffering in working the land on behalf of the *tabinaew,* it is fully within her authority to take the names back from the children. Divesting children of their names removes any claim that they might have otherwise had to that land.

Effort, endurance, labor, service, suffering, and work are the very tissue that serves to connect a person to the land. In fact, it is held that a woman who has endured suffering brought on by her hard work in the service of her husband's clan does so precisely to "anchor" her children to the land—*nga yuluw ea bitiir* (see Egan 1998, 108; 2004, 27). One elder once explained to me that this gendered form of suffering is the reason why mothers are so respected in Yap. This respect *(liyoer)* is clearly evident in the fact that while it is perfectly acceptable to insult another's father, any statement that invokes the mother is considered to be the most potent of insults, one that risks invoking a violent response. After all, it is the mother who thought, planned, and deliberately chose to "plant" her children in the land *(buut)* of her husband's village. It is in the context of this decision-making process, in recognizing the important sacrifices that the mother has intentionally endured in coming to another village in order to plant or anchor her children there, that an individual is able to take pride *(uf)* in saying that he or she is from a specific village.

In addition to her own work, effort, endurance, and suffering, a mother is further held to anchor her children to the land by teaching them to give respect to *(liyoer)* and listen to *(matooyil)* their father. Moreover, she is the one who is responsible for teaching them how to work the land. By working the land, planting and cultivating taro, and giving birth to children who learn through her example to work and

care for the land, a mother is the person whose very planning, deliberation, and forethought transforms the land itself. This transformation
literally occurs in terms of physical alterations produced in the land
through its cultivation. More figuratively it takes place in terms of the
transition of differing peoples and clans over the land, a process that is
enacted through the successive anchoring of new generations of children to that land. These are simultaneously physical and historical
transformations to the land that are mediated by the embodied forms
of suffering and sacrifice of women who came to plant or anchor their
children in a particular village.

Cross-Siblingship and the Structural Dynamics of *Tabinaew* Relations

Women traditionally come from outside of the estate *(bpiin ma feek u
bang)*. Men, in contrast, are responsible for staying on the land and
enacting the authority or voice *(lunguun)* that was inscribed in that
land on behalf of the clan members associated with it *(mafen)*. Here,
cross-siblingship is articulated with land and clan affiliation in such a
way, as Schneider maintains, that "a man and his sisters and the sisters'
children spread across two *tabinaw* but make one *genong* [matrilineal
clan]" (1984, 25). The relationship between men and women in their
complementary roles as brother and sister *(walaag)* directing the
tabinaew affairs, as Egan makes clear, is thus one in which men are
granted the responsibility of overseeing the material resources of the
land, while women are afforded the "right to manage the affairs of the
tabinaw people" (1998, 109). Indeed, it is the women who monitor
the actions of the new clan members who have arrived through their
brothers' marriages.

The goal of a woman in her role as a mother is to seek a better
position for her children than that of her natal family in order to
improve the position of the clan in subsequent generations (Labby
1976, 16). Prior to a daughter being married, her mother will ideally
have in mind the level of village or estate that she should to marry into.
A mother tries to guide her daughter(s) to a marriage that accords with
advancing the status of the clan. As one friend explained, a mother
speaks with her daughters, instructing them to find a husband in a
village and foundation one step higher than theirs. In a mother's role
in advising her daughters to plant their children in a higher-ranked

estate, it is said, *Be yib ngooraed, be puluuw ngooraed*—"She comes to them, she directs them."

A number of elders characterized traditional marriage negotiations as ones in which the participants were engaged in careful planning and maneuvering that would affect many generations to come. The long temporal horizon implicated in such activities led some people to liken traditional marriage to an intergenerational game of chess. In this game, the acts of placing children in certain estates through adoption, while arranging marriages with others, all served the goal of improving the social positioning of the clan in subsequent generations.

In this regard, there is a saying in Yap concerning men and women in their respective roles as *mataam* and *matiin* of a clan associated with a given estate *(mafen)*—roles that Lingenfelter (1975) terms the "public father" and the "public mother" respectively—that speaks directly to this engendered division of *tabinaew* responsibility. According to this saying, the *mataam*, as the highest-ranking man in the clan currently holding title over the *tabinaew*, is the *banood*—one who is *macha'riy* "treasured," *mapiigpiigngeak* "served," *b'gaa fan* "very important," or *mathangelluwol* "sacred." The *matiin*, as the highest-ranking woman of the *mafen*, is in contrast the *puuluw* or "navigator."

As outlined above, it is women who navigate the course of the clan's future in as much as they leave their natal village to live in their husband's village. They are also responsible for teaching their children how to behave in a respectful way toward their father. This is all in an attempt to ensure that the title to the father's estate will be transferred to them. It is also women who are largely responsible for deciding what family or village a particular child should be married or adopted into, as well as playing a crucial role in determining and giving names to their brothers' children.

In contrast, men in their role as *mataam* are held to be the repositories of knowledge associated with the authority, histories of relationships, and land of the *tabinaew*. This is knowledge that is passed down to them by their fathers and their fathers' fathers. Accordingly, when fathers speak, their children should ideally pay careful attention. Whatever knowledge a father is willing to impart concerning the *tabinaew* will prove to be of utmost importance for the children's future dealings with other estates, both within and outside of the village. Such knowledge is considered to be sacred. It is knowledge that should never be forgotten—*dam pagtaline*.[4]

This connection between knowledge, the estate's ancestors, and respect for the father who has possession of this knowledge is inscribed in the very term for listening or paying attention, which is often invoked in the context of respectful relations to the father. The term in question, *matooyil,* includes the morpheme *yil,* which when used on its own refers literally to "bones" and metaphorically to "ancestors." The inclusion of the morpheme *yil* in a term that denotes listening or attention subtly connotes the residue of ancestral knowledge in the voice of the elders. Furthermore, a similar metaphorical elaboration of *yil* is implicated in another Yapese saying that concerns the woman in her role as mother and wife. For in marrying into the estate overseen by another clan, a woman is said to work in order to *thab ii yil ea binaew fa thab ii yil ea magaer*—"cut the bones from the land or to cut the bones out of the work invested" in it (Labby 1976, 19).

The Dialectic of *Gaafgow* and Runguy

The mother, who leaves her natal village to seek out a new estate within which to anchor her children, was characterized by many as the archetypal image of what it means to be suffering and destitute. The Yapese term for suffering is *gaafgow.* It is a concept that is absolutely pivotal to understanding the configuration of social relationships, personhood, and morality in Yap. The term, which is heard repeatedly in everyday conversations and in innumerable different contexts, as one well-respected elder explained to me, is one of the central "teachings of Yap" *(machib nu Waqab).* Indeed, she noted, it is out of *gaafgow* that a number of other important virtuous qualities of a moral person are cultivated, qualities such as: patience *(nuwaen'),* endurance, perseverance, or striving *(athamagil),* self-governance and temperance *(kadaen'),* respect *(liyoer),* concern and care *(taa fan, ayuw)* and humility *(soobuutaen').* Moreover, as another individual observed, the experience of suffering is also understood to be a significant motivational basis for improvement. Without *gaafgow,* an individual will never develop a sense of needing to work to improve him or herself, his or her family, or his or her circumstances.

A particularly articulate elder once told me that in this regard she does not recall her parents ever needing to tell her explicit stories about the virtue of *gaafgow,* since the term was "a period, a semicolon, a comma in all of our sentences—'Don't do that we are *gaafgow,*' 'Don't say that we are *gaafgow*,' 'We are *gaafgow* you should do this,' 'Don't think that way we are *gaafgow*,' and so on." The virtue of suffering was nicely summarized by another woman who recalled, "My elder told me, suffering is good, it shows you humility, it shows you respect, it shows you compassion *[runguy]*, it shows you care, it shows you helping and sharing, it places endurance *[athamagil]* within your mind. If you suffer, you discover how to work and you are given the strength and motivation needed to work effectively."

It is through her experience of suffering that a mother is said to anchor her children to the land. This act of anchoring is enabled through an exchange of sentiment that is metaphorically rendered as "tying" *(m'aag)* the child to the father.[5] It is the responsibility of the mother to "tie the child to the father" *(ma m'aag fa re tiir ko chiitamangin)*. What is held to facilitate this tie is precisely the mother's and her child's experiences of suffering. To this end, one individual I knew quite well recalled his mother often telling him, "You see, son, we are both suffering" *(Me gu tam gadow be gaafgow)*. As another elder attested, "It is true that the mother and her children are both suffering, they have no land, no home, they cannot return to her mother and father's village."

It is out of her experience of *gaafgow* that a mother will try to impress upon her child the precarious position that they both are in. The truth of the matter is that a child is born homeless, without ties to the land. A child is faced with having to learn to work alongside his or her mother in order to eventually earn the right to the title to land from his or her father. In the process, a child will also have to be taught to see the father as someone who should be respected and obeyed *(ma pii liyoer ngaak)*, cared for *(ma pii ayuw ngaak)*, and listened to *(ma matooyil)*.

Without embodying an attitude of respectful deference toward the father, a child risks offending the father's sisters who have the power to take his or her name away in the process removing a child's rights to the land. If this happens, the mother and her children will be forced to return to the mother's natal village. There they will be faced with very little in the way of access to taro patches and gardens given that the mother's brothers and their wives will be the ones using them. In the mother's natal village, the family will have no place or title of their own, and they will have no husband or father to supply them with fish to eat. Without a name, without access to land, individuals are in effect stripped of their personhood. In the process, as an elder once said to me, "you become nothing, you are left to live on a piece of driftwood."

Given this close connection between one's name and one's rights to accessing the land, it is not likely merely coincidence that one of the terms used for "name" in Yapese is *nguchol*. This is a term that also refers to the three rocks that were traditionally used for a hearth to support a cooking pot *(th'iib)*. Without a name, a person is quite literally without a place to put his or her pot since he or she no longer has rights to access "the resources of the land to feed himself and meet social obligations" (Egan 1998, 104).

From the time a woman first leaves her home to marry, give birth, and raise her children, she is faced with the reality that she is suffering, she is *gaafgow*. She is landless and without a title. To gain access to the knowledge that will eventually enable her children to take responsibility for the landholdings of their father's clan's *tabinaew*, a woman has to work. Like Tina, whose recollections frame the beginning of the chapter, a woman has to endure through hardship and suffering in contributing to both estate and village projects. Without this work, a woman (and her children) will never gain access to knowledge of the estate's landholdings. Ultimately, lack of such knowledge will leave a woman and her children landless and suffering.

It is the mother who is said to show her children the land, knowledge that she acquires only gradually by working in the taro patches and gardens of the estate. It is in the process of such work that a woman learns the boundaries of the *tabinaew* from the husband's mother. As a representative of the clan that currently holds title to that land, the mother-in-law is responsible for showing her daughter-in-law the landholdings of the estate bit by bit. The husband's mother does this, however, only after the wife has demonstrated her commitment to working the land, properly raising her children, and caring for and showing respect to her husband.

Traditionally, the mother-in-law begins by showing the new wife one of the estate's lowest-ranking taro patches and a garden or two. After a few years, perhaps after producing a child, the mother-in-law might then bring the wife to an additional taro patch that she could then also claim access to. In time, a woman's sons would have moved through the ranks associated with differing eating classes *(yoogum)*—a complex ritually organized hierarchical system of food-sharing restrictions for men defined by both the status and rank of an individual's *tabinaew* and by his age and maturity (Lingenfelter 1979; see also chapter 3). A son's progress through such eating classes served as an additional indication that the children were themselves respectfully working and suffering for the *tabinaew*. Accordingly, additional higher-ranking taro patches and gardens would eventually be shown to her.

The precariousness entailed in the position that a woman entered into through marriage is made all the more difficult given the fact that she has very little means for support or protection from her natal family without running away from her husband. Such an act of abandonment could very well lead to divorce, which could have dire consequences for her children's access to land. This is made worse because of the restrictions associated with brother-sister avoidance. Such restrictions I witnessed on a daily basis as sisters would physically remove themselves from a space that their brothers entered into, would turn their bodies to face away from their brothers, and would seldom speak to them directly without averting their gaze. In the event of abuse at the hands of her husband, a woman could thus not turn to her brothers for help. As one of Egan's informants noted:

You have to work. And a lot of women, you know, they suffer. All marriages have their ups and downs, and all that stuff. And it's the same for Yapese family: there you have all kinds of problems. But the women will really take all the— you know—whatever is coming to them. Some women will—even through they get beaten up so bad—they still stay, because they're thinking of their kids. Because the way the custom is that, for example, if I leave and then my husband remarries and they have kids . . . then the kids from the second marriage have more say than the kids from my marriage—because it goes back to that thing that their mother didn't really nail them down. Cause everything in Yap is like that. (Egan 1998, 107)

Accordingly, it is said that a mother should always be respected, since she has suffered through great hardship to obtain knowledge pertaining to the landholdings of her husband's estate. Moreover, she can always refuse to tell a disobedient child, or perhaps more likely a child's disobedient spouse, about a certain parcel of land.

Lacking access to explicit knowledge of the location of land is pertinent on two counts. First, given the way that Yapese villages are organized, the boundaries between parcels of land, gardens, and taro patches are in no way clearly demarcated. Instead, a given estate's landholdings are distributed like a mosaic throughout the village. Second, there is also the problem of the historical distribution of residual rights to land that the clan still lays claim to. That is, individuals need such knowledge in order to recognize rights to accessing land tied to previous generations' landholdings in other villages through ties to their clan. Lacking knowledge of the location of land thus makes that land effectively useless.

The great significance of such knowledge of landholdings is tied to the fact that an individual would never think to ask another family about what the boundaries of a particular parcel of land might be. Not knowing the boundaries to one's own land is akin to admitting that you have not effectively endured through suffering on behalf of your estate in order to obtain such knowledge. Not having access to this knowledge is both a moral indictment and tantamount to not having access to the property. Knowledge, land, personhood, and morality are inextricably interrelated.

One elder confided in me that despite these hardships, Yapese women have a subtle but potent power. As a grandmother, she explained, it was her right to tell her children what she wanted done with her grandchildren. "This one should be doing this, that one should be adopted here." She added that in this light, women, despite their suffering and hardships, should not be seen as subservient to men. Translating the term that characterizes the relationship between a woman and her husband, *tapiigpiig,* as "slave" or "servant" is not at all accurate in her opinion. She pointed out instead that a woman is not truly her husband's "slave," since a woman is always acting, sacrificing, suffering, enduring, working, and serving in order to *earn her mother-in-law's title.* "You earn your way!" she exclaimed. She then noted that the term *tapiigpiig* is literally translated as "always turning, turning." Which, she pointed out, has very interesting implications given the fact that it is *tapiigpiig* that propels the turning over of authority and rights from one clan to another as engendered by the work of a woman and her children. In her words, "This work is work that you are doing, and is work for which you most likely will not see the fruits from in this lifetime. You are doing it for your children and your children's children, for they will be the one's who will get the title from their father's mother." In her opinion, a woman's efforts at *tapiipiig* should thus not be construed as servitude since "I have plans, I have *athamagil.* I am earning something for my children and their children's children."

This brings up a crucial point. It is never *mere-suffering* that is construed to be a virtue in Yap. Yapese people, like all people, do not see value in simply suffering for suffering's sake. It is instead *suffering-for* others in the form of self-sacrifice that is construed to be a virtue (see chapter 6). Suffering-for your children, suffering-for your family, suffering-for your estate, suffering-for your community, and suffering-for your chiefs *(piiluung)* is indeed one of the central virtues underpinning models of ethical conduct and moral subjectivity in Yap.

The culturally appropriate response to the perception of suffering, or perhaps more accurately endurance in the face of suffering, is to feel *runguy*—a term that I will gloss as "concern, pity, or compassion" (c.f. Lutz 1988; Jensen 1977a). The concept of *runguy* was first explored in some detail in the context of David Schneider's (1949) dissertation where he translated the term as "love." *Runguy* is a complex term, however, with a broad semantic range that at times overlaps with the English term. Schneider at least partially recognized this when he noted that the "word 'love' *(rungui)* is not confined to heterosexual attraction, but includes the affection between a parent and child and the affection which obtains between two persons of the same sex" (1949, 72). Moreover, much like the usage of "love" in English-speaking Western communities, a great "value is set on love *[runguy]*" (Schneider 1949, 93) in helping to define family relationships.

That said, in the context of his dissertation it seems that Schneider was largely drawing on his own culturally informed interpretation of love in his rendering of the concept of *runguy*—an interpretation, which I argue, does not clearly map onto local meanings. To be fair to Schneider, I should note that while not alluding to his own earlier interpretations of the term in his dissertation, in the context of a much later work he did draw on a personal communication with John Kirkpatrick, one of his former students, to assert that *runguy* is best glossed as " 'compassion' and is . . . not to be confused with amity" (1984, 33). As we will see below, it was also in the same book, *A Critique of the Study of Kinship*, that he perceived, and yet unfortunately did not much elaborate upon, the critical motivational import of *runguy* in establishing, maintaining, and contesting those asymmetrical dependency relationships that play such a significant role in defining so many spheres of Yapese social life.[6]

As a form of compassion, *runguy* is arguably itself a type of suffering, a suffering for the suffering of another (cf. Levinas 1998). In perceiving his wife and children as *gaafgow*, seeing them working for the estate and enduring through hardship, a husband is ideally to feel *runguy*. It is this feeling of *runguy* as a form of compassionate concern or pity in the face of suffering that is held to motivate a husband to care for his

wife and children *(ma piiq ayuw ngooraed)*. It is also compassion that
is ultimately held to bind *(m'aag)* a husband to his children. A husband's care arising from his suffering for the suffering of his wife and
children is implicated in the formation of deep bonds of attachment.
Such bonds are implicated in his eventual decision to share knowledge,
land, and food with his children.

It is out of the dynamic interplay of *runguy* and *gaafgow*, between
compassion and suffering, that titles to land are thus transacted from
one clan to another. While devoting no more than a quick paragraph
to this crucial insight, Schneider did note that it is precisely "*runguy*
that makes a *citamengen* [father] care for his *fak* [child], that holds
together those who are hierarchically related" (1984, 33). And, moreover, it is the dynamics of suffering and compassion that are held to
be the qualities that propel exchange since it is "the motivating feature
of the gift" (Schneider 1984, 33). Accordingly, if any individual
approaches another "saying, '*Ah gafago*' ('I am destitute') then the
other should have *runguy,* and help the destitute person, who will then
be subordinated and owe an eventual return" (Schneider 1984, 34).

One elder once complained to me that in contemporary Yapese
society there are far too many people who are *toelaengaen'* ("high-
minded"). This, she suggested, is because people today do not know
the true meaning of *gaafgow.* Instead of feeling *runguy* in the face of
suffering, people today often become *makankanaen'* ("irritated" or
"frustrated") with people who proclaim that they are *gaafgow.* The
prevalent perspective today, she argued, is that if someone is suffering
it is because he or she is lazy *(malmaal)*. In contrast, in the past, a
person who was *gaafgow* was certain to elicit help from others. Suffering
could open the doors of even the highest chiefs.

As another friend explained, the very basis of social life in Yap is
predicated on the fact that everyone, no matter what the rank of his
or her estate, is born to a mother, a mother who suffers. Mothers,
regardless of the rank of the estate they marry into, have to directly
experience from a firsthand and embodied perspective what it means
to be *gaafgow.* In seeing their mothers suffer, and in suffering themselves, individuals thus learn to feel *gaafgow u fithik ea doway* ("suffering inside of the body"). It is said that without directly experiencing
such embodied forms of suffering, individuals will never truly learn to
feel *runguy* for others who are suffering. Interestingly, it is often held
that those individuals who do not feel *runguy* also tend to be individuals who are always happy *(falfalaen)*.

Now, happiness is certainly a feeling that is valued in Yap. And yet, to some extent, it is also understood to be a barrier to the cultivation of feelings of compassion toward those who are suffering. The assumption here is that if an individual is happy, he or she is not focused on the well-being of others, but is only interested in his or her own success and comfort. Happiness seems to also have a negative connotation inasmuch as it does not engender an orientation to the future. It is instead suffering that orients the individual to future cares and concerns. Suffering and its avoidance are thus tied to planning and thinking about what one can do in the present in the service of bettering one's position (and access to food, resources, and so on) in the future. There is thus a future orientation that is embedded in local understandings of suffering, as well as an emphasis on its moral worth. And the very motivation for helping others, for caring and empathizing with others, is held to be directly rooted in the individual's own embodied experience of *gaafgow*.

It is important to recognize that the dynamic interchange of feeling between a father and his children is held to shift directions once a father has grown too old to care for himself. For when a father (or a mother) faces the sicknesses and physical limitations that often accompany old age, he is transformed into the one that is suffering. At this time, the children who were once the ones considered *gaafgow* are now in the position of feeling *runguy* for their father, and are thus ideally to respond by caring for him accordingly. Again, if the children do not demonstrate the proper care for their father at this time, they risk losing access to crucial knowledge associated with the estate. In the worst-case scenario, they may risk having their names being taken away from them.

Significantly, it is not just land that is understood to be transacted from clan to clan and from one generation to the next, but also a variety of different forms of specialized, culturally valued knowledge. Traditionally, such forms of knowledge included massage techniques, medicines, divining, magic, architecture, and navigation. It is these same ideals underpinning the transfer of landholdings from one generation to the next and from one clan to another that are the foundation for the transfer of these specialized forms of knowledge from parents and grandparents to their children and grandchildren. It is thus sentiment in the form of suffering and compassion that mediates the exchange of knowledge, foodstuffs, and land. Whether manifest in the form of house foundations, gardens, taro patches, medicines, or teachable skills, the exchange of sentiment is mediated through n semiotic vehicles that are ultimately indexical of ongoing histories of social relations. As I wish to demonstrate in the following section, it is in the context of such a dynamic that a great many socially significant relationships are established, defined, and maintained. It is also in the midst of such a dynamic of suffering and compassion that moral sensibilities, forms of virtuous comportment, and ethical ways of experiencing the world are articulated for particular social actors.

The Story of the Two Brothers

To illustrate this dynamic of *runguy* and *gaafgow* and the potential consequences of not fulfilling one's obligations of respectful care for one's father, I would like to share a story that was told to me by a number of different individuals. The story has also been inscribed in the chant of a dance that is performed in the village of Aringel, in the municipality of Dalipebinaw. The chant is called *Soup Ko Nay*. While the details of the story differed slightly with each telling, the basic structure of the tale is as follows:

Long ago, there were many people on Yap and very little food to go around. Everyone was suffering *[gaafgow]*. People were so *gaafgow*, in fact, that many individuals did not have access to a regular supply of food *[ggaan]*. During this time, there were two brothers who were sent out on a daily basis to find food for their family. There was so little food on the island that the boys were often only able to return home with nuts collected from the large spreading branches of a *keal* tree [tropical almond or *Terminalia catappa*].

The eldest of the two boys, while always participating in this work, was selfish *[fal'ngaak']*. When the two boys would find a *keal* tree they would both climb it and collect nuts from the highest branches, which were said to be the best-tasting ones. While the younger boy would always dutifully give the almonds from the highest branches to his father, keeping only the worst tasting nuts for himself, the older brother would always eat the best almonds prior to returning home. The boy's father, of course, recognized the difference between the almonds that were brought home by the two boys, and even though the younger boy was not the eldest, his respect *[liyoer]*, effort *[athamagil]*, and suffering *[gaafgow]* engendered much compassion *[runguy]* in his father. When it came time for the father to pass down his knowledge, which consisted of a form of divining with palm fronds *[chiib]*, he recalled the actions of both of his sons. While he took the time to teach both of his sons the art of divination, he only gave the complete knowledge of the practice to the younger son.

One day many years later, once the brothers had grown, they both set out with their own sons to the sea in two separate canoes. Well into their journey they became increasingly uncertain as to which direction to proceed. They eventually decided that they should divine to find out which path would provide the safest route. Since both had received different forms of knowledge of divination from their father, in the process of interpreting the knots tied in the palm fronds, they ended up with different answers.

The brothers argued for a long time about which one of them had the correct answer, since they both knew that they had conducted their divinations exactly as their father had taught them. Unable to admit that either was mistaken, the brothers decided to go separate ways. In the event that one of their canoes would not make it back safely, they decided to switch their sons; the older brother taking his younger brother's son in his canoe and vice versa. Since the eldest brother had not been given the complete knowledge regarding divination from his father, he misread the palm leaves and as a result took the wrong path. This path was fraught with many perils. The eldest brother and the youngest brother's son were eventually killed by a giant crab. It was said that the younger brother saw the blood carried along by the currents as he and his brother's son made their way back home. He knew immediately that his eldest brother and his own son had been killed.

I believe that there are at least three lessons to take away from this tale. First, there is the fact that social relationships, even within the family, are characterized as predicated upon the maintenance of an ongoing dynamic between suffering and compassion. This is evident in the suffering of the youngest brother who worked for the estate, went without food, and gave the best almonds to his family. These are all acts of self-sacrifice and suffering that engendered feelings of compassion in his father. Second, there is the implication that it is action and not birthright that determines an individual's position in the family and access to knowledge. If an individual does not act in accord with social expectations, like the older brother who selfishly eats the best-tasting almonds while giving the worst ones to his father, he or she can be divested of his or her claim to inheritance and knowledge. Third, the story further points to the fact that an individual can never simply trust the knowledge that is given to them, even if that knowledge was handed down by his or her own parents. The knowledge that is given to another is always based on the recognition that the individual receiving this knowledge has properly endured through suffering for the benefit of the one who currently has possession of it. There is, therefore, entailed in this story the lesson of a double incentive to ensure that sons and daughters respect and care for their parents. It is only by ensuring that actions are in accord with *yalean* ("tradition") and in-line with the wishes and expectations of parents that an individual can be sure to receive knowledge, title, authority, and land.

As one elder pointed out, it is only by cultivating those qualities that are understood to arise from suffering—qualities such as humility *(sobutaen')*, mental strength *(bageel ea taafinay roek)*, and pain, compassion, or attachment for others *(amiithuun)*—that a child will be able to serve his or her father in a way that will guarantee his or her inheritance to the land and its associated *tabinaew* knowledge.[7] As such, it is precisely the cultivation of the feelings of care *(ayuw)*, humility *(soobuutaen')*, endurance *(athamagil)*, and respect *(liyoer)* that constitute the foundational sentiments upon which the relations *(yalean)* of the *tabinaew* rest. The knowledge of a *tabinaew* is therefore transmitted only once a father is able to determine whether or not his children have internalized the correct mix of embodied virtues. It is virtues taking the form of particular dispositions and sentiments that motivate action that are held to ensure the proper transmission and protection of such knowledge in future generations.

In this light, certain structures of motivation and feeling are seen as necessary for cultivating the capacities for memory and responsibility associated with the transmission of *tabinaew* knowledge. For, if a child is not humble or caring, not able to concentrate and expend effort, or not willing to listen attentively to his or her father, he or she will most likely not be motivated to learn, remember, and later transmit the knowledge in question. In addition, the same child cannot be trusted to exact the authority of the position that comes with such knowledge with care and fairness. Without having cultivated the appropriate virtues an individual will be likely to make other people in the *tabinaew* and village suffer if they ever happen to acquire authority.

As a friend explained, the history of relations or *yalean* of a *tabinaew* is a very precious thing. Without it, another person can always work to "rewrite" the history of the estate and in the process take land, authority, or power away from the *tabinaew*. This possibility is made all the more likely given that a person who does not know the *yalean* of his *tabinaew* demonstrates to others in the community that there are problems with his relationship to his father. In the end, this indicates to others that this is a person who has not embodied the values, feelings, motives, and forms of comportment that are recognized as part and parcel of Yapese understandings of virtuous personhood.

Embodying Exertion and Endurance

> The Yapese were a model for other colonies in the eyes of
> the Germans; they were industrious, capable of sustaining
> hard work until the completion of a project.
>
> Hezel, 1995

Central to understanding local conceptions of the formation, perpetuation, and negotiation of social relationships is the concept of *magaer*.
Magaer can be glossed as effort, fatigue, or feelings of physical exertion
that arise from hard work or service. In this respect, *magaer* can be
clearly distinguished from other sensory experiences like laziness
(malmaal), muscle fatigue or soreness from standing or sitting too
long *(magaaf)*, muscle cramps *(galuuf)*, feelings of being tired, very
sick, and unable to move *(awparwon)* or sleepiness *(chuw chuw)*, which
are not necessarily associated with work-based activities. Instead, work-
based activities are activities that necessarily implicate some kind of
social relationship as well as the responsibilities, duties, and expectations that accompany such relationships.

Magaer, as Labby (1976, 19) attests, is understood as an experience
that arises when an individual has expended his or her energy or effort
on behalf of another. It is, as Egan (1998, 93) observes, a concept that
"draws attention to invested labor and to what has been accomplished
through one's effort." As such, *magaer* denotes a morally laden subjective experience. *Magaer* is recognized as an embodied experience that
is comprised of a constellation of sensations that index an individual's
previous effort, labor, and their expenditure of energy on behalf of
other individuals in the clan *(ganong)*, estate *(tabinaew)*, or village
(binaew). Accordingly, it is, in Csordas's terms, an ethically infused
somatic mode of attention in which bodily sensations of effortful exertion and exhaustion "become a mode of attending to the intersubjective milieu that give rise" to those sensations (Csordas 1993).

The centrality of *magaer* in Yapese conceptualizations of social life
is nicely summarized by Schneider when he explains,

The land of the *tabinau* was made, and it took work, *magar*, to make it what
it is. People who lived before built taro pits, planted them, terraced the inland
gardens as was necessary, planted yams and sweet potatoes, built the house
platforms and their surrounding paved areas, paved the paths, and so on, and
those who hold the land today say they are indebted to those who came before
for the work they did to make the *tabinau* what it is. However inherent its

rank may be, it is work that makes and maintains a *tabinau* and people exchange their work for their rights in the *tabinau*. (1984, 27; cf. Labby 1976)

In this light, *magaer* should not merely be viewed in terms of the expenditure of effort, but more precisely as a demonstration of one's feelings of attachment, concern, care, and respect for those of higher status and for the community to which one aspires to belong. Accordingly, *magaer* is imbued with moral value. It is interesting that it is the term *magaer* that is used when an individual wishes to recognize the service, work, or help of another, as the often-heard phrase *kammagaer* attests. This phrase, which can be literally translated as "you have expended effort" or "you have become physically exhausted from your work or service," is rendered in Jensen's (1977a) Yapese-English dictionary as both "you have become tired" and "thank you."

While *magaer* as an embodied sensation or feeling that arises in the face of hard work is directly implicated in local conceptions of "work," it is important to note that there is a distinction made between work understood as a form of intentional activity, called *maruweel,* and the sensory results of such intentional activity in the form of *magaer.* I should also note here, however, that it is a mistake to simply translate the concept of *maruweel* as "work," even though it is true that the term is currently used in everyday talk to refer to all forms of work, including wage labor. Traditionally, *maruweel* was understood in light of the physical exertion *(magaer)* that is enacted in the service of establishing and maintaining *socially recognized relationships* between particular individuals, families, estates, villages, or broader intervillage alliances *(nug)*. Again, the key is recognizing that an individual has suffered through fatigue, pain, and exhaustion *for another's benefit.*[8]

The moral underpinnings of local understandings of work are further implicated in the fact that traditionally work-based activities were ideally only conducted while following a number of important ascetic-like restrictions and abstentions. Most importantly, these included abstentions from sexual activity and restrictions concerning the ingestion of certain foods. These ascetic practices associated with sexual abstention, preparatory seclusion, and periods of fasting associated with work-based activities, as the German ethnologist Wilhelm Müller noted in the early part of the 1900s, were collectively known as *ma koel ea fal ko maruweel* (Müller 1917).

Closely connected to the concept of *magaer* is the concept of *athamagil,* which I gloss here as perseverance, endurance, or striving.

As we will see in the pages that follow, *athamagil* is yet another of Yap's core virtues. The term *athamagil* can be used as an adjective, an intransitive verb, and if modified with the suffix –*liy* can also be used as a transitive verb. Jensen's (1977a) dictionary translates the adjectival and intransitive verb forms as "perseverant" or "patient," while rendering the transitive verb as "to strive for." School report cards in Yap currently use the term as a translation of the English term "effort," although I had numerous people explain to me that this is an inexact translation. Instead, *athamagil* connotes both excellence and perfection in striving or enduring through suffering, hardship, adversity, and challenge. As such, it is held to be one of the most valued qualities in a person. As perseverance, endurance, or striving, *athamagil* is closely linked to suffering.[9] It is *athamagil* that enables an individual to endure in the face of the exhaustion that arises when participating in family, village, and community mandated work projects *(maruweel)*. It is thus *athamagil* that enables an individual to experience *magaer*.

Many elders independently explained to me that *athamagil* is one of the most important values in Yap and that it plays a central role in socializing children *(ma machib naag ea bitiir)*. It is only through *athamagil* that an individual will be able to cultivate the ability to control his or her mind *(k'aedaen')*, be patient *(gumaen')* and work *(maruweel)*. Inasmuch as *athamagil* is directly associated with *maruweel* it is significant to note that the term itself contains the morpheme *aath*, which literally refers to the smoke that rises from a fire. Interestingly, there are a few other Yapese terms that are similarly based upon this root morpheme. When taken together, these terms evidence connotative connections to the embodied experiences of exertion, exhaustion, and effort. The most salient include:

athiithiy: (vi) to sweat

athuwk: (n) sweat, perspiration

athigthig: (v, a) grubby, sweaty from work

athngool: (a) to be bored with, tired of, to be sweaty

As one well-respected elder commented, *Laen ea athamagil baaq magaer u fithik*—"Within endurance there are feelings of exertion, exhaustion, or fatigue in the midst." With *athamagil* comes sweat *(athuwk)*, which serves as an indication to others that an individual is experiencing *magaer*. Accordingly, an individual who is sweating should be recognized for their expenditure of effort with the phrase *kammagaer* ("you have worked" or "thank you").

To sum up, an individual's effort or physical exertion is ideally directed toward the care and cultivation of the estate's *tabinaew*. Such exertion is significantly tied to an individual's ability to *athamagil*, to strive to endure through one's physical suffering, one's exhaustion, fatigue, pain, hunger, and so on. And it is endurance in the face of suffering that is evoked through effortful exertion in the form of work or service for the benefit of the estate that is the basis for evoking feelings of *runguy* or compassion in those of higher status (in this case the husband, his sisters and his mother) for those of lower status (the wife and her children) who are contributing to the estate through their effortful striving in the face of hardship, adversity, and *gaafgow*.

Pain of the Village

Closely related to this discussion of the interplay of suffering, endurance, effortful exertion, and compassion is the concept of *amiithuun ea binaew*, which can be understood as concern, attachment, love, or positive pride for one's village. The phrase *amiithuun ea binaew* can be literally translated as "pain of the village." The phrase is made up of the term for village *(binaew)*, the noun phrase connector *ea*, and the term *amiithuun*, which is a combination of the morpheme *amiith*, a noun referring to the sensation of pain, and the directly suffixed third-person possessive *-uun*.[10] The term *amiithuun* may be used in the context of describing the direct material cause of a physical pain (e.g., *amiithuun ea gargael*—"childbirth's pain"), in referring to pains associated with specific varieties of illness (e.g., *amiithuun ea maath' keenil'*—"*maath' keenil'*'s pain"), or in the case of *amiithuun ea binaew*, in indexing a feeling state very similar to that of *runguy*. Indeed, to say *kab amiithuun ngeak* (literally, "there comes his or her pain") is to evoke the image of great care, love, compassion, and concern for another. The term is also often used in the context of songs of love in which phrases such as *be liyeg amiithuun* (literally, "his or her pain is killing me") are used to generate images of intense feelings of loneliness, longing, attachment, and love in the listener.

One of the first individuals I questioned about the phrase explained that *amiithuun ea binaew* is a concept that is grounded directly in work-based activities *(maruweel)*. As a number of others later concurred, *amiithuun ea binaew* is held to arise from collectively working and suffering together as a community. This collective work, endurance, and suffering is held to be responsible for generating feelings of mutual belonging, concern, and love for one's village. This feeling is only hard earned through effort, suffering, and work and it is often experienced with great intensity.

It is important to note that there seems to be a parallel evident here between the way in which individuals understand the generation of feelings of attachment both within the village and within the family. At the level of the family we have already seen that effortful work and endurance in the face of suffering are ways of cultivating bonds of attachment through engendering an empathetic-like stance in the face of the suffering. This gives rise to a bond of attachment that is later an important basis for transferring the estate's title from one generation to the next. It is similarly a feeling of *amiithuun* that is construed to be the basis for ties to the village, something that can only be cultivated through collectively suffering with other members of the village while working on the land.

Much like one's authority, rights, and title to a particular piece of land are understood to result from one's effort and labor, *amiithuun ea binaew,* one's feelings of attachment, concern, love, and pride for one's village are similarly tied to the suffering, striving, and enduring of a community that is collectively working toward a common goal of building and improving the village. As one elder put it, *Kaakaroom yaed ma athamagil ko maruweel ko binaew*—"Long ago, they put effort, endurance, striving, and perseverance into the work for the village." Indeed, the cultivation of *amiithuun ea binaew* was repeatedly described in terms of a cycle in which striving, enduring, and suffering was seen as the generative source for feelings of attachment generated through collective pain *(amiithuun)* that became the source motivating further works and further efforts for the benefit of the community (cf. Trnka 2008).

Here, there seems to be a recurring theme of suffering and pain as a basis for engendering compassion, attachment, pity, and love in another. This theme indexes a dynamic of morally valenced sentiments that serves to define the generation of social relationships at a number of different levels in Yapese society. As noted earlier, the term *amiithuun* is also often used in ways very similar to that of *runguy*. As such, it is akin to a form of empathetic concern (see Throop 2008b). Although, as one of my research assistants suggested to me, there is an important yet subtle difference between *amiithuun* and *runguy.* As Manna explained, "My picture of the word *[amiithuun]* is that it is more like a bond of attachment that is painful. I think of it as deeply felt strings of pain that do not start from you but comes toward you from the object that is causing your pain. These strings bind you and pull you back toward that object or person. It is something that is felt both ways and is a bit different from *runguy,* which can sometimes be felt only in one direction."

The presence or absence of *amiithuun* has significant consequences for an individual's moral worth. To say *baaq amiithuun roek chaney* ("he or she cares for that person") or *chaney ea baamit ea amiithuun ngaak* ("he or she has the quality of caring, compassion, and concern") is to highlight a person's virtuous qualities. To say that a person is *daariy ea amiithuun* ("without caring, compassion, and concern") is to present a very negative assessment of his or her moral character.

Implied in these statements is the idea that the acquisition of title to land is based on an expenditure of effort in the form of tangible feelings of exertion and ensuing sensations of weakness, soreness, pain, and fatigue. The ability to physically exert energy on behalf of others is itself also predicated upon the ability to plan, to be patient, to defer gratification, and to endure suffering. All of which seems to gain some interesting etymological support when one notes that the morpheme *thag*—"to arrive on top, to surmount, to achieve, to earn"—is included in the term *thagiith,* which refers to the ancestors that inhabit the land of the *tabinaew.* These were the very same ancestors who had previously worked the land and achieved through their own suffering and endurance their rights to that land.

That structures of feeling (Williams 1977) were implicit in the very understanding of the concept of work, is perhaps one of the reasons that present-day wage-labor is seldom taken as seriously as community projects. Exchanging labor for money occurs outside of the morally valenced sentiments at the heart of Yapese understandings of social relations and right action. Indeed, it is not uncommon to hear people in the government or the small private sector, particularly American expats and Peace Corps volunteers, commenting on what they perceive to be an apparent lack of a "work ethic" in Yap. Common complaints include a general inattention to deadlines and workers who spend all their time chewing betel nut and talking. Many people joke about "time *nu Waqab*" or "Yapese time" when someone is late or a deadline is missed. This stands in stark contrast, however, to the way that people pull together to work for community and village projects. Indeed, while I was in the field, I was always truly amazed at how hard people would work for community projects, going without sleep for days, eating very little, and working tirelessly until the project was complete. I participated in preparations for a number of such events and was never able to keep up with the pace and intensity of the work that my friends, family, and neighbors were undertaking.

That said, many of the elders still believe that the way that people engage in community work today pales in comparison to the time of their grandparents. For many, it is precisely this orientation to monetary compensation for one's effort that is responsible for drastically altering the way that people today approach working. To quote one elder, *Kaakaroom, maruweel ea kemus athamagil yi be ngoongoliy, daariy ea puluwon*—"In the past, with work it was only endurance that was made, not money." This statement is made all the more powerful when we consider the fact that the value of Yap's most famous indigenous currency, its "stone money" *(raay)*, is itself calibrated according to the hardship, suffering, and adversity associated with its quarrying and transportation from Palau. As we learned in the last chapter, the most valuable pieces of *raay* are said to be those that were acquired through the greatest hardship. Those acquired after the loss of a human life were of the absolute highest value.[11] Again, we see that in Yap, value, like virtue, is calibrated according to a metric suffering.

CHAPTER 3

Sentiment and Social Structure

The three of us had been sitting across from Fanow's house, talking for the better part of an hour, when Fanow suddenly exclaimed, "Sickness of servants!" She was reflecting on the pain she had been suffering from the past few years. "They say sickness of servants," she repeated. Perhaps in response to my apparent confusion, she turned to Manna and went on, "You know, you know that Yapese saying there about us women: 'You have sickness of servants, because you are sick and you cannot stop working.'" Manna, nodding her head in agreement, added, "It doesn't matter if you are sick because if you are sick you have to move." "If you don't move," Fanow continued, "the household will have to stop eating."

As we saw in the previous chapter, Yapese understandings of ethical modes of experiencing the world are importantly founded upon a dynamic interplay of sentiment. This dynamic is based upon a dialectic of suffering and compassion that is mediated through perseverance in the face of suffering that often takes the form of embodied feelings of exertion-based exhaustion, fatigue, tiredness, and collective pain. In this chapter, I wish to highlight the ways in which such moral sentiments and the actions they motivate articulate with a number of Yap's core cultural idioms. This will include an examination of the idioms of purity and order, hierarchy, relationships, exchange, and food production and consumption. In providing this rather broad introduction to local understandings of social life as mediated through the cultivation, negotiation, and enactment of these core moral sentiments and corresponding cultural virtues, I hope to establish a basis for turning to examine some of the basic ethnopsychological and ethnomedical assumptions that inform individuals' experiences suffering with pain. In particular, it is significant to note the extent to which the practices and beliefs detailed in this chapter are implicated in the virtue of "self-governance" *(kadaen')*. The virtue of self-governance is centrally implicated in local understandings of subjectivity, as well as those forms of expressivity held to simultaneously reveal and conceal the mind's contents, dysphoric or otherwise.

Many of the local understandings of suffering and social life that are explored in this chapter are embedded in cultural idioms that may at times be interpreted as ritually based or religious. That contemporary Yapese communities have sought to reconcile such views most prevalently with Roman Catholic doctrine is a fact that should be kept in mind when thinking through how such understandings come to shape any given individual's experience of pain and suffering (cf. Robbins 2004). The fact that Yapese articulations of Catholic belief and practice do not figure more prominently in this book should thus not be taken to indicate any lack of religiosity on the part of the people I learned from, lived with, and got to know as friends and teachers. Nor should it be interpreted as a desire on my part to downplay the very complex negotiations existing between Roman Catholicism and so-called traditional beliefs that inform contemporary Yapese moral sensibilities.

For instance, there are a number of significant ways that Roman Catholic belief and practice has been influenced by local Yapese traditions. This includes the performance of Yapese dances at church celebrations, the difficult institutionalization and then eventual discontinuation of confession, and the incorporation of a traditional funeral lament *(dolloloew)* into the Catholic liturgy during the Good Friday service held at St. Mary's Church in Colonia. Conversely, the impact of Christianity on Yapese traditions is clearly evident in the singing of hymns, the use of prayer, and the recital of the rosary in the context of church and funeral services performed by one of the island's two priests. At funerals, while mourners often still refer to the ancestors *(thagiith)* of the *tabinaew* during traditional laments, more and more people ask *Got* ("God") to give the blessing to the family in the concluding refrains. Moreover, many of the individuals I knew attended church services and participated in communion regularly (services were held one Sunday a month in their local municipality church). For individuals who lived close to town or who had access to cars there were also opportunities to attend service every week at St. Mary's Church in Colonia.

As we will see in later chapters, the complexity of relations between Roman Catholicism and traditional beliefs is further evident in the context of my interviews with, and observations of, different pain sufferers who seldom overtly evoked Catholic idioms. While prayer was often part and parcel of the activities that families participated in when a relative was ill, often in their absence while in the hospital or off island, individuals rarely cast their own suffering in explicitly religious terms. Certainly, some individuals did evoke the notion of "God's will" when imagining possibilities for recovery or in providing explanations for the causes of suffering. That said, even in such accounts of suffering the accent was strongly placed on describing the individual's specific actions leading up to the illness or misfortune in question and on his or her ability to abide by the restrictions associated with a given treatment regime. The specificity of the individual's social transgressions and the state of his or her social relations were also often deemed significant to interpreting the meaning and moral value of suffering.

With regard to the people that I spoke to and got to know best, personal suffering and pain was rarely explicitly framed in light of Catholic notions of sin, divine grace, salvation, or God's ability to intervene or not in ongoing earthly affairs. Instead, it was most often notions of work, effortful endurance, self-sacrifice, community or familial obligation, collective pain, suffering, and compassion that were the tropes most readily employed when attempting to give meaning to pain. It seems therefore that there are many ways that moral understandings crosscut various modalities of being, with contemporary religiosity being only one such possibility.

On Purity and Impurity

Lingenfelter (1977) argues that the "emic core" of Yapese culture is traditionally articulated according to a number of dichotomous distinctions between land *(arow)* and sea *(madaay)*, spirits *(kaan)* and humans *(girdiiq)*, and male *(pumoqon)* and female *(bpiin)*. In moving from sea to land, spirit to human, and men to women there is a gradated shift from purity to increasing impurity, with the "core of impurity" lying "in the nature of childbirth and menstruation" (Lingenfelter 1977, 333). The overarching distinction defining this continuum of purity is defined by the designations of *tabugul* and *taqay*. While Lingenfelter (1977) and Egan (1998) define these terms according to their contrastive levels of purity, sacredness, and order, I have come to view *tabugul* and *taqay* as further indexing a distinction between controllable and uncontrollable creative power (cf. Shore 1989). Accordingly, *tabugul* is often used to highlight those aspects of existence that have come into being through deliberate action. *Taqay*, in contrast, indexes the effects of power that has at its heart an element of uncontrollability or unpredictability. To understand how *tabugul* and *taqay* are generally situated in Yapese social life as differing modalities of activity and power, it is necessary to revisit the ongoing relationship between people, service, work, and land. Indeed, as Egan notes, the "order" implicated in the concept of *tabugul* is locally construed to be "the legacy of labor" (1998, 134).

While conducting the oral history and GPS mapping project I was repeatedly astounded at the extent to which what appeared to be natural configurations of the landscape were in fact carefully engineered aspects of an expansive and labor-intensive built environment. As I went out each day for the better part of a month to map the village with a group of elders who were helping with the project, it soon became clear that there was very little if any part of the village that had not been deliberately altered. Elders could point out where the shoreline was said to have existed in previous generations. They noted that many of the names for the foundations in those lands reclaimed from the sea indicated that they had been built on top of trash *(dooq)*. Names such as *fitadooq* ("place of trash") and *kanadooq* ("on top of trash") were common in such areas. In fact one of the largest and highest-ranking taro patches in the village was said to be located on an isthmus that was reclaimed from the sea by the hard work of the community.

The elders also told us about the various "streams" *(luul)* that crossed the village, running from the hills in the interior down to the ocean. It soon became apparent that these were not natural streams. They were in fact built up and maintained as an intensive water management system. In some places, the water was directed through stone-lined channels 11.5 feet high. These complex systems of water management clearly required intensive collaborative efforts to construct, along with work allocated to their regular maintenance (Dornan 2004).

Like the water system, the systems of paths, foundations, and platforms found throughout the village were carefully engineered. It seemed that almost every inch of the village was at one point either paved, used as a garden or taro patch, or part of the water management system. Perhaps most astonishing, however, was the evidence we found for the intensive engineering of the coastline. Though previous survey projects (Hunter-Anderson 1983, 1984; Adams 1997) mentioned some degree of alteration of the coastal areas—noting particularly the many impressive stone fish traps found just offshore in many villages—none indicated anything akin to what the elders of the village showed us as we systematically mapped out the coastline. As we learned, practically the entire coastline of the village had been reclaimed from the sea through a process of gradually building up high stone sea walls *(chubog)* that then were used to support man-made structures rising up out of the mangrove swamps. These labor-intensive structures created an intricate network of canals and small man-made "islands" (Dornan 2004).

In a very literal sense then, the land was the direct result of invested, ordered, and intentional human action in the form of collective work. Such collective work was itself only made possible through adherence to *yalean* as the ordered configuration of hierarchical social relations governed by village leadership. It is precisely this image of intentionally organized activity in the form of collective work that permeates many aspects of Yapese social life. It is in this light that Egan (1998, 135) suggests that "the undeveloped was *taay* in that it was low and unclean. Labor, however, lent it order, making it *tabugul* by transforming it into something high, pure, productive, and governed by *yalen*—the prescriptions of Yapese culture. Land was the supreme vessel of order, and different lands became *tabugul* or *taay* with respect to one another in terms of their different histories of invested labor."

Significantly, Lingenfelter recognizes that the distinctions between *tabugul* and *taqay* are not simply perceptibly salient classificatory designations. They are also local ways of categorizing the world that are suffused with motivational force. As he puts it, "The notions of pollution and purity in themselves create significant moods and motivations among Yapese which are further elaborated by the opposition of *fal* ("purifying isolation") versus *tungaf* ("polluting contact"). It is the opposition which defines the rationale for restrictions between human and spirits, and for separation of men and women in the areas of food resources, food preparation and eating" (Lingenfelter 1977, 334–35). The differential ranking of parcels of land, gardens, and taro patches is then importantly predicated upon the ascription of differing degrees of *tabugul* and *taqay* invested in them. This ranking is also the basis for distinguishing between individuals "in terms of the different ways that age, gender, village, and social stratum positioned them in land and the labor invested in it" (Egan 1998, 136). The ebb and flow of everyday life was thus traditionally mediated through attempts at controlling the necessary and inevitable interactions between spirits, people, food, and lands that were differentially distributed along this continuum of "purity." Whether it was understood in terms of distinctions between chiefs and their servants (*piiluung* and *pimilngaay*), status-based distinctions between age-grades, or the various life historical and developmental stages marking the temporal expanse extending between birth and death, Yapese social life could largely be understood as a reflection of such attempts at carefully controlling the interplay of these oppositional forces.

Given that the designations of *tabugul* and *taqay* index differences in the controllability of the powers associated with each, it is interesting to note that those individuals categorized as *tabugul* tended to be the ones who were charged with the responsibility to think, reflect, and organize. They were the ones who had the power to control the actions of others. In contrast, individuals who were categorized as *taqay* were responsible for acting on the basis of other's decisions. They were the ones whose powers were controlled by others. The opposition between spirits and humans, elders and youth, men and women, and *piiluung* and *pimilngaay* all pivot on differences between those who think, reflect, and decide and those who act, work, and serve. It is the *piiluung* ("many voices") who speak and the *pimilngaay* ("those who are running") who carry out their orders.

Birth, death, menstruation, and fertility, all elements of human existence that are understood to be beyond any one individual's abilities to control, are each understood to be *taqay*. Carefully controlled forms of activity, such as ritualized isolation, food restriction, fasting, and sexual abstention, were in contrast thought to help individuals deal with unpredictable and dangerous *taqay* forces. In participating in rigorous ascetic practices, individuals avoided contaminating *(tungaaf)* higher-status community members, paths, foundations, gardens, and taro patches that were held to be *tabugul;* such a breach in purity could very well lead to illness or misfortune (Egan 1998, 145).

Traditionally, the vast majority of major illnesses were tied to such forms of contamination and the inappropriate intermixing of controllable and uncontrollable powers. Perhaps the most common cause of illness was rooted in the intervention of spirits *(kaan)* in human affairs.

The social etiological basis for such illnesses ensured, as Charles Broder argues, that preventative medicine in Yapese communities took the form of the observance of social mores, rules, restrictions, abstentions, and taboos (1972, 35). Indeed, in Yapese medical theory there is "a definite and obvious relationship between breach of taboo and disease. Through the observance of social taboos one can be assured of being free from serious injury or illness, i.e., that [is] caused by a spirit" (Broder 1972, 35). In this respect, Yapese medical theory is intimately connected to not only the appropriate bàlancing of relations between *tabugul* and *taqay* powers but also to morality. The good person, the good life, and right action are each deeply implicated in local under-standings of the cause, onset, trajectory, diagnosis, prevention, and cure of illness. The moral and somatic well-being of persons was thus thought to be mutually influencing.

Importantly, as both Lingenfelter (1977) and Egan (1998) maintain, the designations of *tabugul* and *taqay* forces in Yapese communities were never static or fixed, since communities, estates, clans, and indi-viduals could, and did, occupy very different positions within this continuum of purity through time. As Ushjima argues, there is a lot of oral historical evidence pointing to the fact that Yapese hierarchy was imbued with a "highly volatile propensity for change" (1987, 178; cited in Egan 1998, 134). For example, intervillage warfare could help to alter the rank associated with particular estates. This served to subtly realign the distribution and arrangement of power throughout the island's complex system of political alliances (Labby 1976, 108–11). That said, it is also interesting to note that even something as putatively unpredictable as intervillage warfare was portrayed as carefully ordered and preplanned by the highest-ranking estates, with the victors said to be almost always predetermined prior to the actual battle taking place.

Individuals could also enact certain forms of mobility between these designations. Indeed, a person's life trajectory moving through differ-ent age-grades was significantly understood to reflect a gradual transi-tion from less to more "ordered" or "pure" states of being (Egan 1998, 143). Somewhat similar possibilities for transition were also available to different generations of the same clan as implicated in a woman's efforts to anchor her children in a new *tabinaew*. In Egan's words, "Women attempted to elevate the status of the children they would bear by marrying into *tabinaw* of higher rank, and in so doing, raise their own as well. Since labor produced order, persons could in theory between the states of *taay* and *tabugul* through work and the place their work earned in land. This process was nothing less than a recapitulation of history, as Yapese understood it" (1998, 138). As I will continue to explore in later chapters, traditionally there were truly a remarkable number of ascetic, ritualized, and restrictive practices employed in the service of ensuring that *tabugul* and *taqay* forces did not intermix.

Many of these ascetic practices can be illustrated in the context of a woman's developmental trajectory from her first menses through menopause. Menstruating women were, up until the time of the war, secluded from men for extended periods in women's houses called *dopael*. At the time of a young girl's first menses, when she first entered into the social status of an adolescent or *rugood*, she lived away from her family in a special area of the village called *taminay* ("approach") or *tarugood* ("place of adolescent girls") for as long as a year (Egan 1998; Labby 1976). This was a period of seclusion in which *rugood* adhered to a number of restrictions on their social interactions, food consumption, bodily practices, and uses of space. Upon becoming a *rugood* a girl was no longer able to eat from her mother's pot. She would instead have to gather her own food from one of the estate's lowest-ranked plots of land that was put aside for strictly her usage. She would then have to cook the food she gathered alone in her own kitchen. A *rugood* was often forced to survive on only those foods growing close to the *dopael,* although sometimes she was also given "food of uncertain status that had come to the estate in an exchange" (Labby 1976, 76).

As a number of elders recounted to me, during this time there were also very strict limitations placed on a girl's body, which was considered to be so extremely *taqay* that it was thought to be dangerous to even the girl herself. A *rugood* was required to bathe daily and to wear a special mat around her waist to ensure that she did not place her hands on her grass skirt. During this period of seclusion a *rugood* was also never supposed to touch her head or her hair since these were considered to be very sacred parts of the body. To protect against contaminating her head, a girl's hair was placed within a basket designed to keep it off of her body. She was given a special stick to use in the event that she had to scratch her head (Labby 1976).

Rugood were further forbidden from entering any high status, sacred, or public areas of the village. They were banned from using *tabugul* stone paths. They were forced instead to walk those paths reserved for carrying the corpses of the deceased, death being considered *taqay* and as such another powerful form of pollution and illness. Young and menstruating women were restricted from entering *tabugul* taro patches since their very presence in such places would make any *tabugul* man who ate the taro grown there susceptible to *tungaaf*-based illnesses (Egan 1998, 147). If a *rugood* was ever to meet a group of men, "she could pass them only after asking their pardon and then crawling past on her knees so that they would not catch the *taay* smell of her body" (Labby 1976, 76).

Adherence to such practices and to the use of the *dopael* was largely abandoned after the war. During the time of my fieldwork there was still a sense, however, that menstruation was *taqay* and that precautions should be taken to ensure that *rugood* did not walk on particularly *tabugul* areas or paths and that they did not enter into *tabugul* taro patches. In adhering to such restrictions, young women were importantly seen to be suffering for a higher social and moral purpose in protecting the purity and rank of the community's land.

As a woman matured, married, had children, and worked on the land of her husband's estate she was increasingly viewed to be less *taqay*. By the time a woman had reached menopause she was considered to have entered into the status of *puweelwol* and later *pilabthir*, both designations that marked her effective transition from *taqay* to *tabugul*. While a woman would never be considered as *tabugul* as a man of similar maturity and rank, a woman who had effectively channeled her previously "uncontrolled" creative powers into the *tabinaew* of her husband was seen to have transitioned within her lifetime from the lowest status to one of great respectability (Egan 1998). As Labby summarizes, "A woman who had reached puberty but who had not yet married and produced children was in this sense an *undeveloped* resource and therefore *taay*. It was only as her reproductivity developed on the estate, as she produced children who took on the responsibilities of the land, that she became less *taay*, less undeveloped, and more *tabugul*, a developed resource whose productivity was both reflected by and was reflected in that of the estate" (1976, 74–75).

The oppositional powers of *tabugul* and *taqay* were also reflected in the traditional spatial arrangement of Yapese houses where there were separate kitchens, separate places to sit, and separate sleeping areas for a man, his wife and their children (see Labby 1976, 73; Lingenfelter 1975, 21–24). While adherence to such restrictions in Yapese households has atrophied considerably in recent decades, my Yapese parents still kept separate sets of dishes, cutlery, and cups. My adopted mother, siblings, nieces and nephews used one set and the other was only to be used by my father. My Yapese parents also had separate places *(tagiil)* where they regularly sat, both on the veranda and inside the house, which roughly corresponded to traditional distinctions between *tabugul* and *taqay* areas.

As previously mentioned, another important realm in which careful attention was paid to these distinctions was in the context of death. A corpse was viewed to be *taqay* and thus a number of important precautions had to be followed when dealing with the deceased. Members of the lowest castes, themselves *taqay,* were traditionally charged with the duty of preparing the grave and burying the dead. Traditionally, there was said to be only three main cemeteries for the entire island. These were positioned on very low-ranking lands, far away from high-caste villages. Today, while there has been a proliferation of cemeteries, many of them associated with particular *tabinaew,* these too are most often located well outside village centers in the high lands of the savannas.[1]

In preparation for the funeral, the body was attended to and mourned over by women relatives of the deceased. Again, in being considered *taqay* women were thought to face less potential harm or illness when in close proximity to the corpse, although it is true that this exposure was still construed to be dangerous for them. Traditionally, and still today, women were charged with mourning the deceased with heart-wrenching funeral laments *(dolloloew/dolloloey).* As a number of elders recalled, women also participated in special dances that were performed only during these occasions. Men, being *tabugul,* were required to stay far away from both the women and the corpse. Sitting off in their own area, away from the *waaw* ("scent or odor of the dead") and the sounds of the women's laments, they were responsible for keeping track of the various goods that were brought to honor the title-bearing clan *(mafen)* of the deceased. Men were said to keep their distance from women and the corpse in order to avoid the illnesses associated with the *taqay* of death.

Generally speaking, death would affect two groups of people, those related through clan ties and those who, in some form or another, would inherent rights to access the land of the deceased. As such, representatives from both groups would be responsible for participating in the mourning of the deceased—a period that was said to have traditionally spanned the length of time it would take the corpse to "decompose entirely, such that the smell of the dead was gone" (Labby 1976, 66). At the end of a funeral, participants had to enter into an extended period of seclusion from the *tabinaew* and the village to ensure that the *waaw* did not causes illness and harm to others in the community. Traditionally there were further restrictions placed on all of those participating in the funeral with regard to eating. The most important of these abstentions was avoiding fish, in addition to abstaining from sexual practices.

After the *waaw* had dissipated and individuals had returned to their everyday lives, a portion of the deceased's estate would be set aside from anywhere from six months to a year. This was a time in which there were rigid strictures held against partaking of any of the food that was grown on such land, which was held to sustain the spirit of the deceased (Labby 1976). The period associated with this particular abstention was referred to as *ke aaw ea liiw*—where *ke aaw* means "it falls" and *liiw* refers to the "place" or "position" occupied by a particular individual (Labby 1976). At the end of this period, the food that had accumulated on the land was collected by the clan who were set to inherit it and given to the relatives *(mafen)* of the deceased to eat.

Finally, in discussing low caste, menstruation, birth, and death in terms of *taqay* it is important to note with Egan that these various forms of *taqay* should not be considered unitary in nature. Nor are they held to be necessarily always negative forces. In Egan's words, "[un]like death and the destructive energies radiating from a corpse, menstrual blood was not solely a negative force. The unrestrained energies it represented could cause harm on account of their magnitude, but they were also the source of female procreative power" (1998, 146).

Purity and Hierarchy

Such concerns regarding *tabugul* and *taqay* and their association with particular structures of feeling were also implicated in local understandings of those asymmetrical status relationships embedded in the Yapese "caste" system. While referring to these differing status levels in terms of castes in the context of this book, I would like to caution with Egan that these distinctions should not in anyway be simply equated with the Indian *Jati* systems (1998, 136). Such comparisons occlude the distinct cultural logic of Yapese social classes, which is predicated primarily upon an interplay between compassion and suffering as realized in relations between landed *(piiluung)* and landless *(pimilngaay)* peoples.

Traditionally, there were seven different strata comprising the Yapese sociopolitical system that were at their highest levels distributed between two competing island-wide alliances—*ban piiluung* ("the side of the chiefs") and *ban pagäl* ("the side of the young men"). On the side of the chiefs *(piiluung)* were those villages designated as *bulche'* and those slightly lower-ranked villages of the *methaban*. On the side of the young men *(pagäl)* were the highest-ranked *ulun* villages and beneath them the *tethaban*. Below these were the lowest ranked of the landed classes, the commoner or "warrior" villages, called the *dourchig*. The landless social classes, the *pimilngaay,* like the *dourchig,* were not distinguished according to their alliance membership (see Egan 1998; Lingenfelter 1975). As one moved from lower- to higher-status rankings, one moved again along the continuum of purity from more *taqay* to more *tabugul* states of being.

All of these various villages where ultimately linked to the three highest-ranked villages of the island *(dalip ea nguchol):* Teb in Tomil (representing the grandfather); Ngolog in Rull (representing the grandmother—*tiitaew ko keenggin ea naam*); and Gachpaer in Gaagil (representing the son or father). This threefold division between the three highest-ranked villages was also represented in the threefold distinction between the two island-wide alliances and those foundations responsible for mediating disputes between them: *ulun (ban pagäl), bulche (ban piiluung),* and *luungun somol (ban bpiin).* Each of these three alliances consisted of seven villages, or more accurately seven foundations located in seven different villages. Again, using the family as a basic interpretive framework, the *ulun* were understood to represent the son or father, the *bulche* the grandfather, and the *luungun somol* the sister or mother. This is a threefold distinction replicated again at the village level with chiefs representing the voices of the young men *(luungun pagäl),* the women *(piiluung ko binaew),* and the ancestors or grandfathers *(pilabthir ko binaew).*[2]

While it is common to think of differences between villages generally in terms of their position in this classificatory schema, the reality of such rankings is much more complicated. The complexity and dynamism of this system was based in the fact that it was more accurately the estates and their corresponding foundations *(tabinaew)* and not the village as a whole *(binaew)* that were ranked differentially based on the various *thaaq* ("traditional connection or relationship") they had established to other *tabinaew* both within and beyond the boundaries of the village. Indeed, in relatively low-ranking villages it is

FIGURE 2. Meeting house *(P'eebaay)*. Photo by the author.

possible to find some of the highest-ranking foundations, while even in the highest-ranking villages there are also estates with very little in the way of authority or voice. Moreover, these rankings were never · static since particular *tabinaew* through successive generations, or in some cases in the span of one generation, could also lose or gain *thaaq* ("connections or relationships") with other estates. They could thus accordingly lose or gain status within the village and the island-wide system of ranking.

To understand the significance of the ranks ascribed to estate foundations as well as the foundations of community buildings, it is necessary to grasp the relationship between these foundations and broader political relations both within and outside the boundaries of the village. All of which, I argue, are relationships that are to various degrees implicated in an interchange of the morally valenced sentiments of suffering *(gaafgow)* and compassion *(runguy)*, a connection that again highlights the pervasiveness of idioms of suffering in the dynamics of Yapese social life.

For example, let's look at the case of one community house foundation and one very high-ranking estate foundation in the village I lived in. Both foundations were understood to be material representations of histories of differing relationships generated through past transactions of moral sentiments and work-based activities. In the case of the community house foundation, the status of the foundation was achieved through compensation for suffering endured by the village on behalf of a higher-status village in the context of war *(puluwon ea mael)*. In the case of the estate foundation, the foundation was built through work that was owed to the estate after it had demonstrated compassion *(runguy)* in providing help and shelter to individuals who where suffering because they had been chased out of their own village. The village's evacuation occurred after a few of its members were implicated in a grievous social transgression. In both cases, the actual buildings erected on these foundations reflected these histories of sentiment in as much as the thatching for roofs, materials, and labor involved in their construction were traditionally contributed by the villages connected to the estates in question through the *thaaq* ("connections or relationships") that were established through these previous acts of suffering, loss, service, and compassion.

With regard to the asymmetrical social relations reflected in the differing social strata of the Yapese caste system, the relationship between landless peoples and their chief or *piiluung* is "defined as the relations between a father and his children, following the ideology of the clan estate in which obedient and helpful children are granted land by their fathers" (Lingenfelter 1975, 143). In conceptualizing the relations between higher-status *piiluung* (those who are considered *tabugul*) and their lower-status *pimilngaay* (those who are considered *taqay*) in terms of a parent-child relation, the implied cultural logic is again one in which there is an expression of compassion for suffering that is endured for the benefit of others.

A Yapese Typology of Relatedness

The manner in which transactions of sentiment play a role in articulating the differing relationships interwoven into the texture of Yapese social life is further reflected in the local ways in which relatedness is conceived. In Yapese there are at least three basic terms that can be used to denote the concept of relationship: *thaaq*, *thiliin*, and *yalean*.

While the term *thaaq* is used to describe relations between estates and villages, the concept can additionally refer to relationships played out in the context of socially prescribed roles. Thus an individual's *thaaq* can include being in a relationship of father to child *(chiitamangin-faak)*, mother to child *(chiitinangin-faak)*, brother to sister *(walaag)*, and so on. It is important to note here, however, that in each of these instances *thaaq* describes a relationship or connection between specific individuals that, while socially prescribed, is not necessarily fixed. Instead, there is always the possibility for a given *thaaq* to be made anew or undone, depending on an individual's abilities to continue participating in the dynamic exchange of sentiment and action that serve to enliven and thereby secure its ties. It is true that some types of *thaaq* are pregiven. That is, they existed prior to the individual's birth, having been established in previous generations. Others, however, are newly established, transformed, or ruptured within the lifetime of particular social actors.

As one of my friends explained, when someone asks the question—*Maang ea thaaq roodow?* (What is our relationship?)—they are inquiring about a socially prefigured estate or clan relationship. Importantly, it is often at funerals that *thaaq* are revealed. In the context of a funeral, women are charged with the responsibility of singing funeral laments *(dolloloew/dolloloey)*. Individuals use such expressive forms to explain why they have come to the funeral and what their relationship to the deceased is. While funerals have changed in very significant ways over the past decades (see Egan 1998), traditional funerals were said to be exclusively family affairs in which everyone attending had to justify their presence through explaining their *thaaq*.

All told, there could be *thaaq* between individuals, families, estates, and villages. It was in this lattermost sense that Lingenfelter (1975, 131) translated *thaaq* as "communication channel" and Egan (1998, 177) rendered it "political channel." Lingenfelter (1975, 131) suggests that *thaaq* can be literally defined as "a series of things, tied together with string." Such a definition is evident in the context of its usage in designating a string of shell money as *thaaq ea yaar*. I should also note, however, that more than a few of my teachers pointed to the fact that *thaaq* may also refer to a fiber that runs through a number of different root crops, including *duqōg* (common yam—*Dioscorea alata*) and *theap'* (*Dioscorea nummularia*). In these contexts, the metaphorical elaboration of *thaaq* as a "channel" or "relationship" is founded upon the image of a connecting fiber within these crops, crops that are themselves the result of the hard work and labor of successive generations upon the land that nourished them.

Another term that is relevant to understanding the conceptualization of relationships is the term *thiliin*. In contrast to *thaaq,* this term
refers more specifically to the actual or concrete relationship between
two people. That is, the term refers primarily to whether or not individuals are presently getting along, fighting, or what have you. *Thiliin,*
when rendered in the form of *thildow,* can be literally translated as "the
space between the two of us." This phrase is especially fitting given
that a number of individuals suggested that *thiliin* could refer to the
ongoing face-to-face negotiation of the emotional and practical aspects
of any given social relationship. This is comparable in some ways to
what Alfred Schutz (1967) would have termed the "we-relationship."
Thiliin thus describes the state of the relationship at a particular point
in time. Because of the fact that the concept of *thiliin* highlights
whether individuals in a given relationship are on good or bad terms
with each other, it was not uncommon to hear people ask *Maang ea
ba u thilrow?* ("What is there between them?") whenever someone
might wish to assess the current status of a given relationship.

Finally, there is the term *yalean* which can be understood as indexical of those forms of relationship that incorporate expected behaviors,
feelings, and moral evaluations that fall under the designation of custom
or tradition. As tradition, the term bears a heavier moral weight than
either *thaaq* or *thiliin*. A friend of mine once explained that *yalean* is
viewed as something that precedes your birth by many generations. As
such, it implies practices, ways of thinking and being-in-the-world that
are largely unquestioned and relatively fixed. In this respect, the term
connotes collectively valued residues of previous relationships that carry
forward from the past, through the present moment, and into the
future. When an individual asks *Maang ea yaldow?* he or she is asking
what customary relationship he or she has with another individual. For
example, the question might speak to whether or not two individuals
should be considered in a relationship of chief *(piiluung)* to commoner
(pimilngaay) or "public parent" *(matin* or *mataam)* to child *(bitiir)*.

Before moving on I would like to highlight four further points with
respect to the local renderings of "relatedness" in the context of these
three terms. First, it is possible for an individual to enact different
varieties of relationship with the same person based on these three different designations. For instance, a friend of mine once told me that
her adoption to one of her father's sister's estates had placed her into
a traditional relationship of "public mother" to children *(yalrooraed
matin ea bitiir)* with regard to her "blood" brothers and sisters. That

said, she was still recognized as a sibling *(walaag)* if the same relationships were viewed in the context of their *thaaq*. Finally, she said with more than a little regret that the current status of their relationship *(thiliin)* was often filled with conflict, arguments, and strife.

Second, whether it is in terms of family, estate, or community levels, the concepts of relationship seem to evidence both emotional and active poles. On the emotional side there is the pivotal dialectic between suffering *(gaafgow)* and compassion *(runguy)*. On the active side there is the interchange between those who observe, give, or think and those who expend effort, receive, or act. To exert effort, to expend energy, and to act is to frame oneself in the context of a relationship as an individual who is *gaafgow*. This in turn ideally elicits *runguy* in the individual who is in a position of authority to help the person who is acting and suffering. When represented in this light, we can think of the accretion and social ratification of past exchanges of sentiment as materialized in existing relations between families, estates, and communities. Such existing relations further entail that individuals seek out relations with others with whom such bonds have yet to be forged. *Yalean* and *thaaq* can thus be understood as crystallized residues of exchanges of sentiment between clans that serve to canalize the trajectories of social actors in the present moment. In contrast, *thiliin* can be thought of as representing the real-time evaluation of the status of such exchanges of sentiment in the context of any concrete interpersonal relationship.

Third, local understandings of relatedness are also importantly tied to the significance of monitoring and orchestrating relations between the inner and the outer, private and public, a feeling and its expression, and thought and speech. It is true that in the cases of *thaaq* and *yalean* it is often the outer, public, expressing, speaking, deliberating, and consensus-making side of the person that is emphasized. The *imagio*, in Mageo's (1998) usage of the term, however, is found in the context of those correlated sentiments implied in these relationships. As we will see in this and subsequent chapters, the acknowledgment that there is necessarily an "inner side" to relationships is significant in terms of motivating virtuous conduct. In particular, it plays an important role in an individual's efforts to learn to discipline his or her feelings so that they align with culturally valued repertoires of sentiments implied in family and community relations.

Fourth, all relationships, even those designated under the rubric of *yalean,* are susceptible, to varying degrees, to transformation and change. When looking at inter-estate *thaaq* relationships, for instance, the relative social status of any one *tabinaew* can be greatly affected if it poorly executes its participation in a ceremonial exchange be it in the form of a *mitmiit*, a dance, or a funeral. To this end, the amount of wealth generated for such exchanges—be it wealth in the form of fish, taro, stone money, shell money, woven textiles, or more recently alcohol and tobacco—is an indication of the internal cohesiveness of the estate presenting that wealth (Egan 1998). An estate plagued by infighting, conflict, and poor leadership is ill equipped to navigate the complex web of social ties that could lend support in the event of such an exchange. Yapese individuals, as Egan emphasizes, "recognized this all too well and knew how to read the stock of wealth presented by any *tabinaw* at a *mitmiit* to discern what degree of unity existed within the *tabinaw* itself" (1998, 170).

Relationships are thus understood to be conditional, even when established over multiple generations. This conditionality is tied to the fact that "solid relationships in Yap were the product of *magaer*, of energies carefully and routinely invested." Such conditionality is also evident in the fact that an "estate's display of material wealth at *mitmiit* drew attention only because it demonstrated the estate's wealth in social relationships" (Egan 1998, 175–76). All of this, I would add, is negotiated in the context of ongoing and dynamic interchanges of sentiment between different members of the estate in terms of their alternating experiences of suffering *(gaafgow)*, compassion *(runguy)*, and endurance *(athamagil)*.

Mitmiit and the Exchange of Sentiment in Village Relationships

The dynamic interchange of sentiments implicated in the ties connecting estates and villages through their various *thaaq* are interestingly evidenced in the context of a number of dances *(churuq)* traditionally held in honor of intervillage exchanges—*mitmiit*. As a number of students of Yapese culture have observed, dancing traditionally played a pivotal role in many aspects of Yapese social, ritual, religious, political, and economic life (Brooks 1988; Egan 1998; Konishi 1999; Müller 1917; Noritake n.d.; Smith 1980; see Throop forthcoming a). The chants and movements associated with different dances are recognized as authored by specific individuals who are able to exchange their dances with other estates, much like other Yapese valuables. The most prestigious dances are associated with high-ranking foundations *(daaf)* and as such are considered to be *machaaf ko piiluung* ("valuables of the chiefs") (Egan 1998, 178). Dances are exchanged between estates in differing villages, and such histories of transaction are recalled and recognized, even during the time of my fieldwork, every time the dance is performed in public. Dances that were acquired through such means are only performed publicly after the individuals putting on the dance present shell money *(yaar)* to representatives of the estate of the individual who first composed it.

In the context of *mitmiit,* different types of dances were performed depending on the occasion of the exchange. Variations in the organization of *mitmiit* importantly depended on the occasion for the gathering (e.g., in honor of a deceased *piiluung* versus reciprocating for hosting a previous exchange). That said, most intervillage *mitmiit* were structured in such a way that they began with a form of dance called *tayoer.* Traditionally, this dance was performed by one senior woman from one of the high-ranking *tabinaew* in the village. Given everything that has already been said about the significance of the suffering-compassion dynamic in constituting social relationships, it is interesting to note that the word *tayoer* is made up of the morpheme *yoer* ("to cry") and the prefix *ta-,* which is used to indicate habitual or dispositional forms of activity. The literal meaning is thus, "to be a person who always cries" or "to be a person who is predisposed to cry."

The dance itself included a chant that explained the relationship between the estate and the other estates that have come to the *mitmiit.* As one teacher made clear to me, a *tayoer* explained the existing and traditional relationships *(yalean)* between the two villages participating in the exchange. Part of the content of a *tayoer* included a listing of those items that were and were not given as forms of help and support in past years. As such, it was largely a directive spelling out the context within which the present exchange was about to occur: the *tayoer* detailed the history of the ongoing relationship between the two villages. Past generosity, support, and gifts were honored, while wrongs, slights, and mistakes were brought to the attention of everyone who was in attendance. The *tayoer* was thus seldom an unproblematic affair. Instead, everything about the recounting of the *thaaq* was open to contestation, including references to times when there were disagreements, arguments, social transgressions, or failures to supply aid in times of need.

As the *tayoer* was being performed, the elders of the various estates and the *piiluung* of both villages would listen attentively in order to evaluate the veracity of the events depicted in the chant. If all of the parties agreed on the content of the *tayoer* then the ceremony could proceed to subsequent stages in which valuables would be exchanged as compensation for whatever wrongdoings or debts were enumerated therein. If there was something included in the *tayoer* that the elders did not agree with, however, this would necessitate that both sides sit down to discuss *(puruuy)* the perceived discrepancy. If both sides determined that there was indeed a misrepresentation of the history of the *thaaq*, they would then work to alter the content of the *tayoer* and would request that the newly corrected version be performed. As many noted, this was perhaps one of the reasons why these events were traditionally called *mitmiit* (literally, "getting stuck again and again") since people were continually trying to work out the details of their mutual understanding of the relationship.

Once the relationship had been explained and in some cases discussed and deliberated over in the context of the *tayoer*, there would then be the performance of a second dance known as *taamaen*—the same term that is used to negatively describe an individual who asks for food from people other than his or her own family. In contrast to the *tayoer*, which was performed by one of the elder women (*puweelwol* or *pilabthir*) of the village, the *taamaen* was performed by younger women *(rugood)*. The chant of this dance asked for help for the village in the form of specific food items, goods, and valuables. As Egan (1998) points out, spies were said to have been sent to listen to dance practices well in advance of the *mitmiit* to ensure that the gift-giving village would be able to amass the goods that were being requested. As one of my friends further noted, the spies would also come to listen to the *tayoer* so that they could prepare arguments in advance to challenge any version of the history or current status of the *thaaq* that they did not agree with.

By participating in a *mitmiit* and supplying the goods requested, the giving village was able to provide care and help *(ayuw)* to the village putting on the *tayoer*. As one elder put it, however, if there was no preexisting relationship *(thaaq)* between the two villages, then there could not be *taamaen*. Moreover, the reciprocal nature of *mitmiit* necessitated that *taamaen* could only occur between villages that were of near-equivalent rank, since it would be extremely humiliating for a high-ranking village to request help or aid from a village representing the lower strata of Yapese sociopolitical life.

FIGURE 3. Waiting to dance. Photo by the author.

After the performance of *taamaen* came the ceremonial exchange of goods. This was then followed by other more celebratory dances that could include women's sitting dances *(paer nga buut)*, men's standing *(saak'iy)* and sitting dances, or bamboo dances *(gamaal)*. These dances, associated with the ensuing celebration *(maruuruwol)*, were dances that spoke of historical events and stories, and in some cases were unintelligible because the words were said to have been given by ghosts *(kaan)*. According to the views of one of my teachers, these dances helped to make people feel content and happy *(falfalaen)* after the often-tense deliberations preceding the exchange were completed.

One possible way of looking at this sequence of events is again through the lens of family relationships and the structures of feeling that are implied in these relationships. As we saw previously, parents are the ones who are expected to explain the *yalean* of the *tabinaew* to the children. It is their responsibility to instruct, talk to, and scold the children. Parents are also, however, the ones who should look out

FIGURE 4. Men's sitting dance. Photo by the author.

for the children, providing them with food and care, accepting responsibility for their actions, and apologizing for them to the community
if ever they transgress social rules. In contrast, children are considered
soobuut ("of low status"), without land, and they are accordingly understood to be suffering. In their suffering, they are worthy of pity, compassion, and help. In this framework then, experiences of feeling and
expressing compassion *(runguy)* and shared pain *(amiithuun)* quite
effectively place an individual in the role of a parent or caregiver, a
position that is considered *toelaeng* ("of high status"). Being the one
who is receiving help, who is feeling and expressing *gaafgow* and humility *(soobuut)*, however, is to be put in the role of the child. To ask for
food, help, and goods—in short to *taamaen*—is something that children do with their parents and relatives (and never with strangers).

A parallel logic is apparent in the sequencing of the events at a
mitmiit. Indeed, it seems that *taamaen*—the asking for help, food, and
goods—could only be performed once a relationship had been established wherein one party was instilled with sufficient compassion or
shared pain to be motivated to help the other. This is a form of motivation that is ideally evoked in the context of the performance of *tayoer*.

Since status was, and still is, an important and delicate issue, we can imagine that there would be many opportunities for people to feel upset, hurt, or angry if ever they were made to feel too much like a child *(gaafgow* and *soobuut)* and not enough like a parent *(runguy, amiithuun,* and *toelaeng)*. Herein lies the significance for ensuring the reciprocal nature of these events with villages alternating in hosting *mitmiit,* as well as possible reasons behind the contentious nature of the *tayoer,* which explained the previous history and current status of the relationship.

Notice the structure here, however. First there is deliberation, thinking, and planning in the form of practicing and creating the *tayoer* and the *taamaen.* During the performance of these dances comes the emergence of sentiment. In this case the key moral sentiments of compassion and shared pain are stirred by the perception of suffering and lowliness. Once these two dances have been given, the dances associated with the celebration *(maruuruwol)* would help to evoke feelings of reconciliatory contentment *(falfalaen)*. This, as one of my teachers made clear, was meant to ensure that everyone realizes that "you are suffering, I am suffering" (*kam gaafgow, kug gaafgow*). After all of the negotiations it was time to try to move past any residual feelings of anger *(damuumuw)* and sadness *(kirbaen')*. These dances were thus held to help participants forget past wrongs and move forward with the relationship that they had established together.

From this perspective, the structure of a *mitmiit* can be understood as a play of feeling, an emotion story (Johnson 1998) of sorts, or perhaps more accurately a performance of sentiment at the level of village exchange and ritual (cf. E. Schieffelin 1976). These performances of sentiment were predicated on Yapese ethical modalities of being that rest upon the primacy of thinking, deliberation, and consensus, and the moral sentiments of compassion (*runguy*), shared or collective pain (*amiithuun*), suffering (*gaafgow*), humility *(sobuut)*, and endurance *(athamagil)*.

From Food to Rank

In thinking about the relationship between the sentiments of *runguy* and *gaafgow* and their articulation through work or service *(magaer)* and *athamagil,* we are confronted with a pervasive cultural logic that is deeply implicated in many aspects of Yapese social life. It is not surprising then, that this same logic traditionally figured prominently in local understandings of the significance of food. Scholars like Douglas (1966) and Appadurai (1981) have long noted the ways in which food consumption and production can become crucial sites for culturally marking and constituting social inclusion, exclusion, solidarity, and hierarchy (see also Gupta 1998; Miller, Rosen, and Fiske 1998). Yap in this respect can be viewed, to borrow Appadurai's apt phrasing, as an archetypal example of a society founded upon a "gastro-politics" (Appadurai 1991).

Traditionally, the importance of food in Yapese social life was demonstrated by the fact that each social stratum, gender, and estate had its own foods that were grown on specific lands with specific rankings. In addition, there were different men's eating classes (yoogum) based on age and rank. There was further great value attributed to the suffering and effort involved in planting, caring for, harvesting, and preparing food (Lingenfelter 1979). All of this was associated with a prevalent, if at times implicit, belief that in the process of ingesting foods individuals were held to incorporate the very qualities of tabugul or taqay that were invested in them.

A basic assumption underlying Yapese understandings of food is that the nourishment that comes from the land was a means for the rank, status, and authority inscribed therein to penetrate the body. Accordingly, an individual was imbued with the power of the land through the ingestion of the foods that were grown through the efforts (magaer) of successive generations working upon it. Planting, harvesting, preparing, and ingesting food was only made possible alongside the work, suffering, and endurance of those individuals who helped to prepare the gardens, build and maintain the water works, claim new lands from the sea, and secure the title to specific lands through their service and sacrifice in times of crisis, need, and intervillage warfare. This constellation of efforts was implicated in local understandings of the significance of working and living on the land for ensuring the gradual acquisition of the appropriate amiithuun or forms of attachment arising from collective pain undergone on behalf a particular estate or village.

It is important to note that food in Yap is a vital vehicle for expressing and defining relationships precisely since it also serves as a material index of sentiments. The exchange of food at funerals, within the household, and at inter-estate or intervillage mitmiit, can all be seen as various means through which to express care and concern, as material means for expressing feelings of compassion, shared or collective pain, and suffering. Indeed, in many ways the circulation of food stuffs in Yap serves to remind us of the fact that there are diverse semiotic media available for the expression and communication of feeling states that can go well beyond those associated with bodily and linguistic forms of expression (cf. Munn 1986; Robbins 2003; Schieffelin 1990).

Food was not solely utilized as a vehicle for expressing sentiments, however, since the preparation, acceptance, and ingestion of food was also held to directly affect an individual's subjective life. As one elder remarked to me, if an individual was to consistently eat the wrong type of food (e.g., food taken from a garden that is of higher or lower status), this would have a direct effect on his or her behavior. It would, he suggested, change an individual's habitual ways of thinking and feeling *(taafinay)*. To this end, food, its production, preparation, and consumption were all understood to be an integral part of *yalean* (tradition).

Yalean was, in this respect, likened to a chain in which every link had a special significance. If one link is broken, be it in terms of the food an individual eats, the way that the food is cultivated or prepared, the people that an individual is associated with while gathering or consuming that food, or the land that he or she lives upon, then the rest of the chain would lose its strength and soon fall apart. It is interesting that in this regard some people believed that relatively recent increases in morally reprehensible behavior (e.g., stealing, fighting, drinking, and the like) among younger generations was tied directly to an increasingly acquired a taste for *ggaan nu ngabchëy* ("outsiders' food") and a corresponding lack of interest in eating or preparing *ggaan nu Waqab* ("local food").

As previously mentioned, there is a basic distinction made between two varieties of foodstuffs. There is *ggaan*, which refers to starchy foods such as taro, breadfruit, tapioca, bananas, and yams, and *thum'aeg*, which refers to protein-based foods like fish, shellfish, chicken, pork, and fruit bat. During the time of my fieldwork, rice, ramen noodles, and bread were included in the former category. Canned meats were considered part of the latter. This distinction was further configured by gender; women were largely responsible for the production and collection of *ggaan*, while men were charged with providing *thum'aeg*. While it is true that there were occasions when men would help with clearing gardens and collecting the harvest and times when women were involved in catching land crab and feeding the livestock, there is still, even today, a strong tendency to view these two food-based activities as gender specific.

As ethnographers have long noted (Egan 1998; Labby 1976; Lingenfelter 1975, 1977, 1979; Müller 1917; Senfft 1903; Tetens and Kubary 1873), food production, collection, and preparation were each traditionally associated with strict religiously informed ascetic practices that included strictures on eating certain foods or outright fasting, prohibitions on sexual contact, practices of seclusion (e.g., men would traditionally seclude themselves in the men's house for certain prescribed periods prior to undertaking a fishing expedition), and numerous other rules associated with cleanliness and purification. Moreover, unlike many of the Outer Island cultures where food sharing is often the norm, in Yap the act of ingesting food stuffs was considered to be an extremely private affair, with strict rules against food sharing even within the context of the same household. Citing Tetens's (Tetens and Kubary 1873, 91) early account of eating practices on the island, Egan (1998, 150) notes the apparent antiquity of these local valuations of privacy when it comes to participating in consumptive practices, which are still prevalent, albeit in an attenuated form, in contemporary Yapese society.[3]

Much like Egan, during my time living in Yap I often participated in social gatherings where food was distributed (e.g., funerals, community work projects, parties) and noted repeatedly that food was often rarely eaten in these contexts. While it was true that younger men and women would often eat in public, most of the elders would hold onto their plates, refraining from eating until they had returned to the privacy of their own households. In some cases, if an elder was a man from a particularly high-ranking estate, upon returning home he might simply give the food to his wife and children without eating it himself. I even heard tell of some individuals from very high-ranking estates refusing to eat at some of the restaurants in Colonia. This was said to be on account of the problem of never being able to be certain as to the rank or status of the person who was charged with preparing the food.

It is interesting to note, however, that certain foods have been reclassified in contemporary Yap to allow for the possibility of eating during parties or occasions where people are drinking alcohol (Egan 1998, 151). Referring to a piece of meat or fish as a "chaser" or "sashimi," individuals who are drinking together can, as Egan observes, "bypass customary notions of privacy while ingesting food" (Egan 1998, 151).

This is due to the fact that chasers or sashimi are not considered *thum'aeg* and are thus not classified as part of a meal. Another interesting way of circumventing these restrictions is tied to the order with which food is distributed during such events. Highest-status men ideally receive their food first, prior to lower-status men, women, and children who may otherwise have an opportunity to *tungaaf nag* ("contaminate") the food by preparing their plates.

In reference to these various food-based restrictions it was quite common to hear elders reflecting upon how "strict" life was "long ago." Traditionally, men would have their own pots *(th'iib)* and their own kitchens *(taqang)*, which were kept separate from those of their wives and children. If there were a number of men from the same family living in the same household, they would also each have their own pot to eat from. As previously mentioned, young women *(rugood)* were not allowed to prepare food for elder men or men who had been ritually inducted *(dawaach nag)* into one of the men's eating classes *(yoogum)*. These eating classes, as Lingenfelter explains, were a means by which to "define relative levels of pollution and purity for men and regulate their socio-political contacts and consumption of food" (1979, 416). Once an individual was inducted into a particular eating class, a man could no longer eat with women, children, or men of lower status. He could, however, share food with those men who were members of the same eating class, regardless of their village or community affiliation. The foods that were associated with each eating class were tied to specific gardens, taro patches, fruit trees, and coconut groves that were determined to have a specific level of purity *(tabugul)* appropriate for the eating class in question.

The ability to enter into a particular eating class and move up to higher classes was based on three factors (Egan 1998; Lingenfelter 1979). The absolute limiting factor was tied to the rank of the taro patches *(maqut)* associated with a man's house foundation *(daaf)*. A man could not move higher than the rank inscribed in the lands he was linked to through his estate. The second factor was maturity. As a man aged, married, and had children, he was allowed to move through higher eating classes. Finally, merit and aptitude also played a significant role in progressing through these levels since it was the village elders who ultimately decided if a particular individual was suitable for initiation into a given eating class (this was true especially for the highest-ranking classes). With each progressive movement up the ranks, a man would be confronted with more serious constraints on his social activity and was thus faced with increasing isolation from those who did not share his elevated *tabugul* status (Lingenfelter 1979, 417). This resulted in the fact that even despite the high level of prestige associated with such classes, very few men were motivated to "seek this lofty isolation" (Lingenfelter 1979, 417).

In reflecting upon the many restrictions tied to food preparation, a woman in her mid- to late sixties recalled that when her grandmother went to prepare food for her grandfather she was required to wash her hands in seven different shell bowls filled with water. She also had to change into a grass skirt *(oeng)* that was designated solely for cooking his food prior to entering the kitchen. Her grandfather had been ritually inducted into one of the higher-ranked eating classes. Accordingly, there were numerous restrictions that were also placed on her grandmother while planting, caring for, and harvesting the taro and other starchy food stuffs that were grown in the high-ranking *tabugul* gardens and taro patches that produced his food (restrictions that I will return to discuss in the next chapter). Many older women similarly told me of the effort and suffering that was traditionally entailed in abiding by all of the strictures associated with the production and consumption of food, all the while preparing multiple meals, in multiple kitchens, with multiple pots.

In this respect, one elder asserted that "women hold the base of the breath of the household" *(bpiin ma koel ea michin ea pagoofan ko tabinaew)*. As she went on to explain, this phrase refers to the fact that women are the ones who go to the taro patch, go to the gardens to collect food, and are also the ones who return to prepare the fire, the pot, and the food for its consumption. Women are thus the ones who provide nourishment for their children and their husbands. Without food the members of the family will not have sustenance, and will thus not have life *(yifas)*, a connection that is perhaps implicated in the fact that the morpheme *fas* can be used alternatively to designate "life" and feelings of satiation—*kug fas* ("I am full/alive").

Without the sustenance brought by the production and consumption of food, individuals would literally be without their very breath *(faan/pagoofaan)*. This has very interesting implications given that breath is the source of an individual's voice *(lunguun)*. When people say that *lunguun* does not convey one's own mind or authority, but the wishes and authority of the land *(buut)*, the foundation *(daaf)*, the estate *(tabinaew)*, or the village *(binaew)*, it is also true that a voice cannot be produced without breath. And breath is sustained through nourishment, which is itself only granted through the cultivation and preparation of food. All of which implies forethought, cooperation, sacrifice, suffering, and endurance on the part of those individuals responsible for the land upon which that food is grown.

This connection between food, sustenance, life, breath and voice also implies that one's voice, like one's very breath, relies upon the work and effort of others. Such efforts include the efforts of one's mother, and the countless other generations of people who had worked on the land, whose efforts had lead to acquiring the lands that were associated with a particular foundation. It is precisely these lands that are the very sources for the food that sustains life. To speak for a foundation is thus to speak for those countless others—ancestors, contemporaries, and future descendents—who have worked and will work that land, whose efforts resulted in the fruits that are currently nourishing one's very life breath, the breath that propels one's voice. Voice is thus both figuratively and quite literally given by the land as mediated through breath. The very act of being able to speak signifies that one has access to sustenance, nourishment, support, land, a place, and a family. Without these things, one could not have *fas* ("life"), *faan* ("breath"), or *lunguun* ("voice").[4]

The significance attributed to the power inherent in *lunguun* can also be understood as associated with the premium that is placed on silence and not talking without good reason. To speak without clear purpose is to waste one's breath. Accordingly, it is to waste the effort and work of those who provided the individual with the ability to speak in the first place. Speaking too much, speaking when you have nothing to say, or just speaking to voice your own thoughts and feelings can be construed as a means of disrespecting the labor of those who have worked the land that produced the food that gave sustenance to the breath needed to vocalize those thoughts.

The social significance of voice is further rooted in the fact that it is through voice enabled by breath that one is able to coordinate action, plan with others *(puruuy)*, and notify others of one's goals and plans. One elder told me that when a foundation loses its *lunguun* (i.e., its voice, influence, and authority) it is said that it is due to the fact that the people of that foundation have become *malmaal* or "lazy." They no longer exert effort to work on behalf of their estate. As she put it, "If there is no voice associated with that foundation it is because the people are lazy. There is no endurance, no work, no suffering, so they lose the authority."

It is also interesting to note in this regard that the Yapese word for breath, *faan,* which was also used to refer to the "meaning" or "significance" of an utterance or practice, is phonologically close to the term used for ownership, *fean.* This connection becomes all the more interesting when we recall that breath is needed to invigorate the body while one is exerting effort. It is breath that keeps the body moving, working, and exerting effort, effort that is the basis for acquiring title and possession of land. The term *fean rog* can further be used when somebody wants to let another person know not to touch his or her possession. *Feanog* is literally translated as "it's mine," while *tafean* (habitual prefix *ta-* combined with the morpheme *fean*) is used to refer to one's home.

Hunger and Satiation as Moral Sensibilities

As I will explore in some more detail in the next chapter, there is a great significance placed on the act of eating in Yapese culture, which is tied to the ability to ignore feelings of hunger in the face of cultural and social dictates associated with issues of status, rank, and community obligation. Such gustatory practices are pivotal, I argue, for establishing a foothold for the development of increasingly elaborated emphases on controlling one's somatic, emotional, and psychological expressivity through endurance or *athamagil.* It is this very ability to cultivate mastery over such internal somatic states through enacting *athamagil* that has direct implications for experiences and expressions of pain and suffering.

Traditionally, there were no scheduled times for people to eat. Instead, activities like eating were scheduled according to work projects. Work always held priority over eating. While many of the restrictions traditionally associated with work and food production greatly lessened or disappeared over the last century, I observed that many individuals, particularly those of the older generations, continued to put off eating until they were finished with their work. In a similar light, many elders recounted how common it was in instances when children would complain to their parents of being hungry while working or doing chores, to hear parents say, *M' athamagil, kaed ea n'um, mu shoen* ("You endure, bite your mind, you wait.") This was often contrasted to the way children were said to behave and were treated by their parents in contemporary Yapese society. If a child asks for a soda, if they ask for food or *ocaas* (candies), "it is always *chiiney, chiiney*" ("now, now"), one elder exclaimed. Many complained that it seems that more often than not parents tend to comply with their children's demands.

In contrast, elders recalled being asked when they complained of being hungry while working, *Daabkiy paer be u tafean? Ma kaed ea n'um!* ("Doesn't a person live in his house? You get control of your mind!") The "person" referred to in this case is hunger *(biliig)*. Hunger has its home in the stomach—*Tafean ea biliig ea cheew.* That is, the experience of hunger cannot be found anywhere in the world apart from the stomach, so it is fair to say that the stomach is its home. The implied message is that if the stomach is hunger's home, then there is absolutely nothing to complain about if its presence is sensed. Individuals must learn to accept that this is the way it feels to be human. To be a human is to feel hunger. Accordingly, hunger is not something that should take one's attention off of the work at hand. Instead, individuals should persevere, endure, and keep working.

There is thus a prevalent connection between experiences of hunger and satiation, food consumption, hard work, determination, willingness to suffer in the face of hardship, endurance, thinking through one's actions carefully, and needing to cooperate and coordinate one's activities with others. The upkeep and irrigation of the taro patches and gardens alone necessitated adherence to this constellation of embodied values and ideals. When one considers the fact that a taro patch can take up to as many as five years for it to yield taro of an edible size, not to mention all of the work that has to go into the upkeep of the waterways that feed taro patches and gardens, it is clear that traditional modes of food production were based upon collective labor carried out in light of careful forethought, engineering, and planning. Indeed, the connection between food, its production, harvesting, and its articulation with broader cultural concerns was, as far as I have been able to understand it, a key moral idiom in Yapese culture. As we have seen, food played a role in indexing rank, status, gender, and caste affiliation. It was connected with suffering and the necessity to defer gratification in the context of work, effort, and endurance. It was further tied to forms of disciplining the body that were implicated in various ascetic practices. And it was connected to the high valuation placed on forethought and deliberation in organizing collaborative work projects. Finally, when one considers the fact that in numerous myths and oral histories Yap was said to have suffered through terrible famines driven by overpopulation—such as the famine reflected in the story of the two brothers and the tropical almond tree—it appears that a cultural script linking food production, work, effort, and delayed satiation in the face of planning, deliberation, and social dictates is well ingrained in many levels of local practice, belief, values, and norms.

Of Typhoons and Virtue

In April 2004, seven months after I returned to Los Angeles following my longest stay on Yap, the island was devastated by a direct hit from Typhoon Sudal. Suffering through 125-mile-an-hour winds, Yap sustained severe damage to its communication buildings, hospital, airport, and most of its infrastructure. By some estimates over 90 percent of the homes were also damaged or destroyed. George W. Bush declared Yap a disaster area and it did not take long for the Federal Emergency Management Agency (FEMA) and the Red Cross to respond with aid. In September 2004, when I wrote this chapter's first draft, these agencies had done much to help Yap rebuild its infrastructure and supply families with food and shelter. While this aid was greatly appreciated by everyone who suffered through this devastating experience, it was interesting to hear from a number of my friends that the increased access to *ggaan nu ngabchëy* ("outsiders' food") was also viewed to have a number of negative consequences for the community. As a very close friend of mine wrote a few months after the typhoon:

Yap is suffering at present with all of the goods that FEMA has provided. There are a lot of fifty-pound bags of rice, twenty-five-pound bags of flour, and vegetable oil that Yapese people are eating. I think that Yap is deeply indebted and appreciative of all the excellent food that America has given. We all thank America, but there is now a laziness that has set upon the women of Yap, they no longer go to the taro patch to look for taro. There is a lot of sickness from the American food. The weeds are filling up the taro patches, and we are suffering in Yap.

I believe it is evident from this statement that hunger and satiation are complexly implicated in local moral frames. Depending on the context, hunger and satiation can in fact each be imbued with positive or negative moral valences. For instance, hunger is negatively valenced in as much as it has a number of interesting associations with fear-based illnesses *(m'aar ko marus)*. Satiation, meanwhile, as my friend's reflections attest, may hold a negative valuation especially in relationship to the consumption of nonlocal foods (*ggaan nu ngabchëy*), which are understood to be etiologically tied to numerous "new" illnesses (*m'aar nib biqech*) like diabetes, cancer, and gout.

The connection between a lack of food, hunger, and fear is further rooted in the possibility of linking experiences of extreme hunger to abandonment. Aside from mass famine, being without food is tantamount to being alone and not being affiliated with a *tabinaew*. Such a lack could only result from no longer having someone to witness an individual's suffering and to respond by caringly providing much needed sustenance. In contrast, the experience of hunger also has a positive valence inasmuch as it can indicate that an individual is working and enduring through his or her personal suffering in order to better the lives of his or her family, estate, or community. Similarly, satiation is imbued with a positive moral value to the extent that it indexes the presence of care, nurturance, and compassion (cf. Becker 1995).

Moral Modalities of Being

A former elementary school principal from one of Yap's northern municipalities once explained to me that experiences of suffering, endurance, compassion, and care are at the center of family life, with the husband and his side of the family feeling compassion *(runguy)* and providing care *(ayuw)* when his wife and children are, in the midst of their suffering *(gaafgow)*, perceived to be striving to endure *(athamagil)* to provide service to the estate through working the land. It is, he suggested, only in the context of these feelings that the family can be properly "supported by both sides." Without suffering there is no motivational basis for care *(ayuw)*. There is further no foundation for endurance, humility *(soobuutaen')*, respect or deference *(liyoer)*, and ultimately no striving to better one's *tabinaew*. The centrality of these virtues is such that he often told his students that if they wanted to better their lives, their school, and their communities, all they had to do was to remember three Yapese names. These names represented Yap's core cultural virtues: *Fal'eagar* (a term that connotes excellent work) from Rumuu, *Athamagil* from Nimgil, and *Gaafgow* from Thor.

CHAPTER 4

Subjectivity, Embodiment, and Social Action

When I got back to the village, Yinug was alone in the house. Smiling as I approached, he told me there was some food in the kitchen and that I could eat if I was hungry. I declined and asked how he was doing. "*Maenigil*" (Good), he replied. I noticed that he was wearing his cap, something that he only did when going into town. At the time I found it a little odd, but I did not say anything. I sat down. Yinug sat quietly smoking for a few minutes, getting up occasionally to clean a bit around the veranda. He seemed a little more distracted than usual, I thought, but otherwise appeared to be in good spirits. I reached into my basket and offered Yinug a betel nut. He thanked me, took one, and we both sat quietly preparing our betel nut to chew. We sat together chewing and talking for the better part of an hour.

When it appeared that I might be getting ready to take my leave, Yinug put his cigarette out and began to tell me about what had happened to Tinag. Yesterday, while playing up near Tamag's house, Tinag had fallen out of a tree and had broken her arm. I put my basket back down and waited for him to continue. Looking down, he began to roll another cigarette. Yesterday, he had received a call from Tinag's father asking to speak to his wife, he recalled. When he found out that she was not in, Tinag's father then told him of the accident and that Tinag would be at the hospital getting the bones reset and a cast put on her arm. Yinug had been waiting all morning for his wife to return home so that they could both go visit Tinag. She had yet to return from working in the garden. "Do you need a ride?" I asked. "No," he replied. "It's okay, I'll wait."

To understand actions and events in cultural context, one must first gain some insight into the local "models for experience" that help to organize the life-worlds of particular social actors (Shore 1982). In the case of painful experiences, and individuals' reactions to them, it is especially crucial to develop an understanding of how emotions, feelings, sensations, and other bodily processes intimately linked to pain are broadly figured in local frameworks that are used to understand the nature of subjectivity, psychical and somatic processes, health, well-being, and illness. Anthropologists have traditionally explored this constellation of phenomena under the rubrics of ethnopsychology and ethnomedicine. In the following few chapters, I will outline what I have come to understand of these two overlapping fields of knowledge in an attempt to sketch a general cultural framework within which Yapese individuals are inclined to interpret and give meaning to their experiences of pain in their everyday lives.

In this chapter I will discuss how mind, body, and emotions are configured in local understandings of subjective life, before turning to detail how this particular envisioning of subjectivity is connected to the virtues of suffering *(gaafgow)*, endurance *(athamagil)*, physical exertion *(magaer)*, and compassion *(runguy)*. In the process, I will suggest that the valuation of reflective mental life over impulsive somatic life, which significantly shapes local framings of mind-body relations, is directly implicated in the cultivation of these selfsame core cultural virtues.

As intimated in the previous chapters, a socially competent person in Yap is understood to be a person who is able to sacrifice his or her individual desires, wants, wishes, feelings, opinions, and thoughts to family, village, and broader community dictates. The virtues of self-abnegation and self-restraint as realized through careful reflection and deliberation are deemed essential to the cultivation of those qualities that inhere in a virtuous person, a person who acts thoughtfully, with self-control, humility, and concern for others.[1] A person who is not able to cultivate these qualities, who acts impulsively, who transparently expresses his or her personal feelings and emotions, who speaks without thinking, or acts without regard to the concerns of others, is a person who is thought to have a "weak mind," not unlike a child. To wit, the capacity to master the ability to monitor and selectively share one's emotions, feelings, thoughts, and opinions in the service of wider familial and community goals is one of the essential psychocultural bases of Yapese conceptions of virtuous personhood. It is also one of

the important roots for the valuation of privacy, secrecy, and concealment in Yapese communities.

Not sharing, not expressing, and not acting upon one's "true"
feelings, opinions, or thoughts, a pattern also widely noted in the
context of other Polynesian and Micronesian cultures (Besnier 1994;
Mageo 1998; Petersen 1993; Robbins and Rumsey 2008; Wilson 1995;
White and Kirkpatrick 1985), is at the heart of a number of core cultural values at the basis of Yapese social life (see also Throop 2008a,
2008b; Robbins 2008). Such an ability to monitor and selectively
share information is indeed evident in Yinug's decision to wait until
my imminent departure before telling me about Tinag's accident—an
event that was evidently on his mind given that just prior to my arrival
he was in the process of waiting for his wife to return so that he could
visit Tinag in the hospital.

This understanding of virtuous comportment and ethical subjectivity thus ideally emphasizes a fundamental disconnect between individual expression and an individual's inner life. An individual's inner
states, defined in terms of personal wants, desires, opinions, feelings,
emotions, sensations, and thought-objects, are held to have, in many
contexts, a nondirect, nontransparent connection to action and
expression. It is instead purposeful, goal-directed thought that is oriented toward the consequences of one's actions on the thoughts,
feelings, and desires of others that is ideally to guide one's speech,
expression, and action. An orientation to the consequences of action
and a tendency to go to great efforts to conceal personal motives,
feelings, and opinions is embedded in one of the central Yapese terms
used to refer to an individual's personality—*paqngin* (or *pagniin* in
the dictionary). *Paqngin* encapsulates an emphasis on perceptible
effects for, as Jensen (1977a) notes, it refers both to the observable
trajectories of an object's "effects," "action," or "work" and a person's "behavior" or "personality."

There are, in fact, a number of important ways in which Yapese
ethno-epistemologies are oriented, as Shore (1982) similarly claims for
Samoa, to an emphasis upon "effects" and not "causes." In this sense,
Yapese epistemologies tend to value pragmatic (in the Peircian and
Jamesian senses of the term) orientations to social action and personality structure.[2] It is the perceptual effects of an act and not its hidden
roots that are often the preferred orientation of social actors in judging
or describing the behavior and personalities of others. Well in-line with
this tendency to focus on effects, the morally competent adult is seen

to be an individual who always thinks *(leam/taafinay)* of the consequences of his or her actions and speech before actually engaging in
acting or speaking. More often than not, when an individual does speak
or act, he or she is also thought to be ideally speaking or acting for
another, and not merely for him or herself.

It is in this same manner that both action and voice *(lunguun)* are
ideally taken in Yapese culture to be, at least partially, vehicles of the
collective (see chapter 3). This is not to say that individuals do not
regularly act with personal goals and motives in mind, that they do not
strive to better themselves at the expense of others, or that individuals
are incurious as to others' intentions, motives, and desires (cf. Hollan
and Throop 2008; Robbins and Rumsey 2008). Again, there are some
significant parallels in Samoa where, as Shore maintains, an orientation
to expressive behavior and the perceptible effects of action do not
preclude Samoans from having "a very lively conception of private
experience" (1982, 148).[3]

As I will explore in greater detail, it was widely recognized by my
Yapese friends, family members, and teachers that there are a great
many people who fail to live up to these standards for virtuous ways
of being. Moreover, there are a great number of individuals who are
able to strategically align their personal wishes, desires, opinions, and
feelings with what are putatively broader familial and community needs.
This latter type of person is not necessarily disparaged, however, since
the drive to better his or her own position in life can also have significant positive effects for the family and community. Moreover, a cultural
emphasis on the effects of activity does not perforce entail muting the
saliency of attending to inner motivation. As Egan recounts in discussing some of his frustrations facing well-ingrained habits of secrecy and
concealment with a Yapese friend, "I suggested that Yapese consider
even the most mundane matters to be a case of: 'what is in my head
is my business, not yours.' He corrected me: 'what is in your head is
my business, but you still won't tell me'" (1998, 79).

That said, attempting to balance, reconcile, or integrate personal
ambition or desire with these moral frames for appropriate social action
is never a simple matter. The tensions that arise in the interstices of
these competing motivational frames are, as I will explore in later
chapters, at the very heart of individual struggles to navigate day-to-day
experiences of suffering. As such, it was generally acknowledged that
the disciplining of one's somatically mediated desires, needs, and wants
is a difficult practice, which necessitated the expenditure of considerable effort. It is again *athamagil* or endurance that enables an individual

to perfect those abilities for self-governance entailed in controlling and monitoring the expression of personal desires, needs, and wants in the service of broader community goals. Interestingly, it is also assumed that the effort that is required to achieve such collective goals draws from the individual's wellspring of personal desires and motives. Although in this context, these are desires and motives that have been rarified in light of their expression in the form of intentional actions that, in some way, are viewed as benefiting the collectivity.

Generally speaking, Yapese understandings of subjectivity are importantly configured according to a privileging of mental processes over somatic ones. In fact, the very word for body in Yapese *(doow)* is the same term that is used to designate the detritus resulting from human activity. The body is thus denigrated quite literally as "trash."[4] Much like the "trash" that provides the material for claiming new land from the sea, however, the body can also be transformed into an increasingly purified and ordered *(tabugul)* state. Whereas land is ordered and purified through histories of intentional work and productive labor, the body is purified through being disciplined to serve the ends, intentions, and goals of the socially crafted "mind"—*yaen'* or *waen'*.

Yaen' is a term that foregrounds the subjective processes of thinking, reflecting, deliberating, perceiving, feeling, and willing. This is often held in opposition to the impulsivity, desires, and needs of the body. It is the body, then, that is to be mastered, controlled, and disciplined by the mind, a mind that is oriented to cultural virtues highlighting the value of endurance, perseverance, and effortful striving. Whether evidenced in the proliferation of strict ascetic practices in multiple aspects of Yapese life; the rhetoric of constant deferral of personal desires, wants, and needs in light of obligations to one's family and community; or in terms of the general orientation to work, effort, suffering, and endurance as core cultural virtues, a salient cultural trope in Yap consists of viewing an individual's physical self as ideally subordinated to a mentally governed moral self.

Aspects of Subjectivity

I am certainly entering into potentially contentious ground when I gloss Yapese conceptions of subjective life in light of English terms like "mind" and "body"—terms that most certainly carry the weight of Cartesian (and pre-Cartesian) assumptions concerning the partitioning of experience into putatively separate psychical and somatic domains.

I was repeatedly struck in the context of my everyday conversations, interviews, and observations, however, by the tendency for individuals to reiterate what appeared to be clear distinctions between psychological and embodied states and processes. As Murphy Halliburton (2002; cf. Lutz 1988) argues in the context of his recent work in Kerala, South India, it is important to recall that it is not exclusively "Western" cultures that cultivate distinctions between mind and body. I will leave broader issues concerning the crypto-primitivist ideals entailed in many anthropological renderings of "non-Western" cultures as lacking proclivities to bifurcate experience in such a manner aside. I wish to emphasize instead how Yapese distinctions between psychical and somatic processes, to use Halliburton's apt phrasing, are clearly grounded in a "local phenomenology" in which mentalistic models of experience are generally emphasized and valued over somatic ones.

To this extent, it appears that in some respects Yapese articulations of mind-body relations stand in sharp contrast with Catherine Lutz's (1988) influential characterization of emotion, subjectivity, and personhood on the nearby atoll of Ifaluk. Ifalukians, she argued, do not tend to separate "evaluative and emotional responses from non-evaluative and cognitive response to an environmental event" (1988, 92). Even so, there are a number of important parallels to Lutz's insights inasmuch as the Yapese term *yaen'*, much as Mageo (1989, 1991, 1998) has suggested for the Samoan term *loto*, at times serves to index a relatively undifferentiated constellation of thinking, feeling, and willing that can be opposed to those more clearly delineated distinctions between various aspects of psychical and somatic processes in many Western ethnopsychologies.

Of course, whenever discussing such issues in the context of a society that has been influenced by various colonial regimes, missionary work, and more recently Hollywood movies, popular magazines, American newspapers, the Internet, and books, it is important to recognize the influence that such interactions have had on contemporary renderings of subjective life. Indeed, there are a number of instances—such as evidence I encountered for a shift in metaphorical associations from the liver *(aed)* or stomach *(yael* or *yin)* to the heart *(gum'iirchaq)* as the seat of emotional life—where the impact of Christianity (Roman Catholicism in particular) seems to have importantly informed local discourses pertaining to internal states, somatic processes, and subjectivity.

Catholicism has had a complex and yet significant impact on contemporary Yapese conceptions of morality, personhood, and subjectivity. I would like to stress, however, that historically such translocal influences were seldom met without some resistance. And moreover, local understandings were, in the end, the very lens through which such doctrines and ideas were first filtered (cf. Robbins 2004; Sahlins 1981, 1985, 1995). I would like to suggest, then, that there is still a discernable integrity to indigenous Yapese elaborations of subjectivity and social action. Evidence for this integrity is most readily apparent in the fact that local virtues, ideals, and interpretive frames are highly redundant and are played out in multiple realms of Yapese social life.

As we have already seen, the moral significance of suffering and compassion is evidenced in the structuring of social relations within the family, in defining intravillage and intervillage relationships, and in providing a foundation for many ethnopsychological and ethnomedical assumptions (cf. Levy 1973, 1984). Indeed, the extent of this redundancy indicates, to me at least, an integrity that does not seem likely if present-day configurations were simply the result of a wholesale grafting of Roman Catholic assumptions upon local ways of life (cf. Robbins 2004).

That said, I should note that issues concerning the historical articulation of foreign and indigenous systems in contemporary understandings of psychical and somatic processes are separate from issues pertaining to the *perception* of foreignness or indigenousness in the everyday lived experience of particular social actors.[5] Regardless of the extent to which the ideas explored here have been impacted by translocal interpretive frames (and of course they most certainly have been impacted), it is the various ways in which lived experience is configured by particular social actors that is at the heart of this book. Even when individual actors do perceive distinctions between translocal and local influences on contemporary renderings of subjectivity and social action, the questions that arise most significantly for this particular project are not tied to examining these forms of discernment as such. They lie instead in investigating how these perceptions concretely affect processes of self-articulation and sense-making in the context of everyday practice (cf. Rosenblatt 2004).

Yaen'

While I lived in Yap, there were a number of terms that were utilized in everyday conversation to index aspects of subjective experience that many Western philosophers, psychologists, and social scientists might recognize as relating to properties or processes associated with the concept of "mind."[6] The most central of these was the term *yaen'* (other dialectical versions of the same term were *waen'* and *yaen'if*), which referred generally to the first-person subjective experiences of a particular actor.[7] Indeed, *yaen'* (a directly suffixed third-person singular possessive rendering of the noun) is highly productive, serving as the morphemic foundation for a majority of Yapese terms referring to mental states and processes. It is interesting to note here that grammatically most nouns in Yapese do not follow the same pattern as *yaen'* in utilizing directly suffixed pronouns. Instead, the overwhelming majority rely upon the possessive pronoun suffixes: *roog* (mine), *room* (yours), *roek'* (his or hers), and so on. As Jensen notes with regard to the former, "All of these nouns which are possessed by directly suffixing pronoun suffixes have a very close or intimate relationship to the person or thing which possesses them. The words in this class include most parts of the body [and, I would add, the mind]. This type of possession is sometimes called *inalienable possession*" (1977b, 146). Other notable nouns that fall into the class of "inalienable possession" include most kin terms (e.g., "sibling"—*walaageeg, walaagem, walaagean*) and, of particular significance for this study, the experience of "pain" *(amiithuug, amiithuum, amiithuun)*.

Throughout my time living in Yap, I worked to compile an extensive, but by no means comprehensive, list of "internal states."[8] All told, the final list consisted of: 162 terms referring to general mental processes, including terms that refer to phenomena that might be categorized as emotions, thoughts, memories, and the like; twenty-five terms indexing somatic states and processes, including thirsty *(baleal)*, hungry *(k'iy)*, lethargic *(aaw paa)*, energetic *(pasiig)*, and so on; seventeen terms for active and passive phases of sensory experience, such as looking *(saap naag)* versus seeing *(guy)* or listening *(matooyil)* versus hearing *(rungaqag)*, and for objects of sensory perception, such as sound *(lingaan)*, image *(yaqan)*, and odor *(boen)*; and thirty-two pain-related terms, including physical pain *(amiith)*, burning pain *(ke yik)*, shooting pain *(yip yip)*, and numbness or tingling *(gaamiig)*.

Of the 162 terms that referred to mental processes, ninety-eight were derived from modifications of the morphemic root *yaen'*. For instance, a term like *kirebaen'*, which Jensen translates as "sadness, unhappiness," is constructed by adding the adjective *kireeb* ("bad," "broken," or "ruined") to the nominal morpheme *yaen'* ("mind"). *Kirebaen'* can thus literally be translated as "bad mind" or "broken mind." *Puwaen'*, which resonates with Lutz's (1988) characterization of the Ifalukian term *song* as an observable form of "justifiable anger," results from a combination of the verb/adjective *puw* ("to pull up, stir up, root up, agitate, wake up") and *yaen'*; literally, a "stirred-up or agitated mind." *Ngoochngoochaen'*, which can be roughly glossed as "bored, tired of something, frustrated, depressed," is comprised of the reduplicative adjective *ngoochngooch* referring to something that is very short and *yaen'*; literally, "short, short mind."

A number of different modifications of the morpheme *yaen'* seem to accrue semantic meaning through metaphorical elaborations upon the relative size, position, or state of the mind described. For instance, the term *nuwaen'* ("long mind") was described by many individuals as an ability to persevere in the face of hardship, and as such was held to have a meaning very similar to that of *athamagil*. The opposite of *nuwan'*, *ngoochngoochaen'* ("short mind") is used to describe a person who is quick to anger, lose hope, and become saddened when things are not going his or her way. A person who has a short mind is someone who is not able to endure suffering. He or she is not able to keep up hope in the face of obstacles or challenges. Accordingly, he or she is not able to control his or her emotions. As one elder put it, someone who is *ngoochngoochaen'* is one for whom "sadness stays, one is not able to endure."

While I will return to a more detailed discussion of *yaen'*, let me shift briefly to discuss two other terms that figure prominently in local understandings of subjectivity: *leam* and *taafinay*. In Jensen's dictionary, *leam* is described as a noun or an intransitive verb that means "thought, feeling; to think, to feel." *Leam* can be transformed into a transitive verb by adding the transitivising particle *-naag*, in which case it can be rendered "to think of." The noun and intransitive verb *taafinay* (*tafnay* in the dictionary's orthography) means, a bit more expansively, "mind, thought, to think." This term is also transformed into a transitive verb through the use of *-naag*. In their nominal forms both terms were often used in everyday speech to refer to an individual's "mind," and thus seemed to share at least a partial semantic overlap with *yaen'*.

Throughout the duration of my fieldwork I asked numerous people about the distinction between these two terms (as well as both of their relationships to *yaen'*). Most individuals claimed to use the two terms interchangeably in everyday speech. When I asked them to reflect on whether or not the terms were indeed synonymous, however, the majority of people responded by suggesting that there was in fact an important difference between them. A large but definite minority of individuals claimed that the terms were simply dialect variants of the same concept. *Taafinay* was said to have been traditionally used exclusively in the municipality of Gagil while *leam* was used in the municipalities located in Yap (Marabaaq), the largest of Yap proper's four islands.

With regard to those who believed that there was a salient conceptual distinction between the two terms there was a wide range of variation with regard to how individuals portrayed the differences between them. After talking with well over forty different people at some length who hailed from at least seven of Yap's ten municipalities, it became clear to me that it was very unlikely that a definite consensus regarding the meaning of these two terms could be established. There were, however, some patterns that emerged in individuals' attempts to distinguish between *leam* and *taafinay* that are worth sharing here.

It seems that a central distinction is tied to individuals' epistemic stances regarding their degree of certainty concerning a given topic. Another significant difference concerned the temporal qualities of the subjective states in question. For example, one particularly eloquent elder suggested that *taafinay* could be translated as "opinion," while *leam* had more of the connotation of "will" and "thought." She said that inasmuch as *leam* could be associated with willing or thinking, it should be understood as something that perdures. An individual using the term is suggesting to his or her interlocutor that the topic at hand has been given careful, deliberate thought, and that it reflects a corresponding certitude with regard to his or her epistemic stance. *Taafinay* as an opinion, however, seems to entail a more fleeting, momentary experience *(ma yib ea chiiney)*. It is in some sense light *(baequd)* when compared to the durative heaviness *(toomaal)* of *leam*. *Taafinay* can thus be used to downplay one's certainty about the information, knowledge, or advice being expressed by the speaker. Others, however, reversed these definitions, claiming that *leam* is more akin to a "light" and ephemeral opining, while *taafinay*, in contrast, implies a "heavy," drawn-out process of deliberation.

Some people also sought to distinguish between the two terms according to whether or not either included elements of feeling *(thaamiy)*. Again, there were just as many individuals who suggested that one term was more or less imbued with feeling than the other; some drawing from what appeared to be borrowed Christian metaphors to associate feeling-imbued mentation with the "heart" and strictly ideational mental processes with the "head."

Still yet another distinction that was often invoked was in terms of the metaphorical depth *(tooqaer)* of the experiences referred to by each. In this case, the metaphor of "depth" was employed to indicate the relative clarity or opacity of the experiences so designated to an individual's interlocutors. For example, some individuals suggested that while the contents of one's *taafinay* are quite conscious, easily express-ible, and quickly recognized by others, the contents of an individual's *leam* are much more opaque, even when expressed. Of course, there were individuals who argued that the reverse was true.

Both terms were further portrayed as entailing intentionality in the phenomenological sense of the term (Husserl 1962) as a consciousness directed toward an intentional object. In this regard, one particularly insightful friend of mine emphasized that regardless of how one thinks of the differences between the two terms, *taafinay* and *leam* are both considered active processes. They are, in his words, processes of "putting information together." And yet, an extremely well-respected (and university-educated) man maintained that it was only *taafinay* that implied a process that is directed toward an object, while also entailing some sense of "yearning." *Leam*, he suggested, designates the "mind" in itself, without an object. He added that the term *leam* is seldom used in this way, however, since "thinking of something that abstract is hard for most people." Instead, it is the transitive form, *leam naag*, which does imply an intentional object (e.g., "I am thinking of . . ."), which is most often heard in everyday discourse. That said, I often heard *leam* employed in its nontransitivized nominal form in the context of talk pertaining to an individual who has exerted his or her will over against social dictates: *Kab ea leam roek'* ("His or her mind has come").

While it remains unclear as to whether, and how, *leam* and *taafinay* differ from one another, it is clear that they can both be importantly contrasted with *yaen'*. This is particularly the case when *yaen'* is modi-fied with the noun phrase connector *ii* and the locative relational noun *laen-*, which refers to the interior or insides of an object, space, person, and so on (Jensen 1977a, 1977b). While it was quite difficult to obtain a definitional consensus, almost of all of the descriptions I managed to elicit in interviews and casual conversations centered on the fact that *laen ii yaen'* indexes an individual's innermost desires, wants, feelings, thoughts, opinions, and emotions (although interestingly, in 1913 Sixtus

Walleser translated *laen ii yaen'* as "will" and *yaen'* as "spirit"; see note 7 earlier in this chapter).

Laen ii yaen' was portrayed by many individuals as the emotional, imaginal, volitional, and motivational core of the self, a core that in its uncultivated form is, however, often characterized as a wellspring for socially disruptive acts. *Laen ii yaen'* was also consistently differentiated from *leam* and *taafinay* through a metaphorically based characterization of its greater "depth" and "heaviness." Both depth and heaviness were descriptors utilized to emphasize the opacity of the contents of an individual's *laen ii yaen'* in comparison to the contents of his or her *leam* or *taafinay*.

One Yapese philosopher in his late fifties suggested that in some contexts *laen ii yaen'* reminded him of the English term "personality." As such, he said, it is held to be an attribute of persons. He went on to suggest that *laen ii yaen'* is acquired through socialization and that it becomes crystallized into a perduring form that helps to shape the way an individual "looks at things," as well as their "reactions to events." He added that it is further tied to what a person values or holds to be important. In contrast to *taafinay* and *leam,* which he characterized as both, to varying degrees, context dependant and in perpetual flux, *laen ii yaen'* is instead more akin to a disposition. It signifies a way of being that has perduring effects on an individual's orientation to self, others, and the world. Accordingly, he pointed out that people were often morally positioned as being *fal laen ii yaen'* ("good innermost feelings, thoughts, desires, etc.") or *kireeb laen ii yaen'* ("bad innermost feelings, thoughts, desires, etc.").

What is said to be in another's *laen ii yaen'* is considered information that only that individual can ever truly know. According to the individuals I spoke to about the term, the private nature of *laen ii yaen'* seems to be partially due to the unformulated nature of the experiences that are held to comprise its contents. This is also associated with the fact that, whether formulated or not, these contents are often actively concealed from others and kept secret (cf. Hollan and Throop 2008; Robbins and Rumsey 2008). As such, one older woman explained that *Ma miiith ea laen ii yaen'* ("Innermost subjective experience hides"). When I asked this same woman if it was true that even despite its "hiding" an individual would be able to know the contents of his or her own *laen ii yaen',* she agreed that this was most often the case. She added, however, that an individual would seldom, if ever, express this knowledge to others.

In some ways, then, these descriptions of *laen ii yaen'* resonate with Mageo's characterization of the Samoan concept of *loto* as "the depth of the person . . . always a comprehensive term for personal thoughts, feelings, and volitions" (1998, 10). While it is possible (and laudable) for *laen ii yaen'* to be rarefied through socialization practices that emphasize the virtues of "self-governance," in many ways, much like *loto*, it may in its unrarified form also inspire "all manner of discomforting sentiments, from arrogance to envy to torrents of grief, which cannot be accounted for by social roles" (Mageo 1998, 10, 38–39).

Self-Governance, Self-Articulation, and Innermost Subjective Experience

The significance and dynamics of local understandings of *laen ii yaen'* was something that first became apparent to me in the context of three morally infused distinctions used to discriminate between different types of individuals: *baaq laen ii yaen'*, *ba laen ii yaen'*, and *daariy ea laen ii yaen'*. These three phrases are founded upon grammatically encoded framings of the state or quality, possession, or presence of an individual's *laen ii yaen'*. Due to the many dialectical variants of Yapese, the understudied state of Yapese grammar, and the limitations of my own expertise in formal linguistic analysis, I want to emphasize that even though the connections I am suggesting between Yapese grammar, models of virtuous comportment, and local understandings of subjective experience appear to have some support in Jensen's previous linguistic work and do largely coincide with local speakers' everyday insights into their own language's grammar, they should be taken to be provisional observations at best, and certainly not definitive statements (cf. Silverstein 1981).

The first of these phrases is *baaq laen ii yaen'* (in some dialects, *baey laen ii yaen'*). Here, *laen ii yaen'* is modified by the intransitive stative verb *baaq*, which denotes existence, presence, and may also imply (indefinite) location and possession. Indeed, Jensen, who characterizes *baaq/baey* as an "existential verb" (1977b, 222), translates *baaq* as "there is; there exists; to be or exist in a place; to be located; to have." When using the morpheme *baaq* an individual is thus making a statement of fact about the existence of a person or thing in a particular space or time. It serves to highlight the presence of a phenomenon that exists in the world. Significantly, it does not, at least according to my own observations and to the people I spoke to about the distinction, refer to that phenomenon's qualities or states of being. As modified by *baaq,* this phrase might thus be literally translated as "there are his or her innermost feelings, thoughts, and desires." As I will explore in more detail, however, when used as a person descriptor, the phrase *baaq laen ii yaen'* seems to foreground the possessive connotations of the verb *baaq.* Accordingly, I think that a more accurate translation of this phrase might be "he or she *possesses* his or her innermost feelings, thoughts, and desires."

A second key phrase that is imbued with moral connotations and which utilizes *laen ii yaen'* as a basis for describing an individual's character is *ba laen ii yaen,* or, as it is contracted in the context of everyday speech, *blaen ii yaen'.* In contrast to the stative transitive verb *baaq,* Jensen designates *ba* as a stative tense-aspect marker (Jensen claims that the morpheme *ba* may also be employed in a very different manner as an indefinite article, e.g., *ba kaaroo*—"a car.") As such, *ba* is used in conjunction with nouns and adjectives in a similar way as the English verb "to be." In contrast to *baaq,* which directs a listener or speaker's attention to the simple existence of an object, entity, or person, *ba* denotes the qualities inherent in that object's, entity's, or person's state of being. For instance, to say *Keith ba chignag* ("Keith is drunk"), *Jason ba passig* ("Jason is excited"), or *Jimmy ba ufanthin* ("Jimmy is prideful") is to designate an individual as partaking in a particular state or quality of being.

As a number of my friends and teachers noted when explaining the difference between *baaq* and *ba,* to say *baaq sensey* is to simply state the existence of a teacher in some place or time (e.g., "there exists a teacher"), while to say *cha'nem ba sensey* is to emphasize that a person *is* a teacher (e.g., "that person embodies all of the qualities that are entailed in being a teacher"). The phrase *ba laen ii yaen'* can thus be literally translated as "he or she *is* his or her innermost feelings, thoughts, and desires."

The third phrase, *daariy ea laen ii yaen',* is based on modifying *laen ii yaen'* with the noun-phrase connector *ea* and the intransitive verb *daariy,* which the dictionary defines as denoting inexistence: "there is none; there is nothing." The intransitive verb *daariy* is most often heard in response to the phase *kam magaer* ("you are exhausted from work" or "thank you"). In this context, *daariy* is used to indicate that the work that an individual is being thanked for is in fact not difficult; it does not warrant such notice and does not entail an experience of *magaer*. Literally, the phrase *daariy ea laen ii yaen'* can be translated as "he or she *has no* innermost feelings, thoughts, and desires."

Each of these phrases has very different moral connotations attached to them. First, almost every person I spoke to about the phrase *baaq laen ii yaen'* ("he or she possesses his or her innermost feelings, thoughts, and desires") portrayed it as imbued with an extremely positive valence. As one individual asserted, the phrase *chaqneey baaq laen ii yaen'* describes a person who is patient *(guumaen')*. Even when upset over the actions of another, he or she is able to keep feelings of anger, hurt, sadness, suffering, or pain hidden. A person who is designated *baaq laen ii yaen'* is thus said to be an individual who, even when insulted, never reacts (at least immediately) in kind. Instead, the person is able to keep feelings, thoughts, and opinions to him or herself.

Many others pointed out that a person who is *baaq laen ii yaen'* is also an individual who is able to plan well, organize work projects, and navigate the complexities of village and municipal political life. It describes someone who tends to think ahead, who deliberates carefully prior to acting, and who understands that it is necessary to start preparing for future situations in the present. It refers to a person who knows what he or she wants and who knows what is important. Furthermore, this sort of person recognizes that any acts that are undertaken in the present will necessarily have relevance for the definition and negotiation of future relationships.

He or she is further held to be the sort of person who is motivated to work hard, to endure in the face of suffering, and to defer his or her own personal wants, desires, and inclinations in the service of broader family or community goals. As one elder asserted, a person who is *baaq laen ii yaen'* is also necessarily invested with *athamagil*. Many people pointed out that these individuals are always contributing to community work projects without complaint. They are especially skilled at preparing for and organizing collective activities.

It is interesting that some of the only negative characterizations I heard about persons who were referred to as *baaq laen ii yaen'* came from younger individuals (men and women in their twenties or thirties). These individuals asserted that while all of the above assertions were certainly true, it is not always a good thing to not know what another individual is thinking or feeling. As one man in his early thirties explained to me, the negative side of *baaq laen ii yaen'* is that an individual is holding something back from you. That is, they have "secret thoughts." Inasmuch as the term is used to indicate that a person is in control of his or her mind, however, it is conceived to be a very positive and highly valued attribute of persons. Again, as the intransitive verb *baaq* suggests in marking the simple existence and possession of an individual's *laen ii yaen'*, there seems to be an epistemic distancing implied in this phrase between an individuals actions and his or her innermost subjective experiences.

In contrast to *baaq laen ii yaen'*, *ba laen ii yaen'* is held to describe a person who is partial and biased, a person who expresses favoritism and prejudice. Indeed, a number of individuals translated the term as "prejudice," while emphasizing that a person who is *blaen ii yaen'* will only ever help those people that he or she likes. Such a person will also do everything in his or her power to insult, hurt, or refuse to help those individuals whom they dislike. This phrase describes an individual whose acts are understood to be direct reflections of his or her innermost feelings, desires, wants, and wishes. For an individual who is *blaen ii yaen'* there is no attention paid to the consequences of action, no concern for reflecting on how taking sides and showing favoritism might later affect his or her relationships to others. Nor is there any evidence that the individual in question is able to defer personal gratification for the benefit of others in the family or community. As the stative tense-aspect marker *ba* implies, the individual is seen to be coterminous with his or her desires, wants, opinions, thoughts, and feelings. There is thus no difference between the self and those qualities of being inherent in that self's *laen ii yaen'*. The person *is* his or her *laen ii yaen'*.

It is important to note here that an individual who is *blaen ii yaen'* is characterized as no less motivated than an individual who is *baaq laen ii yaen'*. That said, there is a very significant difference in how people construed the ways in which these two types of individuals tended to translate their motivation into social action. A person who is *blaen ii yaen'* is said to be motivated only to act, work, or invest effort in ways that accord directly with personal inclinations, desires, wants, needs, and feelings. If the individual thinks that the project in question will benefit him or her directly, or will end up benefiting people he or she likes, then that person will invest all of his or her energy into it. Similarly, if a person believes that a certain course of action will hurt, hinder, or disrupt the plans of individuals that he or she dislikes, that person will happily channel all of his or her effort and energy into such actions.

A person who is *baaq laen ii yaen'*, however, is instead characterized as adept at canalizing desires, wants, needs, and feelings into projects, endeavors, and activities that do not merely reflect personal biases. Such an individual will seek out instead courses of action that provide, as much as possible, a fit between personal desires and those of his or her family or community. Through deliberation, careful reflection, and discussion with others *(puruuy)*, an individual who is *baaq laen ii yaen'* is vigilant and has mastery over his or her inner states, motives, and desires. He or she is able to intentionally control forms of expressivity such that they do not merely reflect personal feelings, thoughts, opinions, and needs.

Seemingly positioned between these two morally valenced extremes is the designation of *daariy ea laen ii yaen'*. *Baaq laen ii yaen'* and *blaen ii yaen'* alternatively highlight individuals' differing abilities to enact self-governance over what is ideally represented as occluded aspects of their subjective experience. *Daariy ea laen ii yaen'* emphasizes, by comparison, that an individual is, at least metaphorically, without an inner life of desire, wants, needs, feeling, and opinions. Perhaps more accurately, an individual who is said to be *daariy ea laen ii yaen'* is an individual whose innermost feelings, desires, and needs, are so muted that they do not play much if any role in directing his or her actions. As such, individuals who are deemed to be *daariy ea laen ii yaen'* are regarded as occupying a morally ambivalent space.

On the one hand, such individuals are characterized in a positive light inasmuch as they are held to be individuals who are largely compliant with community goals. Perhaps most positively, they are said to be individuals who do not hold grudges, who do not get upset if they are "scolded," and who never seek to intentionally hurt others. These are also qualities that are at times attributed to individuals who are *baaq laen ii yaen'*. A key difference is found in the fact that the latter are individuals who experience tensions arising from having to conform to social expectations, and yet have the composure, self-control, and forethought to regulate their expressive responses in light of broader social dictates. Individuals who are *daariy ea laen ii yaen'*, in contrast, are not thought to have needed to fully develop such abilities for self-governance since their muted desires, strivings, wants, and needs leave them largely free from tension between their inner life and external expectations and constraints. That said, I should also note that some individuals I spoke to about this designation claimed that while the phrase certainly implies that the individual in question does not experience such inner conflicts, in reality this is never truly the case. Instead, the phrase is perhaps more accurately used to describe a person who always avoids conflict and opposition. This does not mean that the person does not get angry when faced with insults or challenges. It signifies instead that he or she does not express his or her anger directly and further tries to avoid situations where he or she will have to express that anger.

On the other hand, *daariy ea laen ii yaen'* is also infused with a negative moral valence with respect to the fact that individuals who are so designated are perceived to be largely without motivation. The very qualities that lead them to be portrayed in a positive light—their lack of *laen ii yaen'*—is what also leaves them without access to the well-spring of feelings, desires, wants, opinions, needs, and thoughts that are understood to serve as the motivational basis for initiating action. Without such motivation, these individuals are said to be persons who often shirk their community duties if not closely supervised. They do not put in adequate care and effort while working. They do not have the endurance, perseverance, and striving in the face of suffering, hardship, and adversity that is so highly valued in the concept of *athamagil*. In its negative sense, *daariy ea laen ii yaen'* thus marks individuals as disinclined to work, to strive, to expend effort for the betterment of themselves, their family, or their community.

Given everything we have already seen with regard to the high moral value entailed in the embodied concepts of work *(maruweel)*, work-induced exhaustion and fatigue *(magaer)*, and effortful endurance, striving, and perseverance *(athamagil)*, there is indeed much moral ambivalence directed toward the designation of *daariy ea laen ii yaen'*. Finally, this same designation also implies that the person in question can be easily manipulated. Such vulnerabilities to manipulation stem from the fact that the individual's desires, needs, wants, thoughts, feelings, and opinions do not lead him or her to attempt to *strategically* align personal inclinations with social requests and expectations.

In light of these three designations, I believe that we see evidence for a cultural logic in which individual and social goals are variously cast in moral terms. In one case *(daariy ea laen ii yaen')*, there are social actors who are held to be largely unmotivated but not necessarily "bad." These individuals are held to be pliable to social dictates. They are, however, unable to live up to ethical standards associated with the ability to work, endure, and expend effort in the face of suffering. In a second case *(blaen ii yaen')*, there are individuals who are motivated to pursue courses of action based solely upon their own personal agendas. These are often realized at the expense of others' well-being.

The third *(baaq laen ii yaen')* and ideal case appears to be the cultivation of a rarified sensibility in which there is evidence for motivation that is both individual and social at the same time. Here, the inner recesses of individual subjectivity are portrayed as distilled through thoughtful reflection, collective discussion, and patience. Each of these qualities allow the individual to work to determine the best possible course of socially appropriate action given an individual's own personal goals, aspirations, and inclinations.

On Socializing Self-Governance

The cultural emphasis on cultivating mental activity that is ordered, attentive, reflective, and focused is further reflected in the significance attributed to thoughtful, deliberate action, including basic actions that range from speaking and walking to working. Abilities to defer gratification, to think through a course of action prior to enacting it, and to confer and deliberate with others about the merits of possible activities without transparently giving away one's own perspectives, opinions, ambitions, and thoughts, are all rooted in socialization practices and everyday routines that redundantly channel an individual's attention to the significance of thinking before acting (c.f. Schieffelin 1990, 1998).

How do individuals learn to erect a barrier between personal inclinations and actual forms of expression? As George Stocking notes in detailing Franz Boas's insights into the basic organization of mental functions in cultural context, it is a truism that throughout history "all human groups subjected their impulses to the inhibition of some type of customary control and exercised choice among perceptions or actions in terms of some sort of aesthetic or ethical standards" (1968, 220). In Yap, these aesthetic and ethical standards are rooted in abilities to exert inhibition and control in the forms of self-vigilance and self-governance *(kadaen')*. While it is well beyond the scope of this book to provide anything approximating an adequate account of those socialization practices enacted from childhood through adulthood contributing to the cultivation of reflective self-mastery over the expression of one's somatic and psychical states, it is possible to provide some illustrative examples.

During my time living in Yap it was very common to hear parents (as well as other caretakers) telling their children to sit down *(mu paer nga buut),* stop moving *(dammu miithmith),* and stop talking *(dammu noonnoon).* From a very young age—as early as three or four—children were apt to be scolded if they were seen to be expending energies needlessly without an explicit socially sanctioned goal in mind. There were countless times, for instance, that I noted children about to walk off toward the village center (usually to escape their parent's surveying gaze in order to go play) only to be asked: *Ngam man ngan?* ("Where are you going?"). If the children did not respond that they were off to perform a specific task, such as going to help feed the pig, going to deliver a message, or going to the beach (a euphemism for going to the restroom), they would be told to come back to the house. In fact, even if they did have a specific goal in mind, children would often be scolded for not announcing their intended course of action prior to taking their leave.

Ideally, a child is to stand, move, and talk only in the service of following orders from older and higher-status caretakers (cf. Schieffelin 1990; Ochs and Schieffelin 1984). I repeatedly observed parents telling their children to stop performing acts that were being undertaken in order to satisfy their own interests, inclinations, and desires (i.e., watching television or preparing something for themselves to eat) in order to perform a required service that would benefit someone other than themselves. For instance, there were often times when a caretaker, seated on the front veranda of his or her house, within easy reach of an object, would call a child away from whatever he or she happened to be doing in order to come fetch the object in question. A ringing phone, even if positioned immediately beside a caretaker, was a common example.[9] Indeed, one case I observed entailed a child over twenty feet away being called over just to hand a ringing telephone to her paternal uncle, who was seated right next to it (albeit just out of arm's reach).

As one woman I interviewed noted, children are further taught from a very early age not to express their feelings and thoughts to just anybody. Children are repeatedly told that there is a specific time, place, and person with whom to share emotions and thoughts. It is generally acknowledged, however, that children are not able to control what they say, and because of this parents and older siblings are often careful not to talk about things of importance around younger children for fear that they might repeat it. When children do speak their minds, or repeat a potentially significant piece of household information, they are scolded and told, *K'aed ea n'um* ("Bite your mind")!

As was suggested in the previous chapter, another area in which children are trained to defer their own needs, feelings, and desires to the orders and requests of higher-status caretakers is with regard to food consumption. A good example is found in the following excerpt from my field notes:

Today, while a few of us were talking on the veranda one of the children [a boy, age four] got up to get himself a banana. His maternal uncle noticed this and just as the child was going to peel his banana, his uncle told him to stop. He then instructed the child to fetch a basket for the bananas and to bring them over to where I was sitting in order to offer one to me. The child hesitated, looked at me, looked at his uncle, and then, apparently not very pleased with the situation, slowly walked to fetch the basket to offer me a banana. I thanked him and took one. The child then quickly returned to the place he was sitting. He sat and put the basket down. Just as he was about to pick up his banana a second time, his uncle told him to stop and to bring the basket back over to offer a banana to one of the village elders who had stopped by to talk. Again, the child walked across the veranda and offered the food. This same pattern was repeated two more times, the last time the uncle asking that the basket be brought to him, before he finally let his nephew sit down to eat.

At the time, I remember noting both the child's apparent frustration in being ordered to put off his intended consumptive act and his uncle's persistence (and muted amusement) in requiring the child to defer his desire to satisfy his cravings. Again, there is evidence here for concerted attempts to instill in children the ability to delay gratification while engaging in action that is mediated by expending effort in the service of others of higher status.

A central concept associated with socialization practices tied to food consumption is that of *taamaen*. Perhaps metaphorically associated with the dance that bears its same name (see chapter 3), *taamaen* refers to acts of asking or begging for food from an individual who is not recognized as part of the same estate *(tabinaew)* or clan *(ganong)*. Numerous individuals observed that requests that can be characterized as *taamaen* are regarded in a very negative light. This is evidenced in the fact that children from a very early age are taught that they should never ask for, or accept, food from individuals with whom they are not related. Children should refrain from accepting food from nonrelatives even if they are hungry and strongly desire what is being offered to them.

As case in point, when I first moved into my family's house I would often try to offer food that I had purchased in town to my nephews and nieces. For the first three or four months, the children would almost always immediately refuse my offers, often turning to look at their parents (my adopted brothers and sisters) when they did so. Sometimes I would ask two or three times before, with a glint of pride in light of their children's consistent refusals, parents would tell the children that I was now part of the *tabinaew* and that it was okay for them to accept the food I was offering. Their parents reassured them that were not being *taamaen*. The more comfortable the children became with me, the more comfortable they were accepting food from me, especially when there were no adults around to serve as witnesses. That said, my Yapese parents remained very concerned about their grandchildren eating "my" food, particularly in those few instances where they did not first ask my permission. Moreover, the children would often chastise each other with calls of *taamaen* if ever they noticed one of their brothers, sisters, or cousins even doing so much as watching me while I ate or while I prepared my food.

As a socialization practice, accusations of *taamaen* served to help children develop abilities to control and master bodily desires and needs, while further effectively canalizing associations between children's experiences of satiation and hunger with specific individuals within their estate and clan (cf. Schieffelin 1990, 64–70, 177–78). Indeed, in learning to avoid being referred to as *taamaen* a child is faced with an early instance of endurance *(athamagil)* in having to persevere in spite of his or her own bodily urges, desires, and wants. In the processes of deferring gratification, waiting for the appropriate time, place, and person to request food from, sensations of hunger and satiation are configured in light of social values, values that help to orient the child to appropriate social ties and to *yalean*. The designation of *taamaen* thus plays a role in socializing abilities to defer personal desires, wants, and needs in light of social expectations.

The opposite of *taamaen* is the designation of *feekyath* or *feekyathin*. This phrase is used to describe a person who does not give respectful attention to what someone is telling them or refuses to accept something that is offered to them. To refer to an individual as *feekyath* is also considered a very negative thing. In the context of the refusal, the person who has offered something (e.g., food, advice, help, or what have you) is made to feel rejected *(duur)*. This rejection is said to stem from the fact that the potential giver does not feel appreciated for what he or she has done on behalf of another. Through such a refusal an individual is in effect refusing to participate in the relationship. He or she is failing to recognize the effort that was exerted *(magaer)* in preparing the offering, advice, or gift. By not accepting an offering, an individual fails to acknowledge the suffering that was endured by the giver.

The differences between *feekyath* and *taamaen* are significantly articulated around an individual's actions in relation to both established and not (or yet to be) established relationships. The act of inappropriately asking for food can be understood as an attempt to force a relationship where there is not one. The failure to accept food in appropriate contexts can be understood as ignoring or attempting to sever an already established relationship. Even though the ideal for dealing with requests or offers of food resides somewhere between the poles of *feekyath* and *taamaen,* figuring out the appropriate balance in any given interaction is often extremely difficult. As one of my teacher's explained, Yapese tend to error on the side of *feekyath*—saying that they are fine, not hungry, not in need of things from others.

Another example of the socialization of self-governance is found in the context of the value of quietude. Traditionally, there were very strict regulations on making any kind of disruption or noise within the confines of the village. Designated spaces far from the village center were put aside for more uninhibited forms of play *(faafáel).* This was to ensure that the noise emanating from such activities did not disturb those working in the village. As one elder explained to me, while there was consistent attention to avoiding unnecessary noise within the village, these restrictions became increasingly strict after dark. For instance, in times past individuals were not to prepare chestnuts or coconuts after sunset since cracking open their casings is loud work. If an individual wanted to eat these food items after dark, he or she would have to be sure to think of this during the day and prepare the foods accordingly for later consumption.

Many of the older individuals I spoke to recalled their elders telling them that if they made any loud noises within the confines of the village they would surprise and startle the land or the ancestors *(ram gin naag ea buut, fa thagiith).* This was considered a rather inauspicious act given that surprising the ancestors always had the possibility of bringing about misfortune—*aaf machaan.*[10] The term *aaf machaan* is used to describe the fate of individuals who are being punished as a result of a perceived transgression. I was taught that the meaning of the term *aaf machaan* is rooted in those instances when an individual's actions result in rousing negative feelings in others (e.g., *gin* "surprise," *rus* "fear," *damuumuw* "anger"), whether they be human beings, ghosts *(kaan)*, ancestral spirits *(thagiith)*, or even the land *(buut)*. If an individual is making a lot of noise, or doing something that surprises, scares, or angers other people, it is said that the emotions collectively evoked by such acts will likely result in the perpetrator of such transgressions becoming injured, sick, or harmed in some way. Accordingly, it was commonly held that caretakers should never let their children cry in the village—*Dam yoer ea bitiir u laen binaew*. Again, it was common for people to recall their elders exclaiming in such instances, "Children should not cry because something bad will happen" *(Dam yoer ea bitiir, ya ba ang)*.

While concerns about respectful quietude have somewhat lessened in contemporary Yapese society, such an ideal is still highly valued and is in fact currently reflected in Yap state law. As Cyprian Manmaw, Yap State's attorney general, once explained to me, one of the most striking examples of the impact of "traditional values" on the formation of Yap's current penal code is tied to the charge of "disturbing the peace." In the rest of the Federated States of Micronesia (FSM) this charge is only considered to be a misdemeanor. In Yap, however, elders lobbied the legislature to ensure that "disturbing the peace" would be considered a felony carrying a sentence of up to two years in jail!

To avoid disturbing the smooth flow of daily interactions, children, like all individuals, are further required to communicate to others what their intended actions will be prior to setting out to partake in a particular course of action. For instance, in Yap, like in a number of other Pacific societies (see Duranti 1997a; Firth 1972), prevalent communicative forms for greetings and partings include an adjacency pair part of "Where are you going?" *(Ngeam maen ngaan?)* or "Where are you coming from?" *(Keam muub u uw?)*. This is followed by a response that indicates an interlocutor's planned destination or previous whereabouts. In reference to the Samoan "Where are you going?" greeting, Duranti (1997a, 84) makes it clear that "to ask 'Where are you going?' is a request for an account, which may include the reasons for being away from one's home, on someone else's territory, or on a potentially dangerous path. To answer such a greeting may imply that one commits oneself not only to the truthfulness of one's assertion but also to the appropriateness of one's actions. It is not by accident, then, that in some cases speakers might try to be as evasive as possible." Much like Samoa, Yapese individuals are very careful to provide only the bare minimum amount of information possible when confronted with such greetings or partings.

Duranti is quite correct, I believe, in critiquing speech-act theorists like Austin (1962) and Searle (1969) for arguing that these types of greetings are simply a means for the "expression of a psychological state." I would add, however, that the psychological repercussions of having to think of an appropriate response to requests for information about one's past and future courses of action, especially in light of the possible moral implications arising from blatantly deceptive expressions of one's intentions, are arguably tied to a heightening of attention to the merits of engaging in reflection prior to setting off to participate in a particular activity. From a very early age, children are thus conditioned to reflect upon not only an action and its consequences, but further on how others might evaluate the merits of pursuing it. Accordingly, children (and adults) learn ways in which to selectively disclose their intentions for action in order to avoid the moral disapprobation that would most certainly arise if they were discovered to be acting in ways that did not accord with their previously expressed plans.

As Duranti further suggests, these forms of greetings and partings "force participants to deal with a wide range of issues including an individual's or group's right to have access to information about a person's whereabouts, culture-specific expectations about the ethics of venturing into public space, the force of questioning as a form of social control and hence the possibility of withholding information as a form of resistance to public scrutiny and moral judgment" (1997a, 84).

Questions of social control, of concealment in the face of such control, and of rights to accessing certain public (and private) spaces are further tied, in the Yapese case, to the belief that if an individual does not have a definite purpose for engaging in an activity—especially an activity that requires taking leave from the surveying gaze of the other interlocutors who they are engaged with—that they are most likely attempting to conceal nefarious plans (e.g., intentions to steal food or medicine from another person or *tabinaew* or to use harmful magic to injure another or damage his or her gardens, possessions, and so on).

In addition to "Where are you coming from?" and "Where are you going?" greetings and partings may also include the use of the first adjacency pair part *kam magaer* ("you are exhausted, tired, or fatigued from expending effort on behalf of another") and a second pair part, *daariy* ("there was no such effort expended"). Alternatively, an individual may use the adjacency reduplicative paring of *moegeathiin* ("say something").[11] In the former case, the addressee is recognized for having engaged in some prior intentional work-based activity, a designation that highlights the valuation of undertaking morally valenced purposive action. In the latter case, the addressee is faced with a request to speak, which implies again that he or she should provide an account of past activities or an explanation for why he or she has transitioned from one particular location to another.

Greetings and partings are not the only varieties of social interaction that require an explicit expression of one's intentions for carrying out a particular course of action, however. Anytime an individual sets out to make an abrupt or unexpected movement (e.g., standing up to go retrieve something from the kitchen) it is both customary and expected that they first alert others of their impending actions. Such expectations are especially crucial when a person is about to undertake an activity that will bring his or her body into close proximity to his or her interlocutor. For instance, in our family's household I got into the habit of sitting out on our veranda with my back resting against the freezer. Whenever one of my Yapese sisters or mother wished to access the freezer, they would, prior to standing up and walking over toward me, explain that they were about to get up to retrieve some food in the freezer to prepare for dinner. In so doing, they would often specify, in order, the sequence of specific acts that they would undertake to accomplish their particular project (i.e., "Excuse me, I am going to stand up, come over, and reach over you to open the freezer to get some chicken so that I can go to the kitchen to prepare dinner"). Children were often scolded for failing to alert others of their intended actions and especially for failing to say *siroew* ("excuse me," "pardon me") prior to standing or walking past another.

Notifying others of one's actions is further evidenced in subtler ways in the context of norms associated with approaching or passing by another household. In such cases individuals often cough or clear their throats as they approach a residence. This is usually done well before the individual comes into the field of vision of those who might be residing at the household. At night, it was also customary for individuals to carry a light so that others would be able to see them approaching from a distance. Walking in a village at night without a light is a very serious offense, an offense that could result in charges of thievery or the practice of bad magic *(motookan)*. Such accusations could result in severe punishments (sometimes violent) inflicted on the suspected perpetrator.

One interesting embodied consequence of the attention paid to the importance of notifying others of an intended action is that many Yapese individuals have cultivated a highly attuned startle reflex. It may at first seem paradoxical that individuals would have heightened startle reflexes (a seemingly archetypal instance of unreflective, thoughtless action) in the midst of such cultural elaboration of deliberately planned activity. Yet, the very existence of such a deeply visceral response is, as I have come to see it, a somatic reflection of individuals habitually being forewarned of others' actions. As such it represents the body's registering of cultural virtues associated with the virtue of "self-governance."

Most actions are clearly anticipated through announcing to others one's plans for action. This may be accomplished through individuals telling others about where they are going, where they have come from, coughing when they are approaching a household, or carrying a light when they are walking in the dark. By not providing others with such warnings an individual is thus all the more likely to surprise someone with an unannounced or unexpected act. Indeed, as a published guide for teachers in Yap cautions, many Yapese individuals "are easily startled. Males in particular react in extreme ways to a sudden and unexpected touch or loud noise. The Yapese 'startle reflex' implicates alertness, bravery, and protection from injury! Laying a hand gently on a male's shoulder or back is okay, but make sure that the person knows in advance what to expect. The action should never involve an element of surprise" (Kadnanged et al. 1993, 7).

Many individuals exploited this heightened sensitivity to startle in the service of playing jokes on others. Particularly in festive public gatherings like dances, it was not uncommon to see older men taking great pleasure in evoking a startle response in one of their peers. While this sensitivity to sudden movement, touch, or sound could be exploited for purposes of amusement, there was always a risk entailed in evoking such a response. A close friend of mine, recalling his first months attending an American college, told how his roommate (who thought it rather amusing that his new friend was so easily startled) once snuck up behind him. When the young man grabbed my friend's shoulders in an attempt to surprise him, he responded by unintentionally punching his roommate in the face. Needless to say, my friend's peers were careful not to startle him again.

As the quote from the guide for teachers states (see Kadnanged et al., 1993), a highly attuned startle reflex is particularly significant for men. Most individuals I spoke to explained that such a response was important to ensure that men remained alert to the ever-present possibility of an attack in the context of warfare between villages. It was indeed common to hear caretakers chastise boys and adolescents who did not respond with such a startle reflex in the face of sudden, unexpected movement or noise. Caretakers would often tease boys who did not act with such a response by calling them old ladies.

Having a heightened startle reflex also has concrete benefits when confronting the realities of living in an environment where individuals are faced with having to react quickly in response to the slightest sounds, which might indicate, among other things, an impending attack on one's village or a coconut falling to the ground. The latter is indeed a serious and dangerous event, which I was not fully aware of until I was nearly hit directly on the head by a coconut that had fallen from a height of over twenty-five feet!

Decision Making and Speaking-For Others

Yet another way that the virtue of reflective self-governance is cultivated is in the context of prevalent acts of "speaking-for" others. From an early age, children are asked to take messages from older higher-status caretakers to other interlocutors (cf. Schieffelin 1990; Ochs and Schieffelin 1984). Sometimes this consists of asking a child to take a message from a caretaker to someone who is also a part of the same household. Other times, the messages are sent from one household to another. With older children, such requests can also be extended to interlocutors living in nearby villages.

In every case it is imperative that the child transfer the message in its exact form from the speaker to the intended addressee. This focus upon an exact replication of the message is consonant with the high value that is placed upon memory in Yapese culture more generally. There were quite a number of times that I failed to transmit a message in its exact form and was corrected, much to my Yapese parents bemusement, by one of the younger children who had also heard the original message. To this extent, modes of language socialization in Yap seem to run parallel to observations made by Ochs and Schieffelin (1984) with respect to the prevalence of Samoan and Kaluli children being expected to report household news and information to older family members. As Ochs and Schieffelin maintain, "Caretakers use such exchanges to teach children a wide range of skills and knowledge.

In fact, the task of repeating what the caregiver has said is *itself* an object of knowledge, preparing the child for his or her eventual role as messenger. Children at the age of three are expected to deliver *verbatim* messages on behalf of more mature members of the family" (1984, 297–98).

The role of the messenger (*feekthiin*—"take speech") is extended well beyond children's responsibilities for transferring messages within and between households, however. In Yap, sending messages was traditionally a normative practice of communication in the context of intercaste, intra- and intervillage political affairs. The institutionalization of the role of messenger is evident in the fact that specific house foundations are imbued with the "voice" or authority *(luungun)* of *feekthiin*. As such, these households are responsible for sending messages from a higher-ranked chiefly foundation to other such foundations either within or beyond the boundaries of the village.

Recalling the discussion in the previous chapter, it seems that generally speaking, breath *(faan)*, effort *(magaer)*, and voice *(lunguun)* were traditionally perceived to be capacities that should not be wasted in the context of meaningless action. If an individual is going to move, he or she should be working. If he or she is going to speak, such speech should be in the service of planning for what that individual and his or her community are going to do. Or he or she should be speaking at the request of another *(feekthiin)*. Otherwise, the individual is thought to be wasting his or her breath and energy; breath and energy that are themselves afforded by the work of his or her family, community, and ancestors.

As explored in the previous chapters, the concept of chief or *piiluung* further evidences this recurrent theme of the moral worth of cultivating a cleavage between forms of expressivity and sentiment. Indeed, practically every person with whom I spoke about the concept of *piiluung* tried to impress upon me the idea that the person himself is never a chief. It is the foundation and the land that is the chief. Authority and status are inscribed in the land and the person is merely its vehicle, its voice. He is ideally merely acting as a conduit for the power that is vested in the land, land that really represents his ancestors and those who came before him to work on the land and make it what it is today. Recall that even individuals who represent the voice of the highest-ranking foundations are thought to be ideally carrying the voice of the foundation and not thought to be communicating their own personal desires, inclinations, and perspectives.

A similar cultural logic is manifest in the context of community meetings. Community meetings are largely understood to be sites for the expression of decisions that have been made long before the community has gathered to discuss them. In speaking at a community meeting, one elder explained, an individual is ideally merely speaking-for others who, in consultation with individuals both within and outside of the community, have come to a particular decision regarding village affairs. For this reason, meetings are seldom sites for decision-making processes to be worked out. Instead, they are primarily opportunities for the community to come together in order to mend hurt feelings that may have arisen in the face of such predetermined decisions. During meetings only specific individuals associated with certain foundations are able to speak. Moreover, when individuals do speak they often rely upon conventionalized sayings that everyone largely agrees with. These sayings and statements are so clichéd that nobody would ever think of contesting what is being said. Accordingly, talk during meetings is often the talk of consensus making and agreement as opposed to decision making.

When there is evidence for potential conflict during a community meeting, however, the phrases that are most commonly used focus on the importance of taking time to think prior to speaking. Indeed, it is common to hear people say *Daabi gurguur* ("Don't rush"), *Saagël ngoom raam oloobuchiy ea puruuy* ("Slow down, you will make a mistake with the deliberation and discussion"), *Leam gow* ("Let's think together"), and *Biya llowaen' laen ii waay* ("There is wisdom in the basket"). This latter phrase refers to the fact that everyone's baskets contain the materials required to make a betel nut chew *(langad)*. The very process of preparing betel nut—selecting and then breaking open the nut, adding lime, and then rolling the nut and lime in a pepper leaf—takes time. This time allows an individual to take some distance from his or her feelings. In preparing their chew, individuals are afforded an opportunity to think about what they are going to say when the meeting gets back underway. Again, each of these agreed-upon tried-and-true sayings points to the importance of thinking before speaking or acting.

In the context of community meetings, individuals thus have to be very careful not to express themselves in ways that can be interpreted as going against a developing consensus. For example, a friend of mine suggested that occasionally during such meetings a person might say *Gu be leam naag ni mab fael ngoodaed* ("I am thinking that it would be good for us all"). As my friend pointed out, even the expression *Gu be leam naag* ("I am thinking"), however, frames what is being said as a form of opposition to the consensus that is being cultivated in the meeting. This is because the individual is understood to be voicing his or her personal point of view. The expression of such a personal viewpoint goes against the idea that members living in the community are one people: *Gad taab girdiiq*.

An expatriate working for the state government once expressed to me her great frustration with what seemed to be an endless series of meetings in which the focus was only on talking and deliberating with very little, if any, subsequent action (cf. Myers 1986). In the context of day-to-day life in the village, I too noticed that often even the most mundane projects with predictable outcomes would often first need to be subject to collective discussion *(puruuy)* prior to their enactment. This resulted in a common rhythm in daily life consisting of extended periods of deliberation followed by quick transitions from apparent inactivity to intense and prolonged action. Moments of quietude and inactivity resulted directly from the necessity of engaging in collective dialogue and deliberation over the merits of pursuing various projects. Again, this is a replication writ large of the emphasis upon deliberate action generally speaking.

Reflective Social Action and the Path as a Teacher

> People did not move freely between village sections and rarely went to other villages.
>
> Lingenfelter, 1979

Just as one never simply stands up, changes position, or makes quick movements without first alerting others to the intended course of action, traditionally an individual could not walk anywhere he or she pleased in Yapese villages. Aside from its stone money, Yap is perhaps most renowned for its complexly arrayed miles of stone paths that connect estates and villages to one another. Stone paths, like house foundations, have different statuses attributed to them. Some paths are *tabugul*, reserved only for men of the highest-eating classes. Others are publicly accessible, often leading from the peripheries to the center of the village. Still others are designated *taqay*, since they are used only by low caste for the carrying of corpses for burial and by menstruating women and adolescent girls.

FIGURE 5. Stone path. Photo by the author.

A friend of mine once suggested that Yap's stone paths were built to ensure that there was always a fair amount of certainty with regard to the route that an individual would take to get from one village to another, from one estate to the next. In addition, he maintained that unlike other places in the FSM where an individual's path might be uncertain, or might be altered through time, Yapese paths were unchanging. He claimed, for instance, that in other parts of Micronesia if a tree begins to grow in the middle of a footpath, people will often walk around it, letting the tree grow. It is for this reason, he noted, that paths in Pohnpei, Chuuk, and Kosrae are always changing through time as people alter the trajectories of their routes to accommodate their desires or the presence of obstacles. In contrast, Yapese individuals, he argued, will immediately remove any obstacle obstructing a path, and they take great care in tending to the path to make sure that it remains intact.

In many ways, the path *(kanaawoq)* was characterized as a material reflection of the valuation of reflective action. As one elder told me, "The path is a teacher." The very ways in which the rocks are placed on the path serve as a message from the *piiluung* and community to the people walking along it. The path's message is that travelers should always demonstrate respect *(liyoer)* when traveling in the village. Practically speaking, walking along a Yapese stone path is no simple matter. The rocks are very smooth, often covered with moss, and are, as a result, quite slippery. This is especially so during or after a rainfall. Without careful attention to where you are placing your feet, it is quite easy to fall. When walking on a path it is often necessary to look down to see where you are stepping. In the process, individuals are restricted by the design of the path itself to walk deliberately and slowly, with their heads down.

I witnessed numerous people slip while walking on the paths in our village. And I personally slipped or fell more times than I would like to admit. One elder pointed out to me that the use of very smooth rooks, as well as their linear placement, was an intentional design to ensure that individuals who are walking on the paths will keep their minds focused on the task at hand and the purpose of their travels. He suggested that if individuals did not want to slip or fall when walking on a path they had to be conscious of where they are going, and should think through each and every step. Even walking, perhaps the most readily habituated of our embodied daily activities, is construed in the context of navigating village paths to be a very conscious, deliberate act.

Individuals walking to a meeting should focus their attention on that meeting, the topics that they are going to discuss, and what they are going to say. The design of the path is understood to focus individual minds to the task at hand. When walking on a stone path with attention focused on their footing, individuals are also less likely to be distracted by other people's gardens, trees, taro patches, and possessions. As one person put it, building the paths in such a way ensures that *Daamu changar, mu saap ngaa buut* ("Don't you look around, you look to the ground"). By not looking at other people's things, individuals will be less likely to let their minds wander and to feel envy *(awaen)*. They will not *kireeb ea leam* ("have a bad mind.") According to this perspective, individuals are to think of their purposes for traveling, where they are going, and what they are going to do or say upon arrival. The path is conceived to be a teacher inasmuch as it is a recurrent reminder to individuals to be respectful, humble, and focused on the task at hand. The act of walking on a path is a meditation of sorts. It ensures that individuals' minds are clearly focused on what they are going to do. The path ensures that individuals are not distracted by things that are of no consequence to pursuing their particular goals and plans for action.

Mind over Body

As previously noted, the cultivation of self-mastery over the expression of one's internal states is significantly tied to the valuation of mental over somatic processes. This is especially the case when such processes are considered in the context of family- and community-based work projects. As one elder explained to me, traditionally such somatic states as hunger, thirst, and physical exhaustion were not accepted as valid excuses for not working and not contributing to one's family or community obligations. In the face of somatically mediated desires, needs, and wants an individual is told to strengthen his or her mind *(Raam geel naag ea laen ii n'um)* in order to strive, persevere, and endure *(athamagil)* in the face of such hardships. In particular, it is women who are often required to endure in the midst of suffering, effortful exertion, and hunger while expending their efforts on behalf of their husbands' estates.

Such an emphasis on the moral worth of endurance and the disciplining of the body is evident in the traditional use of women's belts. Belts were used in the context of women's work gathering food for their male relatives in high-status taro patches and gardens. The word for belt, *luuqod,* is made up of two morphemes: *luuq* meaning "tear" and *od* meaning "awake." One woman noted that the word *luuqod* conjures up images of a person who is crying and who is not able to sleep *(be yoer, daar ma mool)*. She then added that this association might stem from the fact that a person traditionally tied a *luuqod* when they are suffering and yet they are still trying to stay alert. They are striving to endure in the face of their hardship.

As I discussed in the last chapter, there was traditionally a highly elaborated system of ascetic restrictions tied to the production, collection, and consumption of foods. Whether it was in the context of fishing, gardening, or taro patching, both men and women were often required to follow strict ascetic-like dietary and consumptive abstentions prior to, and during, the undertaking of such activities. In the case of women who were working in high-status taro patches and gardens, gathering food for their high-status male relatives and husbands, such restrictions took the form of individuals being expected to abstain from eating until they had finished their cleaning, planting, and harvesting activities in these *tabugul* locales. Local ideas about food consumption and the embodiment of particular levels of purity may have played a part in such restrictions given that the foods ingested by women were cultivated in relatively low-status gardens and taro patches.

Practically, this would mean that older women (young women were not allowed to enter such areas on account of their being considered *taqay*) would wake up, prepare food for the household, and then leave for a day of backbreaking work in the gardens and taro patches. They were not allowed to eat during any of these activities. Eating had to wait until they returned to the household, sometime late in the evening. As a number of elders recalled, women who were undertaking such labor-intensive practices without access to food used belts made from hibiscus (*gaal'*) in order to help cope with their feelings of hunger. This use of hibiscus may be implicated in the fact that as an intransitive verb the morpheme *gaal'* also refers to the act of "pulling the stomach in."

One elder recalled that women tied these hibiscus belts twice around their stomachs when heading out to work in the gardens and taro patches. They would tighten their belts around their waists whenever they experienced strong feelings of hunger during their work. In fact, there were a number of different activities, events, and occurrences that mandated that individuals go without food and endure the suffering that arises with intense hunger. As previously mentioned, it was quite common to hear people exclaim in response to a person who complained of hunger during an ongoing work project that the stomach is where hunger lives (*Ma paer ea biliig u yal*).

The privileging of psychical over somatic experience in the service of self-governance is further found in the context of those various abstentions that individuals undertook in order to ensure a good outcome for a particular project, plan, or relationship. This was particularly true in the case of practicing local medicine. A medicine's potency is linked in local medical theory to the extent to which the person preparing the medicine follows the many rules and abstentions associated with the period of collection and preparation (*faalngiin ea falaay*). As one elder observed, "If you want the medicine to work you have to respect the medicine." To this end, different medicines have different restrictions associated with them. Most medicines, however, necessitate that both the healer and his or her patient follow str' restrictions on food, periods of fasting, and the avoidan contact. As one healer explained to me, "They both have to respect the medicine and share the burden of its preparation and consumption" (*L'agruw ea koel faalngiin ea falaay*).[12]

One particularly prevalent abstention tied to gathering and preparing medicines is called *daabi aaw ea paaqam* (literally, "do not drop your arm or hand"). This refers to the fact that some medicines should be gathered and prepared immediately upon waking up, before going to the restroom or eating. It is interesting to note here the emphasis placed once again upon disciplining the body. This is yet another instance of a social obligation being placed prior to a physical need. Yet another typical restriction associated with the effective collection and production of medicines is encompassed in the saying *daab mu galimlim*. The dictionary translates *galimlim* as land-based activities that are forbidden for those heading out to sea. In the case of preparing medicines, however, *daab mu galimlim* is tied to not eating, not drinking, and often not working—"not even to cut wood for a fire." Again, there seems to be an emphasis in the midst of these various restrictions in cultivating a form of concentration in which both the healer and the patient will focus all of their attention to the task at hand. Both of them are to concentrate on the medicine, collecting and making the medicine on the one hand, and taking the medicine on the other. Accordingly, anything that is understood to take an individual's concentration away from collecting, preparing, and following the proper prohibitions associated with a particular medicine is thought to take directly away from that medicine's efficacy.

Similar abstentions were tied to sexuality and were evidenced in a practice called *koel faalngiin ea bitiir*. This practice entailed the intentional deferral of sexual desire in service of ensuring the health and well-being of a newborn infant. Ideally, this would entail both parents abstaining from sexual activity for a period that begins roughly four months before the child is born and is carried on for as many as a number of years after the child's birth.[13] One elder explained to me that if this abstention was carried through, the child would be *fool* ("obedient"), *cheag* ("skilled"), *llowaen'* ("intelligent"), *daabi m'aar* ("will not be sick"), and *fal u fithik ea doow* ("good inside the body.")

Two women I spoke to about this practice claimed that in order to *koel faalngiin ea bitiir* that an individual would have to *ke m'ing ea n'ug*—a phrase that might literally be translated as "it broke, my mind." When asked about the meaning of this phrase, one teacher explained that it referred to the feeling of desiring to do something but willfully stopping oneself from following through on those desires: "You want to do it but you stop yourself, you change your mind and you do not do it." Another stated that *ke m'ing ea n'ug* brought to mind the image of a person who had decided to force him- or herself to go against his or her basic needs. She further pointed out that the feeling that was often associated with *ke m'ing ea n'ug* was a sense of extreme deprivation. Again, this is yet another example of a cultural valuing of a deliberate and strict channeling of attention to a specific task at hand.

One woman I spoke to about this practice exclaimed that today, however, "We are all like animals, there is one child held in the basket and another is [already] on the way." In contrast, traditionally there was a great deal of control exercised by the family of the husband and wife in regulating the birth of children. She explained that often the family would choose the number of children the couple could have, as well as the intervals between each child. Anecdotal though it may be, it is interesting to note that both this woman and my research assistant claimed that the women they knew in their mothers' generation (women who would have been bearing their children during the 1940s and 1950s) all had children that were spaced almost exactly four or five years apart from one another. Reproduction, like other modalities of bodily existence, was thus ordered through deliberate and reflective control over one's desires, wants, and needs.

CHAPTER 5

Privacy, Secrecy, and Agency

In the evasion itself... there is something disclosed.
Martin Heidegger, 1927

One's thoughts, one's feelings, one's very mind is private.
Only a fool reveals himself freely.
Bernadette Kadnanged, L. Gilnifrad, and J. Egan, 1993

Buulyäl said that when she asked her grandfather for the medicine, he
was *puwaen'* ("justifiably angry"), although she did not say why.
Instead of giving her the ingredients, he told her to go ask her aunt,
since she also knew some of the family's medicines. He warned Buulyäl,
however, that there was a possibility that her aunt would not give her
the *awochean ea falaay* (the main active ingredient for the medicine).
He told her that the medicine had five ingredients and that if she was
not given five, her aunt was not providing her with the true formula.
When Buulyäl left her grandfather she recalled being absolutely shocked
that there was a chance that her beloved auntie would lie to her. She
was all the more shocked, however, when later that day her aunt told
her only four ingredients for the medicine. At the time, Buulyäl remembers asking her aunt if she was sure that there were only four ingredients, to which she replied that she was not sure, but that if there was
another ingredient she had forgotten it. Buulyäl said that she could tell
that her aunt was lying. When she returned to tell her grandfather what
had transpired, he smiled, nodded, and said that she did not give her
the *awochean ea falaay*. He then told her the fifth ingredient.

In the last chapter I explored some key aspects of Yapese understand-ings of subjectivity, social action, and morality. In particular, I sought to emphasize a Yapese valuation of mental over somatic processes, which is rooted in the merits of engaging in thoughtful, deliberate, and reflective activity. Interwoven throughout this discussion was evidence for a pervasive dichotomy in Yapese cultural logic between thinking and acting. The practical entailments of this bifurcated rendering of thought and action are such that it is often high-status individuals (i.e., high caste, chiefs, elders, and men) who are held to devote most of their attention to thinking, deliberating, and discussing. In contrast, it is often low-status individuals (i.e., low caste, women, young men, and children) who are responsible for engaging in practical activity that is ideally carried out according to directions received from those of higher status, a pattern that has been noted widely throughout Pacific cultures (see Duranti 1994; Ochs 1988; Firth 1970, 1972; Morton 1996; Shore 1982).

In many ways, the idea that action undertaken with careful calcula-tion should be socially valued can be understood to resonate with the practicalities of living life on a small island where individuals are enmeshed in communities where almost everyone is a relative, neigh-bor, acquaintance, or friend. Generally speaking, in such small face-to-face communities it seems very likely that there would be recurring opportunities for an individual's attention to be drawn to the fact that every action necessarily results in consequences, both foreseen and unforeseen, which have concrete social effects for others in the com-munity (cf. Levy 1973).

In response to such tangible access to the trajectories of social effects emanating from an individual's ongoing quotidian activity, it seems reasonable that consultation with others in an individual's family and community concerning specific plans for action would garner some social value. In fact, in this social context it is difficult to imagine how spontaneous, unthinking (re)action could ever rule the day. Acting without attending to the results of one's actions could quite easily lead to hurt feelings and disrespectful behavior at the very least. It might also lead to punishment in the form of abandonment, injury, or death at the very worst. Accordingly, it is not surprising that there would be significant cultural purchase found for understandings of ethical modalities of being that are predicated upon the assumption that individuals should carefully think through the consequences of their anticipated actions.

It is important to highlight, however, that it is not simply the case that social actors could express their intended actions or projects without also placing themselves at some significant social risk. As noted in the previous chapter, in the context of his Samoan research Duranti (1997a) has perceptively observed that in expressing plans for specific courses of action in the case of greetings, individuals set them- selves up as accountable for the truth-value of their utterances and ensuing actions. They are also held responsible for the appropriateness of such activities as configured in moral terms. There are most defi- nitely numerous cultural, interpersonal, and personal possibilities for dealing with such imputations of accountability in differing societies. In Yap, one significant solution to this problem is found in the cul- tivation of privacy, secrecy, and concealment. Indeed, closely tied to the valuation of deliberate activity is a prevalent emphasis placed upon the significance of opacity and nonexpressivity in relation to an indi- vidual's emotions, feelings, opinions, thought-objects, intentions, and the like. Ideally, Yapese moral frameworks thus tend to emphasize a fundamental disconnect between individual expressivity and an indi- vidual's inner life. As such, an individual's inner states are held to have, in many contexts, an indirect, nontransparent connection to action and expression.

These two culturally patterned inter- and intrasubjective emphases, one focusing upon the merits of engaging in reflective action and the other based in a valuation of privacy, can be understood as mutually supporting. The process of evaluating the consequences of one's actions and thinking carefully before acting implies a temporal delay between thought and action. The temporal expanse arising in the context of the delay, however fleeting it may be, gives rise to an opportunity to monitor carefully what an individual chooses to express to others prior to expressing it. Likewise, it is the ability to gain control over the dis- closure of one's emotions and desires that forms the basis of enacting effective strategies of concealment. It is often concealment that makes thoughtful deliberate action itself possible. It is, in other words, an individual's ability to think before acting that affords, and is afforded by, those efforts, often motivated by secrecy, at developing self-mastery over the expression of personal emotions, opinions, and thoughts.

As noted in the previous chapter, there are recurrent and redundant means of canalizing individuals' attention to the significance of think- ing before acting. To act in Yap is thus idealized in terms of recognizing the consequences of one's actions, morally evaluating those consequences as carefully as possible, and then acting accordingly. In contrast, what is patently devalued in light of these local moral sensibilities are individuals who appear to be ruled by an unreflective adherence to personal desires, emotions, feelings, wishes, and wants.

Having broadly outlined some of the key assumptions underlying local understandings of subjectivity, social action, and morality, I wish to shift in this chapter to examine in greater detail the topics of privacy, secrecy, concealment, truth, and agency. I will begin by exploring how secrecy, concealment, privacy, and local orientations to truth are embedded in communicative practices that aim to foster ambiguity. Such communicatively engendered forms of ambiguity are implicated in the dynamics of social relations and the transmission of culturally valued forms of knowledge. This will help to shed some additional light upon the diffuse power structures in Yapese society in which different estates, clans, castes, and genders all have access to socially significant but differing spheres of knowledge.

Following this, I will talk about some of the pragmatic dimensions entailed in the expression of internal states, focusing specifically upon emotions. This discussion will provide a context within which to outline the duplex nature of social agency in Yap, which is predicated upon envisionings of social and personal aspects of "willing" that are at times competing, at times complementary. All of this will provide insight into those culturally salient affordances and constraints informing individuals' experiences and expressions of dysphoric states.

Knowledge, Personhood, and Privacy

In Yap, knowledge is understood to be largely a private possession. Knowledge is only shared with others when those others are deemed to have properly earned access to it through suffering, hard work, service, and care directed toward the possessor of the knowledge. Resulting from this highly personalized orientation to the possession of knowledge is the fact that all forms of knowledge are broadly distributed within communities, clans, and estates (cf. Linstrom 1990, 113–14). As Egan maintains, Yapese ethnoepistemology is rooted in a central cultural assumption that "knowledge had to be fragmented and kept secret to provide bases of power while at the same time curtailing its centralization" (1998, 75). This is evident, as Egan also notes, in the differential distribution of knowledge associated with specific estates.

This knowledge is held to give those estates access to a specific emplacement within the broader sociopolitical organization of the village or intervillage alliances.

The fragmenting of knowledge is not restricted to differences in the forms of knowledge associated with specific estates, however. It is also evident within the confines of given estates in which only certain individuals are chosen to receive particular forms of knowledge. For example, early on Wilhelm Müller noted the very personalized possession of knowledge in the context of traditional Yapese dances. As he explained,

The text and dance figures are regarded as the inviolable intellectual property of their author, who is the only one who can dispose of them and can therefore sell them. In this event, however, all rights pass into the exclusive possession of the purchaser, and the other himself is no longer entitled to have the dance performed. Of course, he, the only one who could provide information about all the details, gradually forgets his own work, while the buyer as a rule is content to memorize the sound of the words purely mechanically at the conclusion of the transaction. (1917, 441)

As Buulyäl's story attests, another good example of this personalized stance toward the possession of knowledge is found in the context of medicinal knowledge. While the most basic forms of medicinal knowledge are often widely shared within a family (e.g., the medicines used to stop bleeding from a small cut or scrape), more powerful medicines (e.g., used to treat wounds inflicted by a stingray) are always very carefully guarded and kept secret by their possessors. A possessor of such knowledge will only share it once he or she has been able to determine that a given individual has sufficiently demonstrated through care, respect, and service, his or her deservedness for acquiring such knowledge. As the story of the two brothers discussed in chapter 2 also makes clear, even siblings should never take for granted that they have received the same accurate or complete information regarding the most powerful and valued forms of knowledge possessed by the higher-ranking members of their estate or clan.

Knowledge of the proper ingredients and preparations for specific medicines is thus highly personalized knowledge acquired only through providing work, service, and care for an individual who possesses it. A person's abilities to approximate expectations concerning ethical modes of experiencing the world are therefore largely implicated in determinations of the strength and breadth of the medicinal knowledge they possess. For example, it is often common knowledge that particular families have access to certain valued medicines. It is seldom common knowledge, however, as to which member of a given family has possession of the active ingredient of the medicine *(laen miit ea falaay)*— recall here the shock Buulyäl expressed that her beloved auntie would hold back just such an ingredient from her when she needed it.

In order to determine who to ask for treatment, people often attempt to discover which of the family members has taken care of the elder who is known to have had possession of the medicine. If this individual is not the eldest, this can present a challenge, however, since it is always considered respectful to first talk to the eldest member of a family if ever there is a request made to a particular estate for help or aid. It is thus not uncommon for people to ask the eldest of the siblings about acquiring the medicine, before trying to meet secretly with the member of the family who is believed to have possession of its most potent form.

Because of these challenges, the first choice for most sufferers is to seek treatment within the family. If a family does not have access to the particular type of medicine necessary to treat the affliction, however, an individual is forced to look elsewhere. When seeking aid from outside the family, it is absolutely necessary to ensure that proper compensation is rendered to the person who is providing the treatment. Otherwise, it is unlikely that the proper care will be received. If adequate *machaaf* ("valuables") are not given to the person supplying the medicine then there is a good chance that the person suffering from the illness will not be given the correct medicine or a medicine of an adequate strength to treat the illness. As one healer attested, this is meant to compensate for all of the "suffering involved in finding and collecting medicine."

In preparing medicines it is essential to find the right plants, collect them in the appropriate manner, and to follow the restrictions necessary to ensure that the medicine maintains its efficacy. As such, compensation for medicine recognizes the knowledge and effort an individual has put into learning and remembering it, as well as the time they have taken to follow the *faalngiin ea falaay* ("abstentions associated with medicine") while they were collecting and preparing it. As one elder asserted, such compensation is never meant solely for the individual preparing the medicine. It is considered instead to also be *mäybil ko thagiith* ("prayer for the ancestors") or *faalngiin ea thagiith* ("propitiation for the ancestors"). That is, the exchange of *machaaf* for medicine is not exclusively *puluwon ko falaay* ("the cost of medicine"). It is also significantly a gift to appease the ancestral spirit (*thagiith*) who is working to imbue the medicine with its *angin* ("efficacy").

I repeatedly observed that medicines given to patients were almost always prepared in such a way as to make certain that the ingredients were not revealed. The process of acquiring medicines is one in which the patient, after having explained the symptoms they are suffering from, will often be told to wait (or return in a day or two) so that the individual providing the medicine can go out on their own to gather the ingredients. Individuals are very careful to collect their ingredients in private. Individuals preparing medicines will often hide the ingredients by wrapping them in an available plant leaf (often palm or taro leaves) to be sure that others will not be able to see the specific plants they have assembled to prepare the medicine in question. Medicines are also similarly wrapped when given to the patient. Even when the wrapping is removed it is still impossible to determine what the exact ingredients are, or how they are prepared. This is due to the fact that a medicine's ingredients are often pounded, crushed, and then mixed together.

The role of secrecy in the collection and preparation of medicine is closely tied to the idea of the medicine's potency. There is, in fact, an active belief held that if too many people know about a particular formula that it will begin to lose its effectiveness. Indeed, a friend of mine once told me of how her aunt had warned her not to give out the formulas for the family medicines since the more people who knew of the medicines the less powerful they would be

This emphasis upon secrecy in the proper transmission of knowledge is further tied to a frequently expressed reluctance to inscribe knowledge in textual forms, even if such inscription is held to be for personal mnemonic purposes. To wit, I heard a number of cautionary tales concerning the theft of notebooks containing medicines. Many individuals pointed out that the only truly safe place to store such knowledge is in one's mind. This concern further extended to attempting to write down or record *yalean* ("tradition") for which there are many tales of such records being destroyed by termites, mold, or water damage. For some individuals, this was an indication of the ancestors' displeasure with such active attempts to inscribe and preserve knowledge outside of the flow of sentiment that helps to define the dynamics of particular social relations. Ultimately, then, issues of privacy, secrecy, concealment, truth, and power cannot be divorced from broader discussions concerning the interplay of the virtues of "self-governance," "suffering-for," effort, work-induced exhaustion, endurance, compassion, and care.

Secrecy, Truth, and Power

> When a people's social life is characterized by a habit of concealment, artful management of the truth is hardly looked upon as deceitful. It becomes, rather, something of a virtue.
>
> Glenn Petersen, 1993

In an important article, Glenn Petersen outlines a culturally informed orientation to privacy, truth, and concealment in another Micronesian society that is well in-line with Yapese moral sensibilities. According to Petersen, the cultivation of the personal quality of *kanengamah*, which he translates as "reserve" or "restraint," is held by many Pohnpeian philosophers to be a central cultural virtue. As a quality, Petersen describes *kanengamah* as the capacity to "keep knowledge, emotions, interests, and possessions concealed" (1993, 335). As a behavior, it refers to the act of concealment. This virtue, both a quality and an activity, Petersen suggests, is largely responsible for ensuring that not-knowing, ambiguity, and dissembling are prevalent features of everyday interaction. Significantly, to this end *kanengamah* "serves as a deliberately constituted safeguard against the encroachment of power" (1993, 335).

In fostering ambiguity, Petersen believes that this particular virtue plays a crucial role in ensuring that "individual autonomy can coexist with patterns of dominance and subordination" (1993, 338). Indeed, in the midst of pervasive not-knowing he holds that individuals are effectively able to question those truth claims that would otherwise confer power to the putative possessors of the knowledge underpinning such claims (cf. Groark 2008). Moreover, he argues that an always selective and partial sharing of knowledge, ideas, feelings, and emotions is importantly predicated upon developing an ability to master the timing of such expressions. By engaging in such practices of concealment individuals are able to forge a space within which to enact their personal agency in the face of what would otherwise be a stifling subordination to existing hierarchies.

Kanengamah has, as one might assume, a complex relation to truth. Efforts to compose one's exterior in order to affect an expressive opaqueness seem to indicate to some North American moral sensibilities untruthfulness or lying. It is an emphasis on the value of mastering one's ability to control the release of information, however, that distinguishes *kanengamah* from outright falsehood. It is through subtlety in the form of strategically managing the timing and contexts within which knowledge is revealed to others that an individual is able to secure a space for his or her personal agency to arise. As Petersen suggests, the "person possessing the knowledge, or an opinion or an emotion, is the one who controls its expression" (1993, 343).

While attention to the contexts within which such strategic revelations take place are certainly important to social actors, *kanengamah* can also be employed as a form of resistance inasmuch as it arises in the service of "not speaking one's mind in response to provocation." It is also interesting that in this regard, the same quality is often explicitly associated with what Petersen describes as a Pohnpeian valuing of "stoicism" in the form of "not showing pain or fear," a connection that has a strong correspondence with Yapese understandings of ethical modalities of being (1993, 342).

Petersen's observations in Pohnpei further align with patterns in other Pacific societies where the opaqueness of actors' intentions (Duranti 1984, 1988, 1993, 2006; McKellin 1990; Ochs 1988, Ochs and Schieffelin 1984; Robbins and Rumsey 2008; Throop 2008b; cf. Duranti 2001) is often rooted in an ambiguity that is fostered by communicative practices predicated upon the prevalence of indirect or "oblique" speech (Besnier 1994; Brenneis 1984a; Goldman 1995; Strathern 1975; McKellin 1990).[1] As Donald Brenneis observes, such oblique communicative practices are often well suited to dealing with dilemmas that arise when an individual wishes to "both act politically and avoid the appearance of such action" (Brenneis 1984a, 70).[2]

As Elinor Ochs observes (personal communication), the ambivalences inherent in indirect speech at least partially stem from the fact that oblique reference is well suited to engendering an explicit shift in interpretive weight from speaker to hearer. In light of the utterance's ambiguity, a hearer is required to actively fill in and thus share responsibility for coconstructing the meaning of the utterance. As such, the explicit assumptions of coauthorship implicated in indirect speech forms may have the effect of ensuring that a given speaker's interlocutors become complicit in the speaker's moral perspective (Besnier 1989). It is this transference of responsibility from speaker to hearer implicated in oblique speech acts that can be held to mark such forms of talk as both potentially strategically beneficial *and* potentially dangerous for speakers and their interlocutors alike.

For example, in Yap it is common in everyday speech to hear inter-locutors discussing the mood or emotional state of a third person through the use of oblique metaphorical reference to the positive or (more usually) negative state of weather conditions. This type of talk is most often heard in those situations where the target of the utterance is either absent or not paying direct attention to the speaker. In this way, such metaphorical statements as *ke kireeb ea madaay* ("the sea is stormy") or *ke kireeb yafaang* ("the weather is bad") are employed as an indirect, often conspiratorial way in which to reference the current emotional state of another.

Yapese orientations to privacy, secrecy, concealment, and truth indeed share a number of strong resonances with patterns noted in other Pacific societies and in particular with Petersen's observations in Pohnpei. In Yap, like in Pohnpei, truth and honesty are categories that are held to have ambivalent moral valences. After confessing that much of his trouble in life had stemmed from trusting too much in others and not being careful to censor himself when sharing personal informa-tion with them, one elder explained that unthinking honesty is consid-ered to be a morally inappropriate practice. While it is certainly good to be *yul'yuul* ("honest"), he observed, it is not good to be *yul'yuul maqay*, a phrase he defined as referring to honesty without forethought. Thus, ideally an individual should be honest, but never completely so. Again, timing the release of information is understood to be at the root of valued forms of truth telling.

As he went on to explain, an individual should always think of the network of social relations within which his or her interlocutors are implicated before sharing any piece of information, even if there is a previously established trust between them. Taking into consideration who one's interlocutors are related to, who their friends are, and who those friends and relatives might talk to is deemed necessary to ensure that potentially powerful or dangerous knowledge does not fall into the wrong hands. He added that unthinking openness is highly disval-ued and is, in its most egregious cases, thought to be equivalent to a type of mental disability. As he explained,

But if honesty is unthinking then you will be overtruthful because . . . this [truthfulness] in Yap, you will be honest, we are friends, you are honest with me . . . I am honest with you but you have yours and I have mine, and neither of us should forget that there will be consequences. So you have your mind and I have my mind, we will be honest with each other but you had your mind and I had my mind. You don't trust me and I don't trust you real full.

But you know that we are honest, but I am thinking of you and I am thinking of me. This person is honest, he is keeping this [a secret]. So there are some things [people or relations] that Jason has in Yap that I don't know if they are good or bad. You two will . . . talk and I will have thought about that thought to the end. Always wondering about what will happen or what will be done . . . and that Jason, can he keep his word? Okay, who is Jason's girlfriend? This person's girlfriend that is a person that has these relations that are like this. And you think and your thoughts return to that and that . . . tiny mistrust comes to . . . That is the way that it is said in Yap: don't be unthinkingly honest. Don't you be unthinkingly honest. You be honest because honesty is good but keep your mind. You are honest with the person, you are wise. Don't you go and jump your mouth . . . you will have breathed a bit before you jump. So that is the way of unthinking honesty. If you are unthinkingly honest then that is how you . . . you trusted that [person] there but you didn't think of other consequences, only that thing [person] that you put your trust in. Unthinkingly honest.

There is an explicit recognition in this statement of the privacy and opacity of individual minds. Along with this is an emphasis on keeping one's attention focused on the potential consequences of revealing knowledge to others who are social actors positioned within a complex web of social relations. Such relations consist of many individuals who may not have the speaker's best interests at heart. It is such an orientation to privacy, opacity, and truth that was characterized by this elder and many others as a central basis for a socially valued form of strategic honesty embedded in, and arising out of, mutual concealment.

Communicative Strategies for Concealment

> It is not easy to investigate the religion of this . . . people.
> The Yapese can be deceptive in this matter as well as in
> others. The superficial observer gets the impression that the
> Yapese, in religious matters, is a pretty indifferent fellow. The
> eager researcher, anxious to get to the bottom of things, will
> be assured, in the friendliest possible way, that his interlocu-
> tor really knows nothing at all about these matters. As a
> proof of his good will, he will refer the researcher to other
> persons, who, he says, are better informed. If you do find
> someone who is willing to talk, you get tales and stories in
> vast quantities; but after you have written until you get finger
> cramps you end up knowing as much about the essential
> matters as when you started.
>
> Sixtus Walleser, 1913

In Yap, indirect or oblique speech is an important means through which to produce and maintain ambiguity in the service of secrecy and concealment. That said, there are in fact a number of different verbal strategies that speakers use, often quite self-consciously, in their attempts to bring into being a communicative context within which personal intentions, motives, feelings, goals, thoughts, and so on are rendered opaque. And it is precisely this opaqueness that helps speakers to ensure that they are able to adhere to expectations regarding a strategic honesty that allows for a morally valued partial disclosure of truth. While there are probably many more such strategies, there are seven whose frequency in the context of everyday interaction makes them worth noting here.

First, there is a practice that many of my teachers and friends labeled (using the English phrase) "talking in opposites."[3] I was repeatedly reminded in the first few months of my fieldwork that I should always be careful not to take what individuals said to me at face value, since the people I would be speaking to would often "speak in opposites." That is, individuals would be likely to say "yes" when they meant "no." They would claim to be poor when they were in fact wealthy. Or they would proclaim that a particular presentation of gifts was worth very little when in fact it was quite valuable. As one friend explained to me, if you are looking for a person who has access to a specific type of medicinal knowledge, for instance, it is almost always the person who claims to know absolutely nothing about medicine who is most likely to have the knowledge in question. In contrast, the person who is readily willing to claim possession of such knowledge probably does not have access to it.

A second strategy is tied to Yapese conversational norms in which asking too many direct questions of another is considered to be extremely impolite.[4] Equally disvalued is the act of interrupting an individual in the midst of speaking. As a result of these norms interlocutors often produce extended stretches of uninterrupted talk with little to no overlapping speech. These particular communicative norms help to create a balance between other-directed and self-initiated speech that is well suited to granting speakers opportunities to provide only the minimal amount of information possible when asked specific questions about intended actions or personal knowledge.

Such communicative norms further grant speakers control over how such information is framed and revealed. That is, individuals seldom provide unsolicited information as to their plans, goals, or thoughts, without first being asked by another—which is rather rare given the constraints imposed upon the appropriateness of direct questioning. Individuals can be certain that even when asked explicitly to part with information, they will often not be asked too many additional questions. Moreover, they will not be interrupted while formulating their responses. In this way, individuals are able to control the direction and content of their responses and as such are often effectively able to restrict themselves to answering only the specifics of the question at hand.

A third communicative strategy employed by interlocutors in an attempt to foster nontransparency between internal states and forms of expression is tied to outright deception or lying *(baen)*. There is certainly a moral valence that is assigned to lying depending on the context within which it occurs (a valence that I am somewhat inclined to see as resulting from colonial and Christian influence). It is, however, also accepted that many people who have access to culturally valued knowledge, such as knowledge having to do with medicines, will, if pressed, lie to keep that knowledge private. Again, recalling Buulyäl's reflections at the beginning of this chapter and the story of the two brothers described in chapter 2, deception in the form of not providing complete or accurate knowledge regarding specific practices is common. This is especially so when the possessor of such knowledge does not believe that the potential recipient has adequately demonstrated sufficient care, service, compensation, or respect in exchange for that knowledge (see also Keenan [Ochs] 1976). In other words, the individual in question has not demonstrated that they are a person of a particular moral worth deserving of that knowledge. Indeed, even within families, individuals told me that they were often quite uncertain with regard to who in the family had received what medicines and the extent to which the knowledge they personally had access to was accurate or complete.

That practices of deception are at times valued is evident in the fact that the term for "lie" or "lying" in Yapese *(baen)* is the same term that is used to designate a traditional form of martial art that is no longer practiced on the island. The ability to intentionally deceive others is, in fact, the basis for a number of stories I heard that are intended to demonstrate the intelligence of the story's main protagonist. Two such stories taken directly from my field notes are as follows:

Tamag then told us a story about his father, who had once invited an Outer Islander over to drink at his house. The two of them got rather intoxicated.

Apparently a fight started when Tamag's father had said that his guest was from a small island and thus had a small mind. The Outer Islander, who knew a form of martial art from his own island, became *damumuuw* ("angry") and challenged Tamag's father to a fight. Tamag's father refused, knowing that there was no way that he could win given that he did not know Yapese *baen* (martial arts). His strategy was instead to stay on his veranda so that he would not have to fight—this was due to the fact that the Outer Islander's lower status ensured that he would not set foot on the house foundation. Remaining on the ground, the Outer Islander raised one of his legs, crossing his foot across his body in preparation to kick. Tamag's father responded by saying that this was just going to make it all the easier to beat him if he insisted on standing on one leg. This enraged the Outer Islander who shouted that Tamag's father should come down and fight. Tamag's father insisted instead that he put his leg back on the ground so that he would have a fighting chance against him; of course, this managed to get the Outer Islander out of position. But at this point the man was so angered that he only wanted Tamag's father to get down on the ground so they could fight. Finally, Tamag's father got off the veranda and in one quick move managed to grab and untie the Outer Islander's *thuw* ("loincloth"), which fell to the man's knees before he caught it. Embarrassed, he was said to have run off.

During the war a Japanese soldier challenged one of the Yapese men renowned for being skilled at *baen* to a fight. The soldier had tried to convince the man to fight him. The Yapese man declined saying that the purpose of his skill was not to fight without purpose. The Japanese soldier insisted. In response the Yapese man took an *uthir* (a base of a palm leaf that is used to sit upon) and sat on the ground. The soldier seeing this was said to have gotten very angry and stood up yelling at the Yapese man to stand up and fight. The man declined a few more times before the soldier screamed that if he did not stand up that he would come over and beat him while he sat helpless on the ground. The Yapese man stayed seated and the Japanese soldier started walking briskly to beat him. As the soldier approached, the Yapese man took his *uthir* out from under himself and threw it on the ground just under the foot of the Japanese soldier. Before he knew what was happening, the Yapese man grabbed and pulled the *uthir* from under the soldier's feet, making him fall to the ground. The Japanese soldier got up and apologized, recognizing that he had been beaten.

In both of these stories there is an interesting theme of the Yapese protagonist remaining calm, not engaging in a fight even when provoked, all the while waiting, watching, and allowing his opponent to get taken over by anger and frustration. Seated, both protagonists refused to act until the time was right for them to move quickly, without hesitation. This strategy allowed them to take their opponents off guard. In each case, the ability to outwit and beat an opponent hinged on the use of deception. Deception is thus valued in as much as it implies the possession of intelligence, patience, and control over one's anger, which allows an individual to take advantage of an opponent's weakness.

A fourth prevalent strategy for eliciting uncertainty in one's interlocutors is tied to the use of what I will call benign and derogatory sarcasm (*moening* and *ke kuuq u waen*). Benign sarcasm (*moening*) was characterized by a number of my teachers as a form of talk in which a speaker's overt utterance is at odds with his or her feelings on the matter; for example, saying *Keam cheag!* ("You are skilled!") in the face of ineptitude. Of course, not all individuals are equally skilled in deploying benignly sarcastic statements. There is always potential for insult. Accordingly, despite the prevalence of benign sarcasm in everyday speech acts the effective use of *moening* is held to be a form of verbal art that is not equally perfected by all speakers. The most skilled are those for whom their interlocutors are never quite certain as to the extent to which their utterances are intended to be interpreted as literal or sarcastic.

Closely related to benign sarcasm (*moening*) is the concept of *ke kuuq u waen*. One teacher described this phrase as indicating a form of expressivity that is, like *moening*, similarly based on a discrepancy between what an individual says and what he or she is thinking or feeling "inside" his or her mind (*mang ea be thaamiy laen ii yaen'*). It seems that a significant difference between *ke kuuq u waen* and *moening* is tied to the fact that the former is held in a more negative light as a form of derogatory sarcasm. In Jensen's (1977a) dictionary the morpheme *kuuq* is defined as "to mock, criticize." A number of individuals explained to me, however, that *kuuq* is seldom delivered in a expressive form that is directly evident to a speaker's interlocutors (*daar ma daag ea kuuq*). Often the only way to discern *kuuq* is through observing an individual's overt behavior (*ngoognol*) in contexts outside of the moment within which an utterance is made. Hence the expression that is used to explicitly highlight this hidden (sarcastic) form of *kuuq* is *ke kuuq u waen'* (literally, "there is mocking or criticism in the mind").

Much like these benign and derogatory forms of sarcasm, a fifth communicative strategy to evoke uncertainty and ambiguity is found in the prevalence of joking (*gosgoos*) and teasing (*galasuw*) in everyday communicative forms. With regard to its impact as a strategy for fostering ambiguity, it is often (although not always) the case that the target of a joke or act of teasing does not find out about it until well after the episode has occurred, sometimes hours, days, or weeks later. Of course, I sometimes found myself at the receiving end of such teasing or joking, often learning about it only well after the fact. The individuals that I knew best, who were my friends, part of my family, and part of my village, all seemed to share a true appreciation for those individuals who could subtly and quickly employ their wit to effective ends in the context of joking or teasing. This was especially so when it was employed in the service of making fun of an individual who was acting in an overly prideful or insensitive manner. The ability to participate in such joking or teasing was also held by many to be tied closely to an individual's intelligence. There is in fact a category of intellectual ability—*maqay* (the same *maqay* evoked in the context of unthinking honesty, *yul'yuul ni maqay*)—that refers to a person who, while they might have knowledge and intelligence "inside" their mind, is unable to speak well, to organize his or her speech in a coherent way, or to participate in joking or teasing with another person (*gosgoos, galasuw*).

As discussed in some detail in previous chapters, the prevalence of "speaking-for" others is yet another communicative means to dissociate overt expressive forms from an individual's personal thoughts, feelings, and emotions. Speaking-for others—whether those others be construed as the ancestors who represent the authority that is vested in a particular estate, parents for whom which children pass messages from one household to the next, or chiefs speaking-for the village during community and municipality meetings—effectively distances an individual's own subjective stance from the explicit content of his or her utterances. Given that it is well recognized that individuals often use their position in speaking-for others to advance their own personal motivations and ambitions, it is often unclear to their interlocutors, however, exactly which aspects of a given utterance reflects a strategic alignment of personal wishes with family or community obligations and which are indeed reflective of a selfless adherence to such obligations.

Finally, paralinguistic aspects of speech are also often aligned with both implicit and explicit attempts to ensure uncertainty in the context of interaction. Eye gaze, body position, volume and tone of voice, are all means by which individuals attempt to conceal their "true" thoughts, feelings, and opinions from others. Indeed, one of the first notes I took when arriving in Yap concerned what I held to be a striking lack of direct eye contact when individuals spoke to one another and a marked tendency for speakers to turn their bodies and heads away from their interlocutors. In fact, it was not uncommon to observe individuals carry

FIGURE 6. A moment's rest. Photo by the author.

on complete conversations with their backs to each other, gazing off into opposite directions. Likewise, during community meetings individuals often sat with their backs against the beams supporting the community house facing out away from the meeting, gazing instead at the horizon, the dance ground, or other parts of the village center. One conversation I noted early in my fieldwork, well before I had acquired the communicative competence necessary to follow an ongoing, multiparty conversation, included six individuals speaking for over an hour, none of whom were facing one another.

In addition to body positioning and eye gaze, individuals are very adept at modulating the volume of their voice in such a way as to ensure that only those who are sitting nearest to them can understand what they are saying. I noticed that individuals who wanted to carry on a private conversation in the midst of a group would often sit side by side, facing neither one another nor the others surrounding them. They would speak only loud enough for their intended interlocutor to discern the content of their talk. This positioning of the body ensures that the stream of sound being produced by a given speaker is directed away from others in the vicinity and that interlocutors' voices remain muted. Such an orientation further makes it unclear to others surrounding them as to whether or not a conversation is in fact ongoing.

An additional benefit to such positioning of the body is that it further occludes an individual's facial expressions from the view of his or her interlocutors. This is especially important given that the face, and more specifically the eyes, are thought to be crucial expressive sites for discerning another's true feelings and thoughts (cf. Robbins 2004, 138). Throughout my time in Yap, I was repeatedly amazed at how sensitive individuals were to the presence of potential unwanted audiences. I was also struck by how skilled individuals were at finding ways in which to carry on conversations that were just below the threshold of audibility for those who were not meant to be intentional recipients of the conversation.

Together, these communicative strategies work to keep interlocutors in a state of uncertainty and not-knowing when it comes to any given speaker's intentions, motives, thoughts, and feelings (cf. Hollan and Throop 2008; Robbins and Rumsey 2008). In such a way, a communicative context is often created within which individuals are left second-guessing the veracity, adequacy, or completeness of what has been told to them. The truth of any given statement is thus something that can never simply be taken at face value. An individual always has to assume that there is most likely a hidden "more" to what an individual expresses in any given situation.

It is a recognized fact in Yap that even if part of what someone says is true, there will also most likely be some disinformation, a lack of information, or outright falsehoods embedded in the utterance. Individuals are never quite certain as to whether what is being said or done in the context of a particular interaction is the truth, a joke (of which they might be the brunt), an evasive tactic, a sarcastic statement, or an outright lie. Often the best course of action in the face of such perduring uncertainty is to wait to see what will actually transpire on the behavioral level. Again, this is a stance that is predicated upon deferring immediate reactions to sensory stimuli, in this case in the form of audible speech (cf. Robbins 2004, 141–42).

By talking in opposites, being elusive, facing metapragmatic restrictions on turn-taking and questioning, only providing the absolutely minimal amount of information necessary, being sarcastic, playing jokes, teasing, avoiding eye contact, or situating the body such that the voice is muted and facial expressions are concealed from the view of others, individuals are able to ensure that their interlocutors can never garner a clear idea as to what they are really thinking or feeling. There is a significant benefit to engendering such communicative opacity. This benefit lies in the fact that by putting interlocutors off guard, off balance, and making them uncertain as to a speaker's true feelings and motives, an individual is granted a strategic advantage. The advantage stems from the fact that the speaker is the only one who truly knows what his or her plans are. Such information can perhaps be importantly used to his or her advantage at some later date. Well in line with this insight, one individual told me that one of the main reasons that people are careful to not say or show what they are thinking or feeling to others is in order to ensure their "safety." For instance, if in a given situation a person becomes very frightened, in working to conceal these feelings, other individuals will not be able to use that information to their advantage against them.

I should note that these habits of concealment are so deeply ingrained that even seemingly important information that would be of some concern for members of a family is often only transmitted at the last minute or well after the fact. It was not uncommon for members of my adopted family, for instance, to return to or depart from Yap in order to conduct work or schooling off island. I was always personally surprised at how many times these events would be shared partially with only certain members of the family and not others. One particularly memorable example concerned the fact that the wife of one friend of mine had left to conduct business off island and had been gone for over a week before the husband's parents found out. During that time, the husband had been to his parents' house numerous times to visit. Not once did he bring up the fact that his wife was off island. In another case, in a family that I was also close to, one of the elders was sick for almost a week before the wife of one of her sons (who lived in the same village) was informed of the situation by her husband who had been making daily visits to see how his mother was doing.

Opacity, Expressivity, and the Meaning of Speaking

In Yap, there is a prevalent language ideology based in part upon the assumption that the meaning of any given speech act is most often hidden (cf. Robbins 2001). A further implication of this ideology is that an audience interested in determining the meanings that lie "behind" overt expressive forms must seek to discover "the meaning of speaking" *(faan ea thiin)* through alternate communicative channels. Much as Robbins (2004, 142–43) and Barth (1975) have noted with regard to a prevalent "epistemology of secrecy" among the Urapmin and Min peoples in Papua New Guinea, the very hiddenness of such meaning underlies its ultimate worth, value, and power (see also Robbins 2008).

Early in my language training I was instructed by two different teachers on separate occasions that an important aspect of everyday communicative forms is tied to something they termed *faan ea thiin.* Examples that they proffered for these expressive forms primarily included hand gestures (i.e., rotating a partially cupped hand that iconically represents an engine propeller, which is used to indicate, often conspiratorially, that an ongoing utterance is somehow deceptive) and facial expressions (i.e., raising one's eyebrows one time to indicate agreement with a request or statement and twice in order to signal disagreement). Because of this, I was initially convinced that the term *faan ea thiin* was a general term for nonverbal or paralinguistic forms of communication, in particular gestures. It was not until I had a conversation with an elder about different forms of "hidden meaning" in Yapese parables that it became clear to me, however, that *faan ea thiin* is not solely restricted to nonverbal communication. It seems instead, quite literally, to refer to the "meaning of speaking."

Given that there is such a deeply rooted assumption that the meaning of speaking is seldom rendered directly in the surface forms of an utterance's explicit content, more often than not the term *faan ea thiin* ends up referring generally to those meanings that arise in the context of indirect, oblique, nontransparent, and hidden aspects of communication. This can be understood in the case of indirect communicative forms that arise out of necessity, such as when individuals are gesturing to each other from a distance. Or in the case of those circumstances in which interlocutors wish to engage in some form of conspiratorial signaling to help each other disambiguate the "true" meaning of a given utterance (e.g., using the "propeller" hand gesture to indicate the deceptiveness of a statement). Indeed, the term *faan ea thiin* is also significantly used to refer in the context of Yapese dances to those bodily movements and gestures that accompany the lyrics of specific chants that point an audience to the deep or hidden meanings entailed within them (i.e., this song is not really about gardening, but about sex).

The value of secrecy, privacy, and concealment is further evident in a much heard aphorism *(ke luul ni baabaay)* used to describe individuals who are unable to attain self-mastery over their expressivity. The expression literally means, "it ripened, a papaya." As one of my teachers explained, this saying is used in a derogatory fashion to refer to people for whom it is possible to tell immediately what they are thinking or feeling. In his words, "You just look at them and know if they are sad or angry."

To help me understand this statement, he explained how a papaya is a fruit for which it is possible to discern the state of ripeness by merely looking at its skin and color. That is, the state of the papaya's "innerness" is reflected transparently in its exterior. In allowing one's inner conditions to manifest directly in one's external forms of expression, an individual is thus comparable to a papaya, and as such is clearly marked as failing to approximate the virtues of self-governance, concealment, and secrecy.

Another person suggested to me that if *ke luul ni baabaay* represents a derogatory commentary on an individual's lack of ability to mask his or her internal states, another phrase, *ke luul ni rowal* ("it ripened, a football fruit") represents the cultural ideal. In contrast to a papaya, a football fruit *(Pangium edule)* is a fruit that has a rough brown exterior that does not in any way clearly evidence the state of its inner ripeness. When looking at the exterior of a *rowal* it is impossible to tell the state of its interior—the fruit could very well be rotten. One of the only ways to determine the state of a *rowal* is to touch it. Touching will still not guarantee, however, that the entire fruit is edible, for this assessment can only be definitively determined by opening the fruit up and looking at its insides directly.

While I heard many conflicting accounts as to whether or not the phrase *ke luul ni rowal* should be considered an idiomatic expression, a dialectical variant of a phrase used in only select municipalities, or merely an idiosyncratic example generated by one particularly perceptive individual who was trying to help clarify the meaning of the more commonly heard phrase *ke luul ni baabaay*, it is regardless interesting to note the extent to which this example draws on the same metaphorical play on relations between the internal and the external.

The contrast between internality and externality is in fact at the heart of a number of other aspects of Yapese cultural logic in which metaphors based upon the images of surfaces and depths, the visible and the invisible, and the apparent and the hidden are recurrently played out. These metaphorically elaborated distinctions between what is directly perceptible and what is occluded from view are operative at both the level of the political system and at the level of individual expression. For instance, during our oral history and mapping project I was told of one house foundation in our village that is responsible for taking care of the various *machaaf* ("valuables") that had come to the village's various estates in the context of traditional apologies or for rewarding services rendered to allies in times of war, conflict, or need. As the elders who were helping with the project maintained, to say that a specific house foundation is responsible for taking care of the village's valuables *(machaaf)*, however, is not to say that this same foundation in anyway possesses or is solely responsible for making decisions that bear directly on the use and allocation of these valuables. Instead, more accurately, the foundation serves merely as the *awochean ea machaaf*—the "face or front of the valuables."

The term *awochean* is defined in Jensen's (1977a) dictionary as "his face, its front." What is most interesting about the term is the extent to which it is used to highlight distinctions between outer expression and inner contemplation or decision making. Just as the term "voice" *(lunguun)* is held to be a sensible surface manifestation of the combination of breath *(faan)* and thought *(leam/taafinay)*, two phenomena that are otherwise hidden, invisible, and importantly connected in Yapese thinking to the effort of others, *awochean* similarly entails the assumption that behind the expressive field of an individual's face lies an inner world of thought and feeling that is occluded from view. To say that a certain house foundation is the "face or front of the valuables" is to imply that, much like a human face, the foundation is responsible for expressing the results of what are otherwise hidden deliberations, negotiations, and decision-making processes pertaining to those valuables.

At the level of the sociopolitical system, the notion of *awochean* is further associated with both *feekthiin* ("messenger") and *lunguun* ("voice" or "authority"). Both of these concepts are implicated in the idea that the people who are actually making decisions and giving orders that later become manifest in the form of overt speech are themselves elided from view. In this system, it is most often lower-status individuals who speak for higher-status decision makers. And it is these same lower-status individuals who then transmit orders to those still lower in rank who are then to undertake the work or service that has been requested. As I pointed out in the previous chapter, at the level of the village, when decisions are discussed at community meetings it is generally held to be the case that the "real" decision-making process has already occurred. Again, decision making, thinking, and discussion are understood to be accomplished largely behind the scenes, hidden from view. The expression of already formulated decisions is, in contrast, something that is publicly accessible and importantly tied to consensus building.

At the level of the individual, *awochean* again importantly points to the dichotomy between outer expression and inner experiences. *Awochean* refers to a person's face. The face's role in mediating between inner experience and outer expression is especially evident in the context of the saying *feal awochean* ("good face"). This phrase is used to refer to those individuals who are skilled at composing their exteriors in such a way that they do not express what they might be feeling or thinking, even when confronted with situations in which their interlocutors might be attempting to provoke an overtly emotional response from them. The phrase is linked to the idea that comprehension of another's feelings and thoughts arises from the horizon of perception. Thus, what lies beyond that horizon must remain unknown. Accordingly, an individual who is able to consistently maintain *feal awochean* is characterized as a person who is able to *ma paag laen ii yaen'*—"he or she lets go of his or her innermost feelings and thoughts."

Even despite this emphasis on maintaining an opaque exterior, it is interesting to note the extent to which the face, and particularly the eyes *(laen mit, laen awochean)*, are held to represent that part of the person that is most susceptible to directly evidencing inner feeling states and thoughts (cf. Robbins 2004, 139). To this end, it is held that to *pii awochaen fa daag awochaen* ("give face or show face") can be very dangerous. Individuals believe that the danger lies in the fact that it is facial expressions that often reveal to others thoughts and opinions that should otherwise ideally be kept hidden. As previously noted, individuals habitually avoid eye contact when speaking. They also often turn their faces away from one another when conversing. Both of these tendencies are examples of the importance of ensuring that one's face does not give away clues as to what an individual is thinking or feeling at a given moment.

The tendency for individuals to look down when walking past another's house can similarly be understood as tied to ensuring that individuals do not readily communicate their thoughts or feelings to others.

Indeed, this idea is hyperelaborated in the prevalent belief that envy *(awaen)* can be readily transferred from the eyes through the direction of an individual's gaze to the object of his or her perception. In this way, whatever objects are perceived through an envious gaze—gardens, taro patches, or personal possessions—are susceptible to destruction or ruin. *Bureag*, the term that is used to refer to this phenomenon (as well as referring in other contexts to "butterflies"), is held to be a largely nonintentional capacity, which certain individuals have more or less of than others. In other words, it is simply a combination of desire and gaze without any necessary intention to destroy another's possession that is sufficient, depending on the individual in question, to pose potential harm to those possessions.

That the face is a somewhat privileged corporeal site for performing practices of expressive quietude is also closely linked to issues of respect *(liyoer)*. It is not surprising in this light that looking at the ground *(awochean nga buut)* when in the presence of a higher-status individual is held to be a way to show respect, whereas looking at such a person directly indicates a lack of concern or outright defiance.

Finally, another, although admittedly tenuous, connection in Yapese cultural logic between inner states and their expression through the face or the eyes is found in the term for child, *bitiir* or simply *tiir*. In Jensen's dictionary the morpheme *tiir* is held to refer to both a "child" and to the "pupil" of the eye. When discussing the term *bitiir* with my research assistant Manna, she argued that the term is actually a contracted form of the stative tense-aspect marker *ba* and the nominal morpheme *tiir—batiir*. If this local etymological assessment is indeed correct (it may not be), the term could be literally translated as "is eyes" or "is child."[5]

When Manna first suggested this interpretation neither of us could quite figure out what, if any, connection there might be between the pupil of the eye and a child. After giving it some thought, however, she suggested that one possible interpretation might be tied to the fact that the eyes are generally held to be a crucial site for expressing internal feelings, desires, thoughts, and opinions, often quite independently of other paralinguistic cues or the actual content of a given utterance. This observation aligns quite well with the assumption that a child has yet to learn how to control or discipline his or her desires, wants, and cravings. Children simply look at what they desire. They show no concern for hiding their intentions, emotions, needs, and cravings from others. They have yet to learn to manage their emotions in an effort to effect forms of expressive opacity. They have thus yet to cultivate the virtue of self-governance.

There is, in fact, a term that is used in Yap to designate the undesirable subjective state that is induced in an individual who witnesses an overly transparent expression of emotion. Particularly in the case of those instances whereby another is inappropriately expressing his or her love, longing, or desire. The term *so ulum* is the same morpheme that is utilized to designate goose bumps. Such a physiological reaction is understood to be a reaction to cold or fear. However, it is also believed to arise when an individual is put in the uncomfortable position of having to experience another individual's emotional outburst. As one elder explained to me, individuals who tend to speak their minds without hesitation and without attention to the possibility of making their interlocutors feel *so ulum* are said to be *dar k'adkaed ea thiin u lunguun*—"words do not cause itchiness in his or her mouth." That is, there is nothing about speaking their mind that is uncomfortable for them.

I should add that the term *so ulum* is not merely a metaphorical elaboration upon a physiological reaction, but is instead experienced as an embodied subjective state. For instance, there were a number of occasions when I heard individuals use the term and gesture to their goose bumps while recalling situations in which an individual failed to live up to local expectations for expressive quietude and muted emotional expressivity. In fact, during my interviews there were often times when my research assistants felt *so ulum* when hearing more personal details of a given individual's life. In one notable case, one of my research assistants was so distraught from hearing a very emotional retelling of an individual's experience of losing a child that she had to physically remove herself from the interview. Later, I discovered that she had become not only *so ulum* but also physically ill as a result of this highly emotionally charged retelling.

The cultural valuation of privacy, secrecy, and concealment appears to be further reflected in a salient lexical distinction that is made with respect to the extent to which, and the communicative channels through which, the emotion of anger is expressed to another. There are a number of terms in Yapese that can loosely be glossed as varieties of "anger." Examples of these terms include: (1) *kaf'aen'*—"angry or upset" but not expressing that anger to others; (2) *malaalngaen'*— "anger," "annoyance," or "irritation" that is not expressed verbally and is often undetectable by an observer, but can on occasion be detected through facial expressions, tone of voice, or the fact that a person is shaking his or her leg while seated; (3) *thung*—"anger" that is readably detectable by an observer through a person's facial and bodily expressions and tone of voice, but is not expressed through explicit utterances; (4) *damuumuw*—"anger" that can be either expressed or not expressed verbally, but is often used to indicated hidden anger; and (5) *puwaen'*—the explicit verbal expression of justifiable "anger" that is often utilized in the context of "scolding" a person who has transgressed local ethical standards of behavior.

While it is true that these terms do index qualitative differences in the type and intensity of "anger," it also appears that an equally salient distinction concerns the extent to which each variety of "anger" is detectable through either indirect/nonverbal or explicit/verbal means. Accordingly, these terms can be understood as culturally elaborated linguistic vehicles highlighting various degrees of explicitness in accessing the contents of another's internal subjective state (in this case their subjective state of anger). In this light, this tendency to hypercognize (Levy 1973) expressivity as a salient dimension of various anger-like emotions seems to be tied precisely to the prevalence of concerns about privacy, secrecy, and concealment in the context of everyday interaction.

A lexically encoded orientation to the channels through which emotions are expressed makes good sense given the social realities faced by individuals who are recurrently reminded of the prospect that what someone says, or the way that they say it, rarely, if ever, transparently reflects that person's feelings, thoughts, or opinions. Because of the pervasive tendency for actors to conceal their thoughts and feelings from others, individuals are confronted with the necessity of having to closely monitor their interlocutor's expressions in the hope of achieving some glimpse, however attenuated that glimpse might be (i.e., a shaking leg), into the "actual" subjective state of the person that they are interacting with.

Motivation and Gossip

That there are such pressures to maintain a nontransparent rendering of one's inner life is not to say that individuals are not interested in determining the content of others' subjective states. Despite the difficulty in determining another's motives for action, or perhaps in spite of it, the people that I knew best clearly recognized that much of importance is missed when they did not attempt to imagine what the possible motives for another's actions might be. In Yap, where motivation is seldom directly asked of another and where it is also seldom freely expressed in the first person, gossip about others' feelings, intentions, motives, and reactions is a central part of everyday talk and interaction (cf. Schieffelin 2008). It is in the context of gossip that a great deal of attention is devoted to analyzing motives for action. Instead of directly asking another why he or she did or did not act in a specific way, individuals often instead wait to covertly speculate with others about the reasons behind, and the consequences of, that person's observed behavior.

A great deal has been written on the social import of gossip in Pacific cultures (see Besnier 1989, 1990, 1994; Brenneis 1984b; Brison 1992; Firth 1967). This work has done much to reveal the key role that gossip plays in ongoing dynamics of conflict and affiliation, while further highlighting its relation to truth-telling and the ways in which gossip may be put to use as a form of resistance. It is not my intention to speak at length here about the broader role of gossip in Yapese society. Nor will I enter into an explicit dialogue with the existing literature on the topic. Instead, I wish to simply point to the ways in which gossip often serves as a privileged means for interlocutors to speculate on otherwise hidden aspects of social actors' motivations, thoughts, feelings, and opinions. An excellent example of this use of gossip to speculate on a third party's motives for acting, as well as the subjective responses in the face of others' actions, can be seen in the following excerpt.

This excerpt was taken from an audio-recorded conversation that occurred between myself (JT) and two older women (AA, AB) concerning a disruption that occurred during a Christmas church service. In the middle of the service a drunken man (DM) entered the community church and walked aggressively toward the priest (Padre), all the while shouting largely incoherent statements to the congregation. Before anything drastic happened, the man's aunt (DG) stood up and escorted him from the church. A few minutes later, however, a cloth depicting Jesus hung in the back of the church fell to the ground for no apparent reason. The following transcribed stretch of talk occurred a few days after the event. In it two older women who had also been present with me at the service discuss what the Padre may have been feeling during the disruption.

001 AA;   *Gube yan gu saap nga laen mit facha ii Padre ya gube taafi-nay naag*
          I went to look at the Padre's face because I was thinking

002   *uug gaar maang ea bayi yoeg ea chaqaney ea . . . ri baye damumuuw.*
          he will reveal what that person was saying . . . he would be angry.

003 AB;   *Maachnea gam naang ni faani noon make thile ton rok Padre ke thile lunguun*
          But you know that when he spoke the Padre's tone changed, he changed his voice

004   *ke thile to' . . . ke . . . wun'ug ke dake keyan lunguun nga buut ke* ((nervous laughter))
          he changed to [tone?] . . . he . . . in my mind his voice went lower [in pitch] . . . he ((nervous laughter))

005   *gumnaang nike gin Padre.*
          I think that it startled the Padre

006 JT;   *Umm, . . . sanaa ke gin*
          Umm, . . . maybe he was startled
                              [

007 AA;   *Ii chanem . . . Gube leam naag . . .*
          That person . . . I am thinking . . .

008 AB;   *Sanaa ke gin, fa ke rus fa, gur ra damumuuw fa*
          Maybe he was startled, or he was scared, or, I would be angry or . . .

009 AA;   *Ra damumuuw daabiy rus, ra damumuuw.*
          He will be angry not scared, he will be angry.

010 JT;   *Umm.*
          Umm.

011 AA;   *Nen gube taafinay naag ea gube wonder ko faanmanga ngaki paer ea chaqaneam ii DM*
          The thing I was thinking, I was wondering what reason **DM** had for staying [in the church]

012   *ma maang ea rariin ea chaqaneam ii Padre . . . ii DG faram ea muguy—*
          and what will the Padre do . . . DG [DM's aunt] is soft [implying quiet, not aggressive]—

013   *maachnea DG ea be nen ma bee roek,*
              but DG she is the one that is responsible

014 JT;   *Umm.*
              Umm.

015 AA;   *Gam naang faram u glasia . . . DG . . . yibe altar ŋeki koel*
              paa facha ii DG,
              You know that church . . . **DG** . . . she came to the alter and
              DG took his [**DM's**] hand

016   *man nga wen, man ŋawen, kenoon nike danumuuw,*
              ere yu . . .
              she went outside, she went outside, she spoke that she was
              angry, so [???] . . .
                                                                          [

017 AB;   *Maachnea DM bbkireeb loeluŋean.*
              But DM is crazy [literally, "has a bad head"].

018 **AA**; *Bakireeb loeluŋean maachnea facha' ea kuma toŋ toŋ*
              ŋaak
              He is crazy but he was singing

019 AB;   *Eh . . .*
              Eh . . .

020 AA;   *Kuma toŋ toŋ ko miti nenir*
              He was singing that [???]

021 AB;   *Ma bineme ea ba chiŋaaw, ere gag ea kuŋ worry naaŋ Padre.*
              But that [was because] he was drunk, so that is why I was
              worried for the Padre.

022   *Nuŋ gaara ri ni lii' Padre fa fa mange ka buuch ku Padre?*
              My mind said that he will beat the Padre or, or, what will
              happen to the Padre?

023   *Ra damumuuw, faŋe rus fa maang . . .*
              He will be angry, or scared, or what . . .
                                                                          [

024 AB;   *Maachnea faani muul fare gi kegin fare gi re nem ni aaw*
              nga buut meŋin.
              But when that cloth [of Jesus] fell to the ground he
              was startled.

025 AA;   *Me gin.*
              He was startled.

As this brief interaction attests, gossip provides an important and recurrent site for individuals to collaboratively discuss possible motives for a third party's activity as well as the possible emotional reactions of interlocutors engaged in and affected by said activity. Of particular interest here is the fact that in lines 001, 003, and 004 we have examples of individuals looking to the face and to other paralinguistic cues (e.g., the tone of voice) rather than to the explicit content of talk or the situation itself in order to attempt to determine the possible feeling states of another. Also of note is that in lines 002, 005, 008, 009, 011, 018, 023, and 025 there are explicit discussions of the possible feelings of the Padre as well as the possible motivations or intentions for DM's behavior. In line 008 there is further a very interesting shift of perspective undertaken by AB who goes from imagining possibilities for what the Padre was feeling to imagining how she might feel in a similar situation ("Maybe he was startled, or he was scared, or, I would be angry or . . . "). Finally, it is important to highlight the fact that such speculation is rendered both as a reflective assessment of DM's and the Padre's possible motives and emotions from the perspective of the interlocutor's present frame of reference (e.g., lines 005, 008, 016, 021, 024) *and* as a retrospective account of what both interlocutors were privately imagining to be DM's and the Padre's self-experience during the event itself (e.g., lines 001, 002, 007, 009, 011, 012, 022, 023). Again, an ethic of self-governance and expressive opaqueness does not thus entail a lack of interest in determining the contents of other minds.

Ultimately, however, if an individual continues to act in ways that are mostly in accord with community norms and values, it is often of little concern as to whether or not his or her personal motivations, opinions, and feelings truly align with community standards. For this reason, many individuals I spoke to highlighted the significance of simply watching and listening to others in an attempt to discern the extent to which their actual behavioral patterns aligned with their directly expressed motives for action.

Ambivalence, Constraint, and Virtue

There is an uncertainty that arises when interacting with individuals who have internalized the virtue of self-governance in the form of control over their emotional states and their expression in the service of community and family obligations. In such a context individuals must recognize the ever-present dangers associated with not knowing what others are thinking or who might be plotting to do what to whom. For instance, oral histories often recalled clandestine plots to murder members of the community who were thought to be plotting against the established order. Such plots were secretively organized by chiefs and were never known until long after there was success in achieving whatever end they sought to accomplish. In light of these plots there was certainly fertile ground for recognizing that things are seldom as they appear on the behavioral level. There is often much that is going on beneath the surface of perceived actions and events.

Given such uncertainties, it is perhaps not surprising that individuals were often quite ambivalent when discussing the benefits of living a life in the midst of such socially orchestrated forms of subjective opacity. While I will revisit such difficulties in greater detail in the context of my exploration of the lives of specific pain sufferers in subsequent chapters, I wish to briefly share the insights of one particularly percep- tive elder who had given much thought to these matters.

In his attempt to describe the significance of secrecy, privacy, and concealment, he pointed out that on a societal level these virtues help to ensure the smooth functioning of the community. He also main- tained, however, that these virtues are also often very difficult on the day-to-day psychological well-being of specific individuals. As he put it, "It is very hard on the emotional life of the person." He explained that this is especially true in the case of intimate personal relationships where individuals are often at a loss for understanding the actions of even those they know best and with whom they live.

This elder had worked for a number years for Yap State's Department of Education. He pointed out that even with the hardships associated with living a life in accord with these models of ethical conduct, it was difficult for individuals to communicate openly, even when made aware of the importance of doing so. For instance, he recalled a workshop that the Department of Education held for teachers on the topic of "communication." He suggested that despite all of the explicit discus- sion concerning the merits of increased "openness" in the classroom, it was very difficult for the participants to feel comfortable communicat- ing their thoughts and feelings to others. He added that in their discus- sions concerning such personal "emotions," he and others found it much easier to use English instead of Yapese terms when talking about their own thoughts or feelings—this was also an observation that I had made.

The difficulties individuals faced in dealing with such forms of expressive opacity, however, also significantly point to local configurations of agency in Yapese communities. As Petersen argues in the case of Pohnpei, there is a close connection between the valuation of secrecy, privacy, and concealment and issues pertaining to social constraint and individual agency. In Yap, I would argue that this is manifest in the context of a duplex understanding of agency, which is imbued with both social constraint and personal efficacy (cf. Robbins 2004, 195). In the case of the former, individuals are expected to continually monitor their subjective experience, their modes of expression, and their choices for pursuing particular courses of social action in the face of social strictures. Through disciplining the body, learning to control the expression of one's emotions, feelings, and thoughts, and in the process crafting one's outer appearance to accord with community expectations, an individual is, at least partially, forsaking his or her personal agency in the service of conforming to community obligations.

This "conformist" pole of social agency contrasts sharply, however, with the multivariate ways in which privacy and secrecy imbue individuals with a sense of autonomy and agency in the midst of what was once, and is still to some extent, a complexly structured sociopolitical sphere of social relations. An individual's "will" is socialized in learning to discipline his or her somatic, expressive, and emotional states to conform to community and family norms and expectations. It is perhaps somewhat ironic, however, that this very conformity to ethical modalities of being affords a space to open up for an individual's agency.

Individuals' power over themselves and others is enabled through their ability to keep feelings and thoughts private. This is true especially in the context of ensuring as much as possible that any unique and specialized forms of knowledge that individuals have acquired remain theirs and theirs alone. It is precisely through ongoing efforts to monitor, limit, and control the expression of internal states that individuals are able to secure a foothold over those aspects of their subjective experience that give them access to forms of knowledge and understanding tied to particular social standings. Such knowledge is kept as much as possible "within" the mind and thus well beyond the reach of another's abilities to directly gain access to it.

In using the term "will" I should make it clear that there is no one word in Yapese that encompasses the range of connotations that are comprised in the English term. According to Merriam-Webster's

Collegiate Dictionary (tenth edition), "will" is used to express (cf. Murphy and Throop forthcoming):

1. desire, choice, willingness, consent, or in the negative constructions refusal; 2. frequent, customary, or habitual action or natural tendency or disposition; 3. futurity; 4. capability or sufficiency; 5. probability; 6. (a) determination, insistence, persistence, or willfulness, (b) inevitability; 7. a command, exhortation, or injunction; 8. a desire, wish as (a) disposition, inclination, (b) appetite, passion, (c) choice, determination; 9. something desired, (a) a choice or determination of one having authority or power, (b) request or command; 10. the act, process, or experience of willing: volition; 11. (a) mental powers manifested as wishing, choosing, desiring, or intending, (b) a disposition to act according to principles or ends, (c) the collective desire of a group; 12. the power of control over one's own actions or emotions

While there is no one Yapese word that includes these various denotative and connotative referents, most of these meanings are, to some extent, and to differing degrees, semantically extended throughout the differing terms for subjective experience that were explored in the previous chapter. For instance, in the case of *taafinay naag* and *leam naag*, the intentionality (e.g., object directedness or definition 11) and future directedness (definition 3) of willing is evoked in the role that thinking and deliberation play in planning out a particular course of action prior to acting. Furthermore, both *taafinay* and *leam* in their intransitive verb or nominal forms are also often used in everyday conversation to refer to "will" in the sense of an individual consciously resisting or refusing (definition 1) the imposition of another's requests, orders, or suggestions (e.g., *kab ea taafinay roek' fa kab ea leam roek'*). Both terms are further explicitly invoked in discussions of how individuals go about controlling their feelings and emotional life (definition 12). Before acting, before speaking, and before allowing one's fleeting thoughts, feelings, likes and dislikes to direct action, an individual should always first *leam naag* or *taafinay naag* about the possible consequences of engaging in that activity.

Laen ii yaen', in referring to an individual's innermost subjective experience, also implies elements of willing inasmuch as it refers to those desires, wants, and yearnings that are often understood to compel or motivate action (definitions 1 and 8). Since *laen ii yaen'* is often characterized as that aspect of one's subjective life that is hidden from others and seldom translated directly into overt forms of behavior, it is perhaps most accurately understood as an incipient form of desire that at times directs action but most often has to be actively suppressed, or at the very least rarified into acceptable forms of activity. As such, *laen ii yaen'* is perhaps best understood as aligned with a sense of inner compulsion to engage or not engage in specific activities. Depending upon the individual's ability to affect practices of self-governance, this inner compulsion can serve as the motivational current responsible for canalizing certain paths of action.

Two further terms whose semantic range also significantly overlap with notions of "will," and which seem to further align with this duplex nature of social agency, are *puuf rogon* and *athamagil*. The former term is often used to designate an inner state associated directly with activity carried out in accord with an individual's desires (definitions 1, 8, 9, 11). The latter term indexes a form of willing tied to conforming to social and familial norms, expectations, and demands (definitions 2, 6, 8c, 12). Since *puuf rogon* and *athamagil* most explicitly encompass a range of meanings that approximate what is often understood by the term "will"—the latter term playing a significant role in sufferers' experiences and expressions of pain and suffering—it will be helpful to examine them both in greater detail.

A number of individuals translated the term *puuf rogon* as "free will," "feel free," or "freedom." Upon first hearing these translations, I was rather certain that the concept was directly derived from Christian influence. It seemed likely to me that it was the result of creatively employing existing Yapese notions in attempting to translate the Bible. The term is partially comprised of the morpheme *puuf*, an intransitive verb with the meaning "to untie" or "to open." In everyday speech, *puuf* is often used to describe the action of a flower opening—*ke puuf ea floras*. The morpheme *puuf* carries the connotation of self-generated or self-initiated action. A flower is able to *puuf* inasmuch as it is understood to open by itself, without any help. The term is also comprised of the morpheme *rogon*, which can be translated as "how" or "the way." *Puuf rogon* can thus be literally translated as "the way of its self-generated opening or untying," or "the way that it is untied on its own." The metaphorical image of "untying" is especially evocative for ideas of gaining freedom from previous constraint.

Puuf rogon was characterized as a way of speaking or acting that is in accord with personal desires, wants, or inclinations. The concept is not characterized as tied to an individual's ability to control his or her desires or emotions (definition 12). It is, in contrast, understood as a form of acting directly upon them (definitions 1, 8, 9, 11). *Puuf rogon* also has a close connection to the concept of *maacham* ("familiar

with," "habitual," "usual," "customary," "comfortable with") (definition 2). As one elder noted, *puuf rogon* could only arise in those contexts where an individual feels comfortable with the people around him
or her. In fact, she recalled her grandfather instructing her when she
was a child that it was imperative to always sit quietly and watch *(mu
saap)* what the people around her were habitually doing before acting,
especially when visiting another person's *tabinaew*. Her grandfather
told her that this was connected to the importance of observing the
way that people in a particular estate usually *mithmiith* (move, comport
themselves), since every *tabinaew* has different ways of being.
Accordingly, whenever a person is not in his or her own estate, he or
she must recall that they do not have *puuf rogon*. That is, individuals
cannot do what they want, say or take whatever they want, or go
wherever they want.

Athamagil as "perseverance," "striving," or "endurance" is, in contrast to *puuf rogon*, the designation that is used to refer to willing in
the form of working to gain control over inner states, thoughts, emotions, and desires. As one teacher explained to me, when children are
being raised they are always told *m'athamagil* or *k'aed ea n'um* ("bite
your mind"). Through *athamagil* they are taught to *mayarmiy ea laen
ii yaen'* ("organize their innermost subjective experience"). *Athamagil*
is thus implicated in the education of sentiment. Through learning
to control their emotional reactions and forms of expressivity children
are taught to *athamagil*. They are taught to organize their feelings
(thaamiy) and knowledge *(naang)* in socially acceptable ways.
Athamagil is in this manner associated with a socially conservative
aspect of willing, a capacity closely implicated in cultivating the virtue
of "self-governance." Accordingly, *athamagil* is at least implicitly represented as a capacity that is closely tied to engendering habits of
thought, motivation, appreciation, and action that are crystallized in
individual actors in the form of durable dispositions; not unlike, in
some respects, Bourdieu's characterization of habitus (see Throop and
Murphy 2002).

It is significant that when I asked two elders about *puuf rogon* and
athamagil, they began by noting that the two terms are antonyms. This
observation led to a very informative conversation between the three
of us concerning local understandings of will, freedom, and tradition—
which, I believe, is well worth sharing here. According to one of the
elders, the concept of "freedom" and "free will" *(puuf rogon u fithikag)*
is not a Yapese concept *(gaathii yalean nu Waqab)*. She believed that

the church and various colonial presences had introduced it to Yap. She added that even with the concept being used regularly in the context of everyday talk, "we are never free." In her estimation, there are always *matoochiyal* ("rules," "laws") and *yalean* ("traditions," "relationships") that restrict an individual's behavior. An individual is never able to do what he or she likes or wants at anytime he or she pleases. It was her position that day-to-day life in Yap is characterized by a lot of "pressure" to do what the community wants. In the final analysis, it is the community that comes before everything else. She acknowledged, however, that things have changed significantly from *kaakaroom* ("long ago") and that today there seemed to be a lot less *matoochiyal* ("rules," "laws") to live with.

That said, today people know that there are alternative ways to live. They are taught about different cultures in school, they read about them in magazines and books, and they see them in the movies they watch. It is, in her estimation, this access to different ways of living that has made the "pressure" and the need to "endure" the lack of freedom all the more difficult. She speculated that in the past people probably did not live with such "pressure." Living with *yalean* was not something that individuals had to "endure." Not knowing any alternatives, this was probably considered to be the way things were.

And yet, she maintained that even today it seems that perhaps the only true "freedom" or acts of "free will" are those occurring when an individual has to go to the restroom. She said that there is in fact an expression that is used on such occasions that translates literally as "my chief is calling" *(be pining ea piiluung roeg)*. When individuals say this phrase, others know that they have to excuse themselves and they are allowed to take leave of their responsibilities. As she explained, the power of this statement is rooted in the idea that when a chief calls upon a person, regardless of what that individual is doing, he or she should drop everything and go. I suggested to her that even this does not imply true freedom. While it may be freedom from social responsibilities, the individual is still being compelled to do something that does not necessarily accord with his or her will since the body is calling them to leave (an insight that both elders found quite amusing).

At this point, the second elder spoke up and said that while she largely understood what her friend was saying, she believes that there is indeed room for *puuf rogon* in the context of *yalean*. She argued that in her opinion, she has *puuf rogog* when she chooses whether or not to answer a question. In this light, she suggested that "freedom" lies in choosing the content and timing of what an individual will share—in terms of personal knowledge, thoughts, feelings and opinions—with others. Since no other person has access to an individual's *laen ii yaen'*, there is a sense of agency that is exerted by social actors in selectively disclosing information about one's self-experience to others. As she put it, "*Bayi'* time *ko puuf rogon*" ("There is a time for free will"). Or, as I might put it, *puuf rogon* is all about timing. She pointed out, for example, that she would seek out the advice of her grandmother, mother, or uncle at different times to talk about different problems. Often it was in the context of these very private face-to-face conversations with people who she trusted that she felt comfortable expressing her "true" feelings on a given matter. Being able to pick particular topics, times, and interlocutors for moments of self-disclosure was the basis for her sense of personal agency even within the confines of the strictures tied to those expected moral ways of being under the auspices of *yalean* (tradition).

CHAPTER 6

Yapese Configurations
of Pain and Suffering

Pain always has a specific language, whether it is a cry, a sob,
or a tensing of the features, and it is a language in itself as
well. As such, it is defined by society's standards of permis-
siveness or its notions of transgression, between what can be
shown or what must be kept quiet or hidden; these norms or
behavioural codes depend upon the cultural foundations of
the societies in which they arise.

Roselyne Rey, 1993

The ocean breeze and the slow rhythmic sound of breaking waves
seemed to have a calming effect on Ma'ar as we sat together in the
comfortable shade provided by his newly built rest house *(koeyeeng)*.
While he still winced when trying to readjust his body to get more
support for his back, he seemed much more at ease than he had been
when we met earlier that afternoon at his family's main house, which
was located much farther inland. He began speaking again while
holding the upper part of his leg for emphasis. "This is something
that I only use the word 'pain' *(amiith)*, that word 'pain,' but that is
not pain." Looking away for a moment, he seemed to be struggling
to find the right words. "Oh, there is pain in the midst . . . I, I
think that it is there in the midst of soreness and pain." And yet, he
conceded, "I don't know the name. But . . . there is something that I
call pain there."

In this chapter I discuss the ways in which experiences of pain are
culturally configured. This initially entails detailing how varieties of

pain are linguistically encoded, at the level of both lexical and grammatical representation. After briefly suggesting what may be interpreted as the initial contours for a Yapese grammar of suffering (see Capps and Ochs 1995; Ochs and Capps 2001), I examine how the conceptualization of pain is situated within the context of local understandings of subjectivity, social action, and morality discussed in previous chapters. In so doing, I argue that pain can either be a form of "mere-suffering," unwanted and without meaning, or it can be experienced as "suffering-for," transformed into a key cultural virtue that provides individuals with a moral connection to others. This translation of pain from an instance of mere-suffering to suffering-for will be illustrated through a particular example: how pain is often framed in light of a prevalent illness category termed *maath'keenil'*.

Perhaps the most basic conventionalized embodied expression of pain in Yap is the interjection *iii*, which is similar to "ouch." The general Yapese term for pain is *amiith*, a noun referring primarily to any noxious or dysphoric physical sensation. Through modifying the morpheme *amiith* with the third-person genitive (possessive) suffix *-uun*, the noun-phrase connector *ea*, and a possessor noun, phrases delineating differing varieties of pain associated with specific objects are represented linguistically. As Jensen (1977b, 188) observes, in Yapese a possessed noun followed by a noun phrase establishes a "construct construction" wherein "the second noun phrase expresses the possessors of the first (possessed) noun itself." For example, through adding the nominal morpheme *nifiy* ("fire") to the possessed noun phrase *amiithuun ea*, one is able to describe the feeling of pain due to fire *(amiithuun ea nifiy)*, literally "fire's pain." This configuration can be utilized to refer to pains associated with specific varieties of illness (e.g., *amiithuun ea gout*—"pain due to gout") or certain activities (e.g., *amiithuun ea gargeal*—"pain due to childbirth").

Possibilities for describing varieties of pain through genitive constructions are notable for the following reason. As Duranti and Ochs (1990, 5–6) have observed in the case of the usage of genitive constructions in Samoan, while genitive constructions "often express a relation of 'possession,' they express other participant roles as well." That is, it is possible for some languages to encode the agency of human participants through the use of genitives that refer, in a more oblique fashion, to the causative role of a human actor in relation to some perceived alteration in a particular property, state of affairs, or quality in the world

(1990, 15). In this light, it may very well be the case that the genitive construction of pain descriptors in Yapese provides a means for individuals to refer more obliquely to the causative role of a given object, phenomena, or state of affairs giving rise to a particular variety of pain. Such constructions may simultaneously background the subject's role as a person undergoing a painful experience. Indeed, there is no explicit grammatical indication of a suffering subject in such genitive constructions. At the level of discourse, at least, the various pain descriptors that can be employed through genitive constructions may thus serve to delimit such dysphoric experiences as separate, or at the very least separable, from a given experiencer.[1]

Yapese does not, relatively speaking, have an expansive vocabulary for differing types of pain (I managed to collect only thirty-four pain-related terms and phrases) (cf. Diller 1980). There are, in addition to the possible modifications of the morpheme *amiith*, however, still other linguistic vehicles through which experiences of pain, or experiences closely associated with it, are described and represented. For instance, the term *gaemiig* (which can also refer to electricity) is used primarily in reference to those various sensations that are associated with losing or regaining tactile sensation, including numbness and the feeling of "pins and needles." This same term, in its past-perfect third-person-singular rendering as *ke gaemiig*, is also at times used to refer to an experience of indescribable pain. As one individual pointed out to me, if someone frames their pain as *ke gaemiig* they are highlighting the fact that the pain is "just too much for words."

The term *galuuf,* which refers to a species of monitor lizard, also denotes pain associated with muscle cramps. This is perhaps a metaphorical reference to the tendency for a lizard's muscles to become paralyzed when it becomes too cold. *Alengeng* and *alengong* are dialectical variations of descriptors for pain associated with headaches, while the term *wup* refers to earaches. *Dilaek,* a term for spear, is further used to describe sharp pains located in the side of the torso or chest, stabbing pains in the side or stomach, as well as a type of chest pain often associated with coughing and loss of breath. Finally, *maal' giil'* ("barracuda" plus "its place, position, seat") metaphorically evokes the image of a barracuda and refers to a "sharp or unexpected pain."

In addition, there are at least four different terms and phrases that can be used to describe "burning pain." These include: the third-person-singular rendering of the intransitive verb *yik'* ("to burn"), for example, *ke yik'* ("it burns"); a suffixed-object-pronoun rendering of the transitive verb *urufeeg* ("to burn, to cook in fire"), for example, *ke urufeegeg* ("it is burning me"); *mithmiith,* a reduplicative morpheme referring to pain associated with sunburn or rubbing the skin; and finally, the phrase *be buul ea nifiey riy* that is used to signify "a pain like a growing fire."

Other pain terms include a handful of reduplicative morphemes that seem to capture some of the temporal and spatial qualities of particular types of pain through a combination of metaphorical extension, iconicity, and sound symbolism. The most prevalent of these terms include the following: *oeb oeb,* a reduplication of the intransitive verb *oeb* "to initiate," which in its reduplicative form means "aching or throbbing pain;" *yip yip* a reduplication of the transitive verb *yip* "to pierce, to sew, to shoot," which in its reduplicative form means "shooting or sharp pain;" *kuruuf kuruuf* a reduplication of the transitive verb *kuruuf* "to pierce through, or make a hole in" which in its reduplicative form means "piercing pain;" *k'aad k'aad* a reduplication of the transitive verb *k'aad* "to bite," which in its reduplicative form means "biting or stinging pain;" and finally, *m'uur m'uur* a reduplicative morpheme signifying "slippery, dull, toothache from eating too much acidic food."

Much like the case of genitive constructions, it is worth noting a possible significance for such reduplicative forms when employed as descriptors of pain states. According to Jensen (1977b, 114), one of the main functions of reduplication in the context of verbs that are also modified with the diminutive prefix *si-* is to express a meaning of "somewhat, a little bit" (e.g., *toey* and *sitoeytoey*—"to chop" and "to chop a little bit"). When employed in the context of adjectives, however, reduplication allows for an inchoative adjective, implying a process of becoming, to be transformed into an attributive adjective, implying a resulting state of affairs (e.g., *roow* and *roowroow*—"to become red" and "to have become red/to be red"). In the case of these pain descriptors I would argue that reduplication possibly serves still yet another purpose, one that highlights the temporal or repetitive quality of the sensations involved, and perhaps additionally the degree of their intensity. Both these temporal and intensive qualities are to some extent described metaphorically through the iconicity implicated in the morphophonemic structure of these various verbs. Indeed, as Geurts (2002, 77) notes in her work with Anlo-Ewe reduplicative morphemes in Ghana, one possible feature of reduplication lies in the creation of ideophones. Ideophones are morphemes whose meanings are at least partially predicated upon their onomatopoeic qualities. Such reduplicative forms, inasmuch as they can be considered ideophonic, may thus function "at a certain level to sensorially evoke that which they repre-sent" (Geurts 2002, 78).

These qualitative aspects of pain are not restricted to representation through reduplicative forms, however. Such qualities can further be captured through constructions that utilize both the stative tense-aspect marker *ba* and the indefinite article *ba*. Here, the former is utilized in order to describe the quality or spatial location of pain. For instance, it is possible to express deep pain through the phrase *ba amiith ni ba tooqaer* ("a pain that is deep"). The intensity of pain is often marked through a predicative adjectival verb phrase in which the stative tense-aspect marker *ba* is combined with inchoative adjectives such as *geel* ("to become strong") or *waer* ("to become weak"), the noun phrase connector *ea,* the noun *amiith,* and the impersonal pronoun *riy,* which often highlights location or the source of motion ("at it, from it"): for example, *ba geel ea amiith riy* ("there is strong or intense pain from it"). Finally, it is also possible to use a third-person descriptive verb, the noun-phrase connector *ea,* and the noun *amiith* to metaphorically describe a particular quality of pain (e.g., *be th'aeb ea amiith*—"it is cutting, the pain").

As will become evident in the remaining chapters, this Yapese grammar of suffering is organized in such a way that pain is rarely identified as coterminous with a given sufferer. In fact, in contrast to those constructions that describe various internal states through the quality or condition of *yaen'* ("mind or subjective experience"), many of which are rendered as verbs (e.g., *kug kirbaen'*—"I am sad"), gram-matical constructions utilized to describe or indicate pain are config-ured in such a way that pain is most typically designated as an object that has a certain distance from the subjective state of the sufferer. Interestingly, this is also quite different from those Yapese terms for other varieties of sensory experience, which are largely rendered verbs. There is a clear distinction in Yapese between those lexical items that mark active and passive phases of sensation, which take the form of either intransitive or transitive verbs, and those sensory objects that are perceived through these various sensory modalities, which are always nouns. For instance, in the case of visual perception there is:

guy (vt.) to see

changar (vi.) to look

yaqan (n.) image

In the case of auditory perception there is:

rungaqag (vt.) to hear

matooyil (vi.) to listen, to pay attention

lingan (n.) sound

In this light, it appears that *amiith* (n.) can be considered more comparable to an object of sensory perception than to a specific way or phase of sensing with or through the body.

One last observation concerning this sketch of the ways in which pain states are encoded linguistically is to point out that one of the most prevalent ways in which individuals refer to their pain in everyday interaction is simply to state *baaq amiith* ("there exists pain") or *kab ea amiith ngoog* ("pain came to me"). What is striking here is again the fact that pain is objectified, made tangible, and fashioned as an entity separate, or separable, from the self who is suffering with it. In the case of the former phrase, there is no mention of the suffering self at all. Instead, the construction, which combines the existential verb *baaq* and the noun *amiith*, simply highlights the existence of pain, without delineating its precise location or its relationship to a particular sufferer (although such utterances were often given a deictic center of an experiencing subject through other nonverbal contextual cues).

In the case of the latter, the experiencer is included in the utterance but is positioned in a passive role as an indirect object toward which the object transferred (*amiith*) is directed. Grammatically, this is accomplished through the use of the impersonal third-person perfect-tense rendering of the verb *yib* ("to come"), the noun *amiith*, the relational preposition *nga* ("to"), and the first person possessive pronoun suffix (*roog*), which when combined are morphemically transformed into *ngoog: ke yib ea amiith ngoog*. In this case then, the focus of the utterance is upon the presence and activity of pain that confronts an experiencer who is undergoing it or perhaps more accurately persevering in the face of it.

At first glance, it appears that the linguistic encoding of pain states in relationship to the somewhat passive experiencers who are undergoing them may contradict the previously articulated moral emphasis upon actively enduring through pain and suffering. While this is certainly one way to interpret this grammar of suffering (see Ochs and Capps 2001), these passive constructions may also be interpreted as a means by which to reconcile the at times competing ethical modalities of being entailed in the virtues of self-governance and suffering-for others. That is, in order for suffering-for others to be construed as virtuous, the experiences of suffering that any one particular individual undergoes must be recognized as authentic. To be authentic, suffering must not be the result of fabrication or exaggeration on the part of the experiencer. In constructing pain as a definite object that is affecting a somewhat passive experiencer, these passive constructions are able to configure pain into just such an authentic form of dysphoric experience. Moreover, a further purpose underlying these constructions may be tied to a speaker's attempts to mitigate statements concerning his or her experience of pain and suffering, which, when directly uttered in a first-person form, breach the virtue of self-governance and its associated restrictions on the first-person expression of internal states.

Mere-Suffering versus Suffering-For

> When one endures suffering, one does so to serve a larger purpose and not because suffering itself is sought out.
>
> Erich H. Lowey, 1991

A significant goal of this book is to explore the ways in which dysphoric experiences like pain can be differentially articulated as meaningful morally valenced experiences, on the one hand, and as fundamentally disjunctive, "world-destroying" experiences on the other. I argue that one of the primary routes through which such a configuration is affected is through providing a framework within which pain, experienced in its immediacy as mere-suffering, is effectively transformed into an experience of suffering-for. As Lowey argues, citing Victor Frankl, it is possible for experiences of pain to "cease to be true suffering when they subserve a person's greater goal and become meaningful" (1991, 3).

It is important to note that for this reason, many scholars have sought to make a careful distinction between pain and suffering (see Lowey 1991; Glucklich 2001). As Glucklich (2001, 11) makes clear, where pain is "a sensation that is tangled with mental and even cultural experiences" and is not always negatively valenced, suffering "in contrast, is not a sensation but an emotional and evaluative reaction to any number of causes, some entirely painless." According to Glucklich and Lowey, suffering, unlike pain, is intrinsically a negatively formulated experience. In making a distinction between mere-suffering and suffering-for, however, I wish to point to the fact that not only pain but also suffering may be cast in a more positive light. As Emmanuel Levinas (1998) also argues, the experience of another's suffering can provide an existential basis for an ethics of mutual recognition. According to Levinas,

There is a radical difference between *the suffering in the other,* where it is unforgivable to *me,* solicits me and calls me, and suffering *in me,* my own experience of suffering, whose constitutional or congenital uselessness can take on a meaning, the only one of which suffering is capable, in becoming a suffering for the suffering (inexorable though it may be) of someone else. It is this attention to the suffering of the other that . . . can be affirmed as the very nexus of human subjectivity, to the point of being raised to the level of supreme ethical principle—the only one it is impossible to question." (1998, 94)

While Levinas suggests that a suffering for the unassumable suffering of another may be an effective catalyst for transforming "useless suffering" into a meaningful and morally valenced experience (see the conclusion), I wish to further advance an argument for the significance of temporality in effecting such a transformation. Briefly stated, the process of fashioning pain into a meaningful experience, that is, transforming it from an instance of mere-suffering to one of suffering-for, is, I suggest, deeply implicated in the ability to temporalize those qualities and sensations that make up such dysphoric experiences so that they stretch beyond the confines of the "longstanding now" of a present moment saturated with pain (see Hellström and Carlsson 1996; Honkasalo 1999, 2000). This temporal stretching is at least partially accomplished through an articulation of ongoing painful sensations with possible images, tendencies, feelings, emotions, and moods that may connect what would otherwise be discrete instances of pain to a double-edged horizon of delimited pasts and possible futures.

Of course, in speaking of the transformation of mere-suffering to suffering-for, it is not enough that dysphoric experiences simply be situated in time. As Lowey notes, the very ability to suffer is at least partially predicated upon "an appreciation of past, present, and future as connected" (1991, 12). And yet, it is very much an ability to extend one's temporal horizons beyond the confines of the present moment of pain that gives rise to possibilities for understanding one's dysphoric experience as undergone or suffered through in light of some broader purpose or goal.

A key way in which this transformation may occur, I argue, is through a process of transitivizing dysphoric experiences through imbuing them with an intentional (in the Husserlian sense of the term as consciousness directed toward an intentional object; see Husserl [1900/01] 2001) "-for" structure. The significance of transitivizing experiences of pain is made all the more compelling given what many philosophers have held to be the nonintentional structure of pain states. For instance, as Scarry asserts,

Physical pain is exceptional in the whole fabric of psychic, somatic, and perceptual states for being the only one that has no object. Though the capacity to experience physical pain is as primal a fact about the human being as is the capacity to hear, to touch, to desire, to fear, to hunger, it differs from these events, and from every other bodily and psychic event, by not having an object in the external world. Hearing and touch are of objects outside the boundaries of the body, as desire is desire of x, fear is fear of y, hunger is hunger for z; but pain is not "of" or "for" anything—it is itself alone. This objectlessness, the complete absence of referential content, almost prevents it from being rendered in language; objectless, it cannot easily be objectified in any form, material or verbal. (1985, 161–62)

Scarry's view of the "objectlessness" of pain is echoed in Levinas's characterization of suffering as a "*datum* in consciousness" that evidences "unassumability." In Levinas's words, suffering

is not only the consciousness of rejection or a symptom of rejection, but this rejection itself: a backward consciousness, "operating" not as "grasp" but as revulsion. A modality. The categorical ambiguity of quality and modality. The denial and refusal of meaning, thrusting itself forward as a sensible quality: that is, in the guise of "experienced" content, the *way* in which, within a consciousness, the unbearable is precisely not borne, the manner of this not-being-borne; which, paradoxically, is itself a sensation or a datum. . . . Contradiction *qua* sensation: the ache of pain—woe. (1998, 91–92)

In the context of ethical modes of being in Yap, it is when pain is understood to arise or result from an individual's efforts to provide for, contribute to, and help his or her family, village, or community that sensations of pain are able to be actively oriented toward an intentional object. Imbued with a -for structure that emplaces pain within local moral sensibilities and models of virtuous comportment, such dysphoric experiences are made significant, valuable, and meaningful. It is notable in this regard that the connection between pain, suffering, endurance, and work, which lies at the heart of Yapese articulations of ethical modalities of being, significantly resonates with Scarry's insights into the general phenomenological relationship between pain and work (cf. M. J. Good 1992; Trnka 2007, 2008). According to Scarry, the activity entailed in work does, "under all circumstances, and regardless of whether it is primarily physical or mental labor, entail the much more moderate (and now willed, directed, and controlled) embodied aversiveness of exertion, prolonged effort, and exhaustion. It hurts to work. Thus, the wholly passive and acute suffering of physical pain becomes the self-regulated and modest suffering of work. Work is, then, a diminution of pain: the *aversive intensity* of pain becomes in work *controlled discomfort"* (1985, 170–71).

Once transitivized as a form of "controlled discomfort," the temporal structure of suffering-for can be compared with phenomenological characterizations of the temporal structure embedded in the experience of hope (Crapanzano 2003). Drawing from Minkowski (1970), Heidegger (1996), and others, Crapanzano (2003, 9) observes that in the phenomenological tradition hope is described as oriented to what Minkowski terms the "mediate future."[2] Poised between the immediate future of expectation and action and the remote future of prayer and ethical activity, hope is held to open for a given experiencer an as of yet unrealized future. Such a future is experienced as just beyond the grasp of the extending tendrils of expectation that suffuse the immediacy of all present moments. In Heideggerian terms, Crapanzano argues that hope can be tied to care *(sorge)*, which is based upon an experience that "something is still outstanding" (2003, 9). There is, therefore, a quality of transcendence that is invested in hope, which as Minkowski asserts, "separates us from immediate contact with ambient becoming: it suppresses the embrace of expectation and permits me to look freely, far into lived space which now opens before me" (1970, 100; cited in Crapanzano 2003, 9). Thus through hope, as Crapanzano summarizes, individuals are "put into contact with a becoming that is unfolding at a distance" (2003, 9). The mediate future of hope can be contrasted with the atrophied futurity that is held to be characteristic of despair and hopelessness. And yet, as Crapanzano argues, despair is rarely divested of temporality since there are still often possibilities for "hope-in-hopelessness."

I believe the temporal structure that is evident in experiences of suffering-for is perhaps best understood as shifting between the mediate futurity that Minkowski characterizes as entailed in hope and the more distal future he attributes to prayer. Moreover, unlike these phenomenological and existential renderings of hope, I would argue that suffering-for is deeply implicated in both distal and proximate pasts, which reach back from the immediate unfolding of the present moment.

It is significant in this regard that the Yapese term that can be most closely rendered as "hope" is *athapaag,* a term that is closely connected with *athamagil.* Indeed, the morpheme *aath* is used in both, and both implicate an orientation to an anticipated future. A key difference between the two terms may be understood in light of what is largely the former's dissociation from practical action, and the latter's embeddedness in ongoing and eventuating activity. As I hope to examine throughout the remaining chapters of this book, it was often a social actor's attempts to endure or *athamagil* that served to imbue suffering with a –for structure.

On Transitivizing Dysphoric Experience: The Case of *Maath'keenil'*

In Yap, an important means through which mere-suffering may be transformed into suffering-for is through designating certain experiences of pain as resulting from work-based illnesses. By situating pain in the context of such illnesses, pain is construed as an indication that a given social actor is approximating the virtues of effortful exertion *(magaer),* perseverance *(athamagil),* and suffering *(gaafgow)* on behalf of others. Generally speaking, in Yapese medical theory experiences of pain *(amiith)* play a significant role in diagnosing an illness's etiology. For instance, pain can supply a diagnostician with an indication of those somatic regions (sometimes occluded from direct view) in which a particular illness is located. This is especially significant given the close connection that exists between particular medicines and specific organs or regions of the body. Moreover, pain also figures prominently in determinations of the efficacy of a particular treatment. Indeed, one of the first signs that a medicine or form of treatment is working properly is held to be found in those instances where pain initially *increases* (sometimes dramatically) in its intensity, before gradually beginning to fade. Many people I spoke to about this idea maintained that a pain that remains unchanged or even initially decreases in intensity after a medicine is administered provides evidence that the medicine or treatment being utilized is *not* effective.

Significantly, pain may also be etiologically and diagnostically linked to work-based activities. One of the most prevalent illness categories in this regard is an illness termed *maath'keenil'*.[3] Quite literally, *maath'keenil'* can be translated as "severed spine," for *maath'* is an adjective that denotes something that has been severed, separated, or cut loose, while the noun *keenil'* refers to the spine or backbone (as well as to a midrib of a leaf or the main stem of a vine; Jensen 1977a). *Maath'keenil'*, however, is an illness category that encompasses a broad range of symptoms, all of which are linked to a common etiological source stemming from hard work. *Maath'keenil'* refers to any illness or painful condition that is caused by an individual's excessive effort *(magear)* or labor *(maruweel)*. As one local healer explained to me, *maath'keenil'* is perhaps the most prevalent illness in Yap. Moreover, while each person who is afflicted with *maath'keenil'* suffers with a different set of symptoms, most share "pain inside the body" *(amiith u fithik ii doowey)*, as well as feelings of weakness *(waer)*. In his estimation, this constellation of pain and weakness is due to a problem with the "veins" or "nerves" *(gaaf)* in the spine that have become damaged through the strain associated with hard work.

It seems fitting that there is also understood to be a relationship between *maath'keenil'* and *magaer*, inasmuch as the latter can be understood as an attenuated version of the former. Given this association, it is possible to think of *maath'keenil'* and *magaer* as representing two ends of the same positively valenced moral continuum wherein hard work, effort, and service are held to have a tangible impact upon an individual's body and sensorium. While the sensations of pain and weakness implicated in both *maath'keenil'* and *magaer* are certainly most often experienced as dysphoric (*maath'keenil'* is held to be an illness after all), they are also imbued with a definite moral valence.

To the extent that an individual's actions—framed in terms of effort and work undertaken in the service of family, estate, village, or community needs—are seen as the generative source for experiences of *amiith*, individuals are able to interpret their pain as a virtuous form of sacrifice or what I am terming here suffering-for. In other words, by adding a -for structure to their suffering, individuals are framing their effort and labor as undertaken for the benefit of another. In so doing, personal subjectivities are aligned with a temporality that positions them between a past defined in terms of commitment to those ancestors who previously worked the land, a present predicated upon continuing service to and respect for those contemporaries who currently hold title to that land, and a future in which obligations to those of a higher status are to be eventually fulfilled.

To the extent that effortful service, endurance, and work play a prominent role in defining local understandings of ethical modalities of being, as well as being implicated in local understandings of disease etiology, it is not surprising that there is also a significant link between illness *(m'aar)*, laziness *(malmaal)*, and an inability to withstand hardship or adversity. This connection is perhaps most clearly crystallized in the concept of *muudul* ("the inability to suffer pain or to endure illness"). Significantly, the term *muudul* is also used to indicate that an individual is lazy *(malmaal)*. This is so particularly in the context of referring to persons who claim to be sick when they are in fact healthy in order to get out of doing work. As such, laziness *(malmaal)* is saturated with moral overtones. Often, a negative moral significance is tied to the belief that individuals abstaining from work on account of illness are perhaps enacting some resistance to community obligations. Alternatively, they may be voicing their displeasure with a given state of affairs or the state of a given relationship.

There is indeed a lot of discussion and gossip whenever someone claims to be ill or in pain and is not participating in community work projects. Much of this talk focuses on questions of whether or not an individual is truly suffering with some affliction, is merely lazy, or is perhaps more accurately angry with the rest of the community. Illness and pain can thus be used simultaneously to highlight an individual's moral worth through demonstrating that he or she is willing to endure through suffering for community betterment, as a means to engender feelings of compassion and care in another individual who is not ill or in pain, as evidence for "laziness," as a means to resist community obligations, or as a way to voice dissention.

Again, it is important to recall that the structure of Yapese understandings of ethical conduct and experience is such that an individual of higher status who is made aware of another's suffering is ideally led to feel compassion *(runguy)*, the suffering-for another who is in fact suffering on their behalf. It is the very mutuality embedded in the –for structure of these two varieties of suffering that enables the constitution and maintenance of social relations (e.g., the ties within *[m'aag]* or between *[thaaq]* particular estates). Here then, those feelings associated with, as well as the expressions of, suffering are always mediated through a third, the individual or constellation of individuals for whom a particular social actor is suffering-for.

M'aar Roog: Pain, Idioms of Distress, and Somatization

One observation I noted early in my fieldwork concerned what seemed to be, at times, a willingness on the part of people to talk about their pain, illness, and physical suffering, while remaining reluctant to speak about other types of personal problems. This was particularly the case in terms of those problems associated with what North American folk models might categorize as instances of psychological suffering.

The director of the Yap Institute of Natural Science, Marjorie Falanruw, once remarked to me that *m'aar roog* ("my illness") is an extremely prevalent topic in everyday talk and interaction. The extent to which illness and physical ailments provide an acceptable idiom of distress when compared to more "psychological" modes of complaint certainly raises the possibility of somatization (see Kleinman and Kleinman 1991; White 1982). It seems to me, however, that in most cases the pervasiveness of *m'aar roog* and the relative ease with which people were willing to talk about physical illnesses is not in fact evidence for somatization strictly speaking; that is, the unconscious translation or misinterpretation of psychical ailments for somatic ones. While this is not to say that somatization does not occur in Yap, I believe that the somatic basis for idioms of distress is often enacted in a fairly self-conscious manner. This is so since such idioms are rooted in a cultural orientation to suffering in which there are times when expressing physical suffering has concrete value. This can be sharply contrasted with the expression of psychical suffering, which is almost always construed to be a mark of failing to live up to ideals associated with moral ways of experiencing and acting in the world.

I believe that the relative ease with which individuals were prepared to talk about their physical illnesses when compared to psychological forms of suffering may be connected to two key values. First, there is the valuing of privacy that is concretely realized in the general tendency for individuals not to share their innermost feelings, thoughts, emotions, or desires with others (see chapter 5). Second, there is the prioritizing of mental capacities over somatic ones, an orientation that is expressed in the privileging of thinking, deliberating, ruminating, and contemplating in opposition to unreflective action (see chapter 4). Indeed, these two values are understood to be mutually supportive in as much as the cultivation of mental capacities associated with deliberate, reflective action is what enables individuals to develop a refined self-mastery over their forms of expressivity. All of which helps to

ensure privacy, as individuals are able to manage their expressiveness
in such ways as to engender mental opacity and communicative ambiguity with their interlocutors. It is often for this reason that strength
of mind is considered to be such a central value in Yapese moral evaluations of personhood. In light of this, the direct, unthinking expression
of an individual's feelings, emotions, and thoughts is correspondingly
devalued, a fact that marks the overt expression of emotional or psychical problems with a definite negative moral valence.

An unwillingness to express what may otherwise be deemed to be
psychological forms of suffering may thus be interpreted as resulting
from the fact that psychical suffering evidences an individual's inability
to enact a mentally refined form of "self-governance." A question still
remains, however, as to what sets of cultural values underpin the more
prevalent, occasionally overt, expression of an individual's physical illnesses and pain in the context of social interaction. It seems that one
way to understand the persistence of this somatic idiom of distress is
in terms of the set of cultural values directly implicated in the virtue of
suffering (gaafgow) more generally, and its relationship to humility
(soobuutaen') and the power dynamics of interpersonal relations
more specifically.

It is quite significant that gaafgow is often characterized in terms of
its opposition to ufaanthiin ("negative pride"). This is because suffering
is connected to the cultivation of humility. More specifically, it is important to recall how the interplay between gaafgow and compassion
(runguy) is played out on a number of levels in Yapese social life, and
how humility is considered to be deeply implicated in presenting a
respectful (liyoer) stance toward others. As detailed in earlier chapters,
a person of higher status (e.g., high caste, men, parents, elder siblings)
is ideally to feel runguy for individuals of lower status (e.g., low caste,
women, children, younger siblings). The demonstration of runguy is
enacted through providing those of lesser status with food, help, shelter,
and access to land and knowledge. In return, those occupying such lower
statuses are to show respect to those of higher status. A means by which
to show such respect is through undergoing suffering: mental, physical,
material, and otherwise. Talk of suffering can thus often be construed
as a communicative strategy to demonstrate respect. Suffering as a form
of honorifics thus foregrounds the humility of the speaker as it places
them in a position of dependency in relationship to the hearer.

As discussed above, people often recognized further rhetorical uses
of illness and pain by individuals who wished to get out of previous

commitments to others or to avoid work. The value of *gaafgow* in connection to the expression of one's suffering through illness and pain, however, may be viewed in light of the important value that is placed on defeating adversity, in facing suffering head on and enduring it. This is a set of values that we have seen to be embedded in the virtue of endurance *(athamagil)*. Individual readiness to talk to others about illnesses and physical pain, I suggest, is thus embedded in attempts to demonstrate that in the face of physical suffering an individual is still persevering and working despite hardship. In so doing, individuals are able to align themselves with three key Yapese virtues: (1) prioritizing psychical over somatic processes; (2) expressing humility through actively working to downplay one's well-being and good fortune; and (3) enduring in the face of suffering—*athamagil*.

Moreover, it is significant that it is the very interplay between suffering and endurance that provides social actors with an accepted means of striving to better their own, their families', or their communities' social position, without the danger of awakening envy *(awaen')* in others. That is, if an individual is seen to be succeeding without suffering or facing obstacles, then it is always possible that they might be seen to be getting ahead at another's expense (another who would be construed to be suffering on their behalf). In so doing, an individual always faces the risk of being faulted for being greedy or selfish, and is further open to the potential deleterious effects that come along with being the target of another's envy (cf. Groark 2008). In the face of suffering, however, ambition can be rarified through its transformation into endurance and effort, both positive qualities encapsulated in the concept of *athamagil*. As such, a principal means through which individuals are able to establish that they are suffering through their various efforts is through the idiom of physical ailments, illness, and pain. Suffering is thus one significant means by which to downplay success.

This is, of course, not an attempt to argue that talk of physical illnesses and pain is merely a rhetorical strategy or that it does not indicate the existence of serious afflictions that have at times devastating effects on individual lives. And yet, it is also true that such a configuration of cultural virtues is certainly at times ripe for strategic manipulation by those who are ambitious and insightful enough to find ways in which to pursue their goals in a fashion that is valued by the community.

It is indeed interesting to think further about the logic of these virtues and their relationship to well-being, and whether or not such a concept can be truly understood as a value in the Yapese context. While it is certainly hard to believe that an individual's well-being would not be valued in some very important ways, it is also true that to be well is to be devoid of suffering. And to be devoid of suffering is to put oneself at risk for being seen to be *ufaanthiin* ("negatively prideful"), *toelaengaen'* ("high minded or arrogant"), and *fal'ngaak* ("selfish"). As one elder from the municipality of Maap explained to me, a significant problem with feeling contentment or happiness *(falfalaen')* is that an individual will not directly experience *gaafgow u fithik ea dooway* ("suffering inside the body"). An individual who is happy is not attuned to the suffering of others. He or she is thus not feeling *runguy* for others who are suffering on their behalf. In this way, contentment and happiness, while subjective states that are valued and sought after, are also at times negatively cast as a potential barrier to engendering feelings of compassion toward those others in the community who are suffering. One of the key assumptions in this regard being that if an individual is happy and content he or she is not focused on the well-being of others, but solely upon his or her own success and comfort. In the face of suffering for another's suffering there is little space for feelings of contentment.

Additionally, it seems that another negative quality associated with happiness is the fact that it is understood to be a subjective state in which an individual is no longer oriented to the future. By comparison, suffering, its avoidance, and suffering-for the benefit of others is tied to planning and thinking through what can be done in the present in the service of bettering one's position (e.g., one's access to food, status, etc.) in the future. There is a future orientation embedded in local understandings of suffering, as well as an emphasis on its moral worth. This orientation to the future, I would add, implicates suffering-for within the phenomenological structure of hope previously discussed.

The very motivation for helping others and for caring and sympathizing with others is held to be directly rooted in an individual's own experience of *gaafgow*. Suffering is therefore virtuous to the extent that it is understood to help orient social actors to future horizons of possibility. In so doing the experience of suffering provides individuals with motivation to better their own, their families', and their communities' positions. Moreover, suffering engenders a stance toward others grounded in compassion. As collectively undergone in community work projects, suffering also provides a means to sediment attachment to others within one's community by means of generating experiences of collective pain *(amiithuun ea binaew)*. All of which prepares individuals to act in accordance with Yapese understandings of ethical modalities of being.

Again, my intention here is not to claim that people who assert to be suffering from physical ailments are not truly suffering from pain or illness. Instead, the point I am trying to advance concerns the notion that illness and pain, which certainly have serious and palpable impacts upon the lives of individual sufferers, can also be, often simultaneously, rhetorically exploited for other means. Suffering may thus present an opportunity for sufferers to highlight their abilities for self-governance. This is the case inasmuch as suffering provides individuals with an occasion to demonstrate to others their strength of mind and their ability to discipline their bodies.

It might seem counterintuitive to suggest that in a community where the capacity to control the body holds such a prominent cultural value, acknowledging physical suffering, pain, or illness can still be linked to virtue. It is important to recognize, however, the fact that it is only in the face of suffering that strength of mind and effective self-governance can be actively realized. Virtue is understood to be rooted in the capacity for an individual to push forward even despite the fact that his or her body is suffering with pain or illness. Without suffering there is no reason for perseverance. And without perseverance an individual's moral worth is never put to the test. This fact also resonates with ambivalent attitudes toward happiness and well-being.

As I will explore in much greater detail in the next chapter—a chapter devoted to investigating the particular ways that individual sufferers sought to reflect upon and narrate past experiences of living with pain—I believe that in talking about physical suffering individuals are often able to fulfill both personal and cultural needs simultaneously. That is, they are able, through their talk of suffering, to make an emotional connection with their interlocutors, while simultaneously marking their suffering as virtuous. Upon hearing of another's suffering, an individual is predisposed to take the stance of a caring and compassionate other. While the content of talk may be presented in a somatic idiom, to the extent that an individual's suffering is also rooted in emotional or psychical pain, an individual is thus afforded a means through which to express, albeit obliquely, such suffering. Moreover, an individual is able to further approximate another important cultural virtue, that of humility (*soobuutaen'*) and respect (*liyoer*) toward another. Such talk is thus not necessarily tied to the misrecognition of psychical suffering for physical suffering on the part of the sufferer (e.g., somatization in the classical sense) but is instead an often recognized way in which to obliquely communicate emotional suffering through morally acceptable somatic means.

Of course, the rhetoric of such talk of suffering may also be used for less beneficent motives. For instance, it was not uncommon at times to witness forms of one-upmanship in the expression of suffering, a competition of sorts in which interlocutors used their suffering as a means to strategically orchestrate the dynamics of a given relationship. As was discussed in earlier chapters, this same tendency was apparent in the context of traditional exchanges or *mitmiit*, as well as in contemporary funeral exchanges. In these situations individuals who gave large gifts to others would verbally attempt to drastically downplay the value of the gift. For example, there were many stories of a person or a family giving fifty or more cases of beer or liquor in the context of an exchange, traditional apology, or funeral, while saying at the time of the presentation that they were merely giving a single beer or bottle of rum. In these instances, the obvious incommensurability of talk and action was used in order to demonstrate respect through humility. All of this occurred in the midst of what was also considered to be a strategic maneuver to competitively gain status.

In more mundane interactions, where there are no physical goods exchanged, there are other possibilities for similar attention to the role of honorific expressions in negotiating social relationships. In this case, however, it is in the form of a suffering-based humility (cf. Irvine 1990). In the context of my interviews, for instance, the most emotionally charged expressions of suffering almost always elicited from my research assistants talk of their own suffering. The desire to share their suffering, I believe, was at least partially a means to avoid being seen as attempting to take on the position of a higher-status person in the context of the interaction. If they had chosen instead to sit silently without speaking of their own suffering when listening to the suffering of another, they would have thus been understood to be taking on the role of a compassionate, and higher-status, listener. For this reason, talk of suffering must be understood as always potentially evocative of experiential, interpersonal, and political truths, sometimes simultaneously so.

CHAPTER 7

Stories Told

There is, in fact, a great deal more . . . than mundane pain in
living close to the land. There are the perennial cuts and
bruises of the day's work, the hands and ankles mangled in
working with wood and stone, the raw chapped hands of the
winter, the blackflies and mosquitoes of the summer, the
joints aching with dampness in the spring and fall. . . . It is
not that pain hurts less here. It does not, nor do wounds
reopened by the strain of continued work heal more quickly.
The pain simply matters less. There is so much more that
matters. When humans no longer think themselves the
measure of all things, their pain is no longer a cosmic
catastrophe. It becomes part of a greater whole.

Erazim Kohák, 1984

In this chapter I will explore largely retrospective narratives of pain that
I collected from eight of the thirty individuals I interviewed for this
project. I have chosen to focus upon the narratives of these particular
individuals because I believe that they represent a range of variation in
orientations to acts of narratively configuring past and ongoing experiences of pain. This range is also evident throughout the interviews that
are not drawn upon in the context of this chapter. Moreover, I believe
that in order to get a sense of the place of pain in the lives of particular
sufferers that we are better served by exploring in greater detail the
narratives of a few people rather than drawing more selectively from a
larger number of individuals.

In transcribing and working through the interviews I conducted for this project, it became increasingly evident that a large majority of individuals I spoke to cast their experiences of pain within moral frameworks that are shaped according to a constellation of virtues associated with hard work, effort, and endurance. Of course, individuals were not equally able or willing to align their pain with local ethical modalities of being. Nor were they equally capable of navigating the tensions embedded in the at times competing, at times complementary, orientations to the virtues of "self-governance" and "suffering-for."

There is, as Douglas Hollan notes (personal communication; see also Hollan 2000, 2001, 2008), a tendency for much of anthropological theorizing and research to flatten out the complexities of an individual's lived experience by focusing too much attention on putatively shared cultural models, narratives, tropes, and idioms. That said, an important aim of this chapter is to demonstrate the prevalence of themes of work, effort, endurance, and perseverance as a central nexus of significance giving shape to individuals' experiences of pain. In so doing, I hope to avoid portraying a featureless rendering of sufferers' narratives. I also hope to avoid presenting an account of their suffering that obscures the ultimate unassumability and nonsubstitutability of their lived experience (see the conclusion; Levinas 1998). Accordingly, I will highlight where possible some of the unique ways in which individuals personalized cultural materials in formulating their experiences of pain and suffering. I will also attempt to make note of those moments wherein the impenetrability of their self-experience is evident in the silences, gaps, and elisions imbricated throughout their narrative recollections (Levinas 1998; see also Das 2007).

It is true, I believe, that the significance of pain in light of local moral modalities of being provide individual sufferers with a set of inherited cultural tropes. These tropes often help individual sufferers to formulate narratives that give meaning to what may in its immediacy, intensity, and uncompromising viscerality be experiences of pain and suffering that actively resist such meaningful elaboration. A central theme to be explored in this chapter therefore is an examination of the extent to which certain cultural tropes may readily serve as possible preunderstandings (Gadamer 1975) that resonate with a particular individual's lived experience of pain. In addition, I will seek to investigate the extent to which such preunderstandings may give meaningful form to what are otherwise unformulated "world-destroying" experiences.

In seeking to highlight the gradated range of experiences arrayed between unformulated and formulated configurations of pain, I hope to shed some light on those marginal varieties of experience that are unfortunately all too often ignored when anthropologists turn to discuss the cultural patterning of subjective life and social action (see the introduction).

While concerns for anonymity have constrained some of the personal details I am able to discuss in this chapter, I hope that the information I have provided will adequately illustrate the power of such tropes in giving meaningful coherence to retrospectively cast narratives of suffering and pain. Such narratives also highlight the extent to which individuals often struggle through time to personalize such inherited preunderstandings. That said, a central goal of this chapter is to demonstrate the extent to which a temporal orientation to past experiences of pain often provides a means for suffering to be configured in terms of more coherent varieties of experience. Moreover, I also wish to highlight the variety of ways in which pain can still obdurately resist such attempts at narrative configuration, thus remaining even within retrospection's distancing glance of attention, a largely disjunctive variety of experience.

Tina: A Life of Suffering and Perseverance

Tina was an affable woman in her early sixties who was suffering with chronic pain in her knees, hands, and back. The eldest of five siblings, she was born in a mid-caste village and later married into a village of comparable rank. After marriage she had given birth to and raised four children. Tina and I knew each other quite well. I consistently found her to be kind, talkative, and quite comfortable interacting with others. Tina evidenced a strength of character and conviction that comes with age and experience. She enjoyed gossiping as much as anyone that I knew. While she was certainly aware of the risks associated with expressing her dislike of others, she often did not hesitate to subtly, and sometimes not so subtly, let her opinions and feelings be known when around people she knew and trusted. Accordingly, many of her friends and family believed that Tina was often too emotional and at times too direct in the way that she expressed herself to others. To this extent, Tina's personality was often at odds with expectations for emotional quietude implicated in the virtue of self-governance.

As I observed firsthand, and as she admitted to me on many occasions, Tina was also known for having a quick temper. Her predisposition to becoming angry was referred to with the borrowed English phrase "high blood." While she often tried to downplay her intelligence, often pointing to the fact that she never went to high school, I found Tina to be extremely bright, curious, and always interested in learning new things. Moreover, many people held her in high esteem because of her knowledge of *yalean* ("tradition").

In talking about her childhood, Tina was quick to focus on the suffering that she and her family endured. Her family was poor; they had no car and few amenities. To make matters worse, for as far back as she could remember, Tina's mother was extremely ill. Upon returning home from school, Tina devoted much of her time to taking care of her younger siblings, as well as procuring and preparing the medicines her mother needed to treat her illness. All of this, she believed, contributed to her failing third grade. To make matters worse, Tina's mother could not deal with any type of intense emotion. This was because such experiences would cause her to have an extreme shortness of breath *(matunguufaan)*. Overall, Tina recalled her childhood as a time when she had to take on great responsibility and hard work. She had to constantly monitor herself and her siblings to ensure that they did not do anything to make their mother's condition worse. Given the extent of her emotional expressiveness and her "high blood," I imagine that this must have been quite difficult for Tina. In her words:

There was a lot of suffering because my mind was suffering *[muug gaafgow kireeb ea taafinay roog]*. During the time between grade two and four, I knew very little English, I had no clothes [laughs], no clothes. When the morning came . . . some days she [my mother] would be so sick, she would take medicine, I would get medicine, so, maybe I would have to go far [to find it] . . . when her shortness of breath would come, medicine would be given. When mother was happy it [her illness] was bad, when she was angry it was bad, if it was really hot, or if coldness came, either persisting or arriving anew, it was really hard. So I was suffering *[Ere gage gub gaafgow]*.

Tina described this period of her life as a time when she was often only able to eat chestnut, taro, and coconut *(ggaan)*, since there was seldom any fish or meat *(thum'aeg)* in the house. Because her mother was sick and her father was often drunk there were many days when she would return home to find that no food had been prepared. On those days she and her siblings would be left to fend for themselves, often only with coconut to eat. The intensity with which she still felt these experiences was evident as she continued.

I was always . . . very sad and I felt . . . if I stayed . . . I stayed and sadness came to my mind, my father was drunk, my mother was always sick, I would go to school, [I had] no or very few clothes, no shoes . . . no clothes mmm—some days I would go and sleep and at night I would cry . . . I was crying because . . . wait I am going to cry [silent for a few seconds while she attempts to hold back her tears] . . . I was crying because . . . I was . . . I knew that my mother was sick. So I saw my very sick mother, I knew what would happen tomorrow, there would be no food, no fish or meat when I went to school, no clothes, my clothes were dirty, so I stayed . . . if I would go play, I would go play but my mind . . . I remained very sad.

Even when she was finally finished with her schooling, Tina stayed for a number of years at her natal village working to help her brothers and sisters and to take care of her sick mother. "Ummm, I was always helping children, my brothers and sisters, and I was always helping my mother by working for them. That was really hard work I did back then, staying with children, my mother, and four of her children. Ummmm . . . four of her children, but she was sick and there were four of her children."

While this was a difficult time for Tina, things did not improve much, if at all, after getting married and moving to her husband's village where she give birth to her own children. Once again, she was faced with hard work and suffering. So much so that she sums up her life to date as a life that was thoroughly rooted in *gaafgow:* "Yes, perhaps, that is how my life is, I, I was suffering. Long ago when I was small I was always suffering, I was suffering, I was suffering, I became an old woman [laughing] I was suffering . . . ooh! There are some people who have good houses, lots of food, lots of money, lots of fish and meat, but I, all the time I was suffering, I was small and suffering, suffering."

Turning to a more explicit discussion of her experience of pain, she explained that she has suffered with back pain for at least ten years. She has had pain in her joints (particularly in her hands) for the past five years. In the last year the pain in her hands became so bad that it was hard for her to pick up heavy objects and she was no longer able to cut open and prepare coconuts. Tina has also been suffering with longstanding pain in her left knee, which was visibly swollen and mis-shapen. This is a pain that she renders grammatically with the impersonal stative-tense marker *ba—ba amiith!* With regard to the latter,

My knee stays very swollen, perhaps it goes . . . two years or one year and a bit the swelling has increased and stayed constant, it stays swollen. I cannot get heavy things, I cannot go around on my knees while I am cleaning. I drop heavy things because of my knee, there is a pain *[ba amiith]*, such pain in my knee and I cannot tell [you] how and then there if there is pain in my back . . . right now there are a lot of problems, a lot of illness.

Recalling how her knee was originally injured, she recounted a time when she was out gardening and was carrying an especially heavy load of food back to her house to feed her children and her husband.

A very long time ago I was gardening during that time . . . I don't know what happened exactly, I went to go and I dropped to the ground, I dropped with one knee on the ground while the other stayed crooked . . . so I stayed . . . I stayed in the path in the rain . . . *iii* [the Yapese equivalent of the English interjection *ouch*] . . . tears were falling from my face because there was pain and pain *iii* . . . I was getting hungry so that is the reason I tried to stand up but I could not . . . something cracked, something or other made a cracking sound. Because there was pain, there was pain and tears there.

Before continuing with Tina's narrative, it is important to note here what appears to be the interweaving of two different ethical modalities of being in this particular passage. On the one hand, there is a fairly explicit understanding of the cause of her pain as resulting from her working in the gardens to procure food for her family. This view of pain as arising from working for her family aligns with the virtue of suffering-for. On the other hand, there is also some evidence of her attempting to approximate the virtue of self-governance through high-lighting her attempts to persevere through her pain to return home after she first injured her knee. And further, although perhaps more subtly, she alluded to this virtue through the indefinite grammatical marking of pain in the final phrase: "Because there was pain, there was pain and tears there" *(Ya baamith, ni baamith be mape luuq riy)*. In using a grammatical construction in which there is no explicit marking of a subject experiencing pain and tears, Tina thus subtly distances the present narrating self from her past self's experience of pain. This marks her current narrative act as one that navigates the thin edge between striving for self-governance and enduring in the face of suffering.

Her narrative configuration of her experiences of suffering with knee pain largely conforms to the Yapese ethics of suffering outlined in previous chapters. In turning to discuss her back pain, however, there are a number of interesting ways that she struggled to give meaning to her pain that, at least initially, seem to stretch beyond the confines of such an ethics. At first, she suggested that her pain was caused by a particularly difficult experience she had giving birth to one of her sons. She added shortly after this, however, that she was not sure if it was childbirth that caused her pain. Instead, she wondered whether or not the act of giving birth may have simply reawoken a previous back injury that she had incurred from lifting food while working on one of her plots of land. "I am usually thinking that is how it was [in reference to giving childbirth], but I don't know it may also be from always lifting things . . . I am thinking that is how, because I am always getting things from my garden in the woods that are very heavy, I am usually thinking . . . I am lifting things that are really heavy . . . that is why there is a problem." Tina suggested that if working did not directly cause her back pain, it certainly made it worse. In so doing she highlighted her struggles to keep working hard despite her pain and discomfort.

I cannot lift a lot of things because of my bad back, there is one, two joints in my back, they move a little from their place, so I cannot lift things that are really heavy. But I usually lift, at that time I tell you I was always lifting but at present, I cannot . . . but it is only just recently that I cannot because of my leg, the injury to my leg has gotten slightly more intense. I don't like that I have to put things down . . . I make my things and I put them down, I take a few and I put them down over there and then I return and get a bit more, it makes me frustrated, [but] I get [one bundle], [and] then I [go on and] get the next.

While there is certainly some evidence of her working to narratively cast her experiences of pain in light of local ethical modes of experience and action, we find in her discussion of attempts to treat her pain some resistance to these self-same models. Here, Tina admitted that while she would prefer to use local medicine to treat her illness, she gets *chaqälbaeg* ("frustrated," "bored," "annoyed") with all of the work that is entailed in finding and preparing it. She was thus not always prepared to *athamagil* to procure the medicines that may help alleviate her pain and allow her to continue working. In her words: "There are some [local medicines] that stay cold, there is cold and with those, I am thinking that if I get them some relief will come. I am frustrated with Yapese medicine, however, because I go and I look for that medicine, there is something I do, but nonlocal medicine you just apply it and you are done. So I [often] don't go looking for Yapese medicine."

That said, at the end of the same interview she attempted to once again invoke her compliance with such models. She explained that her pain's persistence, which is tied to her reluctance to procure local medicines, is further connected to her unwillingness to follow the direction of local healers. In particular, she was reluctant to follow their suggestions to stop working to allow the medicine to take its proper effect. As she put it, "Umm, I think that perhaps it is due to the fact that I do not obey. The healer will say don't lift something heavy, I will lift it. So now, just recently I cannot lift things that are really heavy due to my leg. I have to put the basket [of food] on the ground." Tina thus retrospectively cast her pain as resulting directly from her efforts at enduring in the face of suffering and the self-governance entailed in enacting such perseverance.

Ma'ar: Working, Striving, Hurting

A man in his mid-forties with a stocky build and boyish face, Ma'ar had three brothers and four sisters but was raised as an only child by an adoptive grandfather. Hailing from a mid-ranked village, Ma'ar married in his late twenties and had three children. He was sharp, inquisitive, and had a good sense of humor. I found Ma'ar to be a genuinely caring, calm, and patient person. This did not in anyway diminish his strength of character, however. Nor did it mean that he was incapable of asserting himself at times when the necessity to defend his own interests was warranted. This particular mixture of patience, intellect, conviction, and confidence was indeed recognized in the fact that he was considered to be one of his community's leaders even despite his relatively young age.

In recounting his life history Ma'ar asserted that his close relationship with his grandfather enabled him to learn about *yalean yu Waqab* ("Yapese tradition"). Perhaps more importantly, he suggested that it was his grandfather who taught him the significance of hard work *(maruweel)* and perseverance *(athamagil)*. After graduating from high school, Ma'ar went to college in the United States for three years before returning home to work in a number of government positions. About five years ago, Ma'ar decided to quit his government job to stay and work in the village. During the time of my fieldwork, Ma'ar was making his living selling betel nut and copra.

It was not long after my arrival on the island in September 2002 that Ma'ar suffered a back injury when helping with community work.

The injury occurred while lifting a particularly heavy mangrove tree that had been cut down to use in a community building project. Ma'ar recalled that there were eight other men helping to lift the tree and that he had lost his footing just as they were lifting it off the ground. He knew immediately that he had seriously injured his back. The injury did not stop him from working on the project, however. In fact, it took him almost five months of suffering with chronic and increasingly debilitating pain before he finally decided to seek out treatment from a local healer who specialized in traditional massage.

In his first attempts to describe his pain to me, Ma'ar focused on the pain's progressive trajectory through his body. He pointed out that the pain began in his lower back prior to moving down his hip to his leg. He suggested that the pain was associated with *gaaf* ("nerves" or "veins") that were perhaps damaged when he slipped under the weight of the tree. In terms of the felt quality of his pain, he maintained that the pain in his back was experienced as a fairly constant heaviness *(toomaal)* and the pain in his leg was hard to describe. His leg pain was not really pain *(amiith)*, but something that lay between *magaaf* ("soreness," "tiredness") and *gaamiig* ("pins and needles," "numbness"). Its sensory contours seemed to defy definite description. "It's different that pain, different, I don't know how to explain it but it is different. This is something that I only use the word 'pain,' that word 'pain,' but that is not pain. Oh, there is pain in the midst . . . I, I think that it is there in the midst of soreness and pain. I don't know the name. But . . . there is something that I call pain there."

Ma'ar worked to downplay the severity of his pain, however, by claiming that he experienced his worst pain when he initially injured his back. After that, while there was still pain, soreness, and numbness, he claimed that the intensity greatly dissipated. His pain at the time of this interview, however, was so intense that he had problems walking and sleeping and had great difficulty doing work for the household and participating in community work. This effort at downplaying his experiences of pain certainly resonates significantly with the virtue of self-governance.

After a while, he also admitted, however, that the intensity of his pain increased markedly whenever he tried to work. He revealed that even though he had been told not to work for three weeks while he was undergoing treatment in the form of traditional massage, he had still gone out to look for coconuts to sell for "market." In his words: "Yes, that is a difference there, the pain gets more intense. . . . I stand up and I feel a little bit of pain, I am thinking that it is because of that bundle of coconuts that I . . . moved a bit. Fal [the healer] is right, she said that I should not move around: 'You don't work.' I shouldn't work again, I don't like that, for two . . . three weeks?"

Speaking of the way in which his pain had impacted his life, it was yet again work-based activities that were foregrounded as his most significant concern.

I have difficulty walking and doing things or carrying things, I have difficulty with everything. I go to build something or I go to pull something and then I sleep, there is a problem there . . . if I didn't work hard that day, if I didn't strain . . . and a . . . maybe sometimes in the middle of the night I can sleep on my back. But if I was really working hard the day before I couldn't even sleep on my back, so when I . . . if I'm tired, [and I'm sleeping] on this side and when I try to move then I cannot go to sleep anymore because I was finding a comfortable position but [now I] cannot find [it].

Ma'ar explained that the main reason that he had not sought treatment when he first injured his back was that he knew that he would be told not to work for the duration of the treatment. It was only out of worry that he would not be able to participate in another upcoming community work project that he became motivated to seek treatment.

Umm, and then I think last week, maybe I sleep only a few hours and then was a . . . I was tired . . . and when I start moving, sometimes I . . . find myself shout[ing] . . . then I try to find a more comfortable place, I mean position to . . . to be in and then a just . . . a what . . . sit there or a . . . in that position for . . . maybe . . . sometimes when I . . . maybe almost fall asleep or . . . maybe fall asleep [for a] few seconds and then I get up, it's really bad a . . . I think I'm lucky to . . . and . . . I think one reason why I choose to start this [massage] is because of the working on the community project, because they told me that we're gonna . . . suppose to start sometime this month, and I know that a . . . because doing myself doing my things is different because if I feel pain or tire[d] I can rest but to work like that . . . you know, you cannot rest all the time eh, or take it easy especially [since] we know each other . . . and so this time if we start working and I start laying off, and they'll say, hey what's the matter with you. And a I'm . . . I heard that these people [healers who practice traditional massage], they will ask you not to do anything, do any hard work, eh? Like Fal did, eh? She told me not to start working.

About a month later during a subsequent interview, Ma'ar pointed out that his pain had been gradually getting better with the treatment he was receiving. He had recently ignored the advice of the healer who was treating him, however. As a result he had experienced intense pain after he tried carrying a cooler full of food to his brother's house. Despite this setback, he was still hopeful that he would soon be able to return to work. "It is going, like I went over there to Lowan's house . . . there was pain [in] my leg or just close to the house the pain came, I wanted to rest. . . . This week is the fourth week, third week, yes the third week after Yap Day, perhaps, I am thinking that this [treatment] will go to the fourth week or something, perhaps it depends on today, if she fixes my leg, checks it, a gift will be once she changes the medicine, eh? And then I will be able to work a bit." Ma'ar returned to work that same week, prior to the end of his scheduled treatment regime.

Dammal: Against the Grain

Dammal was a woman in her early fifties who suffered from chronic pain in her legs, joints, back, and head. Low caste, more than any other person I interviewed she was extremely open about her life. Dammal was intelligent, funny, and seemed to genuinely enjoy the interview process. She was very comfortable talking about the troubles that she and her family faced. She was very upfront about her caste affiliation and about caste relations on the island. Generally speaking, she viewed herself to be a nonconformist and felt that she really never did fit the mold for "proper" Yapese conduct. This theme permeated our interviews. Dammal had been married and divorced, had three children, and had spent some years off-island living in Guam and Palau.

Unlike many other interviewees who often characterized their childhood as a time of suffering (*gaafgow*), Dammal stands out as one of the very few who thought of her early childhood as a time when she was happy (*falfalaen'*). She recalled that while her father was still alive she was spoiled with love and affection. When she was ten years old, however, her father passed away under tragic circumstances. She was then adopted by one of her father's brothers. Because of a number of family problems associated with her father's untimely death and the behavior of another uncle who was jailed for beating a man, she remembers this as being a very difficult period for her and her family.

There was sadness in the household, then it turned into hatred. But if I didn't like something I wouldn't let just anybody know, especially the person I didn't like [her uncle]. I don't like to tell him and he wouldn't understand so I sought out my friend and told her. My friend was one of my two grandmothers; I have two grandmothers from my mother and my father. There was much suffering *[Ba geel ea gaafgow]*—that uncle was someone my grandmother cared so much for and she grieved for him because he was her son. She knew that many people didn't like him because of that terrible thing he'd done. . . . But she still felt compassion *[runguy]* for him. We were staying in the village when they put him in jail. So we used to walk from the village every Sunday to attend Mass and bring his food to jail, afterward we walked back.

When her uncle finally did get out of jail, it did not take him long to get into more trouble. One night, drunk and belligerent, he came to Dammal's mother's house where she had been visiting for a few days. After being told to leave by her mother, he responded by attacking the two of them. Dammal was beaten so badly that she passed out. When the rest of the family found out about the assault, they contacted their chiefs and had Dammal and her mother relocated to another village so that they would be safe. During that time, she explained, there was a lot of suffering for both her and her mother. Much of this suffering was not described in emotional terms, however. Instead Dammal spoke of not having enough money to afford proper clothing and school supplies, a theme that was also evident in Tina's case. As she put it, "We moved and I went with my mother. It was terrible, the suffering we went through. There was no one to buy me notebooks for school. At the mission school I had to wear clothes, it's not like the public schools where grass skirts and *thuw*s could be worn. And there was a lot of pressure." In particular, she recalled always feeling pressure to conform to *yalean* while at school, which she found to be stifling.

Unlike the other girls in school, Dammal found it easy to make friends with boys. Most of her cousins were boys and she was used to talking and playing with them as a child. She was comfortable with her cousins *(ke machaam)*. As a result she was often chastised for behaving like a boy. Her affiliation with a low-caste estate and the other children's regular derogatory comments about her *pimilngaay* status made Dammal's school years a very difficult time for her.

. In addition to her feelings of marginality associated with both her caste affiliation and her "tomboy" dispositions, she also expressed ambivalent feelings toward her mother. Dammal blamed her mother for making her life miserable when she was younger. She believed that her mother regularly took out her sorrow and anger on her. This was especially the case in the context of those situations that arose as a result of the death of her father and the troubled relationship with her uncle.

Dammal claimed that her attitude toward her mother changed somewhat, however, as she aged. She explained that when she realized that her mother was frail and dying, she tried to work to keep her "chest free from anger." She did so in order to do her duty in taking care of her mother during her old age and sickness. Dammal also felt that the longer she took care of her mother the more likely it would be that her mother's feelings toward her would begin to transform into something more positive. It was only after a number of years of caring for her, however, that she came to an important realization. One night she realized that a possible reason that her mother might be more kind to her was because of the fact that she knew she was going to die and that she did not want to be judged negatively in the eyes of God. In her words,

But I was always keeping goodness in my chest, I put my chest, I said I will, I am, I put my care [into it], so this will go in a good way not because I was doing it like it's responsibility. I cooked for her, I always washed her and washed her clothes, it changed. That person, she changed. Because at first I was working on things because there was nobody else that was staying with her, nobody wanted to, to help, and I know that she hates me and then her attitude changed [and] I stayed for a long time. [But there remained] a question in my head, there was nobody who told me the answer. It was only after sleeping and waking up that it came to my mind. It's because of that belief in my mind about that religious teaching of the Catholics. I said perhaps that's why . . . it's good [now]. Because that old woman will die . . . I stood up from the ground and there was no more tiredness, I could not sleep, I just stayed and continued to think more and I was crying because I didn't see it [before].

Her mother's increasingly compassionate stance toward her in light of her possible fears of God's judgment seemed at odds, Dammal intimated, with the type of virtuous compassion that arises from simply recognizing that another is suffering on your behalf. Even despite this revelation and the deep ambivalences she felt because of it, she continued to care of her mother for over fifteen years. Given the events that she chose to highlight in reflecting upon her life history, it is interesting that Dammal never did explicitly configure of her experiences of pain in light of her working to care for her mother. Nor did she do so in terms of the suffering she underwent as a child. Instead, she believed that the pain in her joints, legs, and back was primarily tied to her being overweight. In particular, she believed that the pain in her joints resulted from her eating too much rice and nonlocal foods. Indeed, recently she had gotten back in the habit of going to her sister's garden and taro patch in order to prepare and eat more local food. She claimed that after eating local food for only a week the pain in her joints had begun to fade.

I went landward to the outskirts of the village . . . one of my sisters came and we stayed there. I went to my village and I stayed with her for one week and ate local food and ate fish and the pain weakened. . . . The swelling in my leg went away, no more pain there, I came from there and I said that I will not eat rice—oh, I can—she [her sister] took food because she came from the outskirts of the village and she brought food but then it did not take long for that food to be finished, and I have no taro patch of my own, no gardens of my own [so the pain returned].

At first glance Dammal stands out as distinct from many of the other individuals I spoke to about pain. Her narratives of past and ongoing experiences of pain do not overtly focus upon the virtues of suffering-for and self-governance. As I have already discussed in some detail in previous chapters, however, local foods are themselves deeply implicated in local moral sensibilities. The very act of procuring and preparing such foods is often understood as necessarily the result of hard work, suffering-for, and endurance. While Dammal did not articulate the cause of her pain in light of these core cultural virtues, the idioms she evoked to suggest the temporary alleviation of this long-standing pain, and the implicit hope that a return to eating local food may provide a means to escape her pain for good, are once again significantly defined in terms of these self-same moral frameworks.

The extent to which she too tended to align her experiences of pain with these pregiven understandings of ethical modalities of existence and practice was further evident in our final interview together. Dammal talked about the ways in which the pain and suffering that she had to endure have served as important lessons for her. While she had yet to find a way to overcome her pain, in her heart she was happy that she had been able to live through, and learn from, her suffering. "If you learn . . . and you are patient [*ningam k'aedan'um*—"biting your mind"] you will endure and sometime . . . but that [pain] it fixes how I think, it organizes [*ma yärmiy*], you are patient then you can, you see, there are some things that will organize your mind. . . . Not only how you are thinking but how you feel. I organized my feeling and knew . . . eh, ah, how do I say, feel? [I knew how to] 'Feel.'" Well in-line with the virtue of self-governance, Dammal claimed that struggling to persevere in the face of her pain taught her how to "organize" her thoughts and feelings. Enduring through pain thus revealed to her ways to think and feel that are consonant with virtuous modes of being.

Fal'eag: Making and Unmaking a World

Married with six children, Fal'eag was a man in his early sixties who had been suffering with chronic back, joint, and head pain for well over fifteen years. Kind, gentle, and a dedicated worker, Fal'eag was devoted to his family, helping others, and contributing to community projects. Even in the face of his ongoing struggles with pain he was easily one of the busiest and hardest-working people I knew on the island. Fal'eag was also a community leader and was well respected both within his village and in other municipalities.

At the time of our interviews Fal'eag had been suffering with pain in his lower back for at least fifteen years, if not longer. When I asked him to reflect upon what may have been the cause of his pain, he suggested at first that it may have been tied to an accident that he had while he was working for the government. At that time he was often required to climb electrical poles to conduct repair work. On one of these occasions his safety belt broke while at the top of one of the poles. He fell to the ground and believes that it was primarily from this injury that his pain first arose.

In reflecting further, however, he added that some of the pain was perhaps also due to *maath'keenil'*. This was an interpretation that his mother had apparently suggested to him. In his words, "Eh, I think, that is right, my mother said to me that is right, *maath'keenil'*, *maath'keenil.'*" It was at this point that Fal'eag seemed to integrate these two competing explanatory frameworks through suggesting that his pain had perhaps resulted from some combination of injuries tied to his fall and to the hard work he undertook during his youth. And yet, during the years that he first incurred these injuries he claimed that he did not experience much, if any, pain. It is commonly held in Yap, he suggested, that injuries incurred through hard work and labor undertaken during a person's youth result in imperceptible pain that remains dormant inside the body only to emerge later in life. He added that it was because younger people have stronger bodies that they are able to deal with their pain. It is only once individuals grow older, once their bodies become increasingly weak and frail, that the pain begins to emerge.

F;   I think that, Jason, that . . . I don't understand why that pain came, so I will think that the time that I fell I was a young man, twenty-five, twenty-six, and now I am thinking that I feel it now, now I am sixty-two years, years old, sixty-two, and I have heard that they say, they say, when you are a young man you will not feel . . . those things that happened long ago it is only just here [in old age] we will all feel, that is how they say it in Yap.

JT;   So it [the pain] stays inside your body? It stays?

F;   It stays . . . until the body is weakened . . . you feel like that, that is how they say it in Yap, it is what is believed in Yap.

JT;   So what stays?

F;   The way that I interpret it there are things that happen to you when you are a young man, very hard work . . . when it [the work] is finished damage has taken place inside of your body but you will not feel it when you are a young man but becoming an old man that is finally when you will experience those pains there, that is how they believe it to be in Yap, that is how they say it in Yap.

Also suffering from joint pain, Fal'eag explained that his pain was at its worst after long hours of work. "Joints . . . if I work like I am using a machete or a hammer or I use a grinder for a really long time, that is when I feel pain and . . . it . . . I feel that pain come to my hand and I do not know for. . . . If I work for a very long time like I am hammering or I am using a machete or grinding then it will not take long for me not to feel anything [but] I feel pain."

In an attempt to compare these two varieties of pain, he made it clear that his back pain was more of a worry to him than his joint pain. It is telling that it is yet again the idiom of work that serves as a key component in distinguishing between the centrality of these two varieties of pain in the context of his cares and concerns. This is due to the fact that Fal'eag knows that his joint pain is more closely related to the amount and intensity of work that he does. It is also connected to the fact that when he stops working and runs some water over his hands or massages them for a while the pain will eventually dissipate. In contrast, his back pain, while certainly made worse through hard work, is often present even when he is not working. It is also less likely to dissipate when he is resting (although, I should note that I personally did not see much, if any, time when Fal'eag was not working).

Much like Ma'ar, Fal'eag also often had difficulty capturing the sensory quality of his pain. For instance, struggling to articulate the feelings that comprise his back pain he went on to say,

> F;   I feel that it is hard for me to explain to you . . . I feel that there is some pain that is, that is not like the one that stabs like a knife or . . . *[gube thaamiy nib boechi ngi amiith ni baaq ni daathii boed ni kan kuruf ea yaer f . . .]*
>
> JT;   Or spear? *[Fa dileak?]*
>
> F;   Yes, or spear or . . . when I go and I stand up I say that type of pain is, I don't know if it is *gaamiig* or . . . what is *gaamiig,* numb? . . . that pain that is numbness, I don't know how to explain it, the one I feel . . . I feel pain that is . . . you see now but not . . . I feel but it has yet to get to the time when I say *iii* ["ouch"].
>
> JT;   It is like . . .
>
> F;   It is heavy *[ke toomaal]* . . .
>
> JT;   It is heavy . . . okay, it is *toomaal,* it is like having something inside or how do I say . . .
>
> F;   It is heavy . . . pressure.

Even though the pain in his back affected his ability to sleep, move quickly, and sit or stand for long periods of time, he had yet to seek out treatment for it. This, he claimed, was largely due to the fact that he knows that once he begins his treatment he will have to stop working. Again, like both Tina and Ma'ar, this was something that he was not willing to do. As he explained,

> F;   It is said . . . it is said by my mother that there is a type of medicine but I have no time to use medicine and . . . I don't entertain inside [my mind] . . . not that I do not care that I take the effort that I . . . to use Yapese medicine it is just that I do not have the time.
>
> JT;   Why?

F;   Because if I do go see someone, I know in my mind that when I see someone they will give me medicine and will say to me that there are things that I cannot do, but there are a lot of things I would like to do.

JT;   Like what?

F;   There are some people that are building a house and things, there is the house that I maintain and the car, and windows for people and people that . . . I go help with their house and . . .

JT;   Help with work?

F;   Help with work, that is it . . .

JT;   Because of work?

F;   Eh, of course if I went to see someone with my mother's medicine and there is their medicine they will give, it is certain that they would limit me, not certain, there are a few things that I could do and some that I could not do, but it is not good for those types of work that I do and I am not finished, not yet finished, not finished.

Fal'eag's discussion of his back and joint pain resonates in significant ways with the virtues of ethical, reflective self-control and self-sacrifice. Perhaps one of the most revealing retrospective assessments of his past painful experiences, however, is found in the context of recounting his long recovery from a severe head injury incurred after a random, nonwork-related injury. What is particularly striking about his recounting of this experience is the extent to which even in the context of its retelling there is evidence for what Elaine Scarry (1985) has termed the "world-destroying" nature of pain. Also of note is the fact that this particular injury was not initially shared with me when I first asked Fal'eag about his various painful conditions. And yet, its effects were still palpable in the form of chronic headaches, and at times dizziness, that he experienced on a weekly basis. This is Fal'eag's recollection of the time when he first regained consciousness after the injury.

F;   Extremely intense, extremely intense pain there. [Bageel nib geel nib geel ea amiith riy.] When there was a bit of clarity to my mind, I said it would be good had I died. I was depressed [Ke ngoochngoch ea n'ug] it would be good had I died and that I don't feel pain.

JT;   The pain that you were usually feeling was like what?

F;   There is nothing that is like it. *[Daariy banen ni aram rogon.]* I cannot explain [it]. So severe that not only the pain but I don't know where is up and down, I don't know how many days 'cause when I start feeling myself, I was in pain till I could think a little bit and I gave up 'cause when I was in a coma, it was okay, I didn't feel anything but when I start feeling . . . I felt a little . . . I experienced severe pain. It's a horrible feeling, not only pain but . . . I thought I was . . . I couldn't feel . . . I was in a bowl shape, I couldn't feel my legs, I don't know where I am, I don't know my position. Something round . . . I felt very intense pain but I don't feel my body. I feel like a ball turning. I don't know, it's a horrible world. I don't feel my body but I feel just the pain, where the pain is, I don't know, but there's a pain feeling.

JT;   So there is only that pain? Only you and your pain, or not just you, just that pain?

F;   Only pain until I felt my body. I felt something like a ball that was turning, there is pain, there is pain. I am thinking that, I will think that, now I would be thinking that the village is turning in my eyes. All I knew was pain, I don't know my head, I don't know my legs, I don't know my hands, I don't know my body. Only that there is something, a yellow sphere.

The world-destroying intensity of this pain, a pain so horrible that it effaces one's very sense of embodied being, a pain in which it would be "good had I died," a pain so meaningless that "there is nothing that it is like," speaks to the existential limits of Fal'eag's abilities to make sense of the unbearable refusal of meaning inherent in a consciousness engulfed in pain's unassumability. It also, I believe, speaks to the potently transformative nature of such experiences in which Fal'eag's very being-toward-death (Heidegger 1996) had become altered in the face of the unsufferability of such extreme forms of suffering. In so doing, such pain highlights the very real and intense existential struggles associated with attempting to craft ethical experience from such unbearable, brute, and unassumable forms of hurt. To transform such brute pain into an existential embodiment of the virtue of suffering-for is no mere idealized platitude. It involves, instead, a struggle to reconfigure some our most deeply rooted modalities of being, modalities evidencing the often unspeakable recognition of our very mortality and finitude.

In the talk that followed, Fal'eag spoke of the struggles he faced even as he began to regain his sense of self and some semblance of hope in the face of such a completely disorientating and destabilizing pain.

F;   Umm, during the time I felt feelings like that, but if I look [back] now perhaps some improvement arrived during the time that I could think a bit. There was nothing that I could think about, I am thinking, I, I am thinking something will happen that I will not feel pain, it is good that I . . . there came weakness that I . . . I don't know why I still survive[d] and having that pain. I gave up a ((nervous laughing)) I gave up a. . . .

JT;   So, how did you strengthen your mind during the time that you lost hope or you . . . how did it return or it . . .

F;   I don't know if two weeks I . . . I felt my body, my leg and . . . but I was inside that sphere that . . .

JT;   Was spinning.

F;   It's spinning . . . a . . . but perhaps I am thinking that perhaps at that time the pain was weakening or I don't know if that was how it was but that is what I thought. What I was thinking at that time there I could not think that . . . I was aware that I'm recovering, I was not thinking things about that . . . to get rid of myself, to get away from the pain.

Throughout this time, Fal'eag maintained that he struggled to recover hope and to reclaim his desire to remain in this world. In the end, he recalled, this effort was crystallized in his drive to *athamagil*. As he put it, "[I kept] telling myself to *athamagil*. . . . I say inside my mind that I will *athamagil*, I will *athamagil*." Through his effortful striving to endure in the face of such unspeakable pain, he somehow managed to find the inner resources to persevere, to stay alive, to persist, and to find some hope for a return to being without pain.

Paer: Suffering-For

Paer, a large woman with pure white hair in her late sixties living in a mid-caste village, was suffering from chronic back and joint pain. At the time of our interviews together she had been married three times and had had four children. She was recently widowed. Paer's pain left her with a visible limp that necessitated her use of a cane to get around.

While talkative and polite, Paer was often reluctant to disclose much about her personal life. She seemed quite adept at skillfully avoiding questions that she did not wish to address. She was particularly artful in the ways in which she could talk for an extended period of time in response to a given question while providing very little information. That said, as time went on Paer became increasingly comfortable with the interview process and when the mood suited her, she could become quite engaged in reflecting upon her pain in the context of her life history.

Throughout her recollections of her life, Paer framed her narrative in what should now be a very familiar cultural idiom, the idiom of suffering. "Myself, my life, there was very intense suffering in my life, from long ago to present. But now that I have grown, I, I am helping my life. I got married and I became pregnant, myself and my children, we existed, I fell but I helped my and my children's life. But there was my husband who died so right now there is nothing that I can do, I stay and I wait for the time that I will [die]."

Here again we see pain and suffering as implicated in alterations in an individual's being-toward-death as Paer stays and waits for her seemingly endless suffering to finally cease in the wake of physical inexistence. That suffering can become so intimately imbricated in self-experience that its alleviation can only be imagined at the limits of a finite embodied existence speaks again to the very real existential challenges facing attempts to transform pain into virtue.

The theme of suffering took on different shadings in Paer's memories of the war, however. In this context, Paer emphasized the suffering, as well as the hard work, that she and her family had to undertake on behalf the Japanese administration and army. What is most intriguing about Paer's particular articulation of the theme of suffering during the war years, however, is that it appears to have a distinctly different quality than the suffering that is rendered virtuous in the context of suffering-for one's family or community. Indeed, as she makes readily evident, this wartime suffering was coerced and undertaken on behalf of the Japanese occupying forces. Even so, such labor was understood to be an opportunity to demonstrate her and her family's ability to endure, to *athamagil*. Such endurance took on the form of working to protect each other and their community from even worse fates.

Wartime suffering can arguably be viewed as yet another instance of attempting to imbue current experiences of pain with a morally salient narrative framing. Such a framing ties otherwise discrete sensations into a coherent and morally valenced lived experience as memories of pain are understood to index instances of persevering and suffering-for others. In her words:

P;   During that war there was great suffering, suffering that was put upon us. Very great suffering that the Japanese gave to us. We all stayed and we all worked *[Gamaed ma paer riy ni gamaed ma maruweel]*. And there was work and that is how it went *[Ni arme yima maruweel ni arme aram rogon]*. We went to work and we all, we all cooked for them and that, we all, we all cooked their food, so in the morning there was eating and then off to work. And there came work, there came work in the gardens, [to get] food for the Japanese. *[Amre yibe maruweel ni yibe maruweel ea waldug, gaan ea Sapan.]*

M;   Very hard work was put in.

P;   Very hard. Those Japanese I tell you, very hard work there. You could not . . . because . . . you were working it didn't matter . . . you could not . . . you see, you would work and there is pain in your back and you cannot stand straight up, you are told to return to work because there is watching . . . and they will beat you.

The grammatical structure of Paer's talk is noteworthy in these passages in as much as it serves to depersonalize the narrative. The use of the indefinite pronoun marker *yi*, the use of nomic second-person-singular constructions (e.g., *gar ra maruweel*—"you will work"), and the use of inclusive second-person-exclusive habitual plural constructions (e.g., *gamaed ma maruweel*—"we (not you) were all habitually working"), all contribute to mitigating her position as an experiencing, acting, and suffering agent who underwent these experiences firsthand. This form of talk, I believe, can be interpreted as an attempt to once again align her present self with the virtue of self-governance. That is, Paer was able to highlight her mastery over her feelings and memories through grammatically separating her present narrating self from a past self that was suffering at the hands of the Japanese army. Here, existential modalities of being are given voice and articulation through forms of talk that evidence the very self-distancing inherent in the virtue of reflective self-control and equanimity.

In turning to discuss more explicitly her own pain, which she believed to have stemmed from hard work undertaken during this period, Paer further asserted:

I am, because . . . I am thinking how . . . how, I am thinking, heaviness . . . the things I was carrying that I could not carry, I was striving *[athamagil]* while I carried so that is the cause of that . . . of that [pain in], my leg. If I would be taking something heavy in the past, something that I could not [take], I would strive to take it [regardless] and then I would . . . I would feel, I tell myself . . . there was biting here under my leg . . . here to the top. I tell myself, because it touches, touches or I don't know what it does, there is something that bites something there but . . . that is the reason why I will rest my body.

When speaking of the effects of pain in her day-to-day life, it was again work and endurance *(athamagil)* that served as the medium within which her pain was emplaced.

The time that my sickness started I was persevering *[athamagil]*, I could do a little but I am an old person it is hard to go, and, but—so right now it is really hard, I cannot, I . . . there are some things I cannot do. It is only that I think that the children will go gardening but they cannot. I have a problem with gardening, and when I am thinking that I will go I cannot, I cannot go. If I will go so that I garden, you see that little taro patch or the garden over there [close to the house], I go slowly.

The theme of *athamagil* in the face of pain was further extended to Paer's reflections on her use of local medicines and their relative inefficacy. Even despite the fact that the medicines she had tried, and was currently using, for her pain were not effective, she continued to persevere through her suffering while engaging in whatever work-based activities she was still able to do.

Our Yapese medicines there are some, I take one that you put on the ground and sleep on top of it, it is not good, I have yet to feel better, but, perhaps that is because I am old or I don't know what . . . I usually strive a bit *[saathathamagil]* you know, now I have no more responsibilities . . . if there is something, I persevere *[athamagil]* . . . [if] there is something [to do] I persevere a little *[saathathamagil]* to garden . . . if there is someone who is hungry I don't like that they will be hungry, but, at present I am resting, perhaps my mind has fallen [I have lost hope] or I don't know what.

Even despite a suffering that has led to her current loss of hope, she claims that she is only motivated to engage in work in the garden when it is for the benefit of others who are "hungry." That is, her pain is so bad these days that the only way that she will participate in activities that will increase her suffering is on behalf of others—she will suffer-for others but not for her own benefit.

Turning to explain how it is that she is able to *athamagil* in the face of her pain, she stated,

If I go and there is pain in my leg and I will strive *[athamagil]* to go. There is perseverance in my mind that I go over there *[Ba athamagil ea taafinay roog ya nguwan aram]*. But if I go and there is pain, I persevere and I am slow. I go and I use a walker [cane] to go and I see that I will not reach something that is far away. But if I arrive I will sit because if I stand there will be pain, I will stay on the ground I will stay and the pain will go away. If I stay and I stand I cannot because there is pain that will come to my leg. I will stay on the ground. That is the only way it is.

In her struggles to partake in even the most mundane forms of action, in merely trying to walk to fetch something at the other end of the house, pain has reconfigured Paer's very experience of her body's motility in terms of what Drew Leder (1990) has termed pain's centripetal modality. As an embodied registering of restriction, limitation, and resistance, such experiences of pain have shrunk her body's horizons of capability and motility. It is, as she exclaims, "the only way it is." Accordingly, the expanse of the horizons of her life-world has itself been reduced. In the face of such pain, it is only through a virtuous embodiment of perseverance that her body may work to reclaim, even if modestly, the world in which she once felt so intimately at home.

Paer summed up her existential predicament by further framing her suffering in terms of *maath'keenil'*.

But you see, this sickness, these various illnesses of mine, that is the way that I interpret it. In the past there was none, I was at our house and there were no illnesses during the time that I was married to that person, but then my illnesses started. But I took them [the illnesses] to the hospital, and the doctor said you cannot . . . [you have] *maath'keenil'* . . . Because there was something that I should not have carried . . . I strove to carry it. Our way is not a good one . . . no. Us in Yap we carry food in the midst of the bush . . . [I became] sick from carrying, I carried something very heavy. Something that I should not have taken [but] I persevered to take it.

As resulting from the hard work and effort entailed in carrying heavy bundles of food from her gardens to her home, Paer's pain is indexical of her moral enactment of the virtues of suffering-for, endurance, and self-governance as she risked her body's very well-being for the well-being of her children, husband, and estate.

Buulyäl: Compelled to Persevere

Buulyäl was a single woman in her late thirties who had been suffering with chronic, and at times debilitating, head and back pain since she was in her early teens. She had received some postsecondary education off-island and was sharp, inquisitive, and assertive. Graced with fine features, Buulyäl was a very attractive woman who had many male suitors. Her suffering was evident, however, in the dark pools around her eyes that registered her ongoing struggles to sleep in spite of her pain.

In recounting her life history she explained that she spent a great deal of her early childhood living with her grandparents. Her parents were divorced when she was still very young and from the age of four she lived with her father's parents. At the age of ten she left to live with her mother and her mother's new husband in another village. She recalled the move to the new village as being difficult primarily because of the fact that she had very few friends and that one of her aunts (one of her stepfather's sisters) had a quick temper and often beat her when she misbehaved. Whenever her aunt would get angry, Buulyäl remembers running as fast as she could to the forest to escape her aunt's reach and the inevitable beatings that would ensue if she were caught. If she could hide long enough for her aunt's anger to subside, she could often return home to just a verbal scolding.

Of all of the individuals I spoke to about their pain, Buulyäl was easily one of the most detailed in her attempts to describe and identify the sensory quality of her experiences. The following, for instance, was her response when I requested that she enumerate the various of types of pain she currently suffered from.

B;   Only that one that comes to my head, it is pain that is heavy *[nibe amiith ea ke toomaal]*, once in a while there is something that pierces inside my head *[kan kuruuf ban'ean nga laen loelugeeg]*, it aches *[be oeb'oeb]*, aches, my head I tell you it is as if it breaks open, then there is disorder or dizziness in my eyes when there comes very intense pain. There is pain in my back, so that is pain that is like there is something piercing something *[boed ni be*

kuruuf ban'ean] there, or if I cannot stay in one place it will take
me a long time to stand because there is pain that is like that I
told you, it pulls my spine so that it will break. That is how the
pain is, I tell you it pulls my spine there to the point [that it feels
like it might] break. I lie on the ground and I sleep and I try to
rest, but it does not take long for me to turn . . . there is pain,
there is pain, that is how the pain is that I feel *[baaq amiith
nibaaq amiith, aram rogon ea amiith niguma thaamiy].*

JT;   So there are only two types of pain, or . . .

 B;   There are a lot of types, but there is one pain that comes to my
back that pierces something there. One pain is heavy *[Reeb ea
amiith nib toomaal].* There is pain that is inside that is very heavy,
but there is pain inside, one pain that aches. One pain that is like
numbness *[Reeb ea amiith nib gaamiig],* like you cannot feel
things very well. You do not sense things well. That is one type
of pain there. Those all come to my back and head. It is very big,
my back, the pain that usually comes there *[Ribga ni keeruqug
ea mayibe tinem ea amiith nga'].* But once in a while I feel pain
that is hot, very hot *[gube amiith nib gawael nib gawael],* that is
one pain there. And once in a while I feel pain there, but I don't
feel heat there, it is cold, that is one pain something that is very
cold, it is cold . . . in my back.

What is quite notable here is not only the detail that Buulyäl provides
concerning the sensory qualities of her pain, but also the at times relative impersonality of her description. There are a few instances where
she uses a first-person description of her pain states. The remaining
descriptions, however, employ constructions that only imply a suffering
subject through the suffixed possessive rendering of the body part
afflicted with pain (e.g., *Ribga ni keeruqug ea mayibe tinem ea amiith
nga'*—"It is very big, my back, that usually comes the pain there") or
through such impersonal constructions comprised of the existential
verb *baaq* and the noun *amiith* (e.g., *baaq amiith*—"there exists pain").
Perhaps most notable in this regard is her enumeration of different
types of pain states in the second stretch of her talk. In response to my
questioning whether or not she feels only two types of pain, Buulyäl
lists her various pain states according to their sensory qualities without
overtly grammatically referring to her first person experience of them.
Grammatically this is accomplished through using the numeral *reeb*

signifying "one," the noun phrase connector *ea,* and the noun *amiith* (e.g., *reeb ea amiith*—"one pain"). This is followed by the relativizing particle *ni* and a relative clause specifying the variety of pain in question (*nib toomaal*—"that is heavy").

When recalling the initial onset of her pain, Buulyäl, like many of the other sufferers I spoke to, evoked the themes of work, service, endurance, and effort. Hard work itself was not the cause of her pain, however. She believed instead that her pain resulted from her taking an incorrect dosage of medicine that had been prescribed to treat an undiagnosable stomach illness she suffered from as a child. That said, she remembers the time of her pain's onset within the framework of obligations to participate in community work and her endurance to do so despite the intensity of the pain she was experiencing. As she put it:

So, during the time that I was in eighth grade there came a sickness to me, there was pain in my chest, there was pain in my head, and there came dizziness to my eyes. I did not eat, during an entire day there was very little food I ate, I was feeling lazy and then one day I'm told I slept until noon. I slept until noon, I did not wake up in the morning to go to work because I was sick. I was told, "You're sick and you never go to work for the household." I replied that it was because I was sick but then I dropped it [stopped resisting]. I persevered *[athamagil]* and I went to work, eh, when I arrived there was numbness in my leg, and heaviness and pain in my stomach, so it started to rain and I [still] went because they were cleaning the village center. I went and I stayed in the community house, there was numbness in my leg and pain in my back and stomach. So I laid down on the ground and I was crying from the pain. Then there came two women from the village and one of them scolded me . . . she said to me, "You stand up, I am telling you to get up," and she hit me, hit my head and there was pain in my head and my back and so I cried and it was raining. I stood up in the rain and went [to work]. In the evening when the work was done, the people went and she came and said to me: "What are you doing?" I said "Nothing." So . . . I was crying because there was pain in my back like I said before, she said let's go to see a woman in that house and she will give Vix [Vick's VapoRub]. There came a morning that I could not stand up, she [her aunt] told me to stand and I told her, "I cannot!" She said, "You stand up! You find out how and you stand up!" I could not. That is when the sickness came to me very strongly, so they took me to town, to the hospital.

The doctors eventually discovered that the cause of her illness was an incorrect dosage of medicine that had been prescribed at the hospital for her stomach ailment. Even after changing her medication and returning to the village, however, her pain did not go away. What made matters worse was that in addition to the pain she was suffering on a daily basis, her aunt did not seem to understand that her sickness was not simply going to disappear. In the face of her aunt's incredulity, she was forced to continue working for her family. Again, it was her efforts at perseverance in the face of her pain that were foregrounded in her accounts of this time in her life.

When I returned to the village and I stayed at the house, I could not go walking, so I stayed at the house, but still my auntie was not used to it and she told me to go to work, so I would cry and I would work very hard, and I was in pain and I would work . . . I was working in the midst of rain and the sun, I worked under the sun, eh? . . . And there were people in our village who were angry at her . . . because I was sick and perhaps she did not understand or she didn't like to think that it was true that I was sick.

After a brief period of managing to better cope with her pain during the time of her mid-adolescence, Buulyäl was again afflicted with serious back pain in her late teens. So much so that she was unable to work at all. At this time she recalled feeling a range of emotions spanning from anger to sadness. After years of suffering with pain, however, she claimed that today she no longer becomes upset enough to cry when her pain gets too intense for her to work. She has in fact become so accustomed to living with pain that even despite the fact that it continues to remain quite disruptive to her life and her aspirations, she does not allow herself to become saddened by her current condition.

B;   Sadness, I would cry, sometimes I was angry, because it was not me who caused the problems, or I would be angry at myself, I would be angry at myself. So I was sad, and I was angry, and I would cry, I was in pain, anger would come to me and there was pain in my back. And there was very intense pain there and anger would come to me. That is how I stayed.

JT;   And now?

B;   Now . . . I have become accustomed to this type of existence. I understand why. So when the pain comes to me I see how, what I should do to weaken the pain in my back, it is not that I become sad like I did before. I don't cry, only if someone in my family dies, or what, I get sad and cry. But there is nothing that I cry for. And my pain it does not give problems to my thinking like it did at first.

Unlike some of the other narratives explored to date, Buulyäl's account of her pain pivots on her ability to live up to obligations to her family that were, in her estimation, unwarranted given the severity of her illness. In contrast, other pain sufferers I spoke to often focused on the ways in which their current experiences of pain were rooted in what were characterized to be largely *self-initiated* efforts to fulfill family and community obligations. Such obligations necessitated that they put their own personal desires and wishes at bay in the service of deserving others. Buulyäl's characterization of her situation, however, was not centered primarily on efforts to tame her personal desires for the benefit of working for her family. It was instead focused on her efforts to endure an unwanted illness that was held to be completely beyond her control.

This particular framing of her pain focused primarily upon a muted reference to her aunt's moral failings in compelling her to endure in the face of her suffering. In not being recognized by her aunt as authentic, Buulyäl's suffering was rendered in Levinas's (1998) terms a form of useless suffering and not virtuous sacrifice. This contrasts rather sharply, however, with the way in which she spoke of her relatively recent choice to help her sick grandfather. This decision she claims to have made on her own accord. Instead of being compelled to work by an unsympathetic relative, in this case it was her own feelings of obligation to help alleviate her grandfather's suffering that motivated her to endure through her pain and to go back to his village to care for him for over two years. It seems this experience made her rethink the merits of returning to her mother's village in order to help her stepfather, who was also getting older.

In providing care, service, and help to her grandfather and her stepfather, Buulyäl sees her endurance through her ongoing pain as a form of self-sacrifice that has tangible benefits for others. That such endurance in the face of suffering is now largely self-initiated, as opposed to being imposed by an uncaring other, further foregrounds the significance of a particular sort of ethical willing necessary for the embodiment of self-governance.

Fanow: Women's Work, Women's Pain

Fanow was a very well-respected high-caste woman in her mid-seventies suffering from joint and back pain. Her parents had a troubled marriage and she recalled how her family often suffered as a result. There were many days when Fanow and her siblings would go without food. In her early teens, she was very upset with her father in particular, not so much for her own suffering but for her siblings'. Despite her feelings, there was absolutely nothing she could do or say to her father since he was *mathangeeluwol* ("holy, sacrosanct").

It was not long after this that her father suffered a stroke. As a result, she was sent with her siblings to live with one of her mother's sisters in another village. During this period she moved to the dorms at school and spent the majority of her time in town. She would only return to the village on weekends. Even during these short visits home, however, she had a very hard time witnessing her siblings suffering without their father and mother. Not happy with the situation in the village, she found a job in town after finishing school. It was not long after this that she was married.

During the war years Fanow suffered from a very painful injury to her arm caused by shrapnel. She claimed that the pain associated with the injury was still with her, albeit in a much attenuated form. With regard to her most intense and enduring pain, however, she explained that she had been long suffering with pain in her fingers and back, which she at first attributed to arthritis. She attributed the pain in her back to the fact that she was *pilabthir* (an elder). She asserted that the initial cause of the pain in her hands was rooted, however, in her participation in a community project reconstructing one of her village's stone paths. As she recalled, a number of rocks had fallen on her fingers during the many months of hard labor that was invested in the project.

F;   It has been a long time, perhaps when I was fifty years old, there was pain in my back [so] I went to the hospital and they said that sickness from old age came to you, and so . . . it stayed for a while, and then it got worse and now it has really, really shown itself that it . . . my fingers are bent, you know something fell there . . . you know it was very bad from that path.

M;   You think that was what caused it?

F;   Well there was something, there were rocks that fell to [it], there fell rocks to [it] and when it was done and later there was swelling and . . . and . . . you know that it fell on the bone there and it was injured like when something falls there and later . . . there is something that comes to it.

Again, the use of impersonal grammatical constructions, such as the preposition *ngaa* ("to [it]") and the indefinite third-person construction of the intransitive verb *thow* ("to swell"), renders Fanow's hands, fingers, and bones as objects that have no clear grammatical link to a suffering self. It is also interesting to note here that Fanow believed at first that her pain resulted from *maath'keenil'* prior to her receiving a diagnosis from the hospital that she was suffering from arthritis. "Eh, the pain became stronger there . . . you know that *maath'keenil'* of . . . but during the time that . . . when I was fifty years old, the doctor told me that it was . . . that arthritis had come to me, sickness of old age."

Regarding her current suffering, it was primarily in the context of hard work that her pain was at its worst. When she rested the pain would dissipate. "No, when I go, that is when the pain comes, my back it is in pain. If I bend down and I am working that is intense pain, when I don't, when I rest, that is when it lessens a bit."

What is perhaps most striking about Fanow's narratives of suffering, however, is the fact that she often explicitly situated her pain within broader cultural understandings of women's work and the significance of enduring through pain to ensure that food is provided for the family.

F;   Eh, before the pain arrived I would work very well and nothing would give me trouble, because I would think of something to do and I would do it, it was easy, but that pain there that came to my back . . . it is a lot and you know it is a lot all the work that we women in Yap do, bending and stooping, work in the taro patch, work in the garden, if something is made, there is bending and lifting baskets, that is hard and . . . it . . . that is why there is strong sickness there. There is no time that it stops, so that time that there is no sickness and there everything is good, there comes good work, during the time I was a teenager that it [the pain] had yet to arrive . . . it . . . fifty years went by and then the sickness started, all the pain started . . .

M;   So can you explain a bit . . . about how your life was when your pain first started? What I asked before concerned when it had yet to start, but this is when it first came.

F;   Ummm. Nothing, only because there were those pains there and that is how, that is how the pain came but I could not stop working and I could not stop harvesting, I could not stop taro patching, I could not stop gardening, and all the work that women participate in is work of . . . bending over, it . . . so there comes working in the midst of pain and the sickness is not enough to rest, two days or something and the pain in my back stops a bit and then I return to it [work] and that is how . . . there is a time that the pain is really stirred up and all those various types of work become very difficult . . . but it is not possible to drop the work, not possible to stop harvesting, so I am sick but there comes perseverance *[maachnea ii yib athamagil].*

M;   There comes perseverance *[Yib ea athamagil].*

F;   Umm.

M;   So . . .

F;   And you know . . .

M;   No rest . . .

F;   Sickness of servants *[M'aar ni pimilngaay].* They say sickness of servants, you know, you know that Yapese saying there about us women, "You have sickness of servants, because you are sick and you cannot stop working."

M;   It doesn't matter if you are sick, because if you are sick you have to move.

F;   If you don't move the household will have to stop eating.

And again she returned to describe this gendered form of suffering later in the same interview.

F;   That Yapese saying is because . . . because servants, if the chief says to work and make something it is not possible to say no. It doesn't matter if there is sickness, the most important thing is to make it . . . if you don't work the children will go hungry and all of the people in the household. So that is why it is like sickness of servants, you are a servant . . . you are sick but you persevere and work so people come and you are sick, it is due to sickness of servants, you are sick and you cannot stop.

M;   Because it doesn't matter if you are sick since the most important thing is that you persevere and you work.

F;   You will work because there are a lot of people that you give food to, if you don't . . . if you don't work then some people will die.

M;   So that is why they say servant and that is us women and that is
     how it is, it doesn't matter if you are sick you will persevere
     [ngeam athamagil].

F;   You will persevere [Ngeam athamagil].

In sacrificing one's well-being for the well-being of others, in working
and enduring through pain in order to procure the food necessary to
keep others from dying, women's work is virtuous work. Difficult,
backbreaking, unending—this work, this effortful persevering in the
face of pain, leads to a "sickness of servants" that emplaces suffering
within a horizon of virtue.

Gonop: Effortful Concentration and Self-Mastery

Gonop was man in his early sixties and a prominent member of his
community. Married with eight children, his estate held voice or
authority as one the village's *piiluung*. In addition to his status in the
community, Gonop also had long enjoyed a number of high-standing
positions in both the government and private sectors. Gonop had suffered with chronic joint and back pain for over twenty years, and had
chronic headaches for over ten.

Again, the connection between pain and work was salient throughout our interviews. At the beginning of our first interview he asserted
that his pain became increasingly unbearable depending on the extent
to which he engaged in work-based activities.

It is big in the joints of my hand, there are two joints that the pain comes to,
the joint that is here in my hand, my fingers, and the lower part of my back here,
there is something of that pain, the one [the joint?] in my back is in pain. When
that pain goes to my leg, it is strong . . . if I am exhausted from work, if I walk
and I become tired that pain is intense there and I fall to the ground. That one
is very intense pain in my body, the one in my back is very intense pain.

In attempting to describe the pain in his legs and back the focus was
primarily upon its spatial trajectory through the terrain of his body.
With regard to his joint pain, however, Gonop's narrative again returned
to the theme of work-induced suffering.

G;   My pain, I usually fall and the pain goes to my back and then
     goes here under my leg and then goes here to my leg and then

goes to my foot . . . and it goes and stays and that there is intense pain . . .

JT;   And the joints in your hand?

G;   This one in my hand, this joint here it is in pain. There are two [joints] that I have that pain comes to, but it is more intense when I work, when I cut something or when I hammer a piece of wood or . . . that is when I feel the pain there. A while ago there was pain [when] I worked, I worked until it was finished. Once in a while there is pain and I cannot [work] because the pain makes my hand numb and the tools will drop to the ground.

In Heideggerian (1996; cf. Leder 1990) terms, pain at times becomes so intense that it is able to shift Gonop's orientation to the activity of working. Where once his hand and hammer were experienced as ready-to-hand *(zuhanden)*, transparent in their embeddedness in the activity of hammering, in the wake of such pain they are rendered present-at-hand *(vorhanden)*, now discernable objects that pain has brought through their dysfunction into sharp relief (see the conclusion).

Gonop further spoke of chronic headaches that he has suffered with for more than ten years. Again, he pointed directly to a link between the service he rendered to his family as a child and what he later learned was an injury to the joints in his neck.

G;   Long ago in my household we were all suffering . . . to eat food we would come to Colonia and we would cross the island from the other side . . . to our village to get the food and to fix the food and what I, I would take, I would put it [the food] around my neck and I would take it over there [to Colonia] and at that time I was a child not yet grown . . . I was working very hard taking coconuts, all of the bags of copra that were put there, they were big, and myself and my father, the two of us were staying together, and he was old, so if there was a large bag that I . . . it was put in the bag and I would carry it. So I think that is the cause of those things [the pain] is what caused those and . . .

JT;   Yes . . .

G;   Um. Hard work I put in long ago when I was a child.

JT;   *Maath'keenil'*, or . . .

G;   *Maath'keenil'*, that is it. That is my sickness, *maath'keenil'*.

While I was the one to initially bring up the term *maath'keenil'* in this stretch of talk, the description of the cause of Gonop's pain aligned precisely with those that were regularly attributed to this particular illness category.

Gonop described the onset of his pain as very gradual and almost imperceptible. He could not pinpoint exactly when he first felt the pain in his back. It took a number of years for the pain to increase to a level where he began to notice that it was a problem. When I asked specifically about what may have caused the pain, initially he suggested that it was most likely the result of his attitude toward work. In particular, he pointed to the fact that when he was working he did not concentrate on anything else. If he was in the midst of a project he would rarely, if ever, stop working to rest, chew betel nut, eat, or drink.

JT;   So, can you say why you think that the pain started at that time or not?

G;   It is like I said before, that when I was a young man I didn't pay attention to what was or what was bad or, there is an attitude of mine, if I think about something that I will do I don't like to close it, to close it, only that . . . like what my wife does when I am working, when I am working on some carpentry, I am working I am making that [and she says,] "Eh, come because there is coffee." But I don't say anything. "Eh, come and you drink some coffee." But I don't talk because I am concentrating. "Come and eat." I will stand and I will be angry. "You eat the food there" [she will say]. And I will feel in my stomach that I need it but I don't need it yet [so] I will not come, so I want to eat, I eat but I am a bit mental, if I am making something I concentrate especially I will devote my mind to it . . . I don't like if someone bothers me, I will be angry . . . Those things are related to the cause of my sickness . . . because I am stubborn. I am stubborn and aggressive during work . . . because when I, that there, if I work, I like that it is made, it is made, it is made, it is made until it is complete, if it is not completed the way that we are thinking. But I do not tell people to stop or everyone will stop, do not stop working. If it [work] stops then everyone stops . . . so that is one type of attitude I have that I think is a bad cause for all of my sicknesses, if there is work don't stop, if it stops I cannot relax well . . . [My attitude is that of] all [the] types of work there is not one that I cannot [do] because every type of work I can do. If there is something heavy, my mind does not stop at how to do it. So those attitudes I think that those are the things that cause . . . a cause of my sickness, if there is something to be made, I don't like to back away from it or chicken out!

Gonop's attitudes have changed toward work now that he has to face the specter of pain when engaging in it, however. These days he tends put in serious effort only when the work entails something that he is truly interested in. Perhaps most importantly, the work that he is most willing to risk further injury doing is work that is beneficial not just to him, but to his children and the rest of the community.

Everything . . . that will be made I like to make it, I put my mind to it. It is only that in my life at present there is some work that is [??] that I am not really interested in or what is being made doesn't stick in my mind as relevant . . . so I am lazy toward it. But if there is a type of work like the one now . . . that work that we are doing . . . that is something that I think is really good, not good for me, I think that it is good for . . . myself and all of the people and children that will come, so that is why I think that I am going to put my mind to it. I saw how and I gave some help, the way that it is said, but there is some work that I don't really like. But I don't know how, how I appreciated how my life was before I was sick, and what I was . . . what things that I really liked and you know that there was no worry in my mind for it, I tell you.

Generally speaking, a great deal of Gonop's narratives were focused on the themes of work, endurance, and suffering-for in their relationship to his sense of self-worth. And these themes were again revealed in the context of his expression of frustration with regard to his pain and the limitations that it placed upon him. Interestingly, his own frustrations were evoked in the context of discussing his wife's experiences of pain, which were also induced from hard work and labor. To this end, he pointed out that much of the work that he participated in during recent years is devoted to helping her when he can, since he knows that she too is suffering.

My wife, what to say, she is very tired and sick from working, she is overworked but she, the two of us, we try to persevere so that . . . I go to work or to work a bit in the garden or if there is no more work for me to do. So, at this time in my life I am frustrated because the way that my thinking is, I think that there are a lot of things that I would like to make, I do not think that it is difficult or what, that I . . . my disability is very strong at my age, no? Or the sickness. So that is why I am frustrated, because I know that I could do things but if I go to do something there comes my sickness . . . and pain in my body that, so that is [the basis of my] frustration.

Very sadly, Gonop's wife's suffering did eventually come to an end. Despite his efforts to help alleviate some of her pain, his wife passed away a year after I returned to Los Angeles in 2003.

To summarize, with Tina we found a woman who was largely able to configure her dysphoric experiences in light of inherited preunderstandings of virtue and pain. Her narratives drew upon, and were themselves structured by, the virtues of suffering-for and self-governance. Tina retrospectively configured her experiences of pain as indexical of her effortful attempts to persevere in the face of her own suffering in order to help her siblings and sick mother during her youth. There may have been some uncertainty or resistance to fully aligning her experiences with such ethical modalities of being, however. Such ambivalence is evident in Tina's alternating between envisioning the causes of her back pain as derived from childbirth and as stemming from her years of hard work lifting heavy bundles of food.

Turning to Ma'ar, we find a man whose narratives largely aligned with the virtue of self-governance as he stressed his efforts to *athamagil* and attempted to downplay and efface his pain. This was so even despite the very real deleterious effects his pain has had on his everyday life. Work was also a major theme in Ma'ar's reflection upon his pain and in terms of the way that he set out to portray his understanding of what it means to be a healthy self. Interestingly, Ma'ar in his struggles to describe a pain that lies somewhere between *magaaf* and *gamiig*, for which he did not seem to have adequate language to describe, further evidenced pain's unassumability and its obdurate resistance to meaningful categorization. As he put it, "This is something that I only use the word 'pain,' that word 'pain,' but that is not pain. Oh, there is pain in the midst . . . I, I think that there it is in the midst of soreness and pain. I don't know the name."

Dammal, in contrast, first appeared to be an individual who was very reluctant to frame her suffering in light of core cultural virtues. Even despite the fact that Dammal did much to help her mother in her old age, she never did try to configure her pain as an instance of suffering-for her mother. This reluctance may have been tied to the deeply felt ambivalences Dammal experienced toward her mother, a mother who had caused her suffering as a child and whose recent self-transformation may have been motivated by her own being-toward-death and a fear of judgment by a Catholic God. Instead, Dammal focused her attention on how her pain stemmed from being overweight and from not eating enough local foods. It turns out that Dammal's more personalized understanding of the cause of her pain may have arisen from an attempt to reconcile her ambivalent feelings for her mother, the care she had given her, and her own wish to still find a way to embody virtuous modes of being. As we have seen in previous chapters, the virtues of endurance, self-sacrifice, suffering-for, and self-governance, are deeply implicated in practices associated with food production and consumption, activities that figure prominently in Dammal's understanding of her pain.

In some ways, Fal'eag is the person who most readily configured his pain in light of core cultural virtues. Accordingly, Fal'eag's narratives focused much attention on the significance of work, effort, and community obligations. He also directly evoked the category of *maath'keenil'* as a way in which to explain the cause of his pain. And yet, Fal'eag also struggled to articulate the sensory contours of his pain. This was so at first in the context of his attempts to describe his back pain. It was again evident in his efforts to communicate the very intense experiences of pain he underwent after reawakening from a coma. Both of these experiences are examples of pain remaining resistant in its very unassumability to meaningful narrative configuration. In the case of the brute intensity of a pain in which it "would be good had I died" and compared to which "there is nothing that it is like," the torment of Fal'eag's existential struggles spilled forth from the very elisions evident in his fragmentary narration of such experience. Even in light of his retrospective attempts to imbue pain with a narratively articulated significance, his articulations remain largely disjunctive, partial, and incomplete. The closest he came to articulating this experience in a coherent fashion was through the metaphorical, and highly personalized, characterization of his experience of being in pain as likened to a yellow turning sphere in which there was no longer a body, self, or others—only pain.

Both Paer and Buulyäl utilized the virtue of suffering-for throughout their narratives. Both also stood out inasmuch as they sought to portray such suffering-for as imposed upon them. In the case of Paer, her pain and her efforts to persevere were lodged in a discussion of war-time suffering and the work that she, her family, and her community were forced to undertake by the Japanese occupying forces. For Buulyäl it was a focus upon suffering-for and endurance in the face of what she perceived to be unjustly required work on behalf of her aunt. Throughout this time her aunt remained largely insensitive to the debilitating intensity of Buulyäl's ongoing struggles with pain throughout her youth and young adulthood. Both of these cases seem to foreground the significance of a self-initiated form of endurance for realizing virtuous modalities of being. To take on a suffering that is unjustly inflicted by uncaring others inflects that suffering with a different moral worth when compared to forms of suffering emplaced in the compassionate recognition of self-sacrifice and duty on behalf of others. The ambivalences that arise in attempting to situate the particularities of one's own self-experience of suffering in the face of such personal and social histories of injustice speaks to the always complex and nuanced ways that virtues like self-governance and endurance are given meaning for particular social actors.

Fanow, one of the eldest women to be interviewed for this project, was very explicit in aligning her pain with cultural understandings of ethical subjectivity and virtuous comportment. This was so particularly in light of her emphasizing those cultural expectations regarding women's roles and their obligations to obtain food for the family. There is certainly a degree of coercion implicated in viewing her experiences of suffering-for and endurance in terms of obligations to family and her community. As she explained, the pain in her back and joints was due to *m'aar ni pimilngaay* ("sickness of servants"). It is interesting that in contrast to Paer and Buulyäl, however, Fanow seemed to present a slightly more agentive view of her compliance to such obligations. This more agent-centered account of her endurance may be partially interpreted as a result of her foregrounding the virtues of self-governance and suffering-for within a context of ethically recognized duties, obligations, and responsibilities. A suffering enfolded within the compassionate response of others is rendered one that is partially willed as a dutiful and virtuous form of self-sacrifice.

Finally, Gonop connected the cause of his pain directly to his tendency to focus all of his attention and effort *(athamagil)* to work projects that were often detrimental to his physical well-being. Such efforts were especially compelling when work projects helped others in his family and community. Of all the individuals whose experiences of suffering have been discussed in this chapter, Gonop was perhaps the most explicit in linking his past and ongoing pain to abilities and inclinations to embody the virtue of self-governance. In fact, Gonop narratively configured his pain precisely as a necessary result of such self-governance. He regularly ignored his own personal desires, exhaustion, and well-being in order to devote all of his attention and energy to the task at hand.

In this chapter, I believe it is possible to see some indication of the extent to which themes of work, endurance, and effort permeated individual sufferers' attempts to retrospectively constitute their experiences of pain as meaningful, morally valenced experiences. These stories of suffering also provide some insight into the ways that individuals were able to uniquely personalize their narratives. The at times brute unassumability of pain and the complex moral ambivalences arising from taking on unjustified forms of suffering further speak to the very real existential struggles associated with attempting to transform pain into virtue. In this respect, it may be fruitful to view such instances of "pain talk" and the silences, elisions, and opacities often enfolded within them, as pointing to the existence of a continuum of suffering. This continuum of suffering is one in which individuals are differently able or willing to reconcile the existential facticity of their suffering with available cultural resources in configuring their experience in moral terms. In the process, individuals are at times more and less able to transform what might be characterized as largely granulated forms of experience into more coherent varieties.

Indeed, talk of suffering and pain is most certainly being put to different uses throughout these interviews. I would argue that much of this talk indicates attempts by individual sufferers to transform their pain to virtue. At times, however, such talk also appears to be put to use as a rhetorical strategy by speakers to evoke compassion and pity in their interlocutors, a rhetorical strategy that is also in line with local understandings of moral modes of existence and conduct. For others, such talk may be more accurately seen as a rather matter-of-fact indication of what Nancy Scheper-Hughes (1990, 1992) would view to be the brute facticity and viscerality of physical pain that arises from living a life of struggle, poverty, and deprivation. It is certainly also the case that in some instances such talk is evidence for the somatized idioms of suffering I discussed in the last chapter. Finally, there are a number of occasions in these narratives in which past experiences of pain continue to defy meaningful categorization for individual sufferers. Such experiences remain to some extent unformulated even in the face of the impress of cultural and personal preunderstandings.

Of particular interest in this regard is the fact that there appears to be evidence in these various narratives of a number of distinct varieties of unformulated or inarticulate experience. First, there are those forms of experience that may arise in association with moments of perception that are tied to an individual sufferer's real-time immersion in the sensory immediacy of pain. As an intense and immediate confrontation with unassumability, such varieties of pain tend to actively resist the impress of cultural and personal interpretive frames. This is seen perhaps most clearly in the case of Ma'ar's struggles to describe a pain that lies somewhere between *magaaf* and *gaamig*. For Ma'ar there did not seem to be an adequate language readily available to describe such experiences in the immediacy of their unfolding.

Second, there are those varieties of experience that even in the face of a retrospective glance obdurately resist meaningful articulation. Notable here are Fal'eag's attempts to describe an experience in which "all I knew was pain, I don't know my head, I don't know my leg, I don't know my hand, I don't know my body. Only that there is something, a yellow sphere."

Finally, there is evidence, although certainly more tenuous, for varieties of unformulated experiences that arise on what William James (1890) termed the fringe of awareness. Here sensory impressions remain "unnoticed" and yet still somewhat conscious, albeit of a different degree (James 1890; see also Dilthey 1989, 300, 305). This is perhaps best seen in the context of Fal'eag's, Dammal's, and Tina's claims that their pain, which was caused through injury or hard work during their respective youths, could remain "hidden" within their bodies for years. Such pain was held to emerge in the foreground of their awareness only after they had grown older and their bodies had weakened.

The variety of ways in which such dysphoric experiences were articulated (or alternatively remained decidedly resistant to such articulation) provides some interesting material in light of both coherence and granular theories of experience. In both of these theories a retrospectively cast narrative framing of experience is implicated in smoothing out and configuring the contents and contours of subjective life along meaningfully articulated lines. I will return to this observation when I outline a cultural phenomenological approach to morality and experience in the concluding chapter of this book. But first, let us now shift to explore how pain is articulated in the context of what are largely present- and future-oriented narratives arising in the context of real-time interaction.

CHAPTER 8

Dysphoric Moments

A Case Study

Lani gently took Tinag's arm, applied a bit of coconut oil to her hands, and began to feel with her fingers and thumb the length of Tinag's forearm. She asked Tinag to try turning her arm so that it was flat (i.e., with the palm of the hand directed to the ground). Tinag was in terrible pain and was moving her shoulders and her torso instead of her forearm to try to get her arm in the desired position. Seeing her struggle, Lani gently tried to help turning the arm while Tinag looked away, grunted, and winced. With the arm in position, Lani began to press up and down Tinag's forearm and asked whenever she moved to a new location on her arm if there was pain *(Baaq amiith?)*. She finally centered on the area where the break had occurred before stopping.

Lani suggested that Tinag's father come and hold her so that they could try resetting the bone. Her father positioned himself behind Tinag and began rubbing her head and back. Lani explained that it was going to be very painful as she tried to put the bone back into position, but that once it was all over, the pain was going to quickly fade and that she would feel much better. She pointed out that the reason that Tinag was having such a hard time moving her forearm was because the "small bone" in her forearm was misaligned. If they did not reset the bone today, while it was still moving, she cautioned, it would be much harder later when the bone began to heal. Just before resetting the bone, her father whispered in Tinag's ear that there was going to be very strong pain *(ra yib rib geel ea amiith)* but that she would persevere *(maachnea ga ra athamagil)*. He also told her that after the bone had been reset the pain would quickly weaken *(ra waer, ra waer)*.

235

ok hold of Tinag's good arm and showed both Tinag and r what she was going to do. She said that she needed Tinag's o hold the elbow in place as she pulled the arm toward her and pted to reset the bone. As Tinag watched, Lani and her father ticed with her good arm. Seeing this, she started to whimper and ake her head. Lani asked her if she would rather not go through with the procedure and Tinag replied that she could not *(Daabiyog)*. At this point I noticed that Tinag's father was beginning to tear up (as was I). Lani said to Tinag that her father was old and weak and that was why he was crying but that she was strong and that she would be fine. Her father then repeated to Tinag, "*M'athamagil.*" And then, despite her cries and screams, the bone-setting began.

After the bone was finally reset, Lani told Tinag to rest for a minute. Tinag slumped back into her father's lap, who then massaged her head and good arm. Lani wiped the tears from her own eyes and called to her daughter to prepare the medicine. She then began telling us that she had been treating a boy for the last three weeks who had a much worse break than Tinag and that now he was feeling good enough to run around without a brace. Lani then added that the boy had screamed and cried a lot when the bone was reset, but that Tinag was strong and barely cried at all. Her father added with a hint of pride that Tinag did not even cry when she broke her arm after the fall.

In this chapter I will focus on the case of a young girl who received treatment for a broken arm from a local healer who practiced traditional massage. In particular, I will discuss how the brute force of pain experienced purely as "mere-suffering" from the perspective of the sufferer, presented opportunities for the healer and her parents to attempt to shift her frame of reference to understanding her suffering in light of a "-for" structure. Such a structure, I argue, is imbued with a meaningful time-bound intentionality directed beyond the now-point of the painful present. By turning to undertake a microanalytic examination of the narratives arising in the context of real-time interaction between this one young girl, her family, and the local healer attempting to reset the bones in her forearm, wrist, and elbow, I plan to outline an argument concerning the relationship between virtue, temporality, meaning-making, and experience. Most generally, I would like to suggest that an important means through which experience may be imbued with meaning by a given experiencer is significantly tied to temporality. This is so inasmuch as we can understand processes of meaning-making as often implicated in an experiencer's ability to move beyond the confines of the present moment, by linking that moment to past or future orientations, images, concerns, or projects.

More specifically, I will speak to the debates discussed in this book's introduction between two competing theories of experience, what the philosopher Calvin Schrag (1969) has termed the granular theory and the coherence theory. This I will do by suggesting that *indexical markers of cultural virtues*—which can be understood as utterances or signs that point to broader systems of understanding concerning what constitutes the good person and the good life in a given culture (cf. Ochs 1996)—can be understood as meaningful mediating structures between what we might term, following William James (1904a, 1904b), conjunctive and disjunctive varieties of experience. More specifically, I will propose that indexical markers of cultural virtues may organize disparate or disjunctive events, intentions, and actions—that may otherwise seem to be confined to discrete, point-like moments in time—into an incipient and yet meaningfully configured temporal frame. In so doing, indexical markers may thus link such moments to past or future orientations that stretch beyond the confines of the present, a property that has long been ascribed by both philosophers and social scientists to the act of narrative emplotment (cf. Mattingly 1998).

The perspective I am advancing here is based on phenomenological and hermeneutic assumptions that processes of meaning-making are often tied to temporality. In this view, meaning arises through the active linking of a present moment to past or future moments. Accordingly, discrete disjunctive experiences are able to be recast, reorganized, reconfigured, and reframed as significant conjunctive experiences, at the very least retrospectively. That said, where the last chapter highlighted how even in the context of retrospection experiences of pain may still actively resist meaningful articulation, in this chapter I suggest that such indexical markers of cultural virtues may at times actively (pre)configure such dysphoric experiences in real time.

The basis of the argument of this chapter is twofold. First, I plan to outline how indexical markers of cultural virtues may be understood as significant entry points to the temporally configured narrative framing of experience. This is the case to the extent that these markers themselves have a quasinarrative, temporal configuration inherent in their very constitution as *indexes of virtues*. Second, I will suggest that it is due to the very fact that these markers, at least indirectly, index a meaningful, quasinarrativized, temporal frame that they may be particularly salient when an individual is confronted with a radically disjunctive experience, which may be otherwise resistant to narrative framing in the context of its lived immediacy.

But first, let's turn to the case in question.

The Fall

Tinag's injury occurred after returning to her village from school. She knew that she was expected to go straight home to help with household chores and to work on any homework she may have been given that day. Instead of heading home, however, Tinag decided to stay at the top of the hill on the outskirts of the village to play with her friends. It was during this time that she broke her left forearm falling out of a tree. Later, when I had an opportunity to ask Tinag about what had happened to her, she said that she had climbed one of the trees near a neighbor's house and was swinging back and forth on one of the branches. She explained that she lost her grip on the branch and went flying through the air landing on her back with her arm hitting a stone. As she recalled (and as her parents and grandparents later mentioned to me), she did not cry at all when the accident happened.

According to her grandmother, Tinag was certainly in a lot of pain after the fall. She did not cry, however, because she did not want anyone to know that she had hurt herself by doing something that she was not supposed to be doing. In fact, one of her uncles had actually shown up at the top of the hill not long after she fell but was unaware of the injury. This was because Tinag had turned her back to him and kept quiet to make sure that he did not notice her. She managed to keep silent until he arrived at another neighbor's house across the path, at which time she let out a yell. Her grandmother claimed that Tinag had been trying to pretend like everything was all right, but in the end the pain was just too great and she had to express it. Tinag herself told me that she had wanted to cry but that the tears would not come to her eyes. It was not long after this that Tinag's father showed up. Upon seeing her arm, which was obviously broken, he put her in the car and drove her immediately to the hospital.

It is important to highlight the moral implications of the fall that led to Tinag's broken arm. Her accident while playing with her friends after school was interpreted by her parents and her elders as a direct result of her being careless, unthinking, and disobedient. As noted throughout earlier chapters, in light of the virtue of "self-governance," acting without carefully reflecting upon potential consequences and acting without deliberate attention to bodily movements and forms of expression is understood to be a sign of either mental or moral incompetence. In the most egregious cases it is a sign of both. In addition, the fact that Tinag was playing with her friends instead of returning home to do her chores further meant that she had not lived up to the virtue of "suffering-for." In failing to live up to either the virtues of self-governance or suffering-for, Tinag was thus faced with not only the brute intensity of her pain but also with her caregivers' expectations that she should redress these moral failings by now working to approximate these two virtues in the context of her treatment.

The data that will serve as the basis for this case study was taken from two healing sessions that were videotaped during the fall of 2002 about two and half weeks after Tinag's accident. The local healer treating Tinag in both sessions, a woman whom I will call Lani, was an Outer Islander who hailed from the island of Fais, which is located approximately 150 miles northeast of Yap proper. Lani had lived on Yap with her family for the past fifteen years. With a passive fluency in Yapese (that is, she understood Yapese fluently but tended not speak it—her native language was Ulithian) Lani generally communicated to her Yapese patients in English. In both of these sessions, Tinag, who was ten years old at the time of her fall, was accompanied by her father and her mother. On her second visit she was also joined by her cousin, two sisters, and maternal grandmother.

As a result of her fall, Tinag suffered a compound fracture of her radius and ulna in her left forearm, in two places. This was the diagnosis she received when her father first brought her to the hospital where her arm was x-rayed, the bones "reset," and a cast applied. Tinag also suffered a dislocated wrist and elbow. These two injuries did not result from the fall but from what turned out to be the doctor's failed attempt to reset the bones at the hospital. It was only after returning to the hospital a few days later that it was discovered that the bones would have to be reset again. At this point, Tinag's parents decided to take her to see Lani. Lani reset the bones during Tinag's first treatment. She relocated the elbow on her second visit the following day. On the two days that this case material was drawn from, which took place about two and half weeks after the initial treatment began, Lani was attempting to relocate Tinag's wrist.

All told, Lani treated Tinag for over two months. Her treatment consisted of coming for massage every day except Sunday, taking various local medicines that were meant to treat her bones, blood, veins, muscles, and pain, and bathing and exercising in the ocean every morning and evening. Each massage lasted anywhere from fifteen to forty minutes, and with the exception of the first session where Lani first reset the broken arm, and three other sessions that I was not able to attend, I managed to videotape all of the sessions that Tinag underwent during her treatment.

At numerous times during her treatment, Tinag's parents and grandparents reminded her that in order for her arm to heal properly she would have to experience great pain. In the face of that pain, they told her, she would have to endure or *athamagil*. For instance, the morning prior to her first treatment while sitting with Tinag's parents, siblings, and aunt as we were preparing to leave, her aunt told Tinag repeatedly that if she was able to *athamagil* through the pain of the treatment that everything would be fine. Later, on our way to Lani's house, her father took some time to explain to Tinag that the first few days were going to be the most painful, but that eventually the pain would lessen. He also told her that she would probably be going every day for treatment and that even though this would be an unpleasant and difficult experience for her, *ga ra athamagil* ("you will persevere"). He repeated *ga ra athamagil* at least three more times to a very silent and sullen Tinag during the brief fifteen-minute drive to Lani's house.

When I asked her father why it was that he had thought to first bring Tinag to the hospital and not to a traditional healer, he replied that he believed that she was too young to endure the pain that comes with traditional bone setting. He had himself undergone such treatment for a broken leg when he was in his early twenties and he felt that Tinag was just not strong enough to *athamagil* in the face of such intense pain. That said, after the failed attempts to reset the arm at the hospital, he became convinced that they had little other choice but to see a traditional healer. He then added that even despite her young age, Tinag was *be geel laen ii yaen'* ("strong minded").

It is significant to note that Tinag's "strength of mind," while lending itself to her ability to *athamagil*, would later turn out to be conceived as a problem when she began to resist her treatment. During these periods, I was told by her parents and grandparents alike that Tinag had *ba geel ea laem roek'* ("a strong or stubborn mind"). Once she had made up her mind about something, it was very difficult to persuade her otherwise. The distinction between individually and socially canalized willing that was detailed in chapter 5 was thus often at the center of the talk surrounding Tinag's responses to her pain and her treatment. In many ways, part of the moral education being enacted through Tinag's participation in, and her caregiver's responses to, her treatment was tied to attempts to socialize her will. That is, to redirect her strength of mind to the virtuous capacity to *athamagil* and away from an individually motivated attempt to pursue courses of action that went against her caregivers' requests. It was an opportunity for Tinag to engage in moral work directed toward gaining mastery of the self.

To wit, her grandfather often told her that even though the pain she suffered during her treatment was intense, she should not allow her mind to become stubborn. Instead, he instructed that in the face of such pain she should not let her "mind come" but should *athamagil— Dabmu yib ea leam room, fan ra ba amiith kam athamagil.* During the period when Tinag was most actively resisting her treatment, both of her grandparents suggested to me that the best thing to do would be to forcibly hold her down so that Lani would be able to work on her arm. This, they suggested, would ensure that the arm would heal properly as well as helping to teach Tinag to persevere in the face of suffering and not to resist a treatment that would ultimately help her.

Before turning to examine the actual stretches of talk and interaction surrounding the two healing sessions, it is necessary to say a few words regarding the flattening out of experience that tends to occur when the complexities of social action are represented through the constraining medium of text (see Duranti 1997b, 137; Ricœur 1991). It is very much a concern of mine that in representing Tinag's lived experiences of pain in text that readers may tend to overlook the very real intensity and viscerality of her suffering. Indeed, it is important to recall here that transcription is a form of inscription (Ricœur 1991). It is thus necessarily a process whereby only some of the characteristics of a complex action that occurs in real time and space "are fixed into a record that will outlast the fleeting moment of real-life performance" (Duranti 1997b, 137). Unfortunately, it seems that the selectivity and simplification (Duranti 1997b, 137–38) that are necessarily part of fixing fleeting moments of lived experience and social action into a perduring textual form often have the effect of distancing a reader from the potency, tumult, and felt impact that such experiences may otherwise reveal in the context of those full sensory arrays arising with their real-time occurrence (e.g., the positions, proximities, and movements of bodies in space, tonal qualities associated with voices, and so on).

When I have presented this data in public forums, I have often been able to play the accompanying audio along with the transcripts that are presented below. In listening to or watching the original recordings we hear Tinag's screams, shouts, and at times unintelligible calls for the massage to stop. We are able to listen to her sobbing, pleading, and calling out to her parents. We are confronted with the very tangible concern, worry, and care in her caregivers' voices as they attempt to comfort Tinag in the face of what is, if I have ever witnessed it directly, a "world-destroying" moment of pain. In experiencing these recordings first hand, audience members are often visibly shaken up. They are left with an immediate appreciation for the fact that what is represented below in these transcripts is very much imperfectly drawn from actual moments of intense suffering that are the very real experiences of another human being: a ten-year-old girl who wanted nothing more than for her pain to stop. I ask that readers try to keep in mind the difficulties inherent in inscribing such moments of suffering and to recall that the transcription of the interactions that occurred on these two days represents an often very difficult, emotionally charged, and potently upsetting experience for many of the participants involved.

Resistance and the Narrative Configuration of Ethical Modalities of Being

The first interaction that I am going to examine was taken from the first of these two sessions, a session where Tinag was particularly resistant to having Lani work on her wrist. This example will serve as a counterpoint to the second session, since Tinag's resistance to treatment meant that she was not suffering through intense pain in this interaction. It is interesting that in this regard there was significant evidence of attempts by her parents to narratively frame her experience in order to persuade her to stop resisting the treatment.

In the very beginning of this session, Lani had inquired about Tinag's pain. Her father responded that Tinag's pain varied. Sometimes it was less intense, sometimes more so. After removing the medicine that was on Tinag's arm, Lani began to feel the area where the break had originally occurred while Tinag looked on, staring straight ahead and avoiding eye contact with either Lani or her father. In so doing, she was very much approximating the model of self-restraint and controlled expressivity entailed in the virtue of self-governance. As Lani began to apply more pressure, however, Tinag turned to look at her arm and grimaced, before finally pulling back and leaning with all of her weight limply against her father who was holding her from behind. It was at this point that Lani tried to reach out to take Tinag's hand a second time, and it is here that our transcript begins.

((Lani (L) reaches out twice to take Tinag's (T) hand. Tinag does not give her arm but instead sits immobile, leaning with all of her weight, limp, against her father (F), all the while looking down with her eyes closed. Tinag's mother (M) is sitting on her right, watching.))

001 F; *Gabe sasaagël ngaam gurguur nga nge ngaam piiq Lani nga ngaam chamagiy boechquw*
You are going slowly, you will hurry up and you will give Lani [your arm] and you will be massaged a bit

((Lani is wiping something off Tinag's leg and is looking down.))

002 *ya kri geel ea amiith riy me ngaam too . . . ga ra tooffaan.*
because there will be very strong pain and then you . . . you will rest.

003 *Umm? Ga ra chamagiy boechquw.*
Umm? You will be massaged a bit.

((Lani puts her hand out a third time and this time holds onto Tinag's hand and attempts to pull it closer to her. Tinag tries to pull her hand back while her father tries to stop her.))

004 *Kayog ea benir!*
Enough of that!

005 *Tinag . . . gaar paqam iii, ii, . . . paqam Lani.*
Tinag . . . give your arm *iii ii*, . . . your arm to Lani.
[

006 M; *Ngam piiq paqam Tinag.*
You give your arm, Tinag.

((Lani lets go of Tinag's hand and leans back looking at her.))

007 F; *Daa chamagiy paqam,*
         If she doesn't massage your arm,

008   *ra paer paqam arrogon.*
         your arm will stay that way.
                    [
009 M; *Ngaam piiq paqam nge ra chamagiy.*
         You give your hand and she will massage.

((Lani leans forward and points to the area around the wrist and then speaks in English.))

010 L; See, here, it is a little bit soft and (???).

((Lani attempts to grab Tinag's hand again and Tinag uses her good arm to cover her wrist with her hand so that Lani cannot have access to it.))

011 M; *Daa, daa taaq, nga chamagiy nga maaq, paapëy ra fal'eag.*
         Don't, don't put [your arm there], she will massage and she will be finished and it will be fixed quickly.

((Father removes Tinag's good arm and holds it back.))

012 L; Heh. ((short, soft laugh))

013 F; *Da . . . Nga chamagiy boechquw. Bay kri geel ea amiith riy*
         Don't . . . She will massage a little bit. When there is a lot of pain

014   *me goog ngaak nge ngaam tooffaan, hum?*
         I will tell her and you will rest, hum?

((Tinag starts to cry quietly, with her head down, her father starts wiping the tears from her eyes.))

015   *. . . Daab ki yoer, daab ki yoer ((quietly)), gabe yoer me daawor nge chamagiy, um?*
         . . . Don't you cry, don't cry ((quietly)), you are crying and she has not yet started to massage, um?

((Tinag remains motionless covering her injured arm with her good hand.))

016   *Daam koel paqam ni ra paer arrogon. Be geel ea amiith riy?*
        Don't hold your arm or it will stay that way. Is there a lot
        of pain?
                [
017 M; Tin.

((Tinag lies motionless.))

018   *Tinag? Moey nga paqam ni nga chamagiy nge paapëy ra*
        fal'eag,
        Tinag? Give her your hand so that she will be able to massage
        it and fix it quickly,

019   *m'athamagil . . . m'athamagil. Suwan nga laang.*
        you endure . . . you endure. Sit up.

((Her father lightly lifts Tinag's good arm and then sets it back down.
Tinag is still motionless, silent.))

020 F; *Bayi ea chamagiy be waer. Baye taaq gapgip nge ra chamagiy*
        rib waer. Hum?
        She will massage lightly. She will put on coconut oil and she
        will massage lightly. Hum?

021 L; ((speaking English)) We can massage light if you doesn't
        want to. . . .
        It's easy to
                [
022 M; *Suwan nga laang.*
        Sit up.

((Her father tries to position Tinag so that she is sitting upright. She
remains completely limp against him. Lani leans forward to try to take
hold of her arm again.))

023 F; *M'athamagil, ra waer. Kayog ea binir aye . . . Tin!* ((strong
        loud voice.))
        You endure, and then it [the pain] will weaken. Enough of
        that . . . Tin!

((Her father pushes Tinag up slightly again, and she immediately falls
back against him.))

024 M;   *Tinag. Tinag. Daab ki chamagiy paqam me re mog ngu wan.*
Tinag. Tinag. If she's not going to massage your arm then
say so and I will leave.

025   L;   ((in English)) Hum . . . hum, doesn't want me to massage
your hand. No?

There are at least two points worth highlighting in this interaction.
First, there is the fact that Tinag resisted the massage and was thus not
experiencing intense pain. Second, there is the fact that in lines 001–
002, 005–009, 011, 013–016, 018–020, and 023 we see that in an attempt
to convince her to participate in the massage, both Tinag's mother and
father work to narratively frame what is yet to come in the treatment.
They do so in such a way that there is a clear temporally and morally
configured beginning, middle, and end to the interaction.

In the first two lines, Tinag's father tells her to stop resisting; she
will undergo the massage. He further narratively projects a future
horizon of intense pain that she will have to endure. He then suggests
that the pain will not last long and that she will have an opportunity
to rest when the massage is over. In lines 005–009, we witness both of
her parents again narrating the immediate future of her undergoing
the massage, as well as suggesting a possible future of disability with
definite moral repercussions and continued pain if she chooses not to
undergo treatment. By line 011, Tinag's mother scolds her for covering
her arm to stop the massage and then tells her again that the massage
will happen, that it will be over quickly, and that this is the only way
that her arm will be "fixed." Lines 013–016 entail her father narratively
anticipating the impending massage, as well as attempting to encourage
Tinag by bringing up the possibility that Lani will stop the massage if
the pain becomes too great for her to bear. After reminding Tinag that
there is no reason for her to be crying since the massage has yet to
begin (and she is thus not presently feeling any pain), he again reminds
her that continued resistance to the treatment will result in a future in
which her arm will remain injured. Growing increasingly frustrated and
angry with Tinag's continued resistance, her mother then reiterates that
the massage will happen and that it will be over quickly (lines 018–019),
before telling her to *athamagil*, sit up, and stop resisting. Finally, in
line 023, her father again tries to comfort her with the knowledge
that the massage will be quick and that the pain will diminish when it
is over.

The overall structure of the narrative that is coconstructed by Tinag's father and mother in the context of this brief interaction can thus be summarized as follows:

1. You are currently suffering pain because in the past you fell from a tree (the subtext of which is: resulting from the fact that you were neither careful nor obedient).

2. You must now be obedient and stop resisting so that Lani will be able to massage you.

3. During the massage you will be in a lot of pain and you will suffer, but you should persevere *(athamagil)*; you should stop crying, stop resisting, and not express your pain so that she will be able to fix your arm.

4. Once the arm has been fixed the pain will go away, it will heal properly, and you will be able to again return to contributing to your household chores and community work (the subtext of which is: you will be able to look back at this experience with pride in your ability to approximate an ethical way of being).

As we saw earlier, a very similar storyline was provided to Tinag prior to her first massage, and again repeated throughout her treatment. This particular session ended with Tinag effectively resisting her massage altogether, however. Her parents, who were both very upset with Tinag's behavior, decided that if she would not be compliant in allowing Lani to put her wrist back into place that her treatment would end immediately and that she would not return the following or subsequent day(s) for any more medicines or massages.

Acutely Dysphoric Moments and the Articulation of Experience

The following session can be directly contrasted with the interaction just examined. As we saw, the first interaction was one in which Tinag was not suffering through intense pain since she effectively resisted her treatment. It was also a session in which there were many attempts to narratively frame her experience as her father and mother worked to persuade her to participate in the massage. The interaction that occurred on the following day, however, occurred when Lani did actually attempt to put the joint back in place. It was a session in which Tinag was suf-fering through very intense pain. Of central interest here is the fact that in this context, Tinag's parents and her grandmother did not primarily utilize narrative, but turned instead to rely upon what I am terming *indexical markers of cultural virtues* in their attempts to help her through her pain. These indexical markers of cultural virtue, as I will argue below, also entailed a protonarrativized (see Stern 2004) struc-ture. This was so inasmuch as such markers were at least indirectly indexical of a temporal framework. Such a framework was one wherein the present moment of Tinag's pain was positioned between a past of moral inadequacy and a future where Tinag's ability to *athamagil* would allow her to approximate culturally valued modes of subjectivity and comportment. In a way, such markers pointed to a possible means for Tinag to partially atone for her past moral failings.

Indexical markers in their simultaneous coexistence with discrete moments of pain could further play a role in framing such moments as anchor-points for later attempts to more fully configure Tinag's pain in narrative terms. Indeed, as her caregivers later revisited her ability to *athamagil* in the face of her pain, more fully articulated narratives of Tinag's moral worth were able to be rooted in the already fertile soil prepared through the initial framing of her past painful experiences in light of such indexical markers.

While I did not join Tinag and her father on the ride to Lani's house on this particular day, I noticed almost immediately upon their arrival that Tinag's attitude had shifted considerably from the previous session. For instance, when she first sat down on the covered veranda where all of her treatments occurred, Tinag bore a look of serious determination. She quickly settled down to allow Lani to remove her cast (one devised from the split sections of a branch of banana tree that was held in place with a store-bought tensor bandage). As the massage began, Tinag also held her body straight and turned her head away from both Lani and her father. In averting her gaze, maintaining an expressionless look, keeping her body upright and rigid, and in allowing Lani to begin to massage her arm without any of the previ-ous day's resistance, Tinag seemed to be working to approximate the virtue of self-governance. After a few minutes, however, as Lani started to work specifically on her wrist, Tinag moved her body back against her father and tried to stop Lani from carrying through with the massage by once again attempting to cover her wrist with her good hand.

It is at this point that the interaction transcribed below begins. Here, Tinag (**T**) is leaning back against her father (**F**) who is looking at Lani (**L**). Her brother is standing off to the side, watching. Tinag looks to Lani who is holding her injured arm with one hand while reaching to get some more coconut oil in order to begin the process of relocating her wrist. Upon seeing this, Tinag begins lifting her body up and shaking her head with her eyes closed. At this point she exclaims:

001 T; *Daa mu ma teel paqag!*
Don't you pull my hand/arm!

002 F; *Soen, m' . . . m', m' athamagiliy.*
Wait, you, you, you endure.

((At this point, Tinag raises her good hand, and almost simultaneously her father places his right hand over her arm and Lani grabs her hand and looks at Tinag. Her father continues to speak.))

003 *Ke suul daabi geel, boechquw, boechquw.*
It went back into place before, [she will] not [massage] hard, [only a] little, little.

((Tinag is whining quietly.))

004 **L;** ((In English)) Then I know when you feel pain, I stop.
[

005 F; *Boechquw, ah, ma teleag.*
A little bit, ah, she will stop.

((Father leans forward and hugs her. As he does so he grabs her good arm again as Lani prepares to begin the massage.))

006 *M'athamagil. M', m'athamagil, huh? Ra maaq.*
You endure. You, you endure, huh? It will end.

007 L; ((In English)) Ya, you cry, 'cause you feel pain.

((Tinag begins crying louder))

008 F; *Um, um, um.*

009 L; *Um soen.*
You wait.

010 F;   *M'athamagil, m'athamagil. Ma ra ngoongoliy ni ma ra feal'.*
          You endure, you endure. She will fix it so that it is good.

011   *Rayog ni ngaam athamagil? M'athamagil.*
          Can you endure? You endure.

((Tinag shouts))

012 F;   *Ah, boechquw . . .*
          Ah, a little bit . . .

013 T;   *Maaaa papaa* ((screams))!
          But papa ((screams))!

014 L;   If you hadn't ((**F** looks at **L**)) go get a broken bone you won't
          feel pain.

015 F;   *Um. Um. M'athamagil.* ((very quietly))
          Um. Um. You endure. ((very quietly))

((Tinag is now pushing back against her father very forcefully while
screaming and crying.))

016   *Daam yoer. M'athamagil. Daam . . . M'athamagil, Tin.*
          Don't you cry. You endure. Don't . . . you endure, Tin.

017   *Boechquw, boechquw, kri boechquw, kri boechquw, kri boechquw.*
          A little bit more, a little bit more, a very little bit more, a very
          little bit.

((Tinag screaming much louder and struggling intensely.))

018 T;   *Daab kiiiiyooog! Daab kiiyoooog! Paaa!*
          I cannot! I cannot! Paaa!

019 F;   *Daabkiyog? Huh? Daabkiyog?*
          You cannot? Huh? You cannot?

020 T;   ((screaming)) *Paaa!!!!! Staaaaa!!!!*

((Tinag starts whimpering. Father looks up, Tinag's brother (B) sits
down. There is laughter as Tinag's mother (M), two sisters (who
remain away from the massage) and grandmother (G) arrive at the top
of the stairs out of the camera's view. Lani looks back after she hears
the laughter. Something is said that is inaudible. Tinag's grandmother

begins walking immediately from the stairs toward Tinag, but is yet to enter the camera's frame.))

021 G; *M'athamagil, m'athamagil . . .*
        You endure, you endure . . .

022 T; ((screaming))

023 G; *M'athamagil! Be geel ni gem! M'athamagil, m'athamagil!*
        You endure! Make yourself strong! You endure, you endure!

024 T; *Paaapaaaa!!!!!!!*

025 G; *M'athamagil. M'athamagil. M'athamagil, Tinag.*
        You endure. You endure. You endure, Tinag.

((Grandmother appears in the frame walking from the stairs toward Tinag.))

026   *M' athamagil. M'athamagil* (???) ((inaudible because of Tinag's screaming)).
        You endure. You endure ((inaudible because of Tinag's screaming)).

((Tinag is really screaming and struggling now; her grandmother had just sat down and now she stands back up to help Tinag's father restrain her))

027 F; *Eh, eh.*

((Tinag is screaming louder than ever before.))

028 G; *M' athamagil Tin, m'athamagil Tin.*
        You endure Tin, you endure Tin.

029 F; *Be geel nigem.*
        Make yourself strong.

030 G; *M'athamagil, m'athamagil, m'athamagil.*
        You endure, you endure, you endure.

031   *Ra fal'eag paqam. M'athamagil, m'athamagil.*
        She will fix your hand. You endure, you endure.

032   *Ra feal' ea paqam. Ra maaq, ke yan ea* (???) ((inaudible over the crying)).

Your hand will be good. It will end, she went (???) ((inaudible over the crying)).

033   *M'athamagil.*
You endure.

034 T;   *Paaapaaaa!!!!*

035 G;   *M'athamagil. M'athamagil Tin.*
You endure. You endure Tin.

036 F;   (???)

037 G;   *M'athamagil. Bayi feal', daariy ra buuch room, bayi feal' paqam. M'athamagil.*
You endure. It will be good, nothing will happen to you, your hand will be good. You endure.

((Tinag is now screaming, Lani is looking at her face and holding her arm with both hands as she tries to put the joint back in place. Tinag's mother is standing and looking over the shoulder of Tinag's grandmother, who is sitting to the right of the camera watching and helping to hold her leg.))

038 G;   *M'athamagil, m'athamagil, m'athamagil, m'athamagil.*
You endure, you endure, you endure, you endure.

039   *M'athamagil.* ((laughs))
You endure. ((laughs))

040 T;   *Daabyiyoog. Daabiyooog Paaa paaaa!*
I cannot, I cannot, Paaa paaaa!

In looking over this stretch of talk and interaction it is certainly true that there is evidence for narrativized temporal emplotment in lines 010, 014, 032, and 037. Here, Tinag's father and grandmother reiterate the now familiar themes that if she endures the pain, her arm will be fixed, she will get better, and the pain will go away. What is most interesting for the argument I am trying to advance in this chapter, however, is that it is precisely when Tinag was faced with what appears to be moments of having to suffer through her most excruciating pain—moments evidenced by the fact that she was screaming the loudest and attempting to resist the massage most vigorously by kicking and flailing her arms—that both her father and her grandmother were not falling back on fully articulated narratives but on the repeated use of the phrase *m'athamagil.*

As I will suggest below, *m'athamagil* as an indexical marker of cultural virtue that is imbued with an incipient temporal and moral framing of beginnings, middles, and ends, may play a role in transforming disjunctive experiences of brute unassumable pain into increasingly conjunctive and formulated varieties. Indeed, lines 002, 006, 010, 011, 015, 016, 021, 023, 025, 026, 028, 030, 033, 035, 038, and 039, where the phrase *m'athamagil* is uttered no less than *thirty-three times*, seems to coincide most often with those moments when Tinag is most vocally expressing her pain by screaming, crying, and struggling. All of which are acts that, while certainly not giving us transparent access to her subjective experience, at least seem to indicate to those around her that she might be experiencing more intense pain than in those moments when she is sitting quietly before being massaged.

Now, there are a number of possible effects that may be attributed to this repetitive usage of *m'athamagil* in the context of this particular interaction. First, as we have seen throughout the pages of this book, the virtue of endurance or *athamagil* is centrally positioned within the nexus of a number of other core cultural virtues underpinning Yapese moral sensibilities and ideas concerning what constitutes the good person and the good life. *Athamagil* entails a moral view of a person founded upon his or her abilities to endure suffering in the service of carrying on with efforts that will ultimately benefit others. Accordingly, *athamagil* may be viewed as a capacity or enactment of an individual's morally rarified "will" that is oriented to muting or rechanneling personal desires and wishes in light of family, community, and broader social dictates.

To this end, it is important to highlight the fact that the utterance *m'athamagil* is a contracted form of the second-person past-tense rendering of the intransitive verb *athamagil: mu athamagil.* This grammatical form is generally characteristic of directives or imperatives in Yapese. To this extent then, there is a definite evocative force and performative quality that is entailed in uttering *m'athamagil* as a command. As a command, the utterance does not merely represent a particular phenomenon, quality, or state of affairs, but rather is uttered in order to have a direct impact upon a given listener. Indeed, as speech-act theorists have long argued, in addition to its denotative, referential, and propositional functions, language also has an illocutionary function in which utterances are intended to bring about certain effects.

Coined by Austin, the perlocutionary force of an utterance is precisely the notion that illocutionary acts (e.g., stating, commanding, promising, questioning, etc.) have definite consequences or effects on hearers (Austin 1962; Duranti 1993; Searle 1969, 25). That is, language affects a listener, who plays an active role in assigning meaning to a given utterance (Garro and Mattingly 2000, 11). In this way language may serve as a rhetorical tool through its ability to evoke ideas, images, feelings, emotions, motives, and goals in listeners who work to align their own perspective on a given experience or event with those of the speaker. As a command, *m'athamagil* is uttered with the intention of affecting Tinag. It is an attempt at compelling her to conjure up the qualities of mind necessary to persevere in the face of her pain despite her strong desire to resist her treatment and to avoid further suffering.

That said, what may have been evoked for Tinag when hearing these particular utterances—which I wish to suggest may have served as a potentially potent means for stretching her attention beyond the immediacy and intensity of her pain—could entail a number of differing possibilities. At the most basic sensory level, in merely hearing the sounds associated with these utterances, Tinag may have been afforded an opportunity to direct her attention to alternate sensory phenomena beyond the confines of her pain. Engulfed in a wash of painful sensations, it may have been merely in hearing these perhaps indistinct and inchoate utterances that she was made aware of the presence of caring others beyond the confines of her own subjective sphere. In this way, she was perhaps able to envision a horizon of future possibilities beyond the confines of the present.

The very rhythm and repetitive nature of these utterances may have also contributed to helping Tinag see beyond the longstanding now of the painful present. As Ricœur attests in the context of discussing the role of repetition *(Wiederholung)* in Heidegger's discussion of the existential stretching-along of *Dasein*, "Repetition thus opens potentialities that went unnoticed, were aborted, or were repressed in the past. It opens up the past again in the direction of coming-toward [the future] . . . the concept of repetition succeeds at once in preserving the primacy of the future and in making the shift toward the having-been [of the past]" (Ricœur 1985, 76).[1] As Lévi-Strauss (1963) noted long ago in a discussion of the efficacy of symbols in organizing that which "would otherwise be [the] chaotic and inexpressible" pain of a difficult childbirth, the very repetition of chanted phrases may help to organize the immediate lived time of suffering in light of a more distal cultural or mythic time. While I have not sought to graphically represent the rhythmic nature of the repetitive usage of *m'athamagil* in this interaction, the very rhythm of these utterances may have similarly expanded a range of imaginal, emotional, and volitional dimensions of Tinag's subjective experience. In so doing the rhythm of these utterances may have thus provided a nondiscursive means for Tinag to demarcate and thus begin to disambiguate the indefinite, long-standing presentness of her pain (cf. Berger 1997, 470).

I think that it is possible to view the ongoing rhythm, repetition, and pulse of the utterance as providing at least a twofold temporal frame for Tinag's suffering, what I am terming a "dynamic frame" and a "segmentative frame." In terms of the dynamic frame, the pulse of the repetition of *m'athamagil* may be understood to provide a sense of moving forward through time as each evocation of the utterance carries with it an expectation of its continuing repetition. The anticipatory nature of the repetitive pulse of the utterance is imbued with an expectation of an ever-emerging future that may eventually open onto a time when Tinag's pain will eventually subside.

In the case of the segmentative frame, the rhythm of the phrase may be understood to mark out distinguishable moments in time—with each utterance of *m'athamagil* acting much like the ticking of a clock or a metronome in providing a metric by which to orient a consciousness engulfed by pain. Inasmuch as the rhythm and repetition of the phrase is able to extend her attention beyond the long-standing now of her pain, Tinag may thus be understood as having been provided an intersubjective scaffold—also perceivable by the other participants in the interaction—for her attempts to endure, to *m'athamagil*, in the face of her suffering.

Drawing briefly from the phenomenologist Edmund Husserl (1964), we can say that each utterance of *m'athamagil* can be considered a temporal object. That is, it is an object that has temporal expanse or thickness that includes not only the now-point of the present moment but also anticipatory and retained horizons of that moment. This is what Husserl terms protention and retention respectively (1964; cf. Tombs 1990).[2]

As previously mentioned, *m'athamagil* can be understood to provide a dynamic frame for experience. As each utterance arises and gradually fades from the horizon of consciousness, an anticipatory protention awaits the arising of another utterance that is expected to follow the rhythmic contours and patterns of the previous phrase. This rententional projection of an anticipated next utterance allows for the possibility of embedding an otherwise perduring now of intense world-destroying pain within a rhythmic structure that demarcates a time that is objectively and intersubjectively perceivable by both Tinag and her caregivers alike. Such a rhythmic overlay of uttered sound can therefore be understood as an iconic evocation of endurance. Indeed, the rhythm of such utterances are iconic to the extent that the ongoing sonic repetition of *m'athamagil* is suggestive of an extended continuity through time, a property that is a salient qualitative aspect to the idea of perseverance.

To the extent that she was able to register not only the sounds but also the meaning of the utterances, Tinag may also have been made aware of how her present experiences were connected to her previous actions (i.e., her fall from the tree, her failed treatment at the hospital, and her alternating struggles to resist and comply with her ongoing treatment by Lani) and those possible futures that may arise from her current acts (i.e., enduring her pain and being healed, failing to do so and having to live with a disabled arm). As Pierre Bourdieu (1998) argues, such Husserlian retentional and protentional arrays are not only informed by the residues of the immediately passing perceptual now-point but are further impacted by moral orientations sedimented in the form of a habitus (see Throop and Murphy 2002). This is a process that may have possibly enabled an interlacing of Tinag's memory, present perception, and anticipation thus creating a temporal continuum that is at each phase imbued with moral valences.

Moreover, the mere co-occurrence of her father and grandmother uttering *m'athamagil* in conjunction with her experience of excruciating pain and her directly experienced struggles to comply with or resist her treatment, once inscribed in her memory, may have further provided an initial means to begin the work of formulating such experience. As such, the utterance of *m'athamagil* may be construed as a potential point of entry into more fully articulated narratives of the significance of these events, long after they had passed. Indeed, in returning to revisit her ability to endure or *athamagil* on this day in the car ride back to the village, and in numerous subsequent conversations recounting what happened during her massage, Tinag, her siblings, and her caregivers were able to more fully elaborate the important moral consequences of her perseverance in the face of such world-destroying pain. For instance, in telling Tinag's paternal grandmother (who was not present for the massage) about the session, Tinag's father, in the presence of Tinag, said, "*Kab ea amiith machena de yib ea laem roek, ke athamagil. Ke chaag boech Tinag* [Pain came to her but her stubborn mind did not. She persevered. Tinag was a bit more skilled (today)]."

In fact, when Tinag's treatment was finally finished and she was able to return to participating in household and community work projects, there was often talk of both her morally disvalued stubbornness in the face of resisting her treatment and of her ability to finally *athamagil* in the face of such horrible pain. It was this endurance in the face of her pain that contributed to Lani being able to properly finish resetting the bones in Tinag's arm and relocating the joints in her elbow and wrist. Such endurance was directly embodied in even those fleeting moments when Tinag was just still enough, just quiet enough, for Lani to perform the manipulations necessary to relocate her joint.

It is important to note here that Tinag's effort to endure in the face of her pain was significantly seen by members of her family and village alike as an effort to suffer-for her community. Indeed, prior to her accident Tinag was a regular participant in the village's community dances. These dances were often given for visiting tourist groups and were a major source of income for the villagers. Due to the way that Yapese bamboo dances are structured, during the time of her injury three other children from other families within the village had to also sit out during these performances (and were thus not paid for their services). She was, of course, also an important contributor to work in and around her own household. If she had not been able to conjure up the strength of mind to *athamagil*, her disabled arm would have negatively impacted both her family and her community at large. Tinag's injury was thus not hers alone. It was an injury that implicated others to whom she was morally accountable.

In the context of these particular interactions, *athamagil* may be considered an indexical maker of cultural virtue that is potentially evocative of a moral landscape in which past moral inadequacies are framed in light of ongoing present struggles. As such, utterances of *m'athamagil* may serve as a semiotic anchor pointing to a broader moral framework that contains a protonarrativized structure. This framing of present action in terms of past moral failings establishes the basis for impending possible futures that are configured according to local ethical modalities of being. This is an idea that I wish to pursue in greater detail from the perspective of those debates over the structures and dynamics of experience discussed in the introduction to this book.

Narrative, Time, and Metaphor

In his phenomenological description of pain's centripetal and centrifugal modes, Drew Leder (1990) points to the fact that temporality seems to be a significant axis for understanding pain.[3] This is of considerable interest given temporality's centrality in more general discussions of narrative structure and the structure of experience. Indeed, as Desjarlais argues, experience has most often been defined in the West as "an inwardly reflexive, hermeneutically rich process that coheres through time by way of narrative" (1997, 17; see the introduction). Here, I would like to further elaborate on this relationship between narrative, temporality, and experience. This will serve as an entry point into a discussion of some of the ways in which indexical markers of cultural virtue may provide individuals with personal and cultural resources to meaningfully frame their lived experience, especially when faced with the unassumability of some of the most intense varieties of suffering and pain.

Succinctly put, the relationship between narrative and temporality is evidenced in William Labov's minimal definition of narrative as the ordering of two or more events in light of some temporal sequence (Labov 1972). In the context of relating narrativity to temporality, however, Ricœur asserts that it is precisely through narrative emplotment that we are able to "re-configure our confused, unformed, and at the limit mute temporal experience." This is accomplished by unifying into a "whole and complete action the miscellany constituted by the circumstances, ends and means, initiatives and interactions, the reversal of fortune, and all the unintended consequences issuing from human action" (1984, xi, x). For Ricœur, narrative emplotment is thus partially based in a configurational act that "grasps together" "the detailed actions or . . . the story's incidents. It draws from this manifold of events the unity of one temporal whole" in such a way that the act of emplotment "extracts a configuration from a succession." As such, emplotment is defined by Ricœur precisely as the "synthesis of the heterogeneous" or "concordant discordance" wherein beginnings, middles, and ends are meaningfully interpolated in such a way that "one after another" is transformed into "one because of another" (1984, 66, 156).

As Garro and Mattingly similarly explain, through narrative mere sequentiality is transformed into the structure of a plot that imbues sequence with causality, intention, and purpose. By means of emplotment, events are fashioned through a narrative "linking of motive, act, and consequence" (Garro and Mattingly 2000, 10; see also Mattingly 1994, 1998; Garro 1992, 1994). Narrative emplotment is significantly rooted in temporality since temporality is manifest in the very structure of narrative itself. Accordingly, narrative plays a role in shaping the ways an individual is able to reflect on past experience, give meaning to ongoing interaction while also setting a course for future action (see Garro and Mattingly 2000; Ochs and Capps 2001). Temporality, according to Ricœur, is thus "that structure of existence that reaches language in narrativity and narrativity . . . the language structure that has temporality as its ultimate referent" (1981, 165).

Narrative provides us with an important way to imbue our experience with meaning by configuring time according to purpose, intention, and causality. Another such means, however, may be found in nonnarrativized symbolic forms such as metaphor. Indeed, in taking a critical stance toward attempts to theorize the relationship between narrative, temporality, and experience, Laurence Kirmayer (2000) has provocatively argued that while it might very well be the case that narrative is significantly tied to the ordering of events through time, metaphor may more accurately reflect the fragmentary and disjunctive nature of some varieties of experience. Thus, metaphor may importantly serve as a tool through which to imbue such experiences with meaning. Kirmayer points out that to this end, "narratives are not the only constituents of experience" (2000, 153). Even when coherent narratives are used to represent experience they may be quite removed from the immediacy of an individual's life as lived (see also Bruner 1984; Hollan 2000; Wikan 1992).

Kirmayer acknowledges that narratives provide an important means through which experience is codified, represented, anticipated, recalled, and made meaningful. He also believes, however, that there are a number of other "knowledge structures" lacking the overall temporal structure of narrative that may also provide an effective means by which to organize and represent experience. Of these various nonnarrativized knowledge structures, Kirmayer believes that metaphor, by blending what would otherwise be two distinct "conceptual spaces," can be understood to occupy "an intermediate ground between embodied experience and the overarching narrative structures of plots, myths, and ideologies."[4] As such, metaphor may help to convey those forms of "nonnarratized, inchoate experience that resist narrative smoothing and containment" (2000, 155, 169).

The power of metaphor to articulate what may be otherwise the mute viscerality of pain is also suggested by Elaine Scarry. According to Scarry, it is often primarily through processes of metaphorical extension that "the felt-attributes of pain" are able to be "lifted into the visible world but now attached to *a referent other than the human body*" [emphasis in original] (1985, 13). As Scarry argues, the metaphors associated with experiences of pain are routinely predicated upon either specifying an external agent that causes the pain (i.e., a "stabbing" pain) or the "specific bodily damage that is pictured as accompanying the pain" (1985, 15).

On Temporality, Experience, and Virtue

In dialogue with this ongoing discussion of the various means by which experience may be made meaningful through symbolic or linguistic forms, I would like to suggest in concluding this chapter that there is an inherent, yet incipient, temporal structure approximating the temporal structure of narratively configured experience in nonnarrativized indexical markers of cultural virtues. Such markers, which I have argued may be evidenced in the multiple utterances of *m'athamagil*, may thus serve as potential vehicles for defining meaningfully articulated varieties of experience.

The incipient temporal structure found in these indexical markers of cultural virtues is, I believe, reflected in the very definition of virtue itself. While there are many competing philosophical perspectives on how exactly to define virtue, many philosophers, particularly those following some version of Aristotelian virtue ethics (McIntyre 2002; Hursthouse 1999; Nussbaum 2001; Slote 1992), have used the term to refer to those dispositions, discernments, sensibilities, and feelings informing action that is deliberately undertaken by social actors in reference to some commonly valued good.[5] As McIntyre explains in a commentary on Aristotle's *Eudemian Ethics,*

Virtues are dispositions not only to act in particular ways, but also to feel in particular ways. To act virtuously is not, as Kant was later to think, to act against inclination; it is to act from inclination formed by the cultivation of the virtues. Moral education is an "éducation sentimentale." [Thus for Aristotle,] the educated moral agent must of course know what he is doing when he judges or acts virtuously. Thus he does what is virtuous *because* it is virtuous [emphasis in original]. (2002, 149)

In this most general definition of virtue, then, we can see the inter-section of a discerning orientation to a good (implying anticipation), unfolding action and feeling (implying an orientation to the present moment), and dispositions and sensibilities (implying memory and an orientation to the past). Virtues thus entail a threefold temporal struc-ture that figures prominently in many discussions of narrative structure more generally. Indexical markers of cultural virtues also index an incipient version of this threefold temporal frame encompassed in the intersection of past, present, and future self-states. This is a structure that Husserl characterized as inherent in the organization of internal-time consciousness.[6]

Accordingly, indexical markers of cultural virtues can be understood to mediate between two seemingly competing perspectives on narra-tive, experience, and temporality. On the one hand, there is Kirmayer's assessment that there are nontemporally ordered "knowledge struc-tures," such as metaphor, that may help to organize, reflect, or give meaning to disjunctive experience. On the other hand, there are those scholars who have argued for the important role of narrative in struc-turing experience temporally in terms of meaningfully configured beginnings, middles, and ends (see Ricœur 1984, 1985, 1988).

In this respect, indexical makers of cultural virtues have properties not unlike Ricœur's description of Arthur Danto's concept of "project verbs." As Ricœur attests, project verbs, such as "make war" or "write a book," "cover many detailed actions, which may be totally discontinu-ous and implicate numerous individuals in a temporal structure" (1984, 147). In this way, even despite the fact that these project verbs are not narratives, they can be understood as serving to "organize numerous microactions into one unique overall action" (1984, 147; cf. Basso 1996).

In line with what Ricœur has described as the protoconfigurational properties of project verbs, then, I would like to suggest that indexical markers of cultural virtues may have a similar property of being able to organize disparate, otherwise disjunctive, events, intentions, and actions into an incipient, and yet meaningfully configured, temporal frame. This is a frame that is able to orient an experiencer to a past that informs either his or her interpretation of the present moment and of his or her possible futures. In working to mark, select, and thus disambiguate elements of painful experience—thus rendering them experiences ori-ented beyond the present to a past or future configured in moral terms—I am proposing that indexical markers of cultural virtues can serve as potential entry points into narrativized temporal structure. In this light, they can be thought of as semiotic anchors that, while not themselves narratives, succinctly encapsulate what many scholars have characterized as the meaningful more-than-mere-sequentiality that is evidenced in narrative emplotment.

Tied to this, I would like to further offer that when faced with pain in its world-destroying immediacy, these indexical markers of cultural virtues may in some instances be understood to serve as significant organizing frameworks. These frameworks allow sufferers to situate, and perhaps thus transform, their experiences of discontinuity arising in the face of intractable pain. In the process, such disjunctive experiences may be rendered meaningful conjunctive experiences that are articulated according to an orientation beyond the present moment (where sufferers may be otherwise overwhelmed in a wash of unassumable pain), providing access to a meaningfully configured temporal continuum that interleaves the present with the past and the future. As discussed in previous chapters, endurance or *athamagil* plays a key role in transitivizing mere-suffering, transforming it into an experience of suffering-for. Accordingly, *athamagil* may become deeply implicated in a given actor's distal and proximate pasts that reach back from an immediate unfolding of a present moment from which tendrils of expectation extend toward a horizon of possible futures.

My suggestion is that there is a potential phenomenological effect to using this particular indexical marker of cultural virtue in those instances wherein Tinag appears to be facing her most intense world-destroying pain. At the most embodied level, to the extent that these utterances of *m'athamagil* are implicated in keeping Tinag still for even a few seconds, long enough to allow Lani to do her work, Tinag is thereby able to experientially embody the virtue of perseverance, even if only momentarily. Moreover, by suggesting both a temporal and moral framing of her experiences that interpolate an incipient beginning, middle, and end, these markers may help to stretch her attention beyond the present moment that is engulfed in pain. Such utterances perhaps further provide her with an entry point into later moments of narrative emplotment wherein she may come to understand her suffering as valuable as her pain is transformed into virtue. In so doing, they enable her to approximate her culture's models of ethical subjectivity and virtuous comportment, which are intimately linked to notions of what constitutes the good person and the good life.

Finally, indexical markers of cultural virtue may be understood as communicative and cultural resources employed in the dynamic flow of real-time interaction in the service of forming particular ethical modalities of being. In this light, the experiences and events being interactionally framed by these markers importantly corresponds to what Ricœur has suggested are the "enlarged" properties of action in the context of a plot. These properties, he argues, significantly include "the moral transformation of characters, their growth and education, and their initiation into the complexity of moral and emotional existence" (1984, 10).

Conclusion

> While in moral pain one can preserve an attitude of dignity
> and compunction, and consequently already be free; physical
> suffering in all of its degrees entails the impossibility of
> detaching oneself from the instant of existence. It is the very
> irremissibility of being. The content of suffering merges with
> the impossibility of detaching oneself from suffering.
>
> Emmanuel Levinas, 1987

In this book I have sought to demonstrate the pervasive ways in which
experiences of pain and suffering are situated in everyday life in Yap.
This was accomplished by highlighting pain's brute existential facticity
and by examining a number of key cultural virtues that have bearing
on the articulation of experiences of suffering in meaningful moral
terms. In the first half of the book I argued that such virtues have
implications for defining personhood, interpersonal attachment, sense
of place, and the trajectory of familial, social, religious, and political
relationships. When understood in relation to other core virtues, such
as *athamagil* ("endurance"), *magaer* ("work-induced exhaustion"),
and *runguy* ("compassion"), I suggested that suffering and pain are
deeply rooted in various aspects of Yapese social life. This ranged from
exchange and intercaste relations to eating classes, issues of purity and
order, and, finally, to the production and consumption of food.

These same moral sensibilities, practices, and idioms associated with
pain and suffering were then shown in subsequent chapters to be
reflected in local models of subjectivity. Such models encompassed

understandings of the dynamics of inner experience and the communicative forms through which aspects of subjective life are expressed. As we saw, these models were significantly tied to the prevalent practices of concealment and secrecy in everyday forms of social agency. In light of such practices, Yapese understandings of subjectivity and social action were importantly defined in accord with the virtues of "self-governance" and "suffering-for" others.

Following this, Yapese linguistic, semiotic, and symbolic representations of pain states were examined. In addition, the ways that pain is reflected in local illnesses categories was investigated, particularly in the case of the illness known as *maath'keenil'*. Throughout, I attempted to demonstrate some of the cultural processes entailed in the categorization and objectification of pain. In so doing I suggested possible ways in which painful sensations can be transformed from instances of mere-suffering to suffering-for. As a result I worked to establish those local frameworks within which pain could be variously viewed as a form of granulated or coherent experience. Such transformations largely depend upon the extent to which local categories, idioms, and tropes can be employed by individual sufferers and their interlocutors in defining the contours of their suffering.

Finally, in the last two chapters of the book I shifted to explore the narratives of individual sufferers in order to foreground how pain, suffering, endurance, and self-governance are actively configured in the midst of the dynamic and complex texturing of subjective life. This was approached from both the retrospective remove often entailed in interview-based reflections upon past experiences of pain and from the immediacy of living through pain in the context of real-time interaction. Here we were confronted with experiences of pain that seemed to evidence various degrees of articulation spanning a continuum of formulation. Perhaps most importantly there was evidence for the complexity and temporal dynamics of such transformations as individual sufferers were engaged in constantly modifying their attention to relevant aspects of their experience through time. As we have seen, moments of virtuous suffering are subjective and intersubjective accomplishments that may be realized, even if only momentarily, before resolving back into instances of nonvirtuous and unwanted forms of "mere-suffering" and vice versa.

What can we make of the varieties of experience and temporality that have been examined in the preceding chapters? In the case of what were largely retrospectively cast narratives of individuals suffering with various chronic pain conditions, experiences of pain ranged from the unassumability of world-destroying pain, in which individuals may have wished that they had rather died than undergo such unbearable suffering, to coherent moral articulations of a sufferer's self-experience in the form of what was often held to be work-induced varieties of hurt. In the midst of these differing articulations of suffering was evidence for a gradated range of unformulated experiences in which painful sensations were not always readily channeled into available expressive forms.

In the case of Fal'eag, for instance, we saw evidence that pain's unassumability had implications for transforming an individual's lived experience of an embodied time. For Fal'eag this was evident in the way that differing modalities of being-toward-death were evoked in his attempts to face some of the most unspeakable forms of suffering. We also saw much evidence for the moral articulation of suffering in terms of core cultural virtues, however, as individuals like Ma'ar, Gonop, Tina, and Fanow expressed their pain as a form of suffering-for others in their attempts to work on behalf their families, friends, and communities.

With regard to real-time negotiation of intensely disruptive experiences of acute pain on the part of Tinag, her family, and her healer Lani, there was likewise some evidence for an apparent movement toward more fully articulated varieties of moral experience. These varieties of experience arose primarily in the context of attempts to convince Tinag to *athamagil* in the face of her pain. That said, there was further many indications that Tinag's struggles to cope and make sense of her pain were often interrupted and challenged in the face of the immediacy of her pain's brute facticity.

In attempting to offer a way to begin assimilating what in their present unfolding were unassimilatible experiences of pain, Tinag's family worked to direct her attention to efforts at enduring and persevering in the face of her suffering. This was a means to attempt to encode her experience of suffering, not as a world-destroying dissolution, but as an experience imbued with a positive (even if perhaps fleeting and not fully articulate) moral valence. Dysphoric tensions and sensations in the viscera that might otherwise have been ignored, or perhaps categorized as an unwilled response to resist further suffering and pain, may have accordingly been recategorized in such interactions as intentional experiences of exertion and effort on the part of Tinag in order to regain control over her body and mind.

In configuring experiences of pain in light of core cultural virtues—virtues that are deeply implicated in an ethical system that importantly pivots on the nexus of pain and suffering engendered through hard work and service—many of the sufferers I spoke to appeared able to at times recast painful sensations in light of core cultural understandings of what it means to be a good person and to lead a good life. Sensations associated with effortful striving, physical exhaustion, fatigue, suffering, and bodily pain that were able to be linked, either retrospectively or prospectively, to these virtues could thus be re- or precast as morally valenced and meaningful lived experiences. Aligning such experiences of pain with core cultural virtues may have actively worked to stretch a given sufferer's attention from an immersion in the immediacy of a present awash in pain to possible future self-states. This is not to say that a given sufferer's experiences of suffering remained static through time. To feel like one's suffering is virtuous one moment or one day is not to say that one could not again enact a return to experiencing nonvirtuous forms of mere-suffering, of world-destroying pain. Virtuous suffering in this framework is as much dispositional as it is contextual, experiential, and pragmatic.

Articulating Experience

To my mind, these vicissitudes of experience largely outstrip the far too simplistic dichotomous polemics of coherence versus granular theories that were discussed in this book's introduction (cf. Desjarlais 1997; Mattingly 1998). Drawing from the work of William James, Edmund Husserl, and Alfred Schutz, I have elsewhere (Throop 2003a) sought to advance a cultural phenomenological approach to experience that accounts for such complexity. Such an approach situates experience within a continuum of possible formulations, ranging from an immersion in the immediacy of consciousness and action as unfolding in real-time to the mediacy of a distanced reflective assessment of already elapsed events and noticings.

Without getting into the details here (see Throop 2003a), I have sought in particular to highlight how different orientations to time might affect the variegated structuring of experience by means of alterations in a subject's modes of attention (cf. Csordas 1993). To this extent, I argued that while it is true that we often maintain an attitude toward the world that is structured according to a future orientation toward goals, projects, and desires (see Heidegger 1996; Mattingly 1994, 1998; Ochs and Capps 2001), it is also the case that there are moments where it is not merely attention to the future, but attention to the past or the contingencies of the present that directs our action. Indeed, in the context of extreme forms of suffering, it is often the case that individuals have little other choice than to deal with their immediate immersion in the present moment (see Leder 1990; Good 1994; Scarry 1985). As we have seen at times throughout the narratives explored in this book, in the midst of such unassumable forms of suffering and pain, anticipatory protentions may remain unfulfilled as what were previously taken-for-granted properties of self, body, and world are recurrently challenged and destabilized.

In order to better highlight the relationship between these seemingly divergent varieties of granular and coherent experience, such insights can be further situated in the context of Drew Leder's (1990) appropriation of Freud's (1962, 106; 1966, 347) concept of a "complemental series" (Throop 2003a). According to Leder, a complemental series is any gradated series of phenomena that are structured such that the two polar endpoints of the series interact in a way that "the arising of one is necessarily correlative with the other's decline." Leder utilizes this concept to account for differing forms of bodily "disappearance," where a modification of attention works to insure that "as a part of my body is taken up focally, it can no longer play a background role relative to that activity and vice versa" (1990, 28). This same concept is relevant, I have suggested, for accounting for the general relationship between conjunctive and disjunctive varieties of experience which may differentially arise in complex ways through time as individuals continually shift their attention in relation to their embodied, psychical, and social worlds (Throop 2003a).

A "complemental approach to experience" therefore assumes that the *organization of attention* is directly implicated in the dynamic structuring of what becomes either foregrounded or backgrounded in awareness. Such an approach leaves ample room for a range of intermediate experiences that do not display either full coherence or full granularity (Leder 1990; see also Berger 1997, 1999; Csordas 1993, 1994b; introduction). It also helps to explain why it is that absolute coherence and granularity are in the moment of their immediate occurrence mutually exclusive categories.[1] This is not to say that what was once a disjunctive experience cannot be fashioned into a coherent experience through the meaningful structuring entailed in a retrospective glance (see Schutz 1967). Nor that coherence and disjunction cannot follow one another in close temporal succession (Berger 1997, 481; Berger 1999, 124; Berger and Del Negro 2002, 71–72). The stream of consciousness, as James's apt metaphor implies, is in constant flux with attention shifting between more and less coherent forms of articulation from one moment to the next. What this approach does imply, however, is that while there is indeed a spectrum of possible articulations of experience in terms of coherent and granulated forms, it is *not* the case that experience will emerge as coherent and granulated *simultaneously* in either the foreground or background of awareness.

Toward a Cultural Phenomenology of Moral Experience

While I still hold to the basic argument advanced in the development of this complemental approach to experience, in what remains of this book I would like to propose a way to further develop this approach in relation to issues of morality and ethics. This will serve as a means to further discuss issues pertaining to the ways that moral sensibilities are implicated in the articulation of experience. It will also provide us with a means to explore the ways that a cultural phenomenology of moral experience may be implicated in further developing the ethnography of subjectivity.

To address these problems I wish to further elaborate upon a foundational phenomenological insight, namely that social actors are able to shift between different "attitudes"—from a "natural attitude" to a "theoretical attitude" for instance—by engaging in what Edmund Husserl (1962) termed "acts of phenomenological modification" (see Duranti, forthcoming). These acts of phenomenological modification are directly implicated in the patterning of attention and thus the configuration of experience. Significantly, one such form of phenomenological modification is tied to an individual's ability to participate in engagements with other social actors as "beings-like-me"—as meaning endowing, feeling, knowing, and willing subjects who may experience suffering and joy (see also Throop 2008b; Husserl 1993; Stein 1989). Alternatively, social actors may modify their attention to those self-same others by orienting to them as objects, physical entities, or corporeal bodies that have been divested of such subjective entailments (cf. Good 1994).

Husserl understood that the view of a meaningless, inert, objectively given nature set apart from the subjectivities that perceive it is itself a concept that is constituted in a lifeworld, a lifeworld that has a historical specificity and which is also the result of particular acts of phenomenological modification (Husserl 1970). That attitude, in which we are immersed in a taken-for-granted orientation to a physical and social world existing apart from our perception, he termed the natural attitude. Implicated in Husserl's account of the natural attitude is the idea that it, like other attitudes, is constituted subjectively not only in terms of particular ways of seeing, feeling, and acting, but also in terms of particular ways of judging and appreciating (cf. Throop 2009; Geertz 1973). The assumptions underpinning the natural attitude can be destabilized, Husserl argued, by means of enacting the phenomenological epoché, an act of phenomenological modification in which such beliefs can be "neutralized" and put into "brackets" (Husserl 1962).

In his attempts to extend such Husserlian insights to the development of a "moral sense of nature," Erazim Kohák (1984) has argued that scientific orientations to nature often view morality as invested solely within a subject who is made to stand out from the inertness and senseless materiality of the external world. Separating the suffering subject from the world in which he or she is enmeshed leaves the thing we call "nature," Kohák explains, a valueless matter that is inherently distinct from human subjectivity. The resulting depersonalization of nature, the cleaving of the moral from the natural, is tied precisely to unexamined habits of attending to our place in the natural world, claims Kohák (1984). To move beyond such historically bound preconceptions, Kohák argues, we must find ways to initiate a "change in focus" in which we are able to place "radical brackets" around the inert meaninglessness of the natural world.

Also drawing from Husserl (as well as Heidegger, Bergson, and others), Emmanuel Levinas's existentialist moral philosophy similarly seeks to grapple with the way that ethics is grounded in particular attitudes or orientations to experience. Of particular import for the argument I wish to advance here is the fact that in Levinasian ethics a moral claim is made against those orientations to experience in which we come to treat ourselves, and those others with whom we interact, by means of what Martin Heidegger (1996) would have termed a "present-at-hand" ontology (cf. Dreyfus 1990).[2] That is, an ontology that treats a being as an object that has specifiable characteristics, qualities, dispositions, and so on.[3] In contrast to such a present-at-hand ontology, Levinas bases his ethics on a respect for the unassumability of any given being's existence as someone who is independent "of the perception that discovers and grasps them" (1998, 16). If I attempt to understand another solely in terms of her history, habits, knowledge, environment, and character, precisely what escapes my understanding, Levinas argues, is the being of the other that stands in a relation of exteriority to the self-sameness of my being. What escapes typification, what resists a present-at-hand rendering of being as a type of category, quality, or thing, is precisely what Levinas terms "the face." In his words, the face refers to "the way in which the other presents himself, *exceeding the idea of the other in me*" (1980, 50).

In treating another person as a category, in attempting to assimilate the other to the interpretive frames of the self, we engage in an act of violence, Levinas claims, against the very alterity of the other (cf. Butler 2005). In so doing, we no longer partake in the immediacy of the other's concrete presence as a being whose modes of being-in-the-world always exceeds our self-experience. Through acts of representation, generalization, typification, and objectification, the living density of the being who confronts us in the space of the interhuman realm is effaced in all of its concrete particularity, uniqueness, and irreducibility. Recognition of the other's singularity and unassumability speaks instead to engendering a vulnerable passivity in our modality of relating that enables a shift from a present-at-hand ethics to a properly human ethics, one that respects and acknowledges the plenitude and uniqueness of the other being.

That moment of confronting another that evokes in us disquietude, bewilderment, uncertainty, and confusion is precisely that moment that Levinas deems to be the existential foundation of ethics (Waldenfels 2002, 63). It is precisely in such moments of bewilderment and uncertainty that what I term the anthropological attitude and the ethnographic epoché are rooted. I will return to discuss the relevance of these constructs for further developing a cultural phenomenology of moral experience.

In orienting to another it is often only in moments of opacity, where failures in our attempts at understanding reveal the limits of interpretability, that there is a true acknowledgment of the integrity of that other, the alter, the full being that stands before us.[4] Much like the Gadamer of *Truth and Method* (1975), Levinas argues that a view of persons in their typicality is a self-serving infringement on the genuine human bond—a bond of asymmetrical openness and vulnerability. To foreclose such an openness, to predict, to claim to know the other in advance, is to forsake the very inexhaustibility of the being of that other who continually remains a mystery revealing the limits of our expectations, preunderstandings, and prejudices.

While Levinas does not utilize Husserl's terminology in precisely the same way that I have done here, I believe that it possible to see in Levinas the development of an ethics in which the moral is understood to be part and parcel of a particular attitude, an attitude that is thus constituted through particular sorts of phenomenological modification. Without getting into the details of the very real differences between Levinasian and Husserlian approaches in this regard, it is important to note that the particular modes of phenomenological modification advanced by Levinas are those that require a passivity and vulnerability that may at times be at odds with Husserlian notions of consciousness as an active force in constituting reality.

The modality of relating that is required from Levinas's perspective is a relation that is structured in the form of a question, a question that does not anticipate its answer. This is a fully temporalized form of relating. As Husserl's (1964) theories of intentionality, primal impression, and internal-time consciousness also suggest, however, time's very unfolding opens outward toward anticipated horizons that are still undetermined. Time itself, Levinas argues, is organized around the rupture of the predictable, the unsettling of the past in a recurring confrontation with the unforeseeable. This reveals a form of lived temporality that is not equivalent to "the objectivity of theoretical language, which 'gathers' the diachrony of time into presence and representation through accounts and histories" (1998, 165).

According to Levinas, an ethical orientation to the other comes before fully elaborated anticipations of that which is yet to come. It arises instead from the passive unthematized registering of the other's alterity and finitude. Such an orientation to the other reveals a temporal order distinct from, and yet related to, internal-time consciousness (cf. Husserl 1964). What Levinas terms the "futurization of the future" is not a future that is within my grasp. It is a future that is only suggested in the face of the anticipation of the mystery that lies beyond my own and the other's death. It is a future that reveals itself only at the extreme limits of the vanishing point of the horizons marking the finitude of being.

This temporality is one in which responsibility is held to arise not from the particularities of what I have or have not done, nor from the recollected history of my relationship with the other. It is instead "something that never was my presence and never came to me through memory" (1998, 170). This "an-archic responsibility" for the other calls forth from an "immemorial past." It is an imperative from a past that does not stem from a memory of a once-elapsed present moment. It is similarly an obligation that is not oriented to a future state of salvation or redemption (cf. Weber 1946). It is instead an imperative that precedes the temporality of reflexive modes of understanding that are invested with the particularities of a given moral order, a particular theodicy, or a particular eschatology whether narratively, metaphorically, or practically conceived. It is a responsibility that comes not from a rational subjection but from the primordial reality of the asymmetries inherent in the human condition. It is an obligation that breaks upon us as rupture, difference, in the otherwise smooth flowing of temporality in its structure of retention and protention, recollection and anticipation.

From a Levinasian perspective, my present thoughts, feelings, emotions, and moods are held to arise for me in a moment that can only be recognized by *you* in the modality of an after. That is, the expressions you take up as indications of my subjective state are already at that moment retentions or past recollections for *me* of my previously experienced intentions, goals, plans, and desires. My anticipatory horizons, while attentive to your responses, are also feeding forward to the horizons of my own desires, wishes, and hopes for what is next to come. That the synchronization of our two beings even in the most intimate of "we-relationships" (cf. Schutz 1967) is one of a delayed asymmetry constituting an interhuman time that is neither precisely mine nor yours is, Levinas (1987) argues, a basic fact of human existence revealing the necessary excess of being.

It is this very excess of the other's alterity that affects a breach that compels us to reassess the expectations arising from the foreclosure of our being upon itself. In other words, the other's alterity engages an act of phenomenological modification whereby we are compelled to shift our attitude from the platitudes of the familiar, the predictable, and the knowable to the uncertainties of the unfamiliar, the unexpected, and the opaque. There is, therefore, an "adventure," an "intrigue," or what we might call a curiosity that unfolds in response to the opening of being in the face of such forms of rupture so ethically conceived. This is a modality of being in the form of a question that remains beyond any particular existential category.

Each of us is compelled, Levinas asserts, to remain vulnerable to disturbance, to suffer the repeated failures of our expectations in confronting a world that outstrips our attempts at encompassment through understanding. It is in those very moments of passivity, in facing our responsibility for another who exceeds our understanding of them, no matter how fleeting those moments might be, that ethics finds its existential rootedness in the space of the interhuman (cf. Kleinman 1999; Scheper-Hughes 1992).

The Ethics of Suffering

As we have seen, some of the most intriguing and compelling moments revealed in the context of ethical responses to suffering are those associated with the most unassumable varieties of pain and hurt. Suffering is, Levinas asserts, "a *datum* of consciousness" (1998, 91). It is, however, a datum that reflects the reversal of consciousness in its everyday modality of grasping, assimilating, and taking hold. It represents, ironically enough, a sensorial registering of the unrepresentable, the unassumable, and the refusal of meaning. It is rejection, refusal, and denial inscribed in our very sensibilities. Suffering is a form of "backward consciousness," not in a modality of grasping but of "revulsion" (Levinas 1998, 91). It is, for Levinas, a form of pure passivity, a "taking into" consciousness that is no longer an act of consciousness. As a modality of "pure undergoing," suffering renders sensibility "a vulnerability, more passive than receptivity; an encounter more passive than experience" (1998, 92). As such, Levinas takes even the most unassumable forms of suffering as potentially evocative of virtuous modes of being.

He argues that not all suffering is virtuous suffering, however. There is indeed a solipsistic evil to "pure pain" that is pain "for nothing." Such pain, I have argued, can be understood as a form of mere-suffering. The ethical promise posed by pain, however, is that it commands a turn toward, and recognition of, "the other me whose alterity, whose exteriority promises salvation" (Levinas 1998, 93). In the wake of even the most primal moans and cries arising in the face of pain, we witness the initiation of a movement toward a new horizon of experience. Such a movement is effected, I argue, through an act of phenomenological modification in which there is a shift from the incoherent and meaningless solipsism of brute pain, of pure suffering that offers no path of escape, to a beyond that "appears in the form of the interhuman" (Levinas 1998, 94; cf. Scarry 1985). To find a way to position pain within the context of an "end in view," to make suffering a mode of suffering-for, is thus to lose suffering's "modality of uselessness" (Levinas 1998, 95). This, Levinas suggests, is what reveals the ethics of suffering. That is, in the face of the other's suffering, the very unassumability of the other's self-experience is revealed to us and in its self-presencing is evocative of a call to responsibility. This, he claims, is the suffering of compassion.

In the presence of a pain that is not, and can never be, mine, there is a recurrent refusal of my attempts to domesticate that pain to the self-sameness of my being. The suffering in the other, and the suffering that arises in me as the suffering of compassion for the other's suffering, are therefore foundationally incommensurate experiences that are yet articulated through the call to responsibility that they each evoke. Meaningful suffering-for another in the form of compassion or love results from our experiencing the asymmetry evidenced so forcefully, so palpably, in the face of the other's pain. In confronting the stark impenetrability of the other's pain, the integrity of the other being is revealed against the intimate backdrop of our own self-experience. It is at the limits of empathy, Levinas (1998; cf. Kirmayer 2008) asserts, in directly confronting the "ineffaceability" of the other, that a responsibility without concern for reciprocity is primordially recognized, or more appropriately, enacted. It is in this primordial orientation "for-the-other" as other and not as an object or thing—that is, as a being and not a thing to be used—that there exists an ethical obligation, Levinas argues, "prior to the statements of propositions, communicative information and narrative" (1998, 166).

Arising from the nexus of the suffering of compassion and the suffering of the other that can never be my own, there is, ironically, the basis for the most primordial forms of human connectedness. Non-useless suffering, what I have termed suffering-for, is compassion for that which I can never assimilate to my self-experience or fully understand, for that which outstrips the limits of my own particularity. It is in this space of "non-in-difference" to the other's pain that the ethical is realized (Levinas 1980, 1987). Levinas's ethics of suffering is one that is based on the realization that in such moments, however fleeting, we are faced directly with the unassumable integrity of the other "before the astonishing alterity of the other has been banalized or dimmed down to a simple exchange of courtesies that has become established as an 'interpersonal commerce' of customs" (1998, 101).

The ethics of suffering is one that sees the very opacity of the other's self-experience, its recurrent refusals in the face of my call to domesticate its difference to the sameness of my being, as a form of revealing. This is a revealing of the "very nexus of human subjectivity" which, however ironic it may sound, finds its most authentic moments of connectivity in the wonderment that arises in the face of the mystery of the other and the limits of interpretability. This is not a form of recognition that is based in the distancing glance of a theoretical attitude in which the other's expressions serve as indications of his or her character, personality, or history. It is instead a deeper, more primordial recognition of that other's very irreplacibility. In the face of the stark unassumability of another's pain, the finitude, vulnerability, frailty, and nonsubstitutability of the other is thrust forward in all of its unbearable magnitude. In such moments, such as those evidenced in Tinag's incomprehensible screams and Fal'eag's experience of pain in the face of which he would have rather died, there is a shattering of the idea that this suffering now confronting me is the suffering of this or that person who does or does not deserve this, who has or has not done this. This is instead a discerning of the moral worth of the other in their uniqueness and irreducibility that arises when we are no longer oriented to interpreting their existence in a mode of typicality.

But just where does such an existential ethics of suffering leave anthropology? In anthropology we advocate the study of a much different notion of particularity *in* history. We are a discipline that takes the stories of particular persons and communities to be central when we are seeking out, describing, exploring, and at times critiquing in our efforts after meaning, and, dare I say it, truth. It is somewhere in the space between discerning the particularity of the unassumability of being and the understanding of the particularities of historical and cultural beings that lies an answer, I believe, to how it is that we might go about incorporating such a phenomenology of moral experience within an anthropological frame.

I think that many anthropologists would agree that the experiential basis of Levinas's ethics in the face of what can be understood as the enigma and mystery of the other as an unassumable alterity, for instance, is an orientation to others that is in fact not often realized in everyday interaction. As Schutz (1967) and Garfinkel (1967) taught, in our everyday interactions with our consociates it is instead often a mode of typicality, an engagement with others as tokens of particular types of persons, with particular histories, likes and dislikes, dispositions, moods, and proclivities, that characterizes our everyday stance toward our social worlds. It takes, I argue, a particular sort of phenomenological modification that allows us to recognize the mystery of the other in the way that Levinas describes it—as that which breaks in upon and ruptures our experiences of the self-sameness of our being. As Freud's (1949) theories of transference and countertransference have also taught us, those moments within which an encounter with the other is realized as unfettered by traces of past desires, forms of typicality, and anticipations, may be quite rare indeed. Levinas's turn to discuss such limit-experiences as insomnia, suffering, and pain speaks to how extra-ordinary such opportunities to appreciate the integrity and mystery of the other may be. And yet, such moments do still at times occur in even the most ordinary of interpersonal exchanges (cf. Das 2007).

It is, I have argued, only as dispersed through the asymmetries of human relatedness, in the space of the interhuman, that the inert density of meaningless suffering and pain—meaninglessness evidenced in the very phenomenology of suffering as a rupture of the knowable—that suffering may become meaningful as a modality of suffering-for. It is indeed in this region of possibility that Tinag's suffering is arrayed. Just as Tinag is asked to come to interpret her pain as an opportunity to suffer-for others, her suffering is further taken up by others who are compelled to also suffer-for her—to feel compassion for her pain and to recognize a call to responsibility to help her endure.

It is in this relation, in this truly interhuman recognition of an asymmetrical mutuality of suffering and vulnerability, that meaning arises not only as representational and denotational but also as lived. It is precisely the establishment of this existential moral bond, whether by means of indexical makers of cultural virtue, metaphors, or more fully formulated narratives, that is at stake in the interactions I witnessed between Tinag, her caregivers, and Lani. In not delimiting a definitive account of Tinag's final understanding of such attempts at moral self-fashioning—while still attempting to suggest what some of those possibilities might be—I have thus tried to approximate Levinas's call that we recognize the very particularity and complexity of her humanness in such moments by resisting easy attempts at typifying them.

And yet, these moments still call for a movement toward understanding Tinag's self-experience in moral terms that extend from this primordial existential responsibility to more articulated formulations of her moral standing in both personal and cultural terms. The neo-Aristotelian accounts of virtue ethics (discussed in the previous chapter) rely upon an understanding of narrative as implicated in an attempt to mediate the rupture that arises when social actors are confronted with the uncertainties and ambiguities of experience (cf. Mattingly 1998, n.d.). The type of cultural phenomenology of moral experience that I am advancing here is thus one that seeks to take into account both the full plenitude and unassumability of Tinag's being *and* her various modalities of orienting to experience, whether construed in personal or cultural terms. It is thus an approach that seeks to examine primordial structures of human existence in relationship to those forms of cultural and personal understanding that underpin the complexities and ambiguities of a life lived in an effort after meaning and virtue.

The Anthropological Attitude and the Ethnographic Epoché

As I have argued, this account of morality is grounded in the space of the interhuman, a space that both Husserl and Levinas characterize as *not* necessarily one of mutuality and merger (see Throop 2008b; Hollan and Throop 2008; Kirmayer 2008). But yet, it is still one that often does compel us to engage in practices that may lead to empathy, to suffering-for another, to experiences of "collective pain," and to recognizing the other as a self that is similarly vulnerable to the unavoidable call of others' presences in the social scene (Schutz 1967, 1982; Stein 1989). As we saw in previous chapters, cultural idioms, tropes, narratives, and practices play a key role in mediating such forms of ethical self-understanding in relation to our consociates, predecessors, and successors (see Schutz 1967; cf. Geertz 1973).

By comparison, on the existential level, as a point of rupture, unassumability, and resistance, unbearable suffering and pain may engender an act of phenomenological modification in which pain becomes implicated in reorienting an individual to his or her own self-experience in the modality of its immediate unfolding as opposed to its crystallization as a determinable object of awareness. That is, instead of understanding oneself in a mode of typicality, as a person with particular traits, dispositions, needs, wants, and desires, such a confrontation with insufferable pain may evoke a confrontation with the mystery of one's very own being, with the unassumability of subjective experience, and with the palpable reality of our finitude and the proximity of the unknown that awaits us with the coming of our death. In such moments a present-at-hand ontology, one predicated upon a thing-like orientation to human modalities of being-in-the-world, drops away. In its place arises possibilities for an intimate connection with our self-experience in its immediate unfolding, what Bergson (2001) termed the "durée."

As we have seen, this is not the only type of phenomenological modification that may be enabled in the face of pain's unassumability, however. As Drew Leder (1990) maintains, such moments of painful rupture may alternatively lead to a modality of "dys-appearance." That is, in the face of pain what was previously taken to be an unnoticed aspect of our embodied existence—the transparency through which we are enmeshed in the world of our experience—is made present in a new way, now as a noticeable object of experience to be examined. For instance, Gonop's hand that once went unnoticed when grasping a hammer became, in the face of his experience of pain, an object he had to inspect. In this transition, the body itself thus manifests in a modality of the present-at-hand *(vorhanden)* as a thing or an object to be scrutinized. Jarrett Zigon (2007) has productively viewed such moments of breach, which he terms moments of "moral breakdown," as a means for initiating a shift to more self-conscious, reflexive, modalities of being-in-the-world that are realized in instances of ethical reflection. The return to renewed states of familiarity with the world after such moments of moral breakdown give rise, Zigon argues, to possibilities for transformation in the very fabric of the everyday.

When facing the suffering of another, similar shifts in orientation to experience may occur. In confronting the suffering of another, we may be compelled to reorient our attention to the other as a subject and not an object of experience, as a complex self-interpreting being and not a simple determinable thing. The other's unassumability as a suffering subject may bring forth a shift away from interpreting the other as a mere token of a type. Their very mystery being revealed immediately as that which cannot be grasped and which forever eludes our attempts at understanding. In such moments, we are no longer able to flatten out the other's self-experience by subjecting it to our own categories of understanding and expectation. We are no longer able to dwell in the unrecognized typifications orienting us to another as a particular type of person, with particular traits, wants, and desires. It is very much in this spirit that Kohák suggests that when a human "surrenders his pride of place and learns to bear . . . [a] shared pain, he can begin to understand the pain that cannot be avoided as a gift which teaches compassion and opens understanding" (1984, 45).

The opening of being toward the mystery of the other, whether in the face of pain or otherwise, can thus be deemed centrally implicated in realizing an ethical mode of being. In the context of his Tanner Lectures, Arthur Kleinman (1999) provocatively asserts the possibility for advancing just such an openness—an openness that he sees as entailed in ethnographic sensibilities—as a potential mode of moral experience and ethical reflection. Extending some of Levinas's insights, he suggests that

the epistemological scruples, the ontological uncertainties, and the moral sensibilities (and predicaments) of the ethnographer offer themselves up as one means (limited and unpredictable though it be) of sustaining empathy and engagement that deserves serious consideration [by moral philosophers]. That is to say, the ethnographer is "called" into the stories and lives of others by the moral process of engaged listening, the commitment to witnessing, and that call to take account of what is at stake for people." (1999, 418; cf. Benson and O'Neill 2007)

Drawing from Merleau-Ponty's notion of "lateral displacement," Michael Jackson similarly sees the cultivation of such ethnographically grounded moral sensibilities in association with an ability to "critically reconsider one's views from another vantage point." This is tied to the notion that the ethical or moral standpoint is not one that is constructed from the perspective of a "'nowhere' outside of time and circumstance" but is importantly one that "seeks an 'elsewhere' *within* the world" (2005, 48). Terming such an attitude the "visiting imagination," Jackson suggests that a displacement may be engendered in the ethnographic encounter in which it is neither a purely objective orientation to others nor an empathetic merger with others that is at stake. Rather, it is an ability to put oneself "in the place of the other, a way of destabilizing habitual patterns of thinking by thinking . . . [one's] own thoughts in the place of somebody else." The result is neither "detached knowledge" nor "empathetic blending" but rather a taking up of a multiplicity of perspectives in which the individual is able to switch "from one point of view to another without prioritizing any one" (Jackson 2005, 49).

Well in line with these reflections on possibilities for developing an ethics grounded in ethnographic sensibilities, I believe that a cultural phenomenological account of moral experience is further extendable to what I term the anthropological attitude and the ethnographic epoché. Inspired by David Bidney's (1973) insights into an anthropological extension of Husserlian phenomenology, the ethnographic epoché can be understood as an *unwilled* shift in attention that is enacted in the context of the ethnographic encounter, an encounter that is often defined by the recurrent frustration of our attempts at achieving an intersubjective attunement with our interlocutors. As ethnographers of human experience we are often so challenged by our recurrent failures to understand the lifeworlds of those others with whom we learn from and live with in the field that we are forced to engage in forms of phenomenological modification in which we no longer take the true, the good, and the beautiful to be self-evident.

The ethnographic epoché is thus, in Husserlian terms, a form of phenomenological bracketing; however, it is not necessarily restricted to the conscious self-reflection entailed in some of the earliest versions of Husserl's method. The range of reflexive experiences and modifications entailed in moving from experiences of estrangement in our confrontations with unassumable alterity to moments of mutual attunement, where we feel some form of empathy with our interlocutors, is precisely what makes the epoché evoked in such encounters truly an ethnographic one. It is, as Bidney (1973) recognized, the inherently intersubjective nature of fieldwork, of interacting with others who do not necessarily share our beliefs, assumptions, values, moralities, preferred forms of interacting or communicating, that are often responsible for initiating the very particular mode of attention to social interaction that is entailed in what Husserl may have termed the social scientific or anthropological attitude.

It is a very similar attitude that Kleinman recognizes as basic to ethnographic sensibilities and that Jackson sees evidenced in Merleau-Ponty's notion of "lateral displacement." It is also precisely just such an attitude that allows for developing an understanding of the cultural patterning of subjectivity and social action from an anthropological frame of reference. What becomes recognized as "cultural" in the concrete practice of ethnographic encounters is precisely that which destabilizes our otherwise unnoticed assumptions, that which unsettles our usual modes of typification. It is by means of just such a vulnerable, passive, and open orientation to another that we are able to confront some of our most deeply ingrained assumptions about ourselves, our world, and those others with whom we interact. In so doing we are able to envision new horizons of experience. To be compelled by another to interrupt our tendency to assimilate experience to the self-sameness of our being, we thus become opened to possibilities for seeing other ways of being that are not, and yet may never be, our own.

Returning to my own encounters with Tinag as described in chapter 1, it was precisely in those moments where I was made to existentially question my own very presence as a witness, to confront my own interests and plans (interests and plans that led me to participate in the suffering of another that could never be my own), that I was faced with the true integrity of Tinag's being—a being that is not assumable to the self-sameness of my own being. The intensity and viscerality of Tinag's pain, her suffering, her cries, tears, and screams compelled a shift in my orientation to her. In those moments, she could no longer ever simply be a subject of my research, a token of a type of person who suffers pain, even if at times virtuously from a Yapese perspective. Tinag's uniqueness, irreplacibility, and singularity would always outstrip my attempts at understanding her, whether in terms of my own theoretical commitments or in terms of our shared interactional history together. My own tears, my own suffering for Tinag's suffering, was also a point of connection, however, with Lani. My suffering, which could never be Lani's suffering, may have also served to destabilize however briefly the typifications she used in understanding my presence there. At that moment she came to see me as more than a strange outsider, a researcher, an anthropologist, a student, or what have you. I was in that moment uniquely human, vulnerable, and unassumable in my own right.

A Sense of an Ending

> Men, like poets, rush "into the middest," *in medias res*, when they are born; they also die *in mediis rebus*, and to make sense of their span they need fictive concords with origins and ends, such as give meaning to lives and to poems.
>
> Frank Kermode, 1966

According to literary theorist David Morris (1991), our struggles to imbue pain with meaning transform it from a simple sensation to a complex perception. As a perception, painful sensations are organized in an experiential field that is suffused with value, meaning, and emotion. As we have seen, part of what is entailed with this process of fashioning pain into a meaningful and coherent experience occurs when what are otherwise simple sensations of pain that arise in the "middest," are imaginatively imbued with "origins" and "ends" that are implicated in local understandings of virtue. It is my hope that in the pages of this book I have managed to provide an ethnographically rich account of Yapese ethical modes of being. I have done so in an attempt to follow Csordas's (1990, 1994a, 1994b) cultural phenomenological call to pursue in much greater detail those personal and collaborative processes of meaning-making through which pain is able to be fashioned into a perceptible or discursive object through time.

Throughout this book I have attempted to highlight how individuals are able to differentially infuse their experiences of pain with moral, cognitive, and affective valences as articulated in a local model of virtue. Such accounts are inextricably and importantly linked to both personal and collective histories (Morris 1991, 29) and to the shifting temporalities informing particular acts of phenomenological modification. I further hope that I have been able to convincingly point to those varieties of experience that still obdurately resist such configurational processes, while also providing an adequate, if provisional, account of a cultural phenomenology of moral experience that makes room for the existential rootedness of such unassumable forms of experience in the realm of the ethical. Such an account is not one that wishes to ever forget the horrible ends to which pain and suffering are put in the context of torture, violence, warfare, and genocide (see Das 2007; Daniel 1996; Hinton 2002; Scheper-Hughes and Bourgois 2004). It is one that hopes to have shed some light upon the always diverse and complex ways that pain and suffering are necessarily implicated in some of our most human, if not always our most humane, ethical modalities of being. The very real existential struggles undergone by the individuals who so generously shared their experiences of suffering with me speak to the deep significances that such efforts after virtue, even if fleeting, both necessarily reveal and entail.

Notes

INTRODUCTION

1. As Kirmayer (1988) notes, many of these commonsense assumptions are grounded in "a continuous metaphysical tradition in Western thought, traceable from the pre-Socratic philosophers down through the medieval alchemists, expressed by such metaphoric contrasts as active, hot, male and right on the one hand versus passive, cold, female, left on the other. . . . These contrasts reflect an underlying set of values that inform the concept of mind and body, playing one against the other in an unequal contest" (76). Moreover, Schrag (1982) maintains that sensory characterizations of pain in philosophy are rooted in a much broader metaphor of the internal versus external that translates into recurrent debates between introspectionist and behaviorist accounts of pain. As Schrag puts it, for "the introspectionist, pain is an interior psychic state or event, knowable through some species of internal reflection; and the behavior of the organism is at most an exterior sign of an interior happening. For the behaviorist, on the other hand, pain is reducible to the external behavioral reactions, and the language of internal states of consciousness becomes superfluous and suspect" (1982, 113).

2. In psychological literature devoted to the study of pain there is also the acknowledgment that the experience of pain goes well beyond "merely the sensory." For instance, Melzack and Torgerson argue that lexical categories of pain description in English have at least three distinct dimensions that include, in addition to the sensory, cognitive (evaluative) and emotional dimensions (1971; see also Melzack 1975).

3. Although this semantic overlap is interestingly embedded in the very definition of *articulation*, which Merriam-Webster's Collegiate Dictionary renders as "1a: a joint or juncture between bones or cartilages in the skeleton of a vertebrate b: a movable joint between rigid parts of an animal 2a: the action or manner of jointing or interrelating b: the state of being jointed or

interrelated **3a:** the act of giving utterance or expression **b:** the act or manner of articulating sounds **c:** an articulated utterance or sound."

4. I have borrowed this term from the psychoanalyst Donnel B. Stern who defines *unformulated experience* as "mentation characterized by lack of clarity and differentiation." According to Stern, "Unformulated experience is the uninterpreted form of those raw materials of conscious, reflective experience that may eventually be assigned verbal interpretations and thereby brought into articulate form" (2003, 37).

5. I would like to thank Jeff Good for bringing my attention to this quote in the context of the Meta-Epistemology seminar that I coteach with Alessandro Duranti at UCLA.

6. I have undertaken a more detailed examination of this literature elsewhere (Throop 2003a, 2005, 2008a; Throop and Laughlin 2008).

7. The elaboration of Husserl's notion of acts of phenomenological modification as developed in this book and elsewhere (Throop 2008a, 2009, forthcoming a and b) has been worked out in collaboration with Alessandro Duranti with whom I coteach the Meta-Epistemology and Culture of Intersubjectivity seminars at UCLA. While I have for some time now been engaged in an exploration of how Husserl's insights into temporality and the patterning of attention may contribute to anthropological theorizing and practice (see Throop 2003b, 2005; Throop and Murphy 2002; Laughlin and Throop 2008, 2009) it was Duranti who first brought my attention to the significance of the notion of "modification" (*Modifikation*) in Husserl's writing. Since that time we have been working collaboratively to examine the anthropological significance of acts of phenomenological modification (see Duranti forthcoming, n.d.; Throop 2008a, forthcoming a, forthcoming b). Duranti's longstanding interest in Husserl is perhaps first most explicitly evident in his early work on intentionality and truth (Duranti 1993).

8. Arthur Kleinman (1999) has advocated making a distinction between the use of the terms *morality* and *ethics.* "Ethical discourse is reflective and intellectualist, emphasizing cognition (more precisely, in today's jargon, rational choice) over affect or behavior and coherence over the sense of incompleteness and unknowability and uncontrollability that is so prevalent in ordinary life" (1999, 363). In contrast, "moral experience is always about practical engagements in a particular local world, a social space that carries cultural, political, and economic specificity" (1999, 365). While I find Kleinman's distinction to be very useful I have chosen not to follow him in keeping a strict distinction between the two terms in the context of this book. This is partly due to the fact that moral philosophers and social scientists seldom adhere to such a distinction, as well as to the fact that some moral philosophies view ethics (e.g., Aristotelian virtue ethics) to be necessarily tied to such local practical engagements within which social actors are enmeshed (cf. Zigon 2007). I should also note here that in speaking of morality, ethics, and virtue I am not restricting these terms to a usage exclusively tied to religiosity. Indeed, what is recognized as moral or ethical in a given com-

munity of practice often simultaneously crosscuts many different modalities of being, of which religiosity is but one.

I. GIRDIIQ NU WAQAB ("PEOPLE OF YAP")

1. As Egan points out, the designation of these eastern atolls as the Outer Islands in the colonial and postcolonial eras accords well with the hierarchical nature of the relationship between Yap proper and the peoples inhabiting these atolls (1998, 37).

2. According to Egan, "It is noteworthy that these programs have not produced, nor do they appear to have been designed to promote, any industries that could provide local populations with sustainable income" (1998, 45).

3. I cannot help but find it interesting that there are a total of four dissertations written in the 1970s alone (Labby 1972; Lingenfelter 1971; Marksbury 1979; Price 1975) detailing processes of transformation to Yapese kinship, economic, and sociopolitical structures in the face of an ongoing engagement with foreign governments and world economic forces. Moreover, each of these dissertations maintain that such transformations have yet to fully alter or completely displace "traditional" practices, values, and sensibilities.

4. I would like to thank Sheryl Stem, the director of Yap State's archives, for her insight into the issue of the putative "conservatism" of Yapese culture. Her perspective on these matters did much to inform my own.

5. Such interests most likely reflected the influence of the psychoanalytic bent of his early Yale mentor Geoffrey Gorer as well as his Harvard mentors Talcott Parsons and Clyde Kluckhohn. Parsons had entered into formal psychoanalytic training at the Boston Psychoanalytic Institute not long after establishing Harvard's Department of Social Relations and Kluckhohn openly advocated that his students acquire "firsthand familiarity" with psychoanalysis prior to entering the field. Even despite Schneider's rather ambivalent relationship to Freudian theory and psychological anthropology that manifested later in his career, a psychoanalytically honed attention to the complexities of intersubjectivity seemed to be readily reflected in Schneider's detailed description of the ebb and flow of his own "concerns and emotions" throughout the context of his fieldnotes (Bashkow 1991, 175–78).

6. I conducted all interviews with men on my own. When interviewing women, however, Manna or Tiningin (my second research assistant) would be responsible for asking the questions, at least at the beginning of the interview, while I sat and listened. I would often interject with additional questions of clarification or elaboration as the interview progressed. As the person in question became more comfortable with my presence I would gradually take a more active role in the interviewing.

7. It is interesting to note that with the establishment of the current state government and court system at the beginning of the Compact of Free Association between the Federated States of Micronesia and the United States, which currently operates alongside more traditional systems of leadership on

the island, that power and knowledge seem to have been distributed even more diffusely than in the past. For in contemporary Yapese society, village chiefs now have to share power with senators, the state governor, court officials, as well as members of the national government located on the island of Pohnpei.

2. FROM LAND TO VIRTUE

1. See chapter 4; see also Descantes (2002, 232; Egan 1998, 148; Labby 1976, 87–90; Lingenfelter 1975, 1979; Müller 1917, 145, 246–48).

2. As Schneider (1984, 16) and Egan (1998, 100) note, there were over thirty different known matriclans in Yap at the time of Schneider's fieldwork in the late 1940s.

3. As Schneider observes, in Yap the concept of kinship relation is "encompassed in the idiom of land. Land is the rhetoric in terms of which political affairs are conceived, discussed, described, and transacted. Indeed, as we have seen, the Yapese go so far as to say that the land holds the status, while the landholder is merely its transient spokesman; land holds the rank, while its landholders merely act in accordance with that rank; 'the land is chief, not the person'" (1984, 64).

4. An additional way to view this dynamic between men's and women's roles in relationship to the ongoing dialectic of land and people in Yap is that men, with their responsibility for the land's resources as vested in the *lunguun* (voice) or authority of the *daaf,* can be seen as *repositories of the past,* inasmuch as they are thought to hold the knowledge of previous generations associated with that land. In contrast, women, in determining where subsequent generations are going to marry, where children will be adopted, and in planting their children in a particular *tabinaew,* can be understood as cultivating a fundamental *orientation to the future.* That said, a mother in her role as a sister is also importantly oriented to the past inasmuch as she is responsible for overseeing her brother's wife and children in order to ensure that they are all properly working to earn their right to the land associated with her natal *tabinaew* and the title and authority that went along with it. And men, in their political negations, which entail forging, maintaining, or severing links to other *tabinaew* are, of course, also oriented to the future.

5. This is an observation that corresponds well with Schneider's (1984) position that traditionally people did not conceive of a pregiven kin-based relationship between a father and his children.

6. I should note that in Yap there are a number of terms besides *runguy* that overlap, at least to some degree, with those semantic fields encompassed by the English term "love." For instance, there is *adaag,* which refers to anything from "liking" to "wanting" to "desiring," and which can be used equally for objects and people. *Tufeg,* which connotes a form of "cherishing" and "caring," is often used to describe an individual's actions and not necessarily his or her feelings. There is also *taawureeng,* which is more closely related to *runguy* and which is used to refer to those feelings invoked when one is sepa-

rated from one's spouse, lover, close friend, relative, or community. In addition, there is *amiithuun*, which I discuss in more detail later in the chapter, that is literally translated as "pain of," and which refers primarily to feelings of attachment, care, and "love" for one's village or one's community. Interestingly, however, despite these various terms that resonate to some extent with the concept of "love," I often witnessed individuals switching to English when they sought to express their feelings of love or caring for another. For instance, it was very common to hear parents and children say to each other, "love you."

7. Interestingly, this same elder suggested that the transition from landless child to titled landholder is one in which an individual shifted from being *buug buug* ("all curled up") to *kam k'iy ea paam nge em* ("sitting with your legs and arms outstretched"); a bodily position that is only realized when an individual is comfortable in his or her place and no longer feels as if they are merely a visitor.

8. This particular understanding of work was further exemplified in a conversation I had with a friend who once complained to me that her family was always scolding her for never "working." She said that she did not understand this critical evaluation, however, since she believed that she was always "working" very hard to get taro and other foods to give to her friends from low-caste Yapese families and from the Outer Islands. When I asked her why she believed that her family did not recognize her obvious efforts as "work," she thought for a minute before replying that her family did not interpret her activities to be *maruweel*, since the effort she was expending was for the cultivation of what her family considered to be strictly "personal" relationships that were not recognized by her *tabinaew* or by *yalean* (Yapese tradition) as socially significant.

9. The extent to which *athamagil* is held to be a virtue in Yap can also be inferred from the fact that it was quite common to hear people use the phrase "*try naag*," instead of *athamagil*, in the context of everyday discourse. Modifying the borrowed English term "try" with the transitivizing particle *naag* (which is normally used to transform Yapese nouns, adjectives, and intransitive verbs into compound transitive verbs), the phrase *try naag*, as my research assistant Manna first pointed out to me, seems to fill a semantic gap between the concept of *athamagil*, connoting excellence and "giving your absolute best effort" in the face of adversity, and *taafinay naag* ("thinking, feeling, or opining"), which does not implicate a similar moral valence and yet implies, in her words, "no force whatsoever." Here then, it seems that Yapese speakers may have readily incorporated "try" into their everyday discourse in an attempt to fill what was an existing semantic gap between the highly morally valenced concept of *athamagil* and a less morally valenced form of effortfulness that is to some degree captured with the English term "try."

10. I will discuss the grammatical implications of this genitive construction in chapter 6.

11. Pieces of stone money that were considered to be equivalent in value to a human life could be used in the context of a traditional apology in which one individual had taken the life of another.

3. SENTIMENT AND SOCIAL STRUCTURE

1. Concerns of pollution and death are still prevalent in Yap. This is clearly reflected in the gossip I overheard concerning the death of one particularly respected elder whose wife had wanted to bury him near their house. This elicited a great outcry from the other members of the community who argued that it was against *yalean* to have a corpse buried in the confines of the village. In the end, the wife acquiesced to the community's demands and had her husband interred in a local cemetery well outside of the village center.

2. As one teacher of mine recounted, when a person from one of seven *luungun somol* foundations arrives at a meeting it is not uncommon to hear people say *kab ea bpiin ngoodaed*—"a woman has come to us." He explained that this was tied to the traditional role that women play in the family mediating disputes between men: sisters mediating disputes between brothers, mothers mediating disputes between children, and even between children and their father.

3. "Prepared dishes are not eaten in company; each person tries to eat his food outside the house in the dark and in secret at much as possible" (Tetens and Kubary 1973, 91; cited in Egan 1998, 150).

4. The significance of breath, its connection to women's work, nourishment, and sustenance, is perhaps also reflected in a local medicine called *falaay na be*. This is medicine that was traditionally used for treating damage to an infant's umbilical cord, which was held by some local healers to be a cause for asthma *(tunguuufaan, matunguufaan)* later in life. The significance of a connection between breath and nourishment was further suggested in the fact that this type of sickness was thought to be *fuguwan ea m'aar*—"the worst kind of sickness," since it affected breathing, and thus one's very strength to work.

4. SUBJECTIVITY, EMBODIMENT, AND SOCIAL ACTION

1. This moral orientation strongly resonates with Mageo's characterization of Samoa, where she claims that the virtues of personal restraint *(lototele)*, the effacement of personal concerns *(lotomama)*, and personal abasement *(lotofa'amaualalo)* serve to canalize awareness and action toward an ideal of an other-directed, role-conscious individual who "is *not* overcome by the exigencies of inner sentiments, retaining always a calm demeanor and encouraging others to do the same" (1998, 55).

2. As Charles Sanders Peirce ([1878] 1992, 132) explained, pragmatism (or what he later referred to as pragmaticism) should "consider what effects, which might conceivably have practical bearings, we conceive the object of our conceptions to have. Then, our conception of those effects is the whole of our conception of the object" (see also James [1907] 1995, 18).

3. According to Shore, Samoan theories of action are intimately linked to a conceptual distinction between *amio* (a category associated with those actions arising from individual will, desire, or drive) and *aga* (a category tied to socially

sanctioned conduct). As he explains, "*Amio* represents the socially unconditioned aspects of behavior that point away from social norms, toward personal
drives or desires as the conditioning factors" (1982, 154). While in "*aga*, by
contrast, we have the internalization of a set of social forms as an aggregate of
role-based norms for conduct" (1982, 156). In Shore's estimation, Samoans (and
I would add Yapese) individuals view socialization as a process of the "gradual
replacement of purely personal and asocial impulses by a set of socially derived
conventional norms approaching the point where one's inner life is in some
sort of harmony with the demands of social life" (1982, 156). It is important to
note that both Freeman (1984, 1985) and Mageo (1989) take issue with Shore's
characterization of *amio* and *aga*. According to Mageo, Shore's distinction
between *aga* and *amio* is inexact since instead of indexing a distinction between
culture and nature these terms better suggest a distinction between conscious
identity and unconditioned aspects of behavior (1989, 181; cf. Morton 1996).
While it is true that Mageo's definition of *amio* resonates with Shore's, she
suggests that this concept is derivative of a more basic concept in Samoan
ethnopsychology, namely that of *loto*. According to Mageo, *loto* is understood
to be that "subjective dimension of the person, . . . [that] encompasses personal
feeling, thought, and will. Although not necessarily evil, the *loto* is regarded as
all too likely a source of anti-social behavior" (1989, 182). Duranti (2006) has
recently suggested, however, that *loto* does not necessarily connote antisociality
and may perhaps be more effectively glossed as "attitude," "disposition," or
"natural inclination."

4. Jensen (1977a) provides different phonological renderings for "garbage
heap" *(dooq);* "garbage, trash, rubbish" *(dow);* and "body" *(doow).* Given the
prevalence for dialectical variations in the pronunciation of a great many
Yapese terms, I am not at all certain that these particular phonological and
semantic ascriptions are definitive. Moreover, the fact that a number of individuals living in differing municipalities independently pointed out the connection between the term for "trash" and for "body" suggests to me that
regardless of the accuracy of these local etymologies, there was at the very
least a strong culturally elaborated conceptual association between these
two terms.

5. I would like to thank Kevin Groark for a discussion that greatly clarified
some of these issues for me.

6. It is interesting to note that Sixtus Walleser (1913, 5) asserts in the context
of Yapese understanding of the "spirit" and "soul" that "the spirit *(an'i)* has
its seat in the invisible body *(ya'al).* It is equipped with memory and reasoning
power *(tafinai, lem)* and will *(lanian'i).* In this area, however, the Yapese has
as yet come to no clear differentiations." While I will not discuss the concept
of *ya'al* ("spirit" or "soul") in this chapter, it seems that Walleser is using the
locative relational noun *laen* and the noun connector *ii* for "soul." This would
make sense given that his Yapese teachers were most likely using the term *lean
ii yaen',* which Walleser renders as "will." Walleser also translates *taafinay* and
leam as "memory" and "reasoning power" respectively.

7. For simplicity's sake I will use the variant *yaen'* throughout the rest of the book since this was the dialectical variant that was prevalent in the municipalities where I did most of my research.

8. This was accomplished by first listing all of the terms in Jensen's (1977a) dictionary and Elbert's (1946) word-list referring to emotions, feelings, sensation, and thoughts. I then added any terms that came to my attention during my language training or through my everyday interactions and conversations with my family, friends, and teachers. After working on the list for a few months, I then brought everything that I had compiled to the Yap State Department of Education where I received further assistance and input from the department's head linguist, Leo Pugram (who had also helped in putting together Jensen's dictionary), in addition to two men who were responsible for supervising the traditional content of teaching materials produced by the department, Richard Mungwaath and Francis Gaan. Finally, my research assistant Manna took a special interest in this project during the last four months of my fieldwork. During this period, she started her own notebook, jotting down any terms that came to mind, that she encountered in conversing with others, or noted in her work transcribing our interviews that could be added to the list.

9. This example further points to what appears more generally to be a thoroughly human-mediated orientation to "objects" in Yap (Duranti, personal communication). A somewhat similar orientation is insightfully summarized by Schieffelin (1990) for Kaluli children where "children are socialized into the view that particular relationships obtain between people and objects, that objects play a role in the creation and maintenance of social life and in the coordination of relationships" (1990, 178).

10. Interestingly, the Yapese term for misfortune, *aaf machaan,* is comprised of an irregular transitive rendering of the otherwise intransitive verb *aaf,* signifying "to transfer, transport, carry across, translate," and the noun *machaan,* which Jensen translates as "his magical influence" (Jensen 1977a). As Walleser explains, punishment for moral transgressions were traditionally understood to be often rooted in misfortune in which "a disease or some ill, if not death itself, will come to the perpetrator *(af madan)*" (1913, 9).

11. This by no means exhausts the number of different greetings in Yap, which include a number of honorific varieties, including the use of the intransitive verb *siroew,* which Jensen (1977a) translates as "to humble oneself, excuse me, pardon me."

12. For instance, a person taking the medicine *falaay ko marus* should not drink from a coconut that has broken open, should not eat ripe fruit, red fish, raw fish, or barbecued fish. For the persons responsible for finding and collecting the medicine, it was mandated that they should neither sleep with their spouse nor cut wood or hibiscus.

13. Many individuals pointed out that during this time it was accepted that the husband would have sexual relations with other women and there was also the chance that he might have other children with other women. If this hap-

pened, however, the children would not be considered part of the estate, would not be given a name from the estate's foundations, and would thus have no right to the family land.

5. PRIVACY, SECRECY, AND AGENCY

1. Pacific societies are, of course, not alone in privileging indeterminacy and ambiguity in communicative practice. Indeed, Jean Briggs (1995, 1998) and Phyllis Morrow (1990) have noted very similar patterns for Inuit societies, wherein indirection, nonspecificity, and a philosophical orientation to multiple simultaneous references are implicated in social phenomena that range from recognizing limits of human knowledge and avoiding the use of generalizations to deference politeness and transformative metaphors employed in ritual and artistic forms.

2. As Petersen notes, there are also important differences, however, between Pohnpeian epistemology and those Pacific cultures in which "disentangling" is advanced as a means of dispute resolution predicated upon the assumption that while truth is always difficult to discern, with effort there may be ways in which to uncover it (Watson-Gegeo and White 1990). According to Petersen, in Pohnpei (and I would argue likewise in Yap) while the former assumption is shared, the latter is not (1993, 339).

3. Jean Briggs notes a very similar pattern in Inuit communities, where individuals "often say the exact opposite of what they mean—'Don't come to visit!' When they mean 'Do come'; and they often say what they mean in a tone of voice that means something else" (Briggs 1995, 212).

4. There was in fact a derogatory term used to designate such an individual—*feekchilig*. Jensen (1977a) defines the term as "someone who nags, always asking for the same thing over and over." It is interesting, somewhat amusing, and more than a little disheartening that this same term was used to translate the profession of "anthropologist" in the context of an announcement in the October 6, 1967, edition of the *Rai Review* 4 (39): "Sherwood Lingenfelter a ba Anthropologist (Fikchilig) u State University College u Brockport (New York) ni bai yib nga Waab e rofen ni Sunday ko binei e week, ni ngeb i par ni 20 e pul ni nge fil marngaagen yu Waab. Ra fil marngaagen e am nu Waab nike thilthil, salpiy riy nge rogone gidii nibe, par ulan binau. Re marwel rok' nem e ir e ngemang reb e hakese ri. Ra un leengin ngak nge bitir rorow ni 2 e duw yangren ngarabad nga Waab."

5. It is interesting to note in this regard that in their cross-linguistic analysis of high-frequency figurative labels for body parts Brown and Witkowski (1981, 599) include Yapese as an example of those languages that utilize a figurative label equating the pupil of the eye with a human child.

6. YAPESE CONFIGURATIONS OF PAIN AND SUFFERING

1. It is also possible to use the unmodified noun *amiith* in conjunction with the preposition *ko* to make a somewhat more direct statement of the

relationship between a particular variety of pain and its causative object (e.g., *amiith ko nöw*—"pain of a stone fish").

2. Crapanzano is himself critical of what he takes to be phenomenology's lack of attention to the cultural and linguistic structuring of experience. Drawing from Whorf, he holds, for instance, that much of Minkowski's "description of hope rests on a division of time that correlates with the tense structure of Indo-European languages—indeed, with tense structure itself" (2003, 12).

3. Another related pain-based illness is *gubriig*—an illness that some individuals claimed to be caused by hard work, but which most understood to arise from injury stemming from being beaten or being involved in an accident.

8. DYSPHORIC MOMENTS: A CASE STUDY

1. I would like to thank Elinor Ochs for bringing my attention to the possible significance of both Ricœur's and Heidegger's discussions of repetition with regard to this matter.

2. Retention should not be confused with secondary memory or recollection. Where the former is still properly a perceptual process that is modified through time in terms of its continual sinking-back from the present, the former is a presentification—a nonperceptual recreation or reexperiencing of a nonexistent past moment. Similarly, protention is a perceptual given that differs from imagination of nonperceptual future states of affairs in that it extends forward from an existential now-point and thus contains within its grasp the forward facing edge of the perceptual present.

3. In its centripetal mode, as Leder notes, in the face of extreme pain we are rooted in the present moment as "a painless past is all but forgotten . . . [and] a painless future may be unimaginable (1985, 256). In contrast to this centripetal mode, Leder points out that pain's aversive qualities may also lead us to enter a centrifugal mode where our focus and attention is directed outward, away from our dysphoria in a constant seeking for possible future cures or the obsessive dwelling on past causes (1985, 258).

4. It is important to note here that such a strict distinction between metaphor and narrative would not be supported by the likes of Ricœur, who came to view narrative as a form of extended metaphor ([1975] 1997).

5. Generally speaking, modern moral philosophy can be understood as advancing three distinct normative ethical theories. These include those theories that can be classified as virtue ethical, deontological, and consequentialist. Most often traced to the utilitarian thinking of John Bentham and John Stewart Mill, consequentialist theories tend to focus on defining ethical conduct primarily according to an orientation to the consequences of human action. In contrast, deontology, a position most famously advanced by Immanuel Kant, holds that it is not an orientation to the consequences of human action that defines an ethical life, but rather the actor's orientation to specific moral duties, rules, and maxims. Finally, virtue ethics, paradigmatically found in the ethical

and political writings of Aristotle, has often been characterized as agent-centered in as much as it places an emphasis upon those character traits, sensibilities, and dispositions that "enable a person to flourish in a well-run state" (Perrett and Patterson 1991, 185).

6. A somewhat comparable argument is put forth by Daniel Stern in his book *The Present Moment: In Psychotherapy and Everyday Life* (2004). I should make clear, however, that the forms of temporality that are implicated in these virtues are not to be equated with Husserl's notions of protention and retention (see the ensuing discussion of these concepts in the next chapter). Instead, they more accurately align with what Husserl would have termed "recollections/secondary remembrances" and "expectations/hopes."

CONCLUSION

1. See also Ochs and Capps's discussion of the tension between poles of "coherence" and "authenticity" in the context of everyday narratives (2001, 2–6, 17–18, 24, 156, 278–79; see also Ochs and Capps 1997).

2. Levinas's view of ethics is partially derived from Heidegger's (1996) distinction between what is present-at-hand *(vorhanden)* and what is ready-to-hand *(zuhanden)*. In Heidegger's scheme, a tool that is ready-at-hand is not experienced as an object, material or otherwise. It is instead inextricably embedded in the activity and intention of the social actor utilizing a tool to accomplish a given goal. A hammer that is ready-to-hand fades from awareness as an object of experience while the goal of hammering becomes the focus of attention. In contrast, that which is present-at-hand is that which is available to consciousness as an object of awareness. The tool that is present-at-hand is a tool, a hammer that I inspect. It is the object's qualities and properties that become the focus of my attention. Heidegger importantly noted that the tool that appears present-at-hand is often the tool that is no longer functioning to fulfill the actor's goal. When the hammer is no longer working, my awareness is refocused from the task that I am accomplishing to the implement of accomplishment, the object qua object (cf. Dreyfus 1990; Leder 1990, 83–86; Zigon 2007).

3. Levinas goes further than Heidegger, however, in his privileging the otherwise-than-being as the foundation of ethics.

4. It is also, Levinas argues, in such moments of confronting the alterity or excess of the other that we are ironically closest and in most intimate contact with our own subjectivity that is now revealed to us as a standing-out-alone against that which we are not and can never be.

Glossary of Yapese Terms

Alengeng, alengong	headache
Amiith	physical pain
Amiithuun ea Binaew	"pain of the village"
Athamagil	endurance, perseverance, patience; enduring, persevering, striving
Athapaag	hope
Awaen'	envy
Ayuw	to help, to care for
Baen	lie, falsehood, trickery; traditional form of martial art
Bälbaalyaang	crazy, disobedient, naughty (especially of children), dizzy; drunk
Bei	a form of divining performed by tying knots in palm leaves
Binaew	village, community
Bitiir	child
Bpiin	woman; female
Chiitamangin	"father"; a man who holds rights to a given estate and is in a position to pass those rights to a "child" *(faak)*
Chiitinangin	"mother"; a woman who works to earn rights to a given estate for her children or who oversees the transfer of rights in land to a "child" *(faak)*
Chingaew'	drunk

Churuq	dance; dancing
Daaf	stone house foundation
Dolloloew	traditional funeral lament performed by women
Damuumuw	angry; anger
Dopael	village women's house
Faak	"child"; a dependent
Faeluw	village men's house
Falaay	medicine; magic
Falfalaen	happiness, happy, content, satisfied
Gaafgow	suffering, hardship, destitution, poor, pitiful, sad; to suffer, to be destitute, poor, pitiful, sad
Galuuf	a large mangrove monitor lizard *(Varanus indicus)*; muscle cramp
Gamaal	bamboo dance
Ganong	matrilineal clan
Girdiiq	people; humans
Kaan	spirits, ghosts
Kadaen'	"self-governance," "self-control"; literally, "bite your mind"
Kanaawoq	stone path; path; road
Laen ii yaen'	innermost subjective experience
Leam	thought, feeling; to think, to feel
Liyoer	to worship, honor, respect, admire
Lunguun	voice, authority, status
Luuqod	belt, some varieties of which were traditionally worn by women while working in gardens and taro patches
M'aag	to tie, to bind
M'aar	illness, sickness
Maath'keenil'	illness caused by strenuous effort and overwork
Machaaf	valuables
Mafen	clan members who, as direct descendents of a woman who has acquired title to an estate, have authority over its current occupants; individuals of a given *mafen* may retain residual responsibilities and rights over a particular estate for as many as three generations
Magaer	work-induced tiredness, exhaustion, fatigue; also *ka mu magaer*—thank you

Malaal	village dance ground
Malmaal	lazy; laziness
Maqut	taro patch
Maruweel	to work, the intentional activity of working as distinct from its sensorial-based sequelae (see *magaer*)
Mitmiit	traditional intervillage exchange ceremony
Moqoniyaen	evil spirit; malicious spirit that causes illness, misfortune
Nguchol	three stones used to support a cooking pot; three high foundations *(daaf)* at the top of Yap's sociopolitical hierarchy; Yap's three paramount chiefs; a general term referring to an individual's personal name
Nik	founding female ancestral spirit associated with a specific matrilineal clan *(ganong)*
P'eebaay	village meeting house
Piiluung	chief; when used in contrast to *pimilngaay* refers to landed social classes
Pimilngaay	landless classes; servants
Pumoqon	man; male
Puuf rogon	"free will"; acting in accord with one's personal desires, wishes, wants
Raay	a traditional Yapese valuable made of a large aragonite disk; "stone money"
Rugood	age-grade consisting of unmarried adolescent women who have entered menarche
Runguy	to feel compassion, pity, sympathy; to be sorry for
Rus	to feel fear; fear
Sawëy	chain of hierarchically cast exchange relations between islands radiating outward from Yap proper to the surrounding Outer Islands
Soobuutaen'	humble; humility
So ulum	goose bumps; subjective experience arising in the face of another's inappropriate expression of emotion
Taafinay	thought, feeling; to think, to feel
Taamaen	inappropriate request for food; type of dance
Tabinaew	landed estate; including lands, household, and people associated with it

Tabugul	ritual purity; purity arising from culturally ordered development and activity; controllable power; high status; conceptually opposed to *taqay*
Taqay	impurity; disorder, uncultivated, unclean; uncontrollable power; low status; conceptually opposed to *tabugul*
Thaaq	string, fiber; connection; social relationship
Thagiith	an estate's ancestral spirit
Th'iib	cooking pot
Thiliin	between; connection; concrete relationship
Tungaaf	eating restrictions; ritual contamination; type of sickness
Ufanthiin	prideful, arrogant, conceited
Waaw	polluting odor of the dead
Walaag	sibling(s)
Wunbey	stone platform
Yaar	exchange valuable made from shell; "shell money"
Yaen'	subjective experience; mind
Yalean	tradition; custom; customary relationship
Yoogum	ritually sanctioned and differentially ranked system of men's eating classes (men of the same eating class could share food with one another)
Yul'yuul	honesty, truth

Bibliography

Adams, William Hampton, ed. 1997. *Micronesian Resources Study: Yap Archaeology: Archaeological Survey of Gachlaw Village, Gilman Municipality, Yap, Federated States of Micronesia.* San Francisco, CA: Micronesian Endowment for Historic Preservation, Federated States of Micronesia, and U.S. National Park Service.

Agamben, Giorgio. 2007. *Infancy and History: On the Destruction of Experience.* London: Verso.

Appadurai, Arjun. 1981. "Gastro-Politics in Hindu South Asia." *American Ethnologist* 8:494–511.

Asad, Talal. 1993. *Genealogies of Religion.* Baltimore, MD: Johns Hopkins University Press.

————. 2000. "Agency and Pain: An Exploration" *Culture and Religion* 1 (1): 29–60.

Austin, J. L. 1962. *How to Do Things with Words.* Cambridge, MA: Harvard University Press.

Ballantyne, Keira Gebbie. 2004. "Givenness as a Ranking Criterion in Centering Theory: Evidence from Yapese." *Oceanic Linguistics* 43 (1): 49–72.

Barth, Fredrik. 1975. *Ritual Knowledge among the Baktaman of New Guinea.* New Haven, CT: Yale University Press.

Basso, Keith H. 1996. *Wisdom Sits in Places.* Albuquerque: University of New Mexico Press.

Becker, Anne. 1995. *Body, Self, and Society: The View from Fiji.* Philadelphia: University of Pennsylvania Press.

Bensen, Peter, and Kevin Lewis O'Neill. 2007. "Facing Risk: Levinas, Ethnography, and Ethics." *Anthropology of Consciousness* 18 (2): 29–55.

Berger, Harris M. 1997. "The Practice of Perception: Multi-Functionality and Time in the Musical Experiences of a Heavy Metal Drummer." *Ethnomusicology* 41 (3): 464–88.

———. 1999. *Metal, Rock, and Jazz: Perception and the Phenomenology of Musical Experience*. Hanover, NH: Wesleyan University Press.

Berger, Harris M., and Giovanna Del Negro. 2002. "Bauman's *Verbal Art* and the Social Organization of Attention: The Role of Reflexivity in the Aesthetics in Performance." *Journal of American Folklore* 115 (455): 62–91.

Bergson, Henri. 2001. *Time and Free Will: An Essay on the Immediate Data of Consciousness*. Translated by R. L. Pogson. New York: Dover Publications.

Besnier, Niko. 1989. "Information Withholding as a Manipulative and Collusive Strategy in Nukulaelae Gossip." *Language in Society* 18:315–41.

———. 1990 "Conflict Management, Gossip, and Affective Meaning on Nukulaelae." In *Disentangling: Conflict Discourse in Pacific Societies*, edited by Daren A. Watson-Gegeo and Geoff White, 290–334. Palo Alto, CA: Stanford University Press.

———. 1994 "The Truth and Other Irrelevant Aspects of Nukulaelae Gossip." *Pacific Studies* 17 (3): 1–39.

Bidney, David. 1973. "Phenomenological Method and the Anthropological Science of the Cultural Life-World." In *Phenomenology and the Social Sciences*, edited by M. Natansan, 109–42. Evanston, IL: Northwestern University Press.

Biehl, João. 2005. *Vita: Life in a Zone of Social Abandonment*. Berkeley: University of California Press.

———. 2007. *Will to Live: AIDS Therapies and the Politics of Survival*. Princeton, NJ: Princeton University Press.

Biehl, João, Byron Good, and Arthur Kleinman, eds. 2007. *Subjectivity: Ethnographic Investigations*. Berkeley: University of California Press.

Bourdieu, Pierre. 1977. *Outline of a Theory of Practice*. Cambridge: Cambridge University Press.

———. 1998. "Is a Disinterested Act Possible?" In *Practical Reason: On the Theory of Action*, 75–92. Palo Alto: Stanford University Press.

Brenneis, Donald. 1984a. "Straight Talk and Sweet Talk: Political Discourse in an Occasionally Egalitarian Community." In *Dangerous Words: Language and Politics in the Pacific*, edited by Donald Brenneis and Fred Myers, 69–84. Prospect Heights, IL: Waveland Press.

———. 1984b. "Grog and Gossip in Bhatgaon: Style and Substance in Fiji Indian Conversation." *American Ethnologist* 11:487–506.

Briggs, Jean. 1995. "The Study of Inuit Emotions: Lessons from a Personal Retrospective." In *Everyday Conceptions of Emotion*, edited by J. A. Russel et al., 203–20. Dordrecht: Kluwer.

———. 1998. *Inuit Morality Play: The Emotional Education of a Three-Year-Old*. New Haven, CT: Yale University Press.

Brison, Karen J. 1992. *Just Talk: Gossip, Meetings, and Power in a Papua New Guinea Village*. Berkeley: University of California Press.

Broder, Charles M. 1972. Medical Theory: The Yapese Approach. Master's thesis, University of Chicago.

Brooks, Jean. 1988. Ours Is the Dance: A Source and Demonstration of Power on the Island of Yap in the Caroline Islands of Micronesia. Master's thesis, University of Victoria.

Brown, Cecil, and Stanley Witowski. 1981. "Figurative Language in a Universalist Perspective." *American Ethnologist* 8 (3): 596–615.

Bruner, Edward. 1984 "The Opening Up of Anthropology." In *Text, Play, and Story. Proceedings of the American Ethnological Society,* edited by Edward Bruner, 1–16. Washington, DC: American Anthropological Association.

Butler, Judith. 2005. *Giving an Account of Oneself.* New York: Fordham University Press.

Campbell, Keith. 1985. "Self-Mastery and Stoic Ethics." *Philosophy* 60:327–39.

Cassirer, Ernst. 1955. *The Philosophy of Symbolic Forms. Volume 1: Language.* New Haven: Yale University Press.

Castañeda, Quetzil. 2006. "Ethnography in the Forest: An Analysis of Ethics and Morals in Anthropology. *Cultural Anthropology* 21 (1): 121–45.

Crapanzano, Vincent. 1980. *Tuhami: Portrait of a Moroccan.* Chicago: University of Chicago Press.

———. 2003. "Reflections on Hope as a Category of Social and Psychological Analysis." *Cultural Anthropology* 18 (1): 3–32.

———. 2004. *Imaginative Horizons: An Essay in Literary-Philosophical Anthropology.* Chicago: University of Chicago Press.

Csordas, Thomas J. 1990. "Embodiment as a Paradigm for Anthropology." *Ethos* 18 (1): 5–47.

———. 1993. "Somatic Modes of Attention." *Cultural Anthropology* 8 (1): 135–56.

———. 1994a. "Introduction: The Body as Representation and Being-in-the-World." In *Embodiment and Experience,* edited by Thomas Csordas, 1–26. Cambridge: Cambridge University Press.

———. 1994b. *The Sacred Self: A Cultural Phenomenology of Charismatic Healing.* Berkeley: University of California Press.

———. 1996. "Imaginal Performance and Memory in Ritual Healing." In *The Performance of Healing,* edited by Laderman and Roseman, 91–114. London: Routledge.

———. 1999. "The Body's Career in Anthropology." In *Anthropological Theory Today,* edited by Henrietta L. Moore, 172–205. Cambridge: Polity Press.

———. 2002. *Body/Meaning/Healing.* New York: Palgrave.

D'Andrade, Roy. 1995. "Moral Models in Anthropology." *Current Anthropology* 36 (3): 399–406.

Daniel, Valentine E. 1996. *Charred Lullabies: Chapters in an Anthropology of Violence.* Princeton, NJ: Princeton University Press.

Das, Veena. 2007. *Life and Words: Violence and the Descent into the Ordinary.* Berkeley: University of California Press.

Das, Veena, A. Kleinman, M. Ramphele, and P. Reynolds, eds. 2000. *Violence and Subjectivity.* Berkeley: University of California Press.

Das, Veena, A. Kleinman, M. Lock, M. Ramphele, and P. Reynolds, eds. 2001. *Remaking a World: Violence, Social Suffering, and Recovery.* Berkeley: University of California Press.

Descantes, Christopher. 1998. Integrating Archaeology and Ethnohistory: The Development of Exchange Between Yap and Ulithi, Western Caroline Islands. PhD diss., University of Oregon.

———. 2002. "Contained Identities: The Demise of Yapese Clay Pots." *Asian Perspectives* 40 (2): 227–43.

Desjarlais, Robert. 1994. "The Possibilities of Experience among the Homeless Mentally Ill." *American Anthropologist* 96:886–901.

———. 1997. *Shelter Blues.* Philadelphia: University of Pennsylvania Press.

———. 2003. *Sensory Biographies.* Berkeley: University of California Press.

Dilthey, Wilhelm. [1883] 1989. *Introduction to the Human Sciences.* Princeton, NJ: Princeton University Press.

Dodson, J., and M. Intoh. 1999. "Prehistory and Paleoecology of Yap, Federated States of Micronesia." *Quaternary International* 59 (1): 17–26.

Dornan, Jennifer L. 2004. "Preliminary Report on an Oral Historical Survey of Kaday Village, Yap, Federated States of Micronesia." Paper presented at the annual Society for Historical Archaeology Meeting, St. Louis, Missouri.

Douglas, Mary. 1966. *Purity and Danger.* London: Routledge.

Dreyfus, Hubert. 1990. *Being-in-the-World: A Commentary on Heidegger's Being and Time, Division I.* Cambridge, MA: MIT Press.

Duranti, Alessandro. 1984. *Intentions, Self, and Local Theories of Meaning: Words and Social Action in a Samoan Context.* La Jolla, CA: Center for Human Information Processing.

———. 1988. "Intentions, Language, and Social Action in a Samoan Context." *Journal of Pragmatics* 12:13–33.

———. 1993. "Truth and Intentionality: An Ethnographic Perspective." *Cultural Anthropology* 8 (1): 214–45.

———. 1994. *From Grammar to Politics: Linguistic Anthropology in a Western Samoan Village.* Berkeley: University of California Press.

———. 1997a. "Universal and Culture-Specific Properties of Greetings." *Journal of Linguistic Anthropology* 7:63–97.

———. 1997b. *Linguistic Anthropology.* Cambridge: Cambridge University Press.

———. 2001. "Intentionality." In *Key Terms in Language and Culture,* edited by A. Duranti, 129–31. Oxford: Blackwell.

———. 2004. "Agency in Language." In *A Companion to Linguistic Anthropology,* edited by A. Duranti, 451–73. Oxford: Blackwell.

———. 2006. "The Social Ontology of Intentions." *Discourse Studies* 8 (1): 31–40.

———. Forthcoming. "The Relevance of Husserl's Theory to Language Socialization." *Journal of Linguistic Anthropology.*

———. n.d. "Vienna Lecture: Husserl, Anthropology, and the Notion of Intersubjectivity." Unpublished manuscript.

Egan, J. A. 1998. Taro, Fish, and Funerals: Transformations in the Yapese Cultural Topography of Wealth. PhD Thesis, University California, Irvine.

————. 2004. "Keeping-for-Giving and Giving-for-Keeping: Value, Hierarchy, and the Inalienable in Yap." In *Values and Valuables: From the Sacred to the Symbolic*, edited by C. Werner and D. Bell, 3–20. New York: Altamira Press.

Elbert, S. H. 1946. *Yap-English and English-Yap Word Lists with Notes on Pronunciation and Grammar*. Manuscript prepared for the Military Government, CIMA Project, Pacific Science Board.

Farmer, Paul. 1999. *Infections and Inequalities: The Modern Plagues*. Berkeley: University of California Press.

————. 2003. *Pathologies of Power: Health, Human Rights, and the New War on the Poor*. Berkeley: University of California Press.

Firth, Raymond. 1967. "Rumour in a Primitive Society." In *Tikopia Ritual and Belief*, 141–51. Boston: Beacon Press.

————. 1970. "Postures and Gestures of Respect." In *Échanges et communications: Mélanges offerts a Claude Lévi-Strauss à l'occasion de son 60ème anniversaire*, edited by J. Pouillon and P. Maranda, 188–209. The Hague: Mouton.

————. 1972. "Verbal and Bodily Rituals of Greeting and Parting." *The Interpretation of Ritual: Essays in Honor of I. A. Richards*, edited by J. S. La Fontaine, 1–38. London: Tavistock.

Foucault, Michel. 1985. *The Use of Pleasure*. Translated by Robert Hurley. New York: Pantheon Books.

————. 2005. *The Hermeneutics of the Subject: Lectures at the Collège de France, 1981–1982*. New York: Palgrave.

Freud, Sigmund. 1949. *An Outline of Psychoanalysis*. Translated by James Strachey. New York: W. W. Norton.

————. 1962. *Three Essays on the Theory of Sexuality*. Translated by James Strachey. New York: W. W. Norton.

————. 1966. *Introductory Lectures on Psychoanalysis*. Translated by James Strachey. New York: W. W. Norton.

Gadamer, Hans-Georg. 1975. *Truth and Method*. New York: Continuum.

Garcia, Angela. Forthcoming. *The Pastoral Clinic: Addiction and Absolution along the Rio Grande*. Berkeley: University of California Press.

Garfinkel, Harold. 1967. *Studies in Ethnomethodology*. New York: Prentice-Hall.

Garro, Linda C. 1990. "Culture, Pain and Cancer." *Journal of Palliative Care* 6 (3): 34–44.

————. 1992. "Chronic Illness and the Construction of Narratives." In *Pain as Human Experience*, edited by Mary-Jo DelVecchio Good et al., 100–137. Berkeley: University of California Press.

————. 1994. "Narrative Representations of Chronic Illness Experience: Cultural Models of Illness, Mind, and Body in Stories Concerning the Temporomandibular Joint (TMJ)." *Social Science and Medicine* 38 (6): 775–88.

Garro, Linda C., and Cheryl Mattingly. 2000. "Narrative as Construct and Construction." In *Narrative and the Cultural Construction of Illness and Healing*, edited by Cheryl Mattingly and Linda C. Garro, 1–49. Berkeley: University of California Press.

Geertz, Clifford. 1973. *The Interpretation of Cultures*. New York: Basic Books.

Geurts, Kathryn Linn. 2002. *Culture and the Senses: Bodily Ways of Knowing in an African Community*. Berkeley, University of California Press.

Gifford, E. W., and D. S. Gifford. 1959. *Archaeological Excavations on Yap*. Berkeley: University of California Press.

Gillilland, C. 1975. *The Stone Money of Yap: A Numismatic Survey*. Washington, DC: Smithsonian Institution Press.

Glucklich, Ariel. 2001. *Sacred Pain: Hurting the Body for the Sake of the Soul*. Oxford: Oxford University Press.

Goldman, Laurence R. 1995. "The Depths of Deception: Cultural Schemas of Illusion in Huli." In *Papua Borderlands*, edited by Alietta Biersack, 111–41. Ann Arbor: University of Michigan Press.

Good, Byron J. 1992. "A Body in Pain: The Making of a World of Chronic Pain" In *Pain as Human Experience*, edited by Mary-Jo DelVecchio Good et al., 29–48. Berkeley: University of California Press.

———. 1994. *Medicine, Rationality and Experience: An Anthropological Perspective*. Cambridge: Cambridge University Press.

Good, Mary-Jo DelVecchio. 1992. "Work as a Haven from Pain." In *Pain as Human Experience*, edited by Mary-Jo DelVecchio Good et al., 49–76. Berkeley: University of California Press.

Good, Mary-Jo DelVecchio, Paul E. Brodwin, Byron J. Good, and Arthur Kleinman, eds. 1992. *Pain as Human Experience: An Anthropological Perspective*. Berkeley: University of California Press.

Groark, Kevin. 2008. "Social Opacity and the Dynamics of Empathetic In-sight among the Tzotzil Maya of Chiapas, Mexico." In "Whatever Happened to Empathy?" edited by C. Jason Throop and Douglas Hollan. Special Issue, *Ethos* 36 (4): 408–26.

Hage, P., and F. Harary. 1991. *Exchange in Oceania*. Oxford: Clarendon Press.

———. 1996. *Island Networks: Communication, Kinship, and Classification Structures in Oceania*. Cambridge: Cambridge University Press.

Halliburton, Murphy. 2002. "Rethinking Anthropological Studies of the Body: *Manas* and *Bōdham* in Kerala." *American Anthropologist* 104 (4): 1123–34.

Hallowell, Irving A. 1955. *Culture and Experience*. Philadelphia: University of Pennsylvania Press.

———. 1995. *Strangers in Their Own Land: A Century of Colonial Rule in the Caroline and Marshall Islands*. Honolulu: University of Hawai'i Press.

Heidegger, Martin. [1927] 1996. *Being and Time*. Albany: SUNY Press.

Hellström, Christina, and Sven G. Carlsson. 1996. "The Long-Lasting Now: Disorganization in Subjective Time in Long-Standing Pain." *Scandinavian Journal of Psychology* 37:416–23.

Hezel, F. X. 1983. *The First Taint of Civilization: A History of the Caroline and Marshall Islands in Pre-Colonial Days, 1521–1885.* Honolulu: University of Hawai'i Press.

Hinton, Alex. 2002. *Annihilating Difference: The Anthropology of Genocide.* Berkeley: University of California Press.

———. 2005. *Why Did They Kill? Cambodia in the Shadow of Genocide.* Berkeley: University of California Press.

Hollan, Douglas. 2000. "Constructivist Models of Mind, Contemporary Psychoanalysis, and the Development of Culture Theory." *American Anthropologist* 102 (3): 538–50.

———. 2001. "Developments in Person-Centered Ethnography." In *The Psychology of Cultural Experience,* edited by Carmella C. Moore and Holly F. Mathews, 48–67. Cambridge: Cambridge University Press.

———. 2008. "Being There: On the Imaginative Aspects of Understanding Others and Being Understood." In "Whatever Happened to Empathy?" edited by C. Jason Throop and Douglas Hollan. Special issue, *Ethos* 36 (4): 475–89.

Hollan, Douglas, and C. Jason Throop. 2008. "Whatever Happened to Empathy? Introduction." In "Whatever Happened to Empathy," edited by C. Jason Throop and Douglas Hollan. Special issue, *Ethos* 36 (4): 381–405.

Honkasalo, Marja-Lissa. 1999. "What Is Chronic Is Ambiguity: Encountering Biomedicine with Long-Lasting Pain." *Suomen Antropologi* 24 (4): 75–92.

———. 2000. "Chronic Pain as a Posture towards the World." *Scandinavian Journal of Psychology* 41:197–208.

Hunt, Edward E., Jr., Nathaniel R. Kidder, David M. Schneider, and William D. Stevens. 1949. *The Micronesians of Yap and Their Depopulation.* Cambridge, MA: Pacific Science Board, National Research Council, and Peabody Museum.

Hunt, Edward E., Jr., Nathaniel R. Kidder, and David M. Schneider. 1954. "The Depopulation of Yap." *Human Biology* 26 (1): 21–52.

Hunter-Anderson, R. L. 1983. *Yapese Settlement Patterns: An Ethnoarchaeological Approach.* Agana, Guam: Micronesian Area Research Center.

———. 1984. "Recent Observations on Traditional Yapese Settlement Patterns." *New Zealand Journal of Archaeology* 6 (1): 95–106.

Hunter-Anderson, R. L., and Y. Zan. 1996. "Demystifying the Sawei, a Traditional Inter-island Exchange System." *Isla: A Journal of Micronesian Studies* 4 (1): 1–45.

Husserl, Edmund. [1913] 1962. *Ideas: General Introduction to Pure Phenomenology.* New York: Collier Books.

———. 1964. *The Phenomenology of Internal Time-Consciousness.* Translated by James S. Churchill. Edited by Martin Heidegger. Bloomington: Indiana University Press.

———. 1970. *The Crisis of European Sciences and Transcendental Phenomenology.* Evanston, IL: Northwestern University Press.

———. [1931] 1993. *Cartesian Meditations.* London: Kluwer Academic Press.

———. [1900/01] 2001. *Logical Investigations*. London: Routledge & Kegan Paul.

Hursthouse, Rosalind. 1999. *On Virtue Ethics*. Oxford: Oxford University Press.

Irivine, Judith. 1990. "Registering Affect: Heteroglossia in the Linguistic Expression of Emotion." In *Language and the Politics of Emotion*, edited by Catherine Lutz and Lila Abu-Lughod, 126–61. Cambridge: Cambridge University Press.

Jackson, Jean. 1999. *Camp Pain*. Philadelphia: University of Pennsylvania Press.

Jackson, Michael. 1983. "Thinking through the Body: An Essay on Understanding Metaphor." *Social Analysis* 14 (1): 127–48.

———. 1989. *Paths toward a Clearing: Radical Empiricism and Ethnographic Inquiry*. Bloomington: Indiana University Press.

———. 1996. "Introduction: Phenomenology, Radical Empiricism, and Anthropological Critique." In *Things as They Are: New Directions in Phenomenological Anthropology*, edited by Michael Jackson, 1–50. Bloomington: Indiana University Press.

———. 2005. *Existential Anthropology: Events, Exigencies, and Effects*. Oxford: Berghahn Books.

James, William. 1890. *The Principles of Psychology*. New York: Henry Holt.

———. 1904a. "Does Consciousness Exist?" *Journal of Philosophy, Psychology and Scientific Methods* 1 (18).

———. 1904b. "A World of Pure Experience." *Journal of Philosophy, Psychology and Scientific Methods* 1 (20/21).

———. [1907] 1995. "What Pragmatism Means." In *Pragmatism*, 17–32. Mineola, NY: Dover Press.

Jay, Martin. 2005. *Songs of Experience: Modern American and European Variations on a Universal Theme*. Berkeley: University of California Press.

Jensen, John T. 1977a. *Yapese-English Dictionary*. Honolulu: University of Hawai'i Press.

———. 1977b. *Yapese Reference Grammar*. Honolulu: University of Hawai'i Press.

———. 1984. "The Notion of 'Passive' in Yapese." In *Studies in Micronesian Linguistics*, edited by Byron W. Bender, 165–70. Pacific Linguistics C-80. Canberra: Linguistic Circle of Canberra.

Johnson, Allen. 1998. "Repression: A Reexamination of the Concept as Applied to Folk Tales." *Ethos* 26 (3): 295–313.

Kadnanged, B. M., L. Gilnifrad, and J. Egan. 1993. *The Yapese Child: A Teacher's Resource/Bitir nu Wa'ab: Fen e Sensey*. Guam: Multicultural Education Center, College of Education, University of Guam.

Keenan [Ochs], Elinor. 1976. "On the Universality of Conversational Implicatures." *Language in Society* 5:67–80.

Kermode, Frank. [1966] 2000. *The Sense of an Ending: Studies in the Theory of Fiction with a New Epilogue*. Oxford: Oxford University Press.

Kirch, P. V. 2000. *On the Road of the Winds: An Archaeological History of the Pacific Islands before European Contact.* Berkeley: University of California Press.

Kirkpatrick, J. T. 1977. "Person, Hierarchy, and Autonomy in Traditional Yapese Theory." In *Symbolic Anthropology: A Reader in the Study of Symbols and Meanings,* edited by J. L. Dolgin, D. S. Kemnitzer, and D. M. Schneider, 310–28. New York: Columbia University Press.

Kirmayer, Laurence J. 1984a. "Culture, Affect and Somatization (Part I)" *Transcultural Psychiatric Research Review* 21:159–88.

———. 1984b. "Culture, Affect and Somatization (Part II)" *Transcultural Psychiatric Research Review* 21:237–62.

———. 1989. "Mind and Body as Metaphors." In *Biomedicine Examined,* edited by M. Lock and D. Gordon, 57–94. Dordrecht: Kluwer Academic Publishers.

———. 2000 "Broken Narratives." In *Narrative and the Cultural Construction of Illness and Healing,* edited by C. Mattingly and L. C. Garro, 153–80. Berkeley: University of California Press.

———. 2007. "On the Cultural Mediation of Pain." In *Pain and Its Transformations: The Interface of Biology and Culture,* edited by Sarah Coakley and Kay Kaufman Shelemay, 363–401. Cambridge, MA: Harvard University Press.

———. 2008. "Empathy and Alterity in Cultural Psychiatry." *Ethos* 36 (4): 457–74.

Kleinman, Arthur. 1980. *Patients and Healers in the Context of Culture.* Berkeley: University of California Press.

———. 1992. "Pain and Resistance: The Delegitimation and Relegitimation of Local Worlds." In *Pain as Human Experience,* edited by Mary-Jo DelVecchio Good et al., 169–97. Berkeley: University of California Press.

———. 1999. "Experience and Its Moral Modes: Culture, Human Conditions, and Disorder." In *The Tanner Lectures on Human Values,* edited by G. B. Peterson, 20:357–420. Salt Lake City: University of Utah Press.

———. 2006. *What Really Matters: Living a Moral Life amidst Uncertainty and Danger.* Oxford: Oxford University Press.

Kleinman, Arthur, and Joan Kleinman. 1991. "Suffering and its Professional Transformation: Towards an Ethnography of Interpersonal Experience." *Culture Medicine and Psychiatry* 15 (3): 301–91.

———. 1996. "The Appeal of Experience: The Dismay of Images: Cultural Appropriations of Suffering in Our Times." *Daedalus* 125 (1): 1–23.

Kleinman, Arthur, Paul E. Brodwin, Byron J. Good, and Mary-Jo DelVecchio Good. 1992. "Pain as Human Experience: An Introduction." In *Pain as Human Experience,* edited by Mary-Jo DelVecchio Good et al., 1–28. Berkeley: University of California Press.

Kleinman, Arthur, Veena Das, and Margaret M. Lock, eds. 1997. *Social Suffering.* Berkeley: University of California Press.

Köhak, Erazim. 1984. *The Embers and The Stars: A Philosophical Inquiry into the Moral Sense of Nature*. Chicago: University of Chicago Press.

Konishi, Junko. 1999. "The Relationship between the Evaluation and Dance Performance and the Social System in Yap, Micronesia." In *Art and Performance in Oceania*, edited by Barry Craig, Bernei Kernot, and Christopher Anderson, 7–14. Honolulu: University of Hawai'i Press.

Labby, David. 1972. The Anthropology of Others: An Analysis of the Traditional Ideology of Yap, Western Caroline Islands. PhD diss., University of Chicago.

———. 1976. *The Demystification of Yap: Dialectics of Culture on a Micronesian Island*. Chicago: University of Chicago Press.

Labov, William. 1972. "The Transformation of Experience in Narrative Syntax." In *Language in the Inner City*, edited by W. Labov, 354–96. Philadelphia: University of Pennsylvania Press.

Lambek, Michael. 2008. "Value and Virtue." *Anthropological Theory* 8 (2): 133–57.

Langer, Susanne K. 1942 [1996]. *Philosophy in a New Key: A Study in the Symbolism of Reason, Rite, and Art*. Cambridge, MA: Harvard University Press.

Laughlin, Charles D., and C. Jason Throop. 2008. "Continuity, Causation and Cyclicity: A Cultural Neurophenomenology of Time-Consciousness." *Time and Mind* 1 (2): 159–86.

———. 2009. "Husserlian Meditations and Anthropological Reflections: Toward a Cultural Neurophenomenology of Experience and Reality." *Anthropology of Consciousness* 20 (2): 130–70.

Leder, Drew. 1985. "Toward a Phenomenology of Pain." *Review of Existential Psychology and Psychiatry* 19 (2/3): 255–66.

———. 1990. *The Absent Body*. Chicago: University of Chicago Press.

Lessa, William. 1950. "The Place of Ulithi in the Yap Empire." *Human Organization* 9 (1): 16–18.

Lester, Rebecca. 2005. *Jesus in Our Wombs: Embodying Modernity in a Mexican Convent*. Berkeley: University of California Press.

Levinas, Emmanuel. 1980. *Time and Infinity*. Translated by Alphonso Lingis. Dordrecht: Kluwer Academic Publishers.

———. 1987. *Time and the Other*. Translated by Richard A. Cohen. Pittsburgh: Duquesne University Press.

———. 1998. *Entre Nous: On Thinking-of-the-Other*. Translated by Michael B. Smith and Barbara Harshav. New York: Columbia University Press.

Lévi-Strauss. 1963. "The Effectiveness of Symbols." In *Structural Anthropology*, translated by Claire Jacobson, 186–205. New York: Basic Books.

Levy, Robert. 1973. *Tahitians*. Chicago: University of Chicago Press.

———. 1984. "Emotion, Knowing, and Culture." In *Culture Theory: Essays on Mind, Self, and Emotion*, edited by Richard A. Shweder and Robert A. Levine, 214–37. Cambridge: Cambridge University Press.

Lingenfelter, Sherwood. 1971. Political Leadership and Cultural Change in Yap. PhD diss., University of Pittsburgh.

————. 1975. *Yap: Political Leadership and Change in an Island Society.* Honolulu: University of Hawai'i Press.

————. 1977. "Emic Structure and Decision-Making in Yap." *Ethnology* 16 (4): 331–52.

————. 1979. "Yap Eating Classes: A Study of Structure and Communitas," *Journal of the Polynesian Society* 88 (4): 415–32.

————. 1991. "Yap." In *Encyclopedia of World Cultures, Volume II, Oceania,* edited by Terrence E. Hayes, 391–94. Boston: G. K. Hall.

————. 1993. "Courtship and Marriage on Yap: Budweiser, U-Drives, and Rock Guitars." In *The Business of Marriage,* edited by Richard A. Marksbury, 149–74. Pittsburgh, PA: University of Pittsburgh Press.

Linstrom, Lamont. 1990. *Knowledge and Power in a South Pacific Society.* Washington, DC: Smithsonian Institution Press.

Loewy, Erick H. 1991. *Suffering and the Beneficent Community.* Albany: State University of New York Press.

Lutz, Catherine. 1988. *Unnatural Emotions.* Chicago: University of Chicago Press.

MacIntyre, Alasdair. [1984] 2002. *After Virtue.* Notre Dame, IN: University of Notre Dame Press.

Mageo, Jeannette. 1989. "*Amio/Aga* and *Loto:* Perspectives on the Structure of the Self in Samoa." *Oceania* 59:181–99.

————. 1991. "Moral Discourse and the *Loto.*" *American Anthropologist* 93:405–20.

————. 1998. *Theorizing Self in Samoa.* Ann Arbor: University of Michigan Press.

Mahmood, Saba. 2005. *Politics of Piety: The Islamic Revival and the Feminist Subject.* Princeton, NJ: Princeton University Press.

Marksbury, R. A. 1979. Land Tenure and Modernization in the Yap Islands. PhD diss., Tulane University.

Mattingly, Cheryl. 1994. "The Concept of Therapeutic 'Emplotment.'" *Social Science and Medicine* 38 (6): 811–22.

————. 1998. *Healing Dramas and Clinical Plots: The Narrative Structure of Experience.* Cambridge: Cambridge University Press.

————. 2000. "Emergent Narratives." In *Narrative and the Cultural Construction of Illness and Healing,* edited by Cheryl Mattingly and Linda Garro, 181–211. Berkeley: University of California Press.

————. n.d. The Paradox of Hope: Writing against Suspicion. Manuscript.

Mattingly, Cheryl, and Linda Garro. 2000. *Narrative and the Cultural Construction of Illness and Healing.* Berkeley: University of California Press.

Melzack, Ronald. 1975. "The McGill Pain Questionnaire." *Pain* 1 (3): 277–99.

Melzack, Ronald, and Warren Torgerson. 1971. "On the Language of Pain." *Anesthesiology* 34:50–9.

McKellin, William H. 1984. "Putting Down Roots: Information in the Language of Managalese Exchange." In *Dangerous Words: Language and Politics in the Pacific,* edited by Donald Brenneis and Fred Myers, 108–28. Prospect Heights, IL: Waveland Press.

Merleau-Ponty, Maurice. [1962] 1999. *Phenomenology of Perception*. London: Routledge.

Meskell, Lynn, and Peter Pels. 2005. *Embedding Ethics*. London: Berg Publishers.

Miller, Lisa, Paul Rozin, and Alan Fiske. 1998. "Food Sharing and Feeding Another Person Suggests Intimacy." *European Journal of Social Psychology* 28:423–36.

Minkowski, E. 1970. *Lived Time: Phenomenological and Psychopathological Studies*. Evanston, IL: Northwestern University Press.

Morris, David B. 1991. *The Culture of Pain*. Berkeley: University of California Press.

Morrow, Phyllis. 1990. "Symbolic Actions, Indirect Expressions: Limits to Interpretations of Yupik Society." *Etudes/Inuit/Studies* 14 (1–2): 141–58.

Morton, Helen. 1996. *Becoming Tongan: An Ethnography of Childhood*. Honolulu: University of Hawai'i Press.

Müller, W. 1917. "Yap." In *Ergebnisse der Südsee Expedition 1908–1910*, edited by George Thilenius, 1917–1918. (II: Ethnographie, B: Mikronesien. Band 2, Halband 1.) Hamburg: L Friederichsen & Co. Human Relations Area Files. Unedited Translated Munuscript.

Munn, Nancy. 1986. The *Fame of Gawa: A Symbolic Study of Value Transformation in a Massim (Papua New Guinea) Society*. Durham, NC: Duke University Press.

Murphy, Keith M., and C. Jason Throop, eds. Forthcoming. *Toward an Anthropology of the Will*. Palo Alto, CA: Stanford University Press.

Myers, Fred. 1986. "Reflections on a Meeting: Structure, Language, and the Polity in a Small-Scale Society." *American Ethnologist* 13:430–47.

Needham, Rodney. 1973. *Belief, Language, and Experience*. Chicago: University of Chicago Press.

Noritake, Masaru. n.d. "Yapese Tradition" and *Yalen yu Wa'ab:* The Cultural Representation and Practice of Yap Day. Final report submitted to the National Historic Preservation Office, Federated States of Micronesia.

Nussbaum, Martha. [1986] 2001. *The Fragility of Goodness*. Cambridge: Cambridge University Press.

Ochs, Elinor. 1979. "Transcription as Theory." In *Developmental Pragmatics*, edited by Elinor Ochs and Bambi Schieffelin, 207–21. New York: Academic Press.

———. 1986. "From Feelings to Grammar: A Samoan Case Study." In *Language Socialization across Cultures*, edited by Bambi Schieffelin and Elinor Ochs, 251–72. Cambridge: Cambridge University Press.

———. 1988. *Culture and Language Development: Language Acquisition and Language Socialization in a Samoan Village*. Cambridge: Cambridge University Press.

———. 1996. "Linguistic Resources for Socializing Humanity." In *Rethinking Linguistic Relativity*, edited by John J. Gumperz and Stephen C. Levinson, 407–37. Cambridge: Cambridge University Press.

Ochs, Elinor, and Lisa Capps. 1995. *Constructing Panic*. Cambridge: Harvard University Press.

———. 1997. "Narrative Authenticity." *Journal of Narrative and Life History* 7 (1–4): 83–91.

———. 2001. *Living Narrative: Creating Everyday Storytelling*. Cambridge, MA: Harvard University Press.

Ochs, Elinor, and Bambi Schieffelin. 1984. "Language Acquisition and Socialization: Three Developmental Stories and their Implications." In *Culture Theory: Essays in Mind, Self, and Emotion*, edited by R. Shweder and R. LeVine, 276–320. Cambridge: Cambridge University Press.

Parish, Steven M. 1994. *Moral Knowing in a Hindu Sacred City: An Exploration of Mind, Emotion, and Self*. New York: Columbia University Press.

Peattie, M. R. 1988. *Nan'yo: The Rise and Fall of the Japanese in Micronesia*. Honolulu: University of Hawai'i Press.

Peirce, C. S. 1992. *The Essential Peirce: Volume I (1867–1893)*. Edited by Nathan Houser and Christian Kloesel. Bloomington: Indiana University Press.

Perrett, Roy, and John Patterson. 1991. "Virtue Ethics and Maori Ethics." *Philosophy East and West* 41:185–202.

Petersen, Glen. 1993. "*Kanengamah* and Pohnpei's Politics of Concealment." *American Anthropologist* 95 (2): 334–52.

Poyer, L. 1995. "Yapese Experiences of the Pacific War." *ISLA: A Journal of Micronesian Studies* 3 (2): 223–55.

Price, S. T. 1975. The Transformation of Yap: Causes and Consequences of Socio-Economic Change in Micronesia. PhD diss., Washington State University.

Rey, Roselyne. 1993. *The History of Pain*. Cambridge, MA: Harvard University Press.

Ricœur, Paul. 1981. "Narrative Time." In *On Narrative,* edited by W. J. T. Mitchell, 165–86. Chicago: University of Chicago Press.

———. [1983] 1984. *Time and Narrative: Volume I*. Chicago: University of Chicago Press.

———. [1984] 1985. *Time and Narrative: Volume II*. Chicago: University of Chicago Press.

———. [1985] 1988. *Time and Narrative: Volume III*. Chicago: University of Chicago Press.

———. 1991. *From Text to Action: Essays in Hermeneutics II*. Evanston, IL: Northwestern University Press.

———. 1997. *The Rule of Metaphor: Multidisciplinary Studies of the Creation of Meaning in Language*. Toronto: University of Toronto Press.

Robbins, Joel. 2001. "God Is Nothing but Talk: Modernity, Language, and Prayer in a Papua New Guinea Society. *American Anthropologist* 103 (4): 901–12.

———. 2003. "Given to Anger, Given to Shame: The Psychology of the Gift among the Urapmin of Papua New Guinea." *Paideuma* 49:249–61.

———. 2004. *Becoming Sinners: Christianity and Moral Torment in a Papuan New Guinea Society*. Berkeley: University of California Press.

———. 2008. "On Not Knowing Other Minds: Confession, Intention, and Linguistic Exchange in a Papuan New Guinea Community." In "Anthropology and the Opacity of Other Minds," edited by Alan Rumsey and Joel Robbins. Special Issue, *Anthropological Quarterly* 81 (2): 421–30.

Robbins, Joel, and Alan Rumsey. 2008. "Introduction: Cultural and Linguistic Anthropology and the Opacity of Other Minds." In "Anthropology and the Opacity of Other Minds," edited by Alan Rumsey and Joel Robbins. Special Issue, *Anthropological Quarterly* 81 (2): 407–20.

Rosenblatt, D. 2004. "An Anthropology Made Safe for Culture: Patterns of Practice and the Politics of Difference in Ruth Benedict." *American Anthropologist* 106 (3): 459–72.

Ross, M. D. 1996. "Is Yapese Oceanic?" In *Reconstruction, Classification, Description: Festschrift in Honor of Isidore Dyen*, edited by B. Nothofer, 121–66. Hamburg: Abera Verlag Meyer.

Rydstrm, Helle. 2003. *Embodying Morality: Growing Up in Rural Northern Vietnam*. Honolulu: University of Hawai'i Press.

Sahlins, M. 1981. *Historical Metaphors and Mythical Realities: Structure in the Early History of the Sandwich Island Kingdom*. Ann Arbor: University of Michigan Press.

———. 1985. *Islands of History*. Chicago: University of Chicago Press.

———. 1995. *How 'Natives' Think: About Captain Cook for Example*. Chicago: University of Chicago Press.

Scarry, Elaine. 1985. *The Body in Pain: The Making and Unmaking of the World*. New York: Oxford University Press.

Scheler, Max. [1963] 1992. "The Meaning of Suffering." In *On Feeling, Knowing, and Valuing*, edited by Harold J. Bershady, 82–115. Chicago: University of Chicago Press.

Scheper-Hughes, Nancy. 1990. "The Rebel Body: The Subversive Meanings of Illness." *TAS Journal* 10:3–10.

———. 1992. *Death Without Weeping*. Berkeley: University of California Press.

———. 1995. "The Primacy of the Ethical: Propositions for a Militant Anthropology." *Current Anthropology* 36 (3): 409–20.

———. 2002. "The Ends of the Body: Commodity Fetishism and the Global Traffic in Organs." *SAIS Review* 22 (1): 61–80.

Scheper-Hughes, Nancy, and Philippe I. Bourgois, eds. 2004. *Violence in War and Peace: An Anthology*. London: Blackwell Publishing.

Schieffelin, Bambi B. 1990. *The Give and Take of Everyday Life*. Cambridge: Cambridge University Press.

———. 2008. "Speaking Only Your Own Mind: Reflections on Talk, Gossip, and Intentionality in Bosavi (PNG)." *Anthropology Quarterly* 81 (2): 431–42.

Schieffelin, Bambi, and Elinor Ochs, eds. 1986. *Language Socialization across Cultures*. Cambridge: Cambridge University Press.

Schieffelin, Edward L. 1976. *The Sorrow of the Lonely and the Burning of the Dancers*. New York: St. Martin's Press.

Schneider, D. M. 1949. The Kinship System and Village Organization of Yap, West Caroline Islands, Micronesia: A Structural Account. PhD diss., Harvard University.

——. 1953. "Yap Kinship Terminology and Kin Groups." *American Anthropologist* 55:215–36.

——. 1955. "Abortion and Depopulation on a Pacific Island." In *Health, Culture, and Community*, edited by Benjamin Paul, 211–35. New York: Russell Sage Foundation.

——. 1957. "Political Organization, Supernatural Sanctions and the Punishment for Incest on Yap." *American Anthropologist* 59:791–800.

——. 1958. "Typhoons on Yap." *Human Organization* 16:10–15.

——. 1962. "Double Descent on Yap." *Journal of Polynesian Society* 71:1–24.

——. 1984. *A Critique of the Study of Kinship*. Ann Arbor: University of Michigan Press.

Schrag, Calvin O. 1969. *Experience and Being*. Evanston, IL: Northwestern University Press.

——. 1982. "Being in Pain." In *The Humanity of the Ill: Phenomenological Perspectives*, edited by Victor Kestenbaum, 101–24. Knoxville: University of Tennessee Press.

Schutz, Alfred. [1932] 1967. *The Phenomenology of the Social World*. Evanston, IL: Northwestern University Press.

——. 1970. *On Phenomenology and Social Relations*. Chicago: University of Chicago Press.

——. 1982. *Life Forms and Meaning Structure*. London: Routledge.

Scott, David. 1992. "Anthropology and Colonial Discourse." *Cultural Anthropology* 7:301–27.

Scott, Joan. 1991. "The Evidence of Experience." *Critical Inquiry* 17: 773–95.

Searle, John R. 1969. *Speech Acts*. Cambridge: Cambridge University Press.

Shore, Bradd. 1982. *Sala'ilua: A Samoan Mystery*. New York: Columbia University Press.

——. 1989. "*Mana* and *Tapu*." In *Developments in Polynesian Ethnography*, edited by Alan Howard and Robert Borofsky, 137–75. Honolulu: University of Hawai'i Press.

Silverstein, Michael. 1981. The Limits of Awareness. Working Papers in Sociolinguistics 84. Austin, TX: Educational Laboratory.

Slote, Michael. 1992. *From Morality to Virtue*. Oxford: Oxford University Press.

Stein, Edith. [1917] 1989. *On the Problem of Empathy*. Washington, DC: ICS Publications.

Stern, Daniel N. 2004. *The Present Moment: In Psychotherapy and Everyday Life*. New York: W. W. Norton.

Stern, Donnel B. 2003. *Unformulated Experience: From Dissociation to Imagination in Psychoanalysis*. Hillsdale, NJ: Analytic Press.

Stocking, George W., Jr. 1968. *Race, Culture, and Evolution: Essays in the History of Anthropology*. New York: Free Press.

Strathern, Andrew. 1975. "Veiled Speech in Mount Hagen." In *Political Language and Oratory in Traditional Society*, edited by M. Bloch, 185–203. New York: Academic Press.

Tambiah, Stanley J. 1996. *Leveling Crowds: Ethnonationalist Conflict and Collective Violence in South Asia*. Berkeley: University of California Press.

Tetens, Alfred, and Johann Kubary. 1873. "The Carolines Island Yap or Guap, According to the Reports of Alfred Tetens and Johann Kubary," in *Journal des Museum Godeffroy* 1:84–130. Hamburg: Museum Godeffroy.

Throop, C. Jason. 2002. "Experience, Coherence, and Culture: The Significance of Dilthey's 'Descriptive Psychology' for the Anthropology of Consciousness." *Anthropology of Consciousness* 13 (1): 2–26.

———. 2003a. "Articulating Experience." *Anthropological Theory* 3 (2): 219–41.

———. 2003b. "Minding Experience: An Exploration of the Concept of 'Experience' in the French Anthropology of Durkheim, Lévy-Bruhl, and Lévi-Strauss." *Journal of the History of the Behavioral Sciences* 39 (4): 365–82.

———. 2005. "Hypocognition, a 'Sense of the Uncanny,' and the Anthropology of Ambiguity: Reflections on Robert I. Levy's Contribution to Theories of 'Experience' in Anthropology." *Ethos* 33 (4): 499–511.

———. 2008a. "From Pain to Virtue: Dysphoric Sensations and Moral Sensibilities in Yap (Waqab), Federated States of Micronesia." In "Medical Anthropology of Sensation," edited by Devon Hinton, Laurence Kirmayer, and David Howes. Special issue, *Journal of Transcultural Psychiatry* 45 (2): 253–86.

———. 2008b. "On the Problem of Empathy: The Case of Yap, Federated States of Micronesia." In "Whatever Happened to Empathy?" edited by C. Jason Throop and Douglas Hollan. Special issue, *Ethos* 36 (4): 402–26.

———. 2009. "Interpretation and the Limits of Interpretability: On Rethinking Clifford Geertz' Semiotics of Religious Experience." *Journal of North African Studies* 14 (4).

———. Forthcoming a. " 'Becoming Beautiful in the Dance': On the Formation of Ethical Subjectivities in Yap, Federated States of Micronesia." *Oceania.*

———. Forthcoming b. "In the Midst of Action: Phenomenological and Cultural Reflections on the Experiential Correlates of Willing." In *Toward an Anthropology of the Will*, edited by Keith M. Murphy and C. Jason Throop. Palo Alto, CA: Stanford University Press.

Throop, C. Jason, and Charles D. Laughlin. 2007. "Anthropology of Consciousness." In *The Cambridge Handbook of Consciousness*, edited by Philip David Zelazo, Morris Moscovitch, and Evan Thompson, 631–72. Cambridge: Cambridge University Press.

Throop, C. Jason, and Keith M. Murphy. 2002. "Bourdieu and Phenomenology: A Critical Assessment." *Anthropological Theory* 2 (2): 185–207.

Toombs, S. K. 1990. "The Temporality of Illness: Four Levels of Experience." *Theory and Medicine* 11 (3): 227–41.

Turner, Victor. 1986. "Dewey, Dilthey and Drama: An Essay in the Anthropology of Experience." In *The Anthropology of Experience*, edited by Victor Turner and Edward M. Bruner, 33–44. Urbana: University of Illinois Press.

Turner, Victor W., and Edward M. Bruner, eds. 1986. *The Anthropology of Experience*. Urbana: University of Illinois Press.

Trnka, Susanna. 2007. "Languages of Labor: Negotiating the 'Real' and the Relational in Indo-Fijian Women's Experiences of Physical Pain." *Medical Anthropology Quarterly* 21 (4): 388–408.

———. 2008. *State of Suffering: Political Violence and Community Survival in Fiji*. Ithaca, NY: Cornell University Press.

Useem, J. 1946. "Report on Yap and Palau." In *U.S. Commercial Company's Economic Survey of Micronesia. Report 6*. Honolulu: U.S. Commercial.

Wacquant, Loïc. 2003. *Body and Soul: Notebooks of an Apprentice Boxer*. London: Oxford University Press.

Waldenfels, Bernard. 2002. "Levinas and the Face of the Other." In *The Cambridge Companion to Levinas*, edited by Simon Critchley and Robert Bernasconi, 63–81. Cambridge: Cambridge University Press.

Walleser, P. Sixtus. 1913. "Religiose Anchauungen und Gebrauche der Bewohnew von Jap (Deutsch Sudsee)." *Anthropos* 8:607–29. Translated for the Yale Cross Cultural Survey, Human Relations Area Files, 1968.

Watson-Gegeo, Karen Ann, and Geoffrey M. White. 1990. *Disentangling: Conflict Discourse in Pacific Societies*. Palo Alto, CA: Stanford University Press.

Weber, Max. 1946. "The Social Psychology of World Religions." In *From Max Weber: Essays in Sociology*, edited by H. H. Gerth and C. Wright Mills, 267–301. Oxford: Oxford University Press.

White, Geoffrey. 1982. "The Role of Cultural Explanation in 'Somatization' and 'Psychologization.'" *Social Science and Medicine* 16 (1): 1519–30.

White, Geoffrey M., and John Kirkpatrick, eds. 1985. *Person, Self, and Experience*. Berkeley: University of California Press.

Wikan, Unni. 1990. *Managing Turbulent Hearts: A Balinese Formula for Living*. Chicago: University of Chicago Press.

———. 1992. "Beyond the Words: The Power of Resonance." *American Ethnologist* 19:460–82.

———. 2008. *In Honor of Fadime: Murder and Shame*. Chicago: University of Chicago Press.

Williams, Raymond. 1977. *Marxism and Literature*. Oxford: Oxford University Press.

Wilson, Lynn B. 1995. *Speaking to Power: Gender and Politics in the Western Pacific*. New York: Routledge.

Wittgenstein, Ludwig. [1949] 1980. *Remarks on the Philosophy of Psychology*. Chicago: University of Chicago.

Zigon, Jarrett. 2007. "Moral Breakdown and Ethical Demand." *Anthropological Theory* 7 (2): 131–50.

———. 2008. *Morality: An Anthropological Perspective*. Oxford: Berg.

Index

complemental series, 268–69. *See also*
experience
concealment, 15, 36, 37, 69, 103–104, 112,
125, 140–41, 144–45, 147–49, 156, 158,
162, 163, 168, 169, 265. *See also*
secrecy
consciousness, 9, 111, 133, 183, 188, 211,
234, 255, 261, 267, 269, 272, 274, 279,
281, 285n1, 286n4, 295n2; internal
time, 261. *See also* awareness
consequences/consequentialism, 103, 116,
127, 136, 139, 140, 147, 148, 164, 170,
239, 254, 256, 258–59. *See also*
morality
contamination, 72–73, 75–76, 94. See also
tungaf
conversation analysis, xvi
Coordinated Investigation of Micronesian Anthropology, 27
Crapanzano, Vincent, 7–8, 184, 294n2
cross-siblingship, 46, 48–50
crying, 1, 26, 38, 86, 124, 134, 198, 206,
220–21, 236, 238, 244, 246–53
Csordas, Thomas, 3, 10, 12, 41, 61, 283
cultural phenomenology, 3, 13, 16, 234,
267, 269–74, 278–82, 283. *See also*
phenomenological anthropology

daaf, 42–48, 57, 86, 94–95, 159, 288
Dalipebinaw, 35–36, 58
dance, 22, 25, 27, 58, 69, 77, 85–90, 121,
127, 142, 154, 157, 257
Daniel, Valentine, 4
Danto, Arthur, 261
Das, Veena, 4
Dasein, 254. *See also* being-in-the-world
death, 47, 73, 75–76, 77–78, 139, 204, 206,
266, 272, 278; being-toward-, 212,
214, 230
deliberation. *See* action
deontology, 294n5. *See also* morality
Descantes, Christopher, 288n1
desire, 31–32, 37, 102–105, 111–18, 120–22,
129, 132, 134–37, 183, 188, 222, 232,
253–54, 268, 273, 277–80, 290n3
Desjarlais, Robert, 5, 258
destabilizing, 14, 213, 268, 280–83
diabetes, 100. See *m'aar: nib biqech*
Dilthey, Wilhelm, 6
divining, 57–58
divorce, 53, 204, 218
dolloloew/dolloloey, 77, 82

dopael, 24, 75, 76
Dornan, Jennifer, xvii
drunkenness, 150, 164–67, 197, 198,
205
Duranti, Alessandro, 124–25, 140, 176,
286nn5,7, 291n3
durée, 279

eating, 30, 45, 52, 67, 68, 72, 78, 91–97,
99, 121–23, 135–36, 207, 225, 230, 290;
and gender, 52–53, 68, 91, 93, 94–95,
225; restrictions, 52–53, 67, 72, 78,
91–97, 135–36, 290n3, 292n12; and
status, 52–53, 72, 91, 94–95. *See also*
food
eating class, 52–53, 91, 94–95, 131, 264.
See also *yoogum*
efficacy, 136, 143, 144, 169, 185. See also
angin
effort, 44, 46, 47, 54, 58, 60–66, 70, 71,
74, 84, 91, 95–99, 104–105, 116, 118,
121, 123, 125, 129, 134, 143, 145, 159,
183–87, 190, 195, 201, 202, 210, 213,
217, 220–22, 226, 229, 230–33, 253,
257, 266, 267, 289n8, 293n2. See also
magaer
Egan, James, 20, 22, 32, 33–35, 37, 44, 46,
48, 53, 61, 71–72, 74, 78, 82, 87, 93,
104, 141, 287nn1,2, 288n2
Elbert, S. H., 292n8
embodiment, 5, 8, 10–11, 13, 14, 47–48,
56–57, 60–63, 68, 98, 106, 114, 118,
127, 133, 135, 166, 176, 184, 212–17,
222, 231, 232, 257, 259, 262, 266, 268,
279
emotion, 7, 10, 14, 38, 83–84, 90, 97,
102–03, 106, 108–09, 111–12, 120, 124,
140–41, 145–47, 153, 161–63, 167–72,
181–82, 189, 192–93, 282, 285n2,
287n5, 292n8
empathy, 2, 55–57, 63–66, 103, 111, 112, 115,
124, 155, 159–60, 163, 167–68, 191, 253,
254, 269, 270, 276, 278, 280–81. See
also *amiithuun*
endurance, 6, 10, 12, 14, 18, 25, 38, 41, 47,
50, 51, 55, 60–67, 70, 85, 90–91,
96–98, 100, 102, 104, 105, 118, 122,
134, 145, 172, 183, 187, 190, 195, 207,
214–18, 220, 222, 229–33, 264–65. See
also *athamagil*
envy. See *awaen*
epoché, 16, 270–71, 278, 280–81

Text: 10/13 Galliard
Display: Galliard
Compositor: Toppan Best-set Premedia Limited
Cartographer: Bill Nelson
Printer: Maple-Vail Book Manufacturing Group